L.A.'s Ti
of Temple Street

L.A.'s Titans of Temple Street

*Los Angeles County
Government Since 1950*

Tom Sitton

McFarland & Company, Inc., Publishers
Jefferson, North Carolina

This book has undergone peer review.

Library of Congress Cataloguing-in-Publication Data

Names: Sitton, Tom, 1949– author.
Title: L.A.'s titans of Temple Street : Los Angeles County
government since 1950 / Tom Sitton.
Other titles: Los Angeles' titans of Temple St.
Description: Jefferson, North Carolina : McFarland & Company Publishers, Inc., 2023 |
Includes bibliographical references and index.
Identifiers: LCCN 2023006624 | ISBN 9781476688657 (paperback : acid free paper) ∞
| ISBN 9781476649139 (ebook)
Subjects: LCSH: Los Angeles County (Calif.)—Politics and government—20th century. |
County government—California—Los Angeles County—History—20th century. | Los Angeles
County (Calif.)—History—20th century. | Los Angeles County (Calif.)—Social conditions—
20th century. | Social change—California—Los Angeles County—History—20th century. |
Democracy—California—Los Angeles County—History—20th century. |
Liberalism—California—Los Angeles County—History—20th century. | Progressivism
(United States politics)—History—20th century.
Classification: LCC JS451.C29 S5 2023 | DDC 320.809794/930904—dc23/eng/20230301
LC record available at https://lccn.loc.gov/2023006624

British Library cataloguing data are available

ISBN (print) 978-1-4766-8865-7
ISBN (ebook) 978-1-4766-4913-9

Front cover images palm trees © veeterzy/Shutterstock; *background* Los Angeles
County regions map © Rainer Lesniewski/Shutterstock

Printed in the United States of America

*McFarland & Company, Inc., Publishers
Box 611, Jefferson, North Carolina 28640
www.mcfarlandpub.com*

For
Karen, Bill, and Raphe

Acknowledgments

In thanking many of the people who helped to complete this project I must begin with everyone involved with the John Randolph Haynes and Dora Haynes Foundation in Los Angeles. The Foundation advanced this study with two generous research grants. I wish to especially thank Administrative Director William Burke, Administrative Assistant Denia Camacho, and the trustees for their longstanding support for my research.

Since my retirement from the Natural History Museum of Los Angeles County in 2006, I have been aided by the museum staff in this and other research projects. For their assistance I thank my former co-workers John Cahoon, Betty Uyeda, and Brent Riggs at the Seaver Center for Western History Research; William Estrada in the History Department; and Ornithologist Kimball Garrett, who provided me with a wealth of advice on environmental considerations.

The Henry E. Huntington Library in San Marino, California, is the major site for my research, and I was helped by many people there. They include Research Director Steve Hindle and former Library Director David Zeidberg; Sarah Basile and Taline Rumaya in the Corporate and Foundation Relations Office; curators Jennifer Watts, the late Bill Frank, Alan Jutzi, Clay Stalls, and Peter Blodgett; photograph expert Erin Chase; and Reader Services staff members Anne Blecksmith, Sam Wylie, Stephanie Arias, Lisa Caprino, and the many pages who had to shlep all those boxes of documents for me.

I am also indebted to other archival experts working in other important research institutions in the greater Los Angeles area who were always helpful. They include Dace Taube, retired from the University of Southern California Special Collections; Molly Haigh, Simon Elliott, and others at UCLA Special Collections; Todd Godowsky and Mike Holland of the Los Angeles City Records Center and Archives; Christina Rice at the Los Angeles Public Library; and Archivist Azalea Camacho at the California State University at Los Angeles. I also salute Bruce Crochet at the Los Angeles County Board of Supervisors Administrative Office and Katherine Medina at the County Executive Office. Further away, Archivist Elaine Crepeau at Up with People, the staffs of the Bancroft Library at the University of California, Berkeley, the Special Collections Department at the Stanford University Library, the California State Archives in Sacramento, the U.S. National Archives and Library of Congress in Washington, D.C., and the National Archives regional centers in Riverside and San Bruno, California, were graciously helpful to this visitor from Southern California.

My friends and colleagues Raphael Sonenshein and William Deverell read portions of the manuscript and made suggestions for improvement. During the entire course of this project both have been helpful in many ways with their advice and support.

My son-in-law, Andre de la Rambelje, helped throughout the process in solving my many computer dilemmas.

This book could not have reached the final stage without the support of editors Dré Person, Elizabeth Foxwell, Susan Kilby, and other staff members at McFarland.

Finally, as usual, I must express my gratitude to my spouse, Karen, who keeps things together for us during these long book ventures, especially in 2020–2022. Without her love and sacrifices it would not be possible.

Table of Contents

Preface

As I mention in the introduction of this book, studies of local government and urban history usually focus on cities. Counties are rarely mentioned and are perhaps even more important when studying the issues they confront, such as public health, public safety and justice, environmental protection, and many other regional services and the taxes needed to pay for them. Decisions made by county officers have a profound impact on residents in the eighty-eight cities within Los Angeles County's jurisdiction, as well as those living in unincorporated areas for which the county is the primary local government.

My own interest in the history of state and local governments initially centered on the city of Los Angeles leading to my M.A. thesis and PhD dissertation. Later I authored a book on Los Angeles municipal government and politics in the 1930s–1950s era and helped edit a two-volume history of Los Angeles city government from 1850 to 2000.

In those same years I was working in the history department of the Natural History Museum of Los Angeles County which holds a large collection of original documents related to county government and development that made me realize that county government was also important to the growth of the region but that few history sources treated it. That revelation led me to write a book on the history of the county and its government since it was established in 1850. I covered the first century in a book published in 2013 and then moved on to continue the chronology in this one.

This book is primarily dependent on the collections of former county supervisors that contain correspondence with various government officials and constituents, county records for some departments, memos from supervisorial deputies, and court actions. The primary collections are those of four supervisors and several other county officials at the Henry E. Huntington Library in San Marino, California, and of additional supervisors at the Department of Special Collections at the University of Southern California, the Special Collections Department at the California State University at Los Angeles, and the Seaver Center for Western History Research at the Natural History Museum of Los Angeles County. Also helpful are collections of papers of city and state officials at the California State Archives, UCLA Special Collections Department, and the Bancroft Library at the University of California at Berkeley.

Other major sources include city, county, state, and federal documents relating to county issues, minutes of Board of Supervisors meetings (minutes since 1985 are online) and some department records available online, oral history program interviews of participants and personal interviews by the author, and various newspapers, especially my scan of the *Los Angeles Times* since 1950.

L.A.'s Titans of Temple Street (the street including the county's Hall of Administration) is almost unique in studying the history of one county since World War II, Los Angeles County being the most populous in the United States and an innovator in county procedures. I hope the book will provide a better understanding of how county government developed over the last 70 years and how it affects our everyday lives today.

Introduction

County government in the United States has always been an important agency of governance for the nation's population and a participant in national, state, and local history. But the study of the nation's urban history and metropolitan community over the last century has been primarily concerned with cities. Monographs on individual municipalities, urban politics, and specific issues focus mostly on developments within the confines of city limits. Rarely are neighboring municipalities, unincorporated communities, and the further regional hinterlands clearly brought into the analysis of local governance along with decision making at the county level. Studies of counties in the social sciences have been much more prevalent and have focused on specific topics such as transportation, social services, environmental protection, and the structure and process of government.

The same can be said for most studies of Los Angeles County. Few have been concerned with the history of county government, although it has had a significant effect on the numerous municipalities within county boundaries. Just as important is the impact of county government in the unincorporated areas for which it is almost completely responsible for municipal services. In large portions of these entities, county government plays the major role in addressing critical issues such as environmental degradation, regional planning, economic development, law enforcement and courts, the delivery of basic health and social services, and the quality of life.

An examination of the evolution of Los Angeles County since World War II is particularly important because of the size of its population as the nation's most populous county with more residents than forty-one of the states; its geographical space, making it one of the largest in territory; its over $44 billion budget for 2022–2023, more than all but nineteen states; the wide variety of services it provides; and its national role in pioneering "home rule" county government and contracting multiple services for incorporated cities. A study of this county provides historical context for the current relationship of county and city governments in solving regional and local issues. In addition, this context includes the county's role in addressing the myriad events such as financial recessions, civic uprisings, perceived threats from Soviet Russia and other countries, and other emergencies county officials had to respond to.

My first volume in the overall history of the county, *The Courthouse Crowd: Los Angeles County and Its Government, 1850–1950* (Los Angeles: Historical Society of

Southern California, 2013), examined the first century of Los Angeles County government and its role in shaping the political, economic, social, and environmental development of the county since its initial formation. It treated the county's relationship with its cities, the state, a multitude of special districts, and the unincorporated areas completely within its control. It focused especially on public policy and private initiatives for development that have left their mark on the county to this day.

Born in 1850 with twenty-six other California counties, Los Angeles County gradually established the foundation for its future as the predecessor of today's massive bureaucracy. This entity was initially created as an administrative sub-unit of California state government, a supplier of state services at the local level. The basic functions of California counties at their inception in 1850 were few and relatively simple, primarily public health and safety, courts and jails, recording land and vital personal records, collecting taxes, and a few others. In succeeding decades Los Angeles County services expanded as the population grew and the basis for the regional economy changed from raising cattle to agriculture to more urban industries. Its leadership in the official form of the board of supervisors after 1852 meshed public policy with private initiatives in stimulating economic growth, major industries, and opportunity; in addressing the needs of indigents and aiding social institutions; in the expansion of law enforcement and the courts; in providing new services and infrastructure with flood control and water diversion and supply, sanitation, and health facilities; in building roads and transportation networks and subsidizing railroads; in responding to the establishment of communities and demands for the formation of cities and of new counties; and in coping with calls for myriad political reforms. By the early decades of the twentieth century, Los Angeles County had emerged as a national leader in modernizing county functions and administration, although still beset with political conflicts and pressures from outside entities.

After 1920, major changes began to take place in the nation that affected counties and administrative policies. Locally, the tremendous population increase of the Roaring Twenties, the post–World War I economic boom, the formation of the nation's first regional planning commission and county zoning ordinance in Los Angeles County, and other factors called for the expansion and addition of county services. Economic and demographic shifts resulted in massive residential subdivisions and new business centers created as nodes of further activity throughout the county, especially after World War II; the expansion of social services provided with assistance from the federal and state governments during and after the Great Depression; attempts at structural reform of county governance in attempting to increase the number of supervisors and create the office of county executive; and the heightened alteration of the environment as a result of commercial, industrial, and residential development.

The first volume concluded about 1950, when some transformations continued amid further population increase, economic and social changes, and governmental innovations. This second volume picks up the story over the next seventy years as county government responded to increased demands for services by constituents, county department heads, and the state and federal governments with the pioneering Lakewood Plan of contracting for municipal services with new cities; struggled with civil rights issues regarding race relations, gender, and representation; responded to fiscal crises, most notably in the tax revolt and passage of Proposition 13 in 1978 and the reduction of funding for Los Angeles County's medical infrastructure as the county neared possible bankruptcy in the 1990s; and confronted many other major issues. These challenges since 1950 are treated in the present volume, which continues the story of the county's development after its first century.

The overall objective of this book is to demonstrate how the leaders of county government, primarily the county supervisors, coped with change and numerous crises. Most of the chapters focus on four basic themes that help to explain how various decisions were made that affected policies and actions, some of them effective, some not. Personality is one theme, as each supervisor is an individual with personal traits, temperament, attributes, and interests; five different personalities create many opportunities for conflicts in negotiations and final decisions. Ideology is sometimes an overriding theme as evident in cliques on the board voting together, although such groups are not always the dominant element in voting on certain issues. The structure of government is critical as there were many calls for reform to provide improved representation and administration, but always opposition to change by leaders who saw no need for it or disagreed on how it should be accomplished, particularly when it affected their power or even their job. And the power of the supervisors was palpable, as they were both the legislative and executive branches of county government, controlled a budget larger than most states, and could command generous political contributions. They usually left office when they retired, were termed out, or died, rarely after an election defeat. The last theme, outside forces, includes competing interest groups and city officials, the state and federal governments that create additional mandates for the county, environmental changes that must be addressed, and events and movements ranging from California politics to national legislation to international wars and violence that can affect local issues to various degrees. These themes demonstrate the restraints and influences faced by supervisors and other top county officials in their decision-making process.

This study is not an encyclopedia of Los Angeles County government over these years, which would require several more volumes. It is rather an interpretation of the development of this agency of governance based mostly on the actions of the county supervisors, a group of five powerful political figures—"The Titans of Temple Street"—who make decisions affecting well over ten million citizens in the greater Los Angeles region. In the larger national context, it is a case study in how the most populous United States county, the pioneer urban county and leader in innovation in the twentieth century, can provide a better understanding of the development of counties since World War II.

1

The Postwar Era
and the "Five Little Kings"

"Little" they were not, but "Kings" they were, as many observers have referred to the Los Angeles County Board of Supervisors (BOS).[1] It was for good reason, considering the political power of these officials, their longevity in office, and the structure of county government. In the mid-twentieth century, these five men had considerable control of land use, public safety, and many other issues affecting the everyday lives of Los Angeles County residents. Influenced by Cold War fears, state and federal government mandates, other outside forces, the competition between various interest groups, budget considerations, and their own ideologies and personalities, the supervisors and a few other officials shaped the type of services that would be available for millions of county residents and how county government would provide them.

Los Angeles County in 1950

In the century after its founding in 1850, Los Angeles County emerged as one of the nation's leading counties. Located in the southwestern portion of the nation in Southern California, the county encompassed 4083.21 square miles, larger than Delaware and Rhode Island combined. The major population center was the Los Angeles basin, surrounded by mountains and the Pacific Ocean. Almost half of the county's land is mountainous; about eleven percent is desert. The semi-arid Mediterranean climate of the area can be seen by easterners almost every New Year's Day.[2]

The county population in 1950 reached 4,151,687, an increase of 50 percent from 1940 thanks largely to newcomers working in military-related factories during the war, and veterans and their families moving to Southern California after 1945. By mid-century, the county had become the second most populous in the nation behind Cook County, Illinois, and more than five times larger than San Francisco County, the next largest in California. The racial composition totaled 87.3 percent White, 5.3 percent Black, 6 percent Latino, and 1.3 percent Asian.[3]

Initially a "cow county" where raising cattle was the driving force in the economy, Los Angeles County was transformed into the leading U.S. agricultural county by the early twentieth century. After World War II, residential subdivisions and industrial development replaced orchards and fields of planted crops, and the metropolitan area ranked third nationally in industrial production. Two decades later it would be number one. In 1950, the leading industries in the area included aircraft production, petroleum refining, motion pictures, secondary automobile assembly, metals and machinery manufacturing, heating and plumbing equipment, and others that ranked first, second, or third in the nation, many of them served by the largest port complex on the West coast.[4]

As a local government unit of the state of California, Los Angeles County in 1950 comprised the major portion of the third-largest metropolitan area of the nation, behind New York and Chicago. Forty-five incorporated cities were located within the county, including Los Angeles, the county seat, with a population of almost two million. The remaining unincorporated areas, for which the BOS acted as a mayor and city council providing administration and services, included 21 percent of the county population. That number would soon decline with many municipal incorporations in the 1950s and early 1960s. Almost eight hundred special districts in cities and unincorporated communities provided specific services such as flood control, street lighting, and mosquito abatement. These additional governmental units contributed to the confusion of residents regarding responsibility for services, and still do.[5]

The services provided by the county in 1950 far surpassed state mandates when California counties were created a century earlier. Law enforcement and courts, public health and welfare, infrastructure, public records and taxation, and a few other requirements were enhanced over the years with non-mandated services such as cultural institutions, a planning department, and civil defense units created in response to necessity or public demand. By 1950, there were over fifty major units of county government led by eight elected officials and judges and staffed by a huge bureaucracy of full-time employees and appointed commissioners and committee members.[6]

Overseeing most of the county departments and the budget of the entire government was the five-member BOS, each elected in their own district. Without an elected executive administrator such as a U.S. president or state governor, the BOS had both legislative and executive powers, as well as some quasi-judicial powers in cases of appeals. They also had some influence over the three other elected officials since they controlled the county purse. Each supervisor reigned like a king in his own district, as the others would defer to him if an issue existed only within his jurisdiction. If funds were to be spent on a county-wide project, the board would "divide by five" in splitting the total, regardless of where the funds were needed. And since most county government business was conducted outside of public meetings by the supervisors, their staff, and department heads, newspaper reports referred to it as "The Invisible Government."[7]

The Board of Supervisors

The members of the Los Angeles County Board of Supervisors in 1950 and throughout the next two decades resembled those on the board since 1876—White males, mostly Protestants and Republicans born in states other than California.

Primarily attorneys or businessmen, many of them had held local or state elective offices before joining the board, but none moved on to higher positions. For the most part, they retired after long tenures or died while in office; they rarely met defeat in reelection contests.

Los Angeles County's First District was represented by William Allan Smith, a native of Scotland, the only supervisor since 1950 born outside the U.S. Smith came to the U.S. as a child and moved to Whittier in 1921 and was the Whittier State School business manager. In 1931 he was hired as a field secretary for Supervisor Herbert Legg and replaced Legg on the BOS in 1938. Much more conservative than his predecessor, Smith would be defeated by Legg for the same office in 1950.[8]

The 1950 victor in the First District, Herbert Curtis Legg, was a New Yorker who moved to Downey, where he became a building contractor and later a citrus grower and developer. Legg served on the BOS from 1934 to 1938, when he ran unsuccessfully for governor of California. In the following year he was appointed Southern California coordinator for the Works Progress Administration. A liberal Democrat in the 1930s, he turned more conservative in his later service, stained by an indictment for perjury in 1956, but was not convicted. (See Chapter 2.) Toward the end of this term Legg suffered a heart attack and died in 1958.[9]

Following Legg's death, California Governor Goodwin Knight appointed Frank G. Bonelli as Legg's replacement. Bonelli came to Los Angeles from Colorado and became a businessman and developer in Huntington Park. He served on the city council there and as mayor. Elected as a Democrat to the California Assembly in 1953, Governor Knight chose him to complete Legg's term. Bonelli won the election that year and served on the BOS until his death while in office in 1972. A dependable conservative and friend of the region's business elite, he was a major force in the long campaign for reapportionment of the California State Senate, granting more representation to urban counties.[10]

In the Second District, Leonard J. Roach had been a supervisor since 1945. He came to Southern California from Nebraska in 1915, graduated from USC Law School, and became a South Gate attorney specializing in real estate development. In 1945, Governor Earl Warren chose him to complete the term of Supervisor Gordon McDonough, elected to Congress the previous year. Roach was one of the few Roman Catholic supervisors in the twentieth century, a Republican who usually voted with the conservatives until his defeat in 1952.[11]

Kenneth Hahn replaced Roach in December 1952 and would remain supervisor of the Second District for a record four decades. A Los Angeles native, Hahn graduated from Pepperdine College and earned an M.A. degree in education from USC. After serving in the U.S. Navy, he taught high school government and won a seat on the Los Angeles City Council in 1947. In 1952, he took on Leonard Roach in the supervisorial race and defeated the incumbent. A New Deal liberal Democrat and old-school yet young politician, Hahn was a White maverick in the county's increasingly minority district. He fought conservative supervisors and cuts to social services and took care of the needs of the residents in his district, as well as the rest of the county. Health problems finally forced him to retire in 1992.[12]

The Third District Supervisor, John Anson Ford, hailed from Wisconsin, where he taught in a Beloit high school and became a reporter for the *Chicago Tribune*. In 1920, he settled in Los Angeles and operated an advertising agency until his election to the BOS in 1934. A Wilson Democrat in the 1910s, Ford changed his party to Republican in the 1920s while affiliated with liberals, civic reformers, and the Church Federation of Los Angeles as a lay religious leader. By 1934, Ford was a Democrat again and defeated incumbent Harry Baine. After 1938, Ford was the lone liberal until Hahn joined him in 1952. Ford retired in 1958 and ran unsuccessfully for California Secretary of State. He continued to serve in appointed positions in local government until his death in 1983.[13]

Ford was succeeded by Ernest E. Debs, an Ohioan who moved to Los Angeles, where he worked in a small business and became active in Democratic politics in the 1930s. Elected to the California Assembly in 1942, he remained there until his election to the Los Angeles City Council five years later. In 1954, he challenged John Anson Ford, but lost. When Ford retired four years later, Debs ran again, and defeated another city council member, Edward Roybal, in a contested battle based on missing ballots. Part of Debs' legacy after his 1974 retirement included the generous disability payout, he claimed for suffering two years of frustration trying to cope with another supervisor.[14]

In the Fourth District, Raymond V. Darby continued to serve after defeating incumbent Oscar Hague in 1944. Born in Kansas, Darby was a geologist by training, who moved to Inglewood in the 1920s and opened a real estate and construction business. He soon became involved in local politics as a city council member and mayor during World War II. As a supervisor, the Republican Darby voted consistently with the other conservatives. He ran for governor of California in 1950, but lost in the primary and died while in office in 1953, after being assaulted by an irate developer in the boardroom and suffering a stroke.[15]

Darby was replaced by Burton W. Chace, a Nebraskan who moved to Southern California in 1923. He settled in Long Beach, where he owned a lumber business and became interested in politics. In 1933, he was elected to the city's board of education, then to the city council, and as mayor from 1947 to 1953. After Darby's death in the latter year, Governor Earl Warren appointed Chace to the BOS. A solid Republican conservative, he became especially concerned with his beach cities and the Marina del Rey small craft harbor. Chace would not run for reelection in 1972 and died while still in office.[16]

Fifth District Supervisor Roger Wolcott Jessup was born in Utah and moved to Southern California after military service in World War I. He settled in Glendale and established a dairy business. A "staunchly conservative" Republican, Jessup won election to the board in 1932, and remained there until he retired while in the midst of a reelection contest in 1956. In those years he was consistently endorsed by the business establishment and usually followed the wishes of its leaders. He received some elite support in his unsuccessful run for California governor in 1942, and in his quest to become mayor of Los Angeles in 1945. In both contests he lost to stronger candidates also backed by the elite.[17]

Jessup was succeeded by Warren Max Dorn, the victor in the 1956 campaign. After the incumbent dropped out, Dorn won the contest and would serve until his

The Los Angeles County Board of Supervisors in 1959. Seated from left: Burton Chace, Ernest Debs, Frank Bonelli, Warren Dorn, and Kenneth Hahn. CAO Lindon Hollinger stands behind them (Frank G. Bonelli Collection, Seaver Center for Western History Research, Los Angeles County Museum of Natural History).

defeat for reelection in 1972. Born and raised in Pasadena, he became a schoolteacher and then a realtor interested in local politics. In 1949, he won election to the board of directors of Pasadena and served as mayor in 1955–1956. In those years he was active in the Los Angeles County Division of the League of California Cities, at times at odds with county officials on certain issues. Once on the board of supervisors, Dorn was a maverick, who ran unsuccessfully for California governor in the Republican primary in 1966.[18]

The Los Angeles County supervisors in the first two decades of the post–1950 period split into cliques favoring ideology, interest group agendas, and personalities, as local governing units often do. These splits were only occasional, however, since the supervisors usually voted unanimously as issues were discussed and compromises made before BOS meetings. In the early 1950s, Democrat John Anson Ford, a champion of cultural institutions, occasionally cast the only vote on some issues, with the three conservative Republicans and conservative Democrat Herbert Legg opposing him. With the 1952 election of Democrat Kenneth Hahn, the two opposed Legg, Jessup, and usually Darby on ideological issues. Darby's death in 1953 brought in Burton Chace, another conservative Republican noted for his ability to work with department heads, as well as Legg and Jessup.[19]

After the 1956 election, the BOS splits became more personal. The Republican Dorn and Democrat Hahn were reform-minded like Ford, and the three composed a clique on some issues for the short time Dorn and Ford served together. Hahn and Ford disagreed on some projects, however, such as the county's commitment to fund the Descanso Gardens horticultural attraction. Hahn and Dorn would differ on some issues over the next sixteen years, but generally stayed together as they both raised the ire of the more conservative supervisors, Democrat Bonelli and Republican Chace. Bonelli and Dorn would carry on a feud in the 1960s as the two frequently argued during BOS meetings. Democrat Ernest Debs, who succeeded Ford in 1958, considered himself a liberal, although he supplied the swing vote many times for the conservatives. He, too, had frequent problems with Dorn. Occasional supervisor conflicts would increase by 1973, when Hahn, just chosen as chairman of the board, pledged to reduce the growing bitterness and personality conflicts. Unfortunately, it would only get worse. (See Chapter 5.)[20]

The CAO and County Counsel

In carrying out their duties in county governance the supervisors depended on many officers and department heads responsible for the administration of various government units. Among the most important in this era were the chief administrator officer (CAO) and the county counsel. Wayne Allen, appointed the first CAO in 1938, created the template for this position as the liaison between department heads and the supervisors, and acquired increasing influence within the bureaucracy. During World War II, he received an appointment with the U.S. Army overseas and took a leave from the county, which he did again in 1951, before officially retiring in 1954. During the latter leave and then officially until 1957, Arthur J. Will served as CAO. A graduate of USC who rose through the county ranks since 1932, Will was lauded for his organizational skills and establishing cooperation among the departments. His successor, Lindon S. Hollinger, joined the county workforce as a messenger in 1929 and rose through the ranks like Will. Hollinger was especially concerned with budget matters and the public perception of county leadership, and he experienced several setbacks in his relations with the supervisors. He was followed in 1970 by Arthur G. Will, the son of Arthur J. Will. Arthur G. admitted that he "lived in the civil service tradition" while growing up and became well-known for his trimming the county budget during lean years in the early 1970s. In 1974, the stress of the "punching-bag role" he had to play in dealing with board members in a contentious era led to his accepting a similar job in Contra Costa County, where the pressure was not as severe. These CAOs played an important role in the administration of a growing government as the county population, workforce, infrastructure, and budget mushroomed over the thirty years following the war.[21]

Of even more importance to the supervisors at various times was the county's lawyer, County Counsel Harold W. Kennedy, Mr. Fixit in many respects. Born in Colorado and raised in Pomona, Kennedy earned his law degree at UC Berkeley and worked in the district attorney's office for two years. He then moved to the county counsel's unit and took over monitoring state legislation affecting the county during sessions of the legislature in Sacramento, drafting laws for the county's benefit, and lobbying state legislators, many of them from small rural counties competing with Los Angeles. In 1945, the BOS appointed him county counsel, and his major activities over the next few years included drafting the 1947 Air Pollution Control District Act for Los Angeles County, and, with the CAO, composing the county's Cold War loyalty check program for its employees in 1947 and ordinances for the registration of communists in 1950. In the early 1950s, Kennedy emerged as the leading figure in defending California counties from incorporated cities challenging the amount of taxes paid to county general funds that were used to support unincorporated areas; Kennedy devised a new special district category to meet those inequalities. Asked to assist in shaping California's overall water plan in 1954, he was loaned to the state legislature to analyze water issues. He performed all of these tasks and many more besides wide-ranging legal work for the supervisors and department heads. Kennedy finally retired in 1967, succeeded by John Maharg, who served until 1973.[22]

Cold War Politics

One of the most profound political issues affecting county government after World War II was international—the Cold War. Postwar events such as the testing of an atomic bomb by the Soviet Union, escalation of the conflict in Korea, and revelations of espionage heightened global tensions and influenced American politics, from national to local. Los Angeles County politics reflected those tensions as issues became more contentious in the Cold War atmosphere that seemed to cast many debates in ideological terms.[23]

In the five years before 1950, most supervisors were supporters of the regional entrepreneurial elite leaders and the anti-communist crusade aimed at expanding business opportunities, restricting labor unions, and crushing the influence of the Left. In most cases they would pursue measures to oppose ideas and persons deemed to be threats to security with little regard for constitutional rights. That would include requiring loyalty oaths by county employees and issuing resolutions in support of outlawing the Communist Party in 1947. The county counsel advised that such actions would be found to be unconstitutional, but the supervisors, except John Anson Ford, approved a loyalty check requiring county employees to swear their loyalty and list "subversive" organizations to which they had been a member. This loyalty oath, the first such county ordinance in the nation, resulted in the discharge of thirty-three employees who refused to sign it. The supervisors were shocked when informed by the county counsel that nine employees admitted their current membership in the Communist Party and could not be fired since they signed the form truthfully.[24]

The Cold War heated up in late 1949 through 1950, with the Soviet test of an atomic bomb, investigations of alleged Communists in the U.S. government, and U.S. troops fighting in Korea. In the summer of 1950, Congress considered a bill to require the registration of communists to keep track of their movements. Not to be outdone, the county supervisors decided to require the registration of Communists and their sympathizers in Los Angeles County. This first county "Red Registration" ordinance in the nation passed in 1950, and several arrests of resistors were made before the ordinance was ruled unconstitutional by local judges. The county did not stop trying to investigate possible subversives, however, as the supervisors ordered county employees to testify before the House Un-American Activities Committee (HUAC) if subpoenaed to do so in 1952. At least one county social worker was fired for refusing to testify at a HUAC hearing that year.[25]

Housing became a major county issue during the era of the Red Scare. The housing shortage during the war had forced the supervisors to step up the county's public housing program, as did officials in many cities. Immediately after the war most local governments continued to expand emergency and public housing to meet the needs of the growing population as long as the federal government subsidized most of it. In 1946, the BOS appropriated an additional $100,000 for housing relief, as well as voting to allow the Los Angeles County Housing Authority (LACHA) to use any appropriate parcels in unincorporated territory for the temporary placement of Quonset huts as long as the federal government paid for everything except utilities. At the same time the board had to settle the problem of rent control. Apartment owners had been complaining of federal control of rents, and tenants in county territory were being evicted. When federal rent controls lapsed in the summer of 1946, the board followed the lead of the Los Angeles City Council in approving a rent control ordinance capping increases at 15 percent as the two agencies awaited further legislation from Congress.[26]

During the county loyalty oath campaign in 1948, the housing program became associated with radicalism as business forces opposed to both public housing and rent control initiated a campaign to defeat the statewide Proposition 14. This initiative, backed by housing advocates, progressives, labor, and other groups, would create a state housing authority to support city and county public housing agencies in California. A Committee for Home Protection became the local unit of a growing movement in the nation led by real estate interests to cast public housing as a "communist scheme" to create further government intrusion on private enterprise. With generous contributions from wealthy developers, Proposition 14 suffered defeat. But in the following July, President Truman signed the Taft-Ellender-Wagner Act providing for 810,000 units of public housing across the nation. The Los Angeles City Council unanimously approved an application for funds to build 10,000 units as the city became the first government entity to receive a contract. Los Angeles continued to move forward swiftly on its housing program, while proponents of public housing complained to the supervisors that LACHA did little other than keeping housing projects racially segregated while violating federal regulations.[27]

By late 1949, most of the supervisors appeared as anti-public housing as their housing commissioners. In several BOS meetings the majority voted 4–1 against approving a federal loan application. The supervisors were reminded that at that same time 30,000 rental units were being destroyed for construction of freeways and the civic center, over 75,000 unemployed veterans did not have decent housing, and that slum clearance for public housing could provide thousands of jobs, reducing the county relief load. The vote did not change, and thus the county halted its commitment to federally subsidized low-cost housing in the year the city enthusiastically embraced it.[28]

At the same time, the board majority moved to end rent controls in unincorporated areas.

This effort coincided with a nation-wide crusade of real estate interests and landlords to abolish all rent controls. In August 1950, the supervisors voted 4–1 to urge the local federal rent control office to end the regulations in unincorporated areas. When President Truman finally signed a bill containing a local option, the county and most of its cities quickly ended rent control within their jurisdictions.[29]

With the rent control battle over, business interests pushed to end construction of any more public housing in Los Angeles. The fight in the city would continue until 1953, when Mayor Fletcher Bowron was defeated by Norris Poulson, who made "government socialism" in the form of public housing the major campaign issue. Meanwhile, the county's Regional Planning Commission reported in November 1950 that the housing shortage had ended.[30]

After 1950, like officials in counties and cities throughout the nation, the Los Angeles County supervisors continued to pursue earlier initiatives in combating possible subversion and attacks on the homeland. Wartime programs such as a block warden system composed of volunteers, air raid planning, and appointing a civil defense agency were revived in cities and the county. An air raid system was installed in 1955 with financial help from the state after the supervisors were warned that a Soviet attack was likely. In the same year the supervisors ordered the distribution of a booklet entitled "You and the H Bomb" to all private homes in unincorporated areas. At a time when some residents began building private bomb shelters on their property, the supervisors began to study sites for large shelters for the population. By 1961, Kenneth Hahn provided leadership on this issue at a time when city officials in Santa Barbara and Palm Springs assured residents of Los Angeles that they would welcome Angelenos in case of a nuclear attack. (At the same time, the civil defense coordinator of Riverside County raised the ire of his supervisors for recommending that Riverside residents "arm themselves to repel possible hordes of Los Angeles refugees.") Hahn developed a program designed to build shelters in county school yards to protect up to six million people from fallout in the event of a nuclear attack and hoped county taxpayers would vote for it with the slogan "A dime a day will keep the fallout away!" The board liked his idea but agreed that the $400,000 to pay for it should come from the federal government, not county residents. Hahn asked President Kennedy for his support as part of a federal initiative to finance such projects, but the president and Congress declined. The supervisors did establish shelters in some existing buildings during the rest of the decade with federal help in stocking them with supplies.[31]

The BOS also continued its fight against communists and allied groups, including county workers and candidates for county offices. Inspired by the Congressional House Un-American Activities Committee and Senator Joseph McCarthy's investigations, as well as those of California's Tenney Committee, the supervisors and other county officials were active in suppressing the local Left. The previously mentioned "Red Registration" ordinance of 1950 was immediately ruled unconstitutional by local judges, as well as being ineffective as it only applied to those living in unincorporated areas. The supervisors then requested that the state legislature pass a similar law affecting the entire state, but an appellate court ruling in 1951 declared it unconstitutional. Hahn turned to making sure that the Communist Party label appeared on ballots of these candidates, even though county elections were non-partisan. (The *Times* pointed out in earlier stories the Communist affiliations of candidates running for sheriff and assessor in 1950.) The interest in 1964 was generated by Hahn, then facing an opponent who worked for the Communist Party in his reelection race and wanted to be sure voters knew it. He introduced motions to recommend state legislation for Communists to be identified on ballots, and to urge the California Bar Association to deny membership to party members. Neither would be approved.[32]

Loyalty oaths required of county employees, were also defended, and held up as models for other government agencies. Refusing to complete or sign the oaths led to discharges of county employees, as well as city and state workers in the 1950s. The list of organizations that an employee had to note if a past or present member posed a particular problem for Supervisor Ford, who admitted that he belonged to two of them, as well as being a proud member of the American Civil Liberties Union and a past member of the Friends of the Abraham Lincoln Brigade during the Spanish Civil War in the late 1930s. Both groups were considered by conservative politicians and others to be to be dominated by communists. After being upheld in courts on several levels through almost two decades, the county loyalty oath was finally struck down in 1967.[33]

The supervisors also had to contend with other political groups on the far right and far left. Their predominant interest was communism, which they pursued in the actions mentioned above, plus ordering a 1964 report by the county counsel to study U.S. Supreme Court cases relating to the Communist Party, which they distributed to members of Congress and the public. The report was highly critical of the court, charging that it aided communist subversion. Other county officials blamed groups on the Left for county problems; a former County Grand Jury foreman suggested that the supervisors should sue the Black Panthers and other groups for damages resulting from rioting. On the other hand, the supervisors also requested the county counsel to report on methods to control the activities of the American Nazi Party which acquired a house in Glendale for its national headquarters in 1964, as well as similar hate groups. Critics of state and county mental health programs described them as communist plots and demanded that socialized medicine be abolished. The list of complaints about groups on both ideological ends seemed endless.[34]

Censorship was also a weapon of anti-communist groups in preventing certain publications from reaching the eyes of children and adults. One example was the campaign to keep advocates of United Nations Educational, Scientific and Cultural Organization materials from the Los Angeles City Board of Education in 1952–1953 and later. Opponents considered the human rights organization to be an anti–American "One World" agency spreading its propaganda in teaching materials.[35] In unincorporated Hacienda Heights in 1971, the local Republican Women's Club complained that the county library program showed propaganda films that "contain Communist-Socialist, Marxist-Leninist viewpoints of our society" followed by discussion periods lacking opposing viewpoints. Bonelli asked the county librarian to review the films in question, and the librarian pulled them from circulation. This decision faced criticism by other California librarians and newspaper editors for caving into the censors; Bonelli responded with a temporary hold on financing for another county library building already approved.[36]

The influence of Cold War politics was also evident in the county art scene. As historian Sarah Schrank has observed, in the years immediately following World War II, abstract art produced by modernists, some of them returning veterans, competed with more traditionalist landscape and still-life works offered by members of art clubs in county and city exhibitions. As county art institutions displayed more of the modernist pieces, the conservative artists objected. At the 1947 annual exhibition of works of local artists at the County Museum of History, Science, and Art, the winning abstract pieces were called "degenerate junk" inspired by communism by the losers, who organized demonstrations and demands for the museum director's resignation until the county supervisors ordered the abstract art to be removed. A similar situation occurred at the All-City Art Show in 1951, when conservative artists called winning abstract pieces "communistic" as they had in other shows. They had the Los Angeles City Council up in arms until Mayor Bowron helped to downplay the controversy and it eventually dissolved. Four years later the council became alarmed again with the installation of the abstract Bernard Rosenthal sculpture, *The Family*, at the new Los Angeles Police Department headquarters, generating protests but not removal of the piece.[37]

The county supervisors faced more protests of art in county facilities in the early 1950s.

In 1951, the Los Angeles Coordinating Committee for Traditional Art objected to a county museum exhibition including twenty paintings by artists listed in a Michigan Congressman's speech "Communists Maneuver to Control Art in the United States." The Congressman also described a certain gallery in New York City that was invited to contribute pieces for the exhibition as "adhering strictly to the Communist Party line." The chairman of the committee claimed that it represented 7769 members and called for its supporting organizations to protest to the museum's board of governors, the supervisors, and city newspapers; but little more would be heard from them. Another controversy arose in 1953, when a conservative political activist protested the appearance of a USC assistant professor's prize-winning painting on display in the county museum. The modernist painting was a "monstrosity," she claimed, and might even be "Communistic propaganda." A *Times* art critic thought it had "delightful color," a bright red that must have convinced the activist of its inspiration by communism. Since the activist was a frequent critic of the supervisors, they apparently decided to have the painting removed from display to appease her. It was just as well, for in the following year the painting became part of a national exhibition of contemporary art at the Art Institute of Chicago. And in 1956, members of the American Legion post in Malibu protested the inclusion of two members of the jury chosen by curator and noted artist Millard Sheets for an exhibition at the county fair. Both had been described as "Marxist evaluators posing as critics" by the aforementioned member of Congress. In this instance the supervisors were able to pass the protest along to the County Fair Association.[38]

The Supervisors and the Entrepreneurial Elite

As in the years before 1950, most of the county supervisors acceded to the requests of the regional business and social elite whenever possible. Dependent on election campaign contributions and financial and political support for county issues, BOS members were also motivated by the same drive to develop the county's industrial and residential expansion in working closely with the regional leadership. This would include the appointment of business and professional leaders to powerful county agencies such as the Regional Planning Commission and the boards of governors of cultural institutions favored by the elite. Contributing county support for a regional transit system, assisting with the location of a new Ford assembly plant in Pico Rivera, and helping business and political leader Asa Call to obtain a contract to fund USC medical services for the county hospital because of a USC financial emergency comprised a few of these types of favors that encouraged the business establishment to support the supervisors.[39]

As usual, the supervisors worked closely with major business organizations, especially the Los Angeles Chamber of Commerce, whose directors were friends of BOS members. For decades the supervisors approved budget appropriations for the Chamber to attract industries to the area. Supervisors were invited to speak to the directors every year to seek support for county initiatives and to accompany directors on proselytizing junkets; at least by 1970, all five and their spouses were invited to annual retreats to play golf, be entertained, and talk business. A related organization was the All-Year Club, which attracted tourists to the area through publications, advertisements, and such. This agency invited the supervisors to annual luncheons in the 1950s to lobby for funding which reached $800,000 in the 1960s and had to be cut back by 1970. Several smaller organizations with similar objectives received much less, and chambers of commerce in cities outside Los Angeles were usually left out.[40]

In a BOS conflict in supporting the business elite in the early 1950s, the board had to face choosing a site for a new county courthouse, a dilemma that had festered since the old courthouse suffered significant damage in the 1933 Long Beach earthquake. After failed attempts to obtain federal subsidies or win bond elections, the supervisors decided to save excess funds each budget year until enough could be amassed to start the project. By 1951, they were ready to go, but faced opposition to the original site by retailers who wanted to move it further south to increase their downtown property values. Roach, Legg, and Jessup voted for the move, while Ford and Darby opposed it because of the $2.5 million already expended for architectural planning and land acquisition. As Legg stated that day, "In a case like this I think we should help the downtown business interests." But Ford and Darby refused. The standoff continued for over a year, when Hahn joined Ford and Darby in voting for the original site, and Legg and Jessup refused to supply the necessary fourth vote. The issue was finally settled in January 1953, after the Los Angeles City Planning Commission disapproved of the original site and the BOS voted for a compromise location nearby. A courthouse committee of the local elite was appointed to study the new plan, and the building would be completed in late 1958.[41]

Another situation demonstrating a difference of supervisor opinions relating to the entrepreneurial elite involved the Los Angeles County Museum of Art in 1966. One of its earliest exhibitions, produced by local artist Edward Kienholz, included two sections that enraged several supervisors: one was the back seat of a 1938 Dodge with mannequins of two teenagers exploring sex, the other contained a number of objects arranged inside a brothel. Dorn objected to a portrait of General Douglas MacArthur in the brothel as "unpatriotic," and demanded that the door of the Dodge be closed as the scene was "pornographic." Bonelli threatened to withhold county funding from the museum, and Hahn joined him in a motion to lease the museum to a private support group. The *Times* and other newspapers questioned the supervisors' place to judge art, while Edward Carter and other members of the business elite on the museum's board of governors refused to close the exhibit. The supervisors eventually voted 4–1, with Bonelli opposed, to support their appointed governors and honor their legal commitments. Dorn, however, who announced that he "knows pornography," kept up his public condemnation of the exhibition. He was criticized by Debs, who stated that Dorn was just doing it for publicity in his campaign for California governor. In the end, they agreed that there would be tight security for the exhibit, and it would be limited to those eighteen and older.[42]

Cooperation between the elite and the supervisors was completely copasetic in the creation of the Music Center. The drive for such an entity began in the 1940s, but public funding could not be secured. In 1955, Dorothy Chandler—a well-known philanthropist, president of the Hollywood Bowl Association, regent of the University of California, and spouse of *Times* publisher Norman Chandler—was chosen by the supervisors to lead a citizens' committee to obtain private financing for such a structure. She would be instrumental in the choice of the members of this group, which included Asa Call and other powerful business, political, and social leaders. Her ability to convince them and others to contribute to the fund raised over $19 million by the early 1960s. The effort was also aided by the Chamber of Commerce, whose president lauded her efforts and urged businesses to contribute the remaining amount needed. This fund, along with county government lease-back bonds, allowed noted architect Welton Becket to design the structure completed in 1964 and named the Dorothy Chandler Pavilion. Two additional buildings, the Mark Taper Forum and Ahmanson Theater, were added to the property in the next few years. During the entire time, the supervisors worked closely with Mrs. Chandler and awarded her with a Los Angeles County Distinguished Service Medal for her heroic efforts. The supervisors received an outstanding county music and theatrical venue and, according to a former *Times* reporter, a respite from the publication of county scandals in the 1950s and 1960s that appeared in other papers but were squelched in the *Times* because of the association of the supervisors and the publisher's spouse.[43]

In the above situations and others, such as enticing the Brooklyn Dodgers to move to Los Angeles, in which Supervisor Hahn worked with city officials and the Chamber of Commerce to convince Dodgers owner Walter O'Malley to move, county supervisors supported the business establishment in numerous ventures to increase industrial and residential development in the region. This partnership of boosters was advantageous for both groups.[44]

County Law Enforcement

The preservation of law and order in the county since 1950 has been in the hands of two elected officials—the sheriff and the district attorney—as well as the elected judges of the Superior and Municipal (to 2000) courts. These officers are assisted by the Probation Department, public defenders, the County Grand Jury, and until the 1990s, by county marshals who served as bailiffs in the Municipal courts.

In the 1950s and 1960s, the Los Angeles County Sheriff's Department (LASD) was headed by Eugene Biscailuz and Peter Pitchess. Biscailuz, born in Boyle Heights, joined the department in 1907, and rose in the ranks until his appointment to head the California Highway Patrol in 1929. Shortly after, he returned to his previous position in Los Angeles, and was appointed sheriff in 1932. His career as sheriff lasted until his retirement in 1958. Over those years he was hailed for modernizing the department and participating in many county initiatives such as heading the civil defense committee during and after World War II. He worked well with the business community and became a local celebrity as he displayed his love of Western lore in appearing at parades atop a horse with decorative saddlery. On the other hand, he received criticism in newspaper stories for lax oversight of the department's liquor control efforts during Prohibition, and by the state attorney general and County Grand Jury regarding LASD vice squad scandals in the 1940s.[45]

Pete Pitchess also loved riding horses but was much less of a showman. Born in Salt Lake City, he earned his law degree and worked as a special agent in the Federal Bureau of Investigation. He moved to Los Angeles in 1952 and joined the LASD the following year as undersheriff to Biscailuz. When the latter retired in 1958, he supported Pitchess as his successor, and Pitchess's tenure would last until he retired in 1981. In those years he was noted for further modernizing the department and carrying on a more contentious relationship with the BOS. He became adept at playing the supervisors against each other and currying support from the business elite in obtaining more funding for his agency. In the 1970s, he would have to confront the conduct of his deputies in the Latino protests that included the death of reporter Ruben Salazar, and scandals revealed by Supervisor Baxter Ward and the *Times*. (See Chapters 4 and 5.)[46]

During these years, the LASD would confront many issues from the past as well as the present. With the growing population in the county the sheriff demanded more resources to fight increasing crime. After several critical reports of grand jurors describing deplorable jail conditions, the situation had to be redressed with the construction of the Men's Central Jail and the Sybil Brand Institute for Women in 1963. Both required more staff to guard the increasing inmates, as did the new contract system to provide services for new cities. (See Chapter 3.) The costs of adding contract services were the subject of many disagreements between the sheriff, the BOS, and officials in the new cities and the older cities that kept their own municipal departments. The conflict was a major issue in the gradual personal conflict between Pitchess and the supervisors and CAO. Pitchess appeared much more confrontational than Biscailuz, and frequently demanded more staff and funding months after the county budget had already been approved, as well as publicly criticizing supervisors during their reelection campaigns. Juvenile crime also increased in this era, as it did throughout the nation, attracting the attention of the state legislature, the county's Human Relations Commission and the ACLU on the Sunset Strip riots of 1966 involving youths protesting curfews in Hollywood. Sheriff's deputies were also accused of racial discrimination, although much less than the LAPD. (See Chapter 4.)[47]

The Sheriff's Department acquired additional duties in enforcing "morality" ordinances passed by the supervisors and occasionally investigating the supervisors themselves. Gambling had always been an interest of the BOS, and in the 1950s the board outlawed "claw machines" available in some areas of the county. In the early 1960s, the BOS voted to ban draw poker, even in one's home if it involved money, and established a commission on pornography to eradicate racy movies and comic books. In 1951, the board approved a "burlesque control" ordinance, followed it up in 1965 with an effort to regulate topless bars, and tried to ban nude dancing in bars in 1970. In some cases, these actions might also focus attention on the supervisors themselves, as the "claw machine" issue convinced some residents that Legg and Jessup might be beholden to gamblers; they both voted against the ordinance and the machines could only be found in their districts.[48]

Another challenge for law enforcement was the continued presence of organized crime related to vice and other opportunities. In the early 1950s, several representatives of the New York and Chicago organizations, as well as home-grown mobsters from the previous decade, were still engaged in various rackets, including prostitution, bookmaking, narcotics distribution, extortion, grand theft, and various forms of gambling. When not in prison in the 1950s, Mickey Cohen could be found at the top of the list, as noted in a state investigation in 1957, which included notes on many of his gangland associates, some of them in various units of the Mafia. Another local racketeer listed was Ray "Whitey" Christl, a gambler and "good friend" of Legg and of Chace's chief deputy. Christl was involved with the Los Angeles County rubbish change from burning in home incinerators to burying in dumps to reduce air pollution. In this situation Legg was indicted but not convicted for perjury in accepting bribes in 1956. (See Chapter 2.)[49]

Organized crime figures also partnered with local hoodlums in various rackets, particularly gambling. Groups of the two were always active in Hollywood and other areas of the city of Los Angeles, in Culver City in the late 1940s and early 1950s, and in unincorporated areas such as Bell Gardens in the early 1950s and 1960s. Some of these activities included the involvement of LASD deputies accepting bribes to protect vice operations in the late 1940s that resulted in an investigation by state authorities and the County Grand Jury in 1949 and 1950. The 1950 report "The Pattern of Vice Protection" documented the actions of deputies in a major gambling operation leading to the firing of the chief of the vice squad and bribery convictions of the chief and a retired captain. Several other LASD deputies were also implicated in accepting loans and gifts from the mobsters involved, but not charged with any crime. Sheriff Biscailuz was criticized for not conducting an investigation until forced to.[50]

The LASD vice protection scandal and the perjury and bribery trials related to Legg's involvement in the rubbish collection issue were two of several major charges of county government corruption in the 1950s. A more sweeping accusation was offered by television news reporter George Putnam in 1956. Putnam began a crusade calling for an investigation of county government after scandals including payoffs for liquor licenses to a member of the board of equalization, the rubbish hearing, and an on-going state legislature investigation of it, the "mockery of justice in the Supervisor Legg perjury case" and related probes, reports of a "captive Grand Jury" unable to investigate, and a 37.8 percent rise in crime. He invited the district attorney to appear on his show to explain these incidents and his office's inadequate reviews of them and asked the governor for a full investigation and to reactivate the state crime commission of the 1940s. For almost three months he supplied listeners with a long list of alleged crimes and the names of local underworld figures. The television shows probably kept his audience interested but did make a difference. As the *Times* editorial title appearing at the end of the campaign, "Rumor, Gossip, Innuendo Not News" opined, Putnam's program "exceeded the dictates both of journalistic responsibility and of good taste." The editorial's blanket defense of county officials attacked by Putnam saved some reputations in the region but did not resolve the charges.[51]

Putnam was not the only critic of a county district attorney the 1950s. District attorneys of that decade were responsible for investigating such incidents, but some had various problems in meeting those duties. Several of the past district attorneys had questionable reputations, especially Asa Keyes (convicted of accepting bribes in the 1920s), Buron Fitts (indicted but not convicted in the 1930s), and Fred Howser (associated with gamblers in the 1940s and suspected of colluding with them while state attorney general). The district attorney in 1950, William E. Simpson, initially blocked the investigation of the LASD vice protection case and an earlier wiretapping case involving the LAPD Vice Squad and mobster Mickey Cohen but was forced to proceed with both. After Simpson died in 1951, the supervisors appointed Ernest Roll to the office, and he served until his death in late 1956. Roll was accused by a member of the 1954 County Grand Jury of blocking the investigation of bribery regarding the granting of liquor licenses and ignoring charges that asphalt the county paid for was never received. He was also one of Putnam's many targets. After Roll's death the supervisors faced 30 contenders to the office, including Jack Tenney, the former liberal-turned-conservative assemblyman who chaired the state's Un-American Activities Committee during the 1940s. After lobbying by supporters of the nominees, the supervisors chose Superior Court Judge William B. McKesson as the D.A.[52]

McKesson was an improvement over his three predecessors in that the only major criticism of him revolved around his role in campaigning for state attorney general candidate Pat Brown in 1958. He won his own election campaign that year and again in 1960, both times as a moderate with the endorsement of the conservative *Times*. He decided not to run again in 1964, and the victor that year was Superior Court Judge Evelle Younger, who would have a distinguished record in his six years in office. In 1970, Younger was elected California attorney general, and he ran unsuccessfully for governor in 1978. His successor, Joseph Busch, Jr., was known as a nice guy, but not a very able administrator. Busch would die after a heart attack in 1975, one of three district attorneys who died while in this stressful job since 1950.[53]

The district attorney's office also supplied a legal mentor for the County Grand Jury, which reviewed county and city government operations and had responsibility for hearing criminal proceedings that could lead to indictments and trials. The annual sessions were particularly interested in law enforcement, the conditions of county jails and the treatment of juveniles in county care, among other issues. The vice protection report previously mentioned was one of its major accomplishments of this era, reminiscent of the 1928 jury and the "runaway" juries of the 1930s that led to the indictments of district attorneys and others. Each jury appointed by superior court judges are aided by a legal advisor, investigators, and funding for auditors that always seemed to be too little yet produced some important results. In fact, the board did not always respect the contributions of some of the juries. In 1972, a supervisor described the overall process as "We give them [the jurors] a dinner and a badge, and a scroll when they leave. We say, 'Thank you for your service, and God bless you.' And then the next group comes in."[54]

While the BOS worked with judges to improve court procedures, the period was a stormy time for the relationship. On several occasions the supervisors refused to consider adding additional judges because of the added costs to county government, even though the numbers of criminal and civil cases increased with the added population. In other issues, one or all supervisors tried to limit judges lobbying on county time and expense for laws in Sacramento, especially laws the BOS unanimously opposed. The supervisors disagreed at times on whether to approve travel expenses for judges to attend professional conferences, or tried to at least limit the number of attendees, except for allowing a judge in one's district. By 1970, Hahn wanted a freeze on all travel for judges because of overcrowded case calendars. And in 1973, he demanded an investigation of a Municipal Court judge in Santa Monica who ordered two county maintenance workers to a holding cell for forty-five minutes because they refused to adjust a thermostat they were not allowed to access, as it was ordered as part of a conservation program. The supervisors had other contentious moments with some judges at the same time they sought to improve the judicial process. The rest of the 1970s decade would not be much different.[55]

Busting Budgets

The annual county budget included estimated revenue and expenditures for all its operations, and capital projects were an especially costly group in this era. During the Great Depression and World War II, few massive and expensive structures could be built because of the press of rising welfare and public safety considerations. The construction of a new county courthouse after the 1933 Long Beach earthquake damage to the existing edifice was not completed until 25 years later.

With the increasing population in far-flung suburbs after 1945, the supervisors had to catch up with buildings and services for those residents and an expanding county workforce. Budget deliberations continued as they did in the 1940s, although the funding totals were much higher. Various interest groups and individuals demanded new necessities and amenities, prices for goods and employee salaries were on the rise, and taxpayer associations and residents protested if supervisors raised their property taxes and service fees. The entrepreneurial elite expected taxes to be kept low while the supervisors were supposed to subsidize industry, business expansion and tourism. City officials complained that county expenditures on generous salaries and other items forced them to raise their municipal taxes as well. (See Chapter 3.)[56]

The years following 1950 would witness huge increases in spending and property taxes which resulted in taxpayer protests and critical editorials in newspapers. Supervisor Chace sought to explain why taxes were rising so high in 1958 with the construction of schools for the children of new residents, the rising overall population, inflation, state mandated spending and other contributors, but his statement probably fell on many deaf ears. Other supervisors tried to limit some expense items such as subsidies to the Chamber of Commerce as advocated by grand jurors and Supervisor Ford since his first election; Hahn demanding an investigation of County Road Department appropriations from state gasoline taxes not being spent on construction; and of several supervisors arguing in 1957 over whether to sell most of Descanso Gardens to raise revenue. In the same year, Hahn recommended deleting a few $23 decorative waste baskets for the new courthouse when most county offices had seventy-five cent baskets, as the supervisors strived to reduce the preliminary budget by $16 million. The final budget would include the restoration of most of the proposed cuts.[57]

The 1960s were even more fiscally challenged for county administrators. In early 1961, CAO Hollinger reported that 774 county jobs *could* be cut temporarily to save funds but recommended against it as it would also cut services and would be expensive to replace them later. The final budget that year would see an increase, as usual. In 1962, the supervisors pledged to hold the line on an austerity budget, but it rose by more than $200 million when finally approved. A month after the *Times* printed an editorial on the rapid rise of employees at all government levels, the supervisors approved a generous pay raise that would necessitate a tax hike. In the following year they were informed that state and federal mandates required hiring almost 4000 new employees when the supervisors already faced another austerity budget and the usual protests from the Property Owners Tax Association and others. In 1966 the BOS brought an order for more budget cuts, and the CAO responded that they would have to come out of health and capital projects in several of the districts in which supervisors were running for reelection, so much for those cuts. In 1967, the county tax rate and assessed value would, as usual, reach new highs. And in 1969, Hahn demanded reimbursement from the state for taxes lost to the county by the state highway commission in purchasing land for freeways to help balance the budget.[58]

The 1970s were even more difficult. In August 1970, the situation was so bad that the county treasurer reported that he had only enough funds to get into the next week with no reserve left. By December, the supervisors feared a financial crisis, so they delayed a health insurance subsidy for employees and postponed some capital projects just before they approved millions for other infrastructure. In January 1971, CAO Will reported that the county faced a "critical period of financial distress," as did the state. He predicted a massive deficit if budgetary changes were not made immediately, recommending cuts in welfare, health, and sheriff's budgets and raises in revenue sources. The plan evidently worked as the county could almost balance its budget by April. At the end of June, the final budget was approved, again at the "highest level in history," even with many capital projects delayed. While cities and school districts had problems with cash on hand later that year, the financial situation improved so that in 1972, the supervisors, some of them running for reelection, approved a lower budget for the first time in decades. The rest of the 1970s, however, would revert to expanded budgets and tax revolts. (See Chapter 7.)[59]

Despite these budget restrictions and expansions, the BOS found ways to build county buildings after 1950. With the absence of construction before then and the population boom in the suburbs and older cities, the need for new infrastructure was evident. Besides roads, flood control, storm drains, and other such projects, the construction program included many structures in the Civic Center district of the county seat in Los Angeles, and branch offices, courthouses, Sheriff's stations, small

The Los Angeles County Hall of Administration in 1970 (Herald Examiner Collection / Los Angeles Public Library).

airport terminals, and a plethora of other county service facilities. A few built in or near the Civic Center in the 1950s and 1960s included the Law Library (1953), Courthouse (1958), Fort Moore Memorial (1958), Sports Arena (1959), Hall of Administration (1960), Hall of Records (1962), Men's Central Jail and Sybil Brand Institute for Women (both 1963), Music Center Buildings (1964–1967), and the Criminal Courts Building (1972). Most of these buildings are still extant and functional, some even architecturally pleasing, especially the Hall of Administration. Ironically, Hahn and Debs thought the building *too* elegant when it was completed; several decades later it was re-named the Kenneth Hahn Hall of Administration.[60]

Along with setbacks and funding problems, many county buildings arose in these decades, many more were to come. The *Times* reported in May 1972, that the county "owned or leases about 700 major structures; it had sixty-eight projects under construction, and it was planning 274 more." As such the county's infrastructure reflected its rising population and provided many opportunities for jobs and economic growth touted by county management.[61]

One more proposal for county infrastructure that was not successful was offered by John Anson Ford. In the 1940s, Ford proposed that a heroic statue of "Democracy Uniting the World" and an Academy or Institute of Democracy be erected on the Pacific Coast to complement the Statue of Liberty on the Atlantic Coast. The monument, he wrote, was "conceived in an atmosphere of human liberty, in a day when liberty is in need of emphasis, even as it is in need of defense." As Ford envisioned it, the statue would depict "three races of man—all as equals—supporting the world" and would be located on a 1500-foot hill along the Palos Verdes Peninsula. The statue would extend above the monument base comprised of three museums, and a library and lecture room. The monument was designed with the assistance of artist Millard Sheets, sculptor Albert Stewart, and architect Harold Field Kellogg.[62]

In early 1950, Ford began a serious funding campaign for the monument. He received what he thought to be an agreement with a representative of the landowners to donate the site if funds for construction could be obtained. He then wrote to a few possible supporters, including President Harry Truman, General Douglas MacArthur, historian Will Durant, businessmen Conrad Hilton and Howard Hughes, and others for private donations and to become members of the committee to guide its success. He even contacted government officials in Japan and Europe to seek their support. The effort would prove fruitless, however. The trust owning the property had been acquired by a company whose sympathetic board chairman died in a plane crash. The company directors then decided to develop the land for residential subdivisions. In October 1958, just weeks before Ford would retire from office, the supervisors considered purchasing the original site for park purposes and for the monument, and they began negotiating the acquisition the following year. But Ford was not around to promote it, and other budget needs increased, spelling the end for his monument.[63]

County Elections

Elections for Los Angeles County officers have been non-partisan since a state law approved in 1913. Federal and state candidates are also included on these ballots with their political party affiliation, while county contestants are not listed with theirs. For most candidates, however, media attention before elections can make clear which party the candidate belongs to, or at least his or her general positions on important issues.[64]

For the major elective county offices, particularly the supervisors, losing a reelection contest after the original victory is rare. In most cases members of the "Board of Eternity" left office either by retiring after many years in office or dying while on the job. Of the eleven supervisors serving between December 1950 and December 1971, four died while in office, four retired after long terms, and three met defeats in an election. The reasons stemmed mostly from the power of these positions in attracting political support, tremendous amounts of campaign funds, and publicity in metropolitan and community media. The challengers had fewer resources unless they were wealthy, well-known, or well-connected, or there was a major scandal involving the incumbent, which normally made little difference in the outcome. Sheriffs at this time were in a similar position, as the incumbent in 1950 served for twenty-four years before his 1958 retirement, and his successor served for twenty-two years. The elected assessor in 1950 served for twenty-four years in that position, as well as six years previously as a supervisor, and his successor held the position for sixteen years.[65]

Candidates for supervisorial elections usually included politicians or those in businesses or some form of administration, most of them mainstream in their politics. Occasionally, one who did not fit those descriptions became involved. As mentioned earlier, in 1950 one candidate for sheriff and one for assessor were identified as being affiliated with the Communist Party USA. In the primaries of both 1964 and 1972 Supervisor Hahn was opposed by an official of the Communist Party USA proud to announce his position, and he agreed with Hahn on certain issues. And in 1976, Hahn was opposed by a member of the Trotskyite Socialist Workers Party.[66]

The increase in voters and changing technology in preparing for elections and counting votes posed new challenges for those responsible for implementing the process. In some elections from 1950 to 1970, there were major problems that caused local and national embarrassment. In the 1958 general election, Los Angeles City Council members Ernest Debs and Edward Roybal fought for Ford's Third District seat. Roybal, who had opposed the city's Bunker Hill redevelopment project that displaced low-income residents in favor of government-subsidized wealthy developers, as well as the Chavez Ravine removal of residents for a baseball stadium, was endorsed by Ford and many liberal groups. Debs was more conservative and pro-development by this time in his political career and endorsed by the *Times* and the AFL. On election night Debs seemed to be the clear winner, but as the vote counting continued, Roybal moved to the front. At least for a few hours Roybal appeared to be the first Latino to be elected to the BOS in the twentieth century.[67]

That would soon change. On the following day the registrar-recorder ordered a recount and determined that 10,000 votes had mistakenly been added to Roybal's total, which put Debs back in the lead. Debs eventually had 12,000 votes to spare when the absentee ballots had been added. Roybal objected, asking for a grand jury investigation of the counting, and claiming over 100 of his supporters in East Los

Angeles had been intimidated by poll workers who challenged them and denied their votes. His case was also forwarded to a state civil rights committee, but neither agency took action. For many citizens on the Eastside, the entire count was believed to be a fraud, and Latino politicians resurrected it often over the next few decades to remind their supporters to be diligent in casting their vote.[68]

In the 1960s, the voting problems were both human error and computer inadequacy. The county's handling of the 1960 general election was seen as an embarrassment to the rest of the nation as the results for president were announced long after those of many other governments. Hahn investigated and found problems of outdated state requirements, a needed reorganization of county staff, and an electronic system that had yet to be fully tested. In 1968, the county was tardy in processing the June primary election returns. Some ballots did not leave voting precincts until hours after the polls closed. The problems were identified as late delivery of sample ballots, the largest voter turnout in county history (71.16 percent), and an inadequate computer capacity. The assassination in Los Angeles of candidate Robert F. Kennedy on the night of the national primary upstaged the embarrassment of the voting delay. In the following year the supervisors were alarmed by a report of several computer experts playing a software game to test their ability to rig an election by distorting the results. Board members were especially concerned that the experts were successful three out of three times. They ordered Registrar-Recorder Ray E. Lee to investigate and advise them of safeguards necessary "to preserve the sanctity of elections in Los Angeles County." Presumably that situation would be taken care of, although Lee would face a more significant problem in the next election.[69]

The 1970 state primary would be the last under Lee's leadership. Unfortunately for him, Supervisor Hahn was running for the U.S. Senate and furious with the local chaos. As it turned out, there were also major problems in three other California counties causing delays in the tabulation of votes. Orange County suffered a power failure and overburdened computers; San Diego County staff could not operate vote-counting machines properly; and Fresno County staff could not program computers to handle the ballots so that it took almost twenty-four hours after the polls closed to start counting them. In Los Angeles County, Lee reported that the problems included a wild-cat strike that delayed delivery of paper, delay in getting paper and sample ballot information to the printer, delays by the data processing department, and a total of 1660 different styles of ballots needed because of the large number of schools and special districts. These problems resulted in the delay of sample ballots to 40,000 voters; 500,000 sample ballots never arrived. On election day, the wrong ballots were given to voters in a different district and/or in a different political party, and some precincts ran out of ballots; the magnetic tapes for the computers tabulating the votes were not prepared on time, and some of the results were accidently dumped. As could be expected, the supervisors were livid when informed of these problems and the many complaints of residents, and they blamed Lee for the embarrassment. Hahn and a judge on the ballot sued Lee for allowing the problems and demanded a new election, but neither suit went to trial. As a result of this disaster, the CAO temporarily took charge of the coming general election, Hahn came in third in the Democratic primary race in the county and the state, and Lee retired early the following year.[70]

As an added note on this era, county officials did their best to protect the good name of Los Angeles County. But occasional problems prevented it. In 1968, the Parks and Recreation Department asked Louise Huebner, a writer and media celebrity who professed to be a witch, to appear at a county "Folk Day" event at the Hollywood Bowl. On that day she received a county scroll signed by Supervisor Debs which certified that she had been designated as the "Official Witch of Los Angeles County" to reign over the event and cast a spell over all of Los Angeles County. She not only cast a spell to ensure the sexual vitality of county residents but decided to use her new title to promote her writings, appearances, and a record album. When Debs and County Counsel John Maharg heard of Huebner's use of the title for promotional purposes, Maharg informed her that the scroll was "purely ceremonial" and asked that she "immediately discontinue use of the title."[71]

Ms. Huebner declined Maharg's request, stating that she received no pay for her appearance, which "only added to the much-needed sophisticated image of this County." She asked that Debs return the gift she gave him of "a Magical Golden Horn that was meant to insure his Romantic Vitality." Huebner then appeared at a press conference to publicize the county request to refrain from using the title, which Maharg stated was just a "gag," and she concluded that she would have to "de-spell all of Los Angeles County" if Maharg and Debs continued this "first witch persecution in America since the 1690s," as she described it. Apparently, her threat "to withdraw her spell which gave Los Angeles amazing sexual vitality," as noted in a newspaper ad for her new book, convinced Debs and Maharg to drop their witch hunt.[72]

2

Messing with
the Environment

Every animal but man must adapt to its own environment or die. However, man chose centuries ago to change his environment rather than adapt to it.... It has now become obvious that some of these changes have resulted in many more problems than existed before man altered his environment to suit his desires.—Los Angeles County Grand Jury, Final Report

The above quote,[1] which continues with the observation that "the environmental dilemma is as much the 'doer's' [county government] problem as it is the 'receiver's' [the environment] problem," was the determination of the Los Angeles County Grand Jury in 1973. In the two decades before and for some time after, the county supervisors paid lip service to protecting the natural features of the county, while allowing massive development and its alteration of the environment. The Regional Planning Commission had a reputation for approving most plans for more industrial and business structures and residential subdivisions that transformed large swaths of land previously devoted to agriculture. If the commission occasionally denied a project, the supervisors frequently overrode that decision for favored developers. As the population increased, so did air and water pollution; the supervisors had to address these problems in balancing the competing demands of industrialists and residents.

In the century before 1950, the BOS was responsible for approving most of the environmental changes taking place in the county outside and sometimes inside incorporated cities. From the mid–1800s cattle era, through the succeeding agriculture period and the early 1900s, the BOS had tremendous power and influence in shaping the landscape, in what was introduced, retained, altered, and lost. Population booms in the 1860s, 1880s, and 1920s spurred many of the changes to the land once described in its early 1900s condition as "the old rural American Dream in full romantic maturity. The valleys afforded views of snow on peaks, forested slopes, citrus groves below, vineyards and fields lower still, and towns, roads, and railroads in the foreground."[2]

Despite many changes to the county landscape, in 1950 it was still diverse with a unique flora and fauna. Farming remained the major land use as the county led all others in the U.S. in the production of agricultural products. But the increase in population of some three million in the 1950–1970 decades would change that as orchards and crop fields gave way to residential subdivisions, commercial districts, and industrial entities. The Regional Planning Commission estimated that agricultural land in the east San Gabriel Valley portion of the county dropped from 72 percent to 19.5 percent in the period from the late 1940s to 1960, when the county was no longer the nation's top producer. Trees disappeared quickly after World War II as one county supervisor recalled a developer admitting in the mid–1950s that an average of 1000 trees per day were uprooted and burned to make room for subdivisions. Further concretization of rivers in the county for flood control eliminated flora in the beds and forced out fauna. The residential explosion also exacerbated air and water pollution, as well as the massive increase in concrete and asphalt for driveways, sidewalks, freeways, and more roads. Development would only slowdown in the 1970s because of a downturn in the national economy, a reduced population increase in the decade, and a moratorium on building in some areas as a result of state legislation and a court order.[3]

Final decisions allowing zoning changes for land use, subdivision and commercial developments, and other actions to alter the landscape in unincorporated areas and sometimes in the cities rested with the BOS. As in the past, most of the supervisors in the 1950–early 1970s era were in favor of expansive growth, particularly since they depended to a large degree on contributions from developers. In fact, Frank Bonelli and his successor, Peter Schabarum, were developers themselves; Herbert Legg, Raymond Darby, and Warren Dorn were realtors, dependent on residential and commercial growth for sales. Legg created an extensive network of developers for political support in his district that carried on to his successors, Bonelli and Schabarum. (After Bonelli's death, the large amount of cash he left to his family became the basis for a lawsuit questioning the source of the funds and resulting in splitting the proceeds between the family and the county.) Ernest Debs, the chair of the planning committee while a member of the Los Angeles City Council, had a reputation as the "strong man of Los Angeles zoning," even accused of bribery at least once as a supervisor. Burton Chace led the first phase of an effort by Malibu developers to force residents of the unincorporated area to pay for a massive sewer system to accommodate the thousands of new homeowners that might flock to the many subdivisions they intended to build with Chace's help. On at least several occasions Warren Dorn introduced zoning change issues in meetings after the full agenda had already been completed. Almost all of the supervisors were noticeably sympathetic to developers during their terms.[4]

The perils of not listening to developers were obvious—campaign contributions might dry up. Other drawbacks could become evident. In a zoning change hearing regarding a residential project proposed in the Antelope Valley, the supervisors voted 4–1 against the change. After the vote, Raymond Darby reportedly said something derogatory to the defeated developer and his wife, resulting in the developer striking Darby in the face. The supervisor collapsed in his office ten minutes later and died of a brain hemorrhage. Ironically, the project was revised and approved several months later by the Regional Planning Commission (RPC) and the BOS.[5]

To implement their desires regarding which development to approve, the supervisors relied on the RPC, a board appointed by the supervisors. Los Angeles County was the first to create such a body which began to meet in 1923; over the years the members responded to the general and specific demands of the supervisors frequently influenced by developers. Over most of the 1950–1975 period and after, the RPC was usually dominated by those members who had a personal stake in regional growth based on their occupation or profession. Many were developers, real estate brokers, or banking officials appointed because of that experience, and susceptible to conflicts of interest. For example, in 1975, two of the five were bankers involved with mortgages and two others were realtors. Critics pointed out that the commissioners consistently acted pro-development, ready to approve any proposal to build in almost any area, regardless of the situation and expense to county taxpayers and future homebuyers. The deputy of one supervisor advised his boss that the RPC "is so developer-oriented that when they do deny a variance request.... I have to conclude that the variance is really not warranted."[6]

By the 1970s, reformers on the BOS started to question their colleagues' appointments of RPC members. One appointment for the Fourth District was successfully blocked because he was developer. In late 1979, environmentalists opposed the reappointment of developer Owen Lewis, the RPC chair or vice-chair for eighteen years, as a means to "reduce the majority development bias" of the RPC. Lewis, the "official sprawl champion" of the county, fought for his position while under investigation by the district attorney for possible criminal self-dealing. In January 1980, he finally resigned for health reasons. Lewis's health seems to have improved as he continued his association with soon-to-be convicted City of Industry developer James Stafford, a former RPC commissioner appointed by Herbert Legg.[7]

In the meantime, the staff of the Regional Planning Department continued research and compilation of detailed plans for unincorporated areas, investigations of many specific issues such as housing, noise pollution, illegal formations of subdivisions, zoning changes, new subdivision proposals, and a host of others affecting the environment. In the 1970s, it was influenced by a pro-development director, as well as supervisors, to the point that some of its recommendations were ignored or overturned when expediency dictated. Despite political and administrative interference, the department did make headway in protecting some features of the county environment in this era.[8]

The County General Plan

The 1950s and 1960s were years of runaway development in the county; the 1970s were different. New housing subdivisions and commercial structures did appear throughout the incorporated cities during the downturn in the national and local economy. But development was limited in the non-urban unincorporated areas because of a challenge to the county's overall plan for them.

The change began in 1967 with a call by the County Grand Jury for a study of planning and zoning practices as a means of preventing conflicts of interest on the part of county officials responding to the requests of developers. In the next year the Regional Planning Department initiated its five-year program to create a countywide plan for zoning and development, the first phase being the Environmental Development Guide (EDG) adopted in 1970. This guide described the county as "a maze of billboards, tract houses, hamburger stands, freeways, automobiles, smog and an endless skyline of telephone poles." It went on to lament water pollution "by discharges of untreated waste," the "loss of natural features and open spaces and inadequate facilities of all kinds," along with other maladies that needed to be addressed. "Unless a bold new commitment is made to correct existing social and environmental problems in the very near future, additional growth will be disastrous." The supervisors approved the EDG and agreed to appoint a fifty-member citizens' advisory council to monitor it.[9]

Shortly after the adoption of the EDG, the state legislature passed the Open Space Lands Act requiring California counties to prepare a plan with specific areas identified and strict controls to protect them. The counties had to submit these plans in 1972, with the deadline later extended to the end of June 1973, and an interim plan had to be submitted in the meantime. The supervisors hoped to use the EDG as the interim plan and held hearings after being criticized for allowing the RPC to make EDG plan revisions favoring developers. The hearings were attended by over sixty environmental, homeowner, planning, and other groups protesting the EDG as inadequate. The BOS approved a moratorium on land use permits in open spaces but allowed exceptions on appeal. The Regional Planning Department gathered information for further revisions as environmentalists argued before the RPC that the original EDG should be filed with the state as the basis for a stronger final plan. Developers and their allies insisted that the revised EDG (more sympathetic to development) should be filed instead. A court decision brought on by a suit by the Sierra Club and other groups ruled that *no* development could take place in the 775,000 acres of "Open, Rural and Agricultural Land" in the unincorporated areas of the county. With that ruling the supervisors ordered county department heads to "move at top speed" to create an open space plan.[10]

In 1973, the process continued with more hearings attended by environmentalists and development interests. California Attorney General Evelle Younger added to the deadline pressure by informing the BOS that if an interim plan was not adopted by the end of June, the county would not be allowed to issue valid building permits or receive state subventions from the open-space program. In April, the RPC submitted a revised interim plan to the supervisors which reduced 178 square miles of open space, among other amendments, to the EDG. During the review period, representatives of the Coalition for Planning in the Public Interest protested that the new plan was "a blueprint for urban sprawl" devised to help developers, and that the RPC shielded alternative plans from the group and left little time to study it. Under the looming deadline, the supervisors reviewed it quickly and approved it with two days to spare. The Coalition then filed suit against what county officials would soon call the county's General Plan. In August, Superior Court Judge David Thomas issued a preliminary injunction to freeze development in the open and sensitive areas until his final decision. That would finally come in 1975, when he ruled the General Plan to be void, finding it internally inconsistent and in violation of the State Open Space Act. However, he allowed the 1973 General Plan to remain effective until the new plan could be approved, causing much confusion for county planners in knowing which stipulations would be in effect.[11]

With this defeat, county officials embarked on a new effort to create an acceptable General Plan. Supervisors receiving continual requests from developers and threats of lawsuits for delays to earlier construction approvals poured more money into the planning department for staff and other resources to devise a plan that would also include incorporated cities and more elements. Research and hearings were conducted in 1975–1977 with a preliminary draft of the new general plan completed in early 1978. More hearings and revisions continued with the environmental coalition leaders and developers and their allies, including organized labor, still not happy with the changes. By late 1980, the plan finally came before the BOS for approval. It was still contentious for the opposing sides, but as one supervisor deputy opined, if it was radically changed in either direction Judge Thomas might void it again. And since two new development-oriented supervisors had just been elected, it might not be approved and could cause further confusion. Two supervisors in favor of limited development had just been defeated, and would soon be gone, so the vote came up just before their terms ended. Despite further protests by environmentalists, the board majority voted to approve it. Judge Thomas accepted the new General Plan and lifted his moratorium on development in areas where it had been restricted.[12]

The Anti-Smog Crusade

Los Angeles and Southern California have been synonymous with air pollution since the 1940s. Smoke from oil refineries and other industries in the region were already noticeable. But during World War II, various defense industry firms in central Los Angeles spewed additional noxious fumes that darkened the city at daytime and became a serious health hazard. After the war, the supervisors attempted to control "smog" as it became known, but only had jurisdiction in the unincorporated areas. This was a major problem since the primary source of smog was believed to be the industrial areas of Los Angeles and the western cities of the county. From there the heavy smoke blew eastward to the San Gabriel Valley, eventually trapped in front of the mountains, and further into other counties. Smog was thus a regional problem, so the county created a special district designed to limit air pollution throughout the county without restricting industrial expansion. After a long battle in the state legislature with petroleum and other industries opposing the district and regulation, the supervisors established the Los Angeles County Air Pollution Control District (APCD) in 1947 and placed themselves in charge of it.[13]

Balancing the health of residents and the by-products of industrial processing would not be easy. The staff of the APCD faced opposition to many of its regulations, even though it was usually supported by county newspapers and Chamber of Commerce leaders concerned with industrial growth, but also with the region's image portrayed to the rest of the nation. The supervisors hired Dr. Louis C. McCabe, head of the Coal Division of the U.S. Bureau of Mines, as the director, and created a Citizens' Smog Advisory Committee which included attorney James Beebe, a longtime director of the Chamber of Commerce, and former California Institute of Technology President Robert A. Millikan, to oversee it. Over the next two years the APCD staff worked diligently to reduce smog but faced myriad obstacles with the opposition of industrialists who thought the regulations too restrictive, and of suffering residents who thought the program moved too slowly. McCabe resigned in May 1949, replaced by former Army Corps of Engineers Col. Gordon P. Larson. In the meantime, the supervisors searched for other methods to control smog as the population increased and thousands of new industrial plants sprouted in the county.[14]

Nineteen fifty would prove to be a watershed year for the anti-smog crusade. In that year Caltech Professor A.J. Haagen-Smit was hired as a consultant to study air pollution in the county. His research proved automobiles to be a more significant contributor to smog than other researchers believed. This conclusion, which was not accepted immediately by some experts, would change the course of agency testing, enforcement, and the politics of smog.[15]

The 1950s witnessed continued protests from residents in the San Gabriel Valley, especially in Pasadena, concerning the lack of progress. Several private citizen groups formed to force county officials to step up the program, even threatening the recall of a supervisor if he did not fire Larson in 1954. Pasadena city official Warren Dorn became a spokesman for these groups, as well as the League of California Cities, and worked with the supervisors before his election to the BOS in 1956.[16]

The city of Los Angeles also dueled with the supervisors in this decade over county inaction. Mayor Fletcher Bowron criticized the program, and later Mayor Norris Poulson and city council members threatened to enforce the city's own ordinances instead. In 1953, Poulson appealed to California Governor Goodwin Knight for help in forcing the county to move quicker, and Knight appointed a committee to investigate both the county program and the dispute over the chief sources of smog. For the next several years Poulson fought the county's ban on backyard incinerators as one cause of smog because of the added expense to residents and the possibility that gangsters would control rubbish transportation and dumpsites.[17]

On the other side of the smog issue, the California Incinerator Association, petroleum industries represented by the Western Oil and Gas Association, and other groups lobbied the supervisors and state legislators to protect industries being accused of producing smog. They also funded and published research that contradicted some of the early scientific studies of smog.[18]

In the middle of this conflict sat the Los Angeles Chamber of Commerce, devoted to industrial expansion, but also public health and the region's image for tourists and businesses. The Chamber supported the 1947 air pollution district bill and the agency but did not endorse some of the most restrictive controls on industry. In 1954, four Chamber committees worked with the APCD on research and securing citizen and industrial cooperation. Chamber directors such as Asa Call, Arnold Beckman, John McCone, and USC president Fred D. Fagg served as trustees of the Southern California Air Pollution Foundation, a respected organization although supported mostly by oil companies, as well as metropolitan newspapers, other major businesses, and one brewery.[19]

Amid this discontent and support, as well as research on the scientific, medical, industrial, and other facets of the issue, the APCD had a mixed record in the 1950s. Since its leadership initially saw the automobile as just a minor cause of smog until 1953–1954, the staff concentrated on industrial and other causes. Victories such as a record number of smog permits denied in May 1953, were few. Charges of mismanagement of the department by Gordon Larson, favoritism, and inadequate staffing and research led to Larson's removal. The gradual acceptance of automobile exhaust trapped by an inversion during the hot summer as a major source increased the agency's responsibilities by 1954. The APCD certainly limited some smog, but keeping up with the expansion of industries, the influx of a population that depended on the automobile for transportation, the expectations of smog-weary residents, and the demands of five supervisors proved difficult. One writer described Larson's successor, Smith Griswold, as "The man with the least envied job in county government." Griswold "never gets off the hot seat." Those who preceded him "either have been fired or had the good sense to resign."[20]

The county supervisors were generally supportive of the APCD, but quick to demand changes when constituents complained. The BOS provided additional funding for research, but residents claimed it was wastefully redundant. An enforcement officer was hired in 1954 to increase inspections and fines; the number of both quickly increased. But the supervisors had their favorite interests and individuals to consider, along with their personal rivalries, which might make them move slowly on the issue. Ford spent a lot of his time on this issue in the 1950s, and Warren Dorn brought his activism to the board during his sixteen-year term.[21]

Kenneth Hahn made smog a primary concern for much of his long career. Hahn was sworn into office in early December 1952, and in that month, he began sending requests to Gordon Larson to investigate air pollution from factories and other sources. In some cases, he made inspections on his own and directed Larson to take over enforcement. He wrote letters to mayors of U.S. cities asking how they were coping with smoke and fumes. Most notably, in 1953 he began a two-decade crusade to convince major American automakers to develop anti-smog exhaust devices. General Motors replied that company engineers were working on it; Ford answered that its exhausts did not contribute to air pollution. These responses spurred another inquiry from Hahn the following year and became an annual epistle to automakers which the writer printed in a booklet he distributed every few years to publicize the inadequate responses. He also requested an opinion from the county counsel on whether the supervisors could require any new automobile sold in the county to be equipped with an exhaust device that would eliminate smog, and to set a deadline for autos, buses, and trucks to be so equipped. The council agreed it could be done if there was such a device. Thwarted in that attempt, he would try in 1964, only to be denied again.[22]

Smog Control in the 1960s and Early 1970s

County officials and others in California had asserted in the 1950s that smog was prevalent in many parts of the state, especially in urban areas and the Central

Valley. Legislators responded in 1960 with passage of a law that created the Motor Vehicle Pollution Control Board. This agency was tasked with the responsibility of reducing smog produced by automobiles, trucks, and other vehicles. One facet of the law set up a timetable for them to be equipped with anti-smog devices beginning the year after the approval of at least two effective devices. With this division of responsibility, local air pollution control agencies concentrated on stationary sources of air pollution such as factories and refineries. The Los Angeles County APCD did much better in reducing smog emanating from sources other than vehicles, which led to fewer complaints from residents and the county supervisors. In fact, the County Grand Jury estimated stationary-source smog at only 10 percent of the total by 1972.[23]

Although the state assumed responsibility for reducing vehicle smog, Dorn and Hahn continued their battles against automobiles as polluters. Among Dorn's noteworthy contributions was his resolution stating that four exhaust devices had been certified in 1964 and automakers needed to install them on their 1966 models. Dorn made sure to ask the U.S. Attorney General to investigate the actions of the major automobile manufacturers in this regard and authorized the county counsel and county air pollution control officer to travel to Washington, D.C., and Detroit to assist the Department of Justice in its investigation.[24]

Hahn was even more active. He continued to send suggestions and requests for inspections of smoking factories and refineries to the APCD and sent more of his annual letters to the carmakers, as noted in a New York City newspaper. In January 1965, and again in 1966, Hahn asked U.S. Attorney General Nicholas Katzenbach to investigate collusion among the three major automakers "to restrain the development of effective devices" for reducing smog. In 1967, he asked California Governor Ronald Reagan to appoint a special committee of experts to study the state's smog program after the Los Angeles County APCD director testified before Congress that the devices allowed for use in California did not meet the state's standards. That same year he and Dorn led the supervisors to stop purchasing new automobiles for the county if a Congressional amendment to prohibit California from setting higher clean air standards than federal regulations would pass, which it didn't. By 1968, Hahn also tried to obtain authority to control jet aircraft pollution in the county that would be regulated by the federal government.[25]

The 1966 letter to Katzenbach finally spurred him to convene a federal grand jury to investigate the alleged conspiracy. After a long delay the jury found that there was indeed a conspiracy to refrain from conducting research. By this time the Nixon Administration had taken over and in March 1969, the county and state offered assistance to the Department of Justice (DOJ) in pressing this issue. With little federal action, the BOS approved Hahn's motion to sue the DOJ for blocking California's efforts to control smog in automobiles. The supervisors then instructed the counsel to sue the three major automakers for $100 million in damages to compensate for the treatment of health problems of county residents caused by smog. In September 1969, the DOJ gave up further investigation and opted for a consent decree to force automakers to make their research and patents available to anyone. This decision sparked court filings by Los Angeles County officials and Hahn's request that consumer advocate Ralph Nader be hired by the county to assist its lawyers.

It also spurred support from members of Congress and officials in cities and states throughout the nation. The consent decree was approved and upheld by the U.S. Supreme Court in March 1970.[26]

The federal government became more involved in air pollution restrictions in the 1970s. Amendments to the 1967 Clean Air Act approved in 1970 created the Environmental Protection Agency (EPA), which set and enforced standards for prevention of air and water pollution. It also allowed California's Air Resources Board (CARB), which replaced the Motor Vehicle Pollution Control Board in 1967, to take over the operation of local air pollution control boards if those agencies did not demonstrate sufficient progress in meeting EPA standards. Automakers were mandated to begin installing emission controls on all vehicles in 1975, and the Los Angeles County supervisors urged the president and members of Congress to strictly enforce this mandate.[27]

As part of its program to meet federal standards, or the even stricter California requirements, the CARB had to enforce a 1974 state law that required anti-smog devices on 1966–1970 automobiles only in the southern counties. In this case, Hahn led the fight *against* the installation because these devices were deemed to actually increase smog and decrease gasoline mileage. In addition, they were only required for some cars in just six counties, and he believed they would be too expensive and should be paid for and installed by automakers. In September 1974, Hahn made an approved motion to request that Governor Reagan call the legislature back in

Smog covers and chokes downtown Los Angeles in 1973 (Fitzgerald Whitney, photographer, *Los Angeles Times* Photographic Archive [Collection 1429], Library Special Collections, Charles E. Young Research Library, UCLA).

session to repeal this law. Reagan refused, so the county supervisors filed suit to stop enforcement, and in January 1975, Hahn's former deputy, state Senator Nate Holden, offered a bill to repeal the law. Hahn then stirred up support for his mission with letters to state legislators and newspapers, resulting in radio and print editorials, consumer letters to state officials, and support from civic groups. The campaign was successful; Holden's bill was passed and signed by Governor Jerry Brown.[28]

Meanwhile, changes taking place in the early 1970s that would alter the state's anti-smog program in Southern California. The Los Angeles County APCD came under increased criticism for protecting polluters and was under investigation by the state attorney general in early 1973, leading to the resignation of its director. The county supervisor responsible for overseeing the APCD was accused of protecting his favorite political contributors. Cities and adjacent counties complained of Los Angeles not doing enough to reduce smog flowing into their jurisdictions. With state and federal agencies assuming more powers over local officials, the drive to transfer responsibility for stationary pollution to a regional organization picked up momentum.[29]

Hahn and his fellow supervisors had been in favor of a more regional agency in 1955, arguing that smog was a state and regional problem and should be handled that way. In the 1970s, however, they were more concerned about losing local control in a decade of increasing encroachment by larger agencies. State legislators had a different view as it appeared that the Los Angeles County APCD failed in its mission. In 1973, several bills to create a regional agency were offered in the state legislature, none of them advocated by the Los Angeles County supervisors. To head off further legislation, the supervisors joined their counterparts in Orange, San Bernardino, and Riverside counties to form the Southern California Air Pollution Control District (SCAPCD) in mid–1975. This agency would be dominated by Los Angeles County with more votes in decisions and restricted input by the others. Assemblyman Jerry Lewis of Riverside was not satisfied, however, and offered a bill that same year "to dilute the influence of the L.A. County Board of Supervisors." The Lewis bill would create the South Coast Air Quality Management District to replace the SCAPCD by February 1, 1977, governed by fewer county supervisors and the inclusion of city representatives and one appointment by the governor. Supervisors from all four counties opposed the bill, especially those in Los Angeles, which would pay about 70 percent of the annual budget. Hahn and others complained that the agency should be funded by the state, not county taxpayers, but Governor Brown disagreed. For the supervisors it marked the beginning of a rocky relationship with this agency including attempts to refuse paying county dues, ignoring meetings, and much later vowing to protect industries spewing smog. (See Chapter 9.)[30]

Dirty Water

Besides the increase in air pollution, the 1950s growth in population and industry also affected the county's water supply as more pollution from factories and sewers spewed into rivers and the ocean. The supervisors had begun attempts to prevent the disposal of industrial and residential waste into the Los Angeles River and the Pacific Ocean in the late 1940s and succeeded in suing polluters and requiring permits to discharge waste into waterways. In 1949, the county committed its resources to aid Los Angeles and Long Beach in responding to serious pollution at the harbor.[31]

After 1950, county officials continued to respond to pollution in water sources. In 1954, the county engineer touted county protection of underground water supplies that could escape detection since it is not as apparent as in surface water. In the same year the supervisors fought the city of Los Angeles over the latter's dumping sewage in the Los Angeles River. Supervisor Hahn offered motions approved by the board in 1968 and 1969 to strengthen the enforcement of river pollution by oil companies and for officials to study ways to strengthen the power of the State Water Pollution Control Board. In 1970, the supervisors ordered all DDT to be recalled from county departments so that it would not be dumped in the ocean and endanger marine life and humans. "Strict procedures prevent the discharge of untreated waste into the sewer system" that empties into the ocean, Supervisor Debs wrote to a constituent.[32]

Despite these and other actions, water pollution remained a problem. The harbor area would continue to receive petroleum-based pollution from ships loading and unloading cargo, as well as various wastes from rivers reaching the ocean there. Garbage and industrial waste were still dumped in the concrete-lined Los Angeles River. In 1968, the *Times* reported that pollution in California waters was getting worse, especially with coastal oil spills at the Los Angeles Harbor, that the state moved too slowly to help, and that the regional boards responsible for enforcing pollution control did little except to protect industries. (One of the members of the Los Angeles area board at the time was Supervisor Frank Bonelli.) Even with the environmental movement gaining steam in these years, the protection of water resources and associated fauna proved difficult; it would remain so for many more decades. (See Chapter 9.)[33]

Trashing the Land

The disposal of rubbish was one element in the county's riddance of waste in the 1950s and 1960s. Since early in the century, edible garbage had been shipped to farms to be consumed by hogs. By 1950, garbage disposals became popular, so these wastes were flushed into the sewer system. Rubbish was burned in backyard incinerators or in various dumpsites where larger rubbish was then burned. The process ended when the increase in smog convinced the supervisors to abandon it and require the cut and cover method of burying rubbish in canyons and other depressions. This decision meant that rubbish had to be hauled away by private or public transport to dumpsites by the mid–1950s, creating an additional expense for residents and arguments over who would operate the transport and dumps.[34]

Enforcing the change in rubbish disposal offered the supervisors many opportunities to argue with municipal officials in the county and among themselves. The BOS was not even unanimous on cut and cover, as Supervisor Darby claimed it would attract rodents and affect the health of residents more than smog. But once the decision had been made to require that process, the supervisors moved forward. Los Angeles City officials led by Mayor Norris Poulson fought the change for years based on where the dumpsites would be located and who would operate them.[35]

In fact, characters such as Ray "Whitey" Christl, who had "long been identified by law enforcement authorities as a shadowy, but powerful figure in gambling operations in Southern California," tried to "muscle into" the disposal business in 1955–1956. As mentioned in Chapter 1, Christl was also a friend of Supervisor Legg and other county officials whom he depended on in acquiring permits and approvals for private waste disposal. Legg was one of the most adamant supervisors in supporting the change from burning rubbish to burying it in dumpsites (perhaps not for environmental reasons) and assigning disposal to private enterprise instead of a government service. When Mayor Poulson charged that the county's 1955 ordinance attracted Eastern gangsters to run rubbish collection with bribes for those in charge, Legg demanded evidence, which would eventually be presented. At the same time the County Grand Jury was investigating the issue as the ban on incinerators drew near and the county extended the deadline for another eighteen months so the city would comply.[36]

Shortly after the ban went into effect the County Grand Jury investigation of "Eastern gangster" involvement in rubbish collection monopolies bore fruit, although not as Legg expected. Legg himself was indicted for perjury in testifying that he did not know a rubbish contractor who claimed to have paid the supervisor a $10,000 bribe to obtain five county rubbish collection contracts; witnesses testified he met with the contractor on at least four occasions. Legg's chief deputy and another contractor were also indicted for participating in the alleged bribery. Legg's trial began in January 1956, and by its end, three of the four charges were excluded because of lack of corroboration and differences in the testimony of key witnesses. For the remaining charge it appeared that the memory of one of the two witnesses was hazy and Legg's memory cast doubts on whether he had knowingly lied. Along with skepticism of the testimony of the key accuser, the jury found reasonable doubt of Legg's guilt, so he was acquitted. The trial of his deputy and the indicted contractor ended after the key accuser refused to testify as his statements might incriminate himself. With that the entire episode was over, but not forgotten by local news broadcasters and others.[37]

Increasing need for more rubbish space required new dumpsites, and even before the incinerator ban became effective, the county faced opposition from the city of Monterey Park. The county and the sanitation district for that area wanted to locate a large dump in that city to serve Los Angeles and surrounding cities. The Monterey Park City Council objected to having the dump in their city and the county condemning land for it, while residents in adjoining cities supported it at BOS meetings. In the ensuing negotiations a city councilman threatened to take the issue to court, noting that the city already received 40 percent of the county's rubbish in private dumps within the city limits and did not want to be "a dumping ground for most of the city of Los Angeles." Most supervisors thought their responsibility to establish dumps trumped local protest and voted 4–1 to approve this one.

Monterey Park officials fought the decision in court as a violation of home rule and endorsed a bill currently in the state legislature to prohibit counties from establishing such facilities in cities that ran counter to local ordinances. While the suit and the county's counter action worked their way through the court system, the proposed law was approved and signed by the governor, ending county plans for that site.[38]

The question of whether the dumpsites should be operated by private enterprise or government entities erupted in 1959, when the supervisors argued over the issue in several meetings. In that year, they had to decide whether to acquire Scholl Canyon land in Glendale, where city officials and the sanitation district had made plans for a public dump in close proximity to San Gabriel Valley cities and Los Angeles, or in privately-operated gravel pits in Sun Valley, far to the west, or in Irwindale, far to the east. Glendale officials protested the possible abandonment of the Scholl site and organized a multi-city opposition that demanded a grand jury investigation. Los Angeles Mayor Poulson again charged that "rubbish racketeers" wanted to control the operation for huge profits. Bonelli and Chace continued to favor private operation, but Hahn changed his mind and joined Dorn and Debs in upholding the board's 1956 policy to support public dumps. After the final hearing attended by representatives of private dumps, the vote for public operation changed to unanimous.[39]

Another dumpsite considered by the county at the same time was one in the city of Los Angeles located in Mission Canyon. Amid protests by various homeowner groups in the area, the Los Angeles City Council approved a conditional use permit in 1957, authorizing the county to use it for a dumpsite for fifteen years. The county purchased the property two years later, and the landfill began operation in 1960. It continued until 1964, when the sanitation district and county made a deal with developers to transfer county operations to adjacent canyons and fill them at a lower cost. That would be even more profitable to the developers who would not have to fill the canyons themselves for their own use. According to reporter Bill Boyarsky, the county eventually paid over $2 million for the right to fill and in lost property taxes, installed a sprinkler system, and built a road and other facilities. When combined with Metropolitan Water District purchases the total to taxpayers was estimated at almost $13 million. With this transfer the original main canyon dump would be reserved for future use.[40]

While the main dump was operating between 1960 and 1964, developers completed two subdivisions at the top of the canyon. Bel Air homebuyers were told that the main canyon below would become a recreation area including a golf course, baseball fields, and other amenities. With the dump closed in the latter half of the 1960s, even more homes were built along the ridge and residents put up with the view of the dump in anticipation of the recreation area. In late 1972, the county's use permit to operate in the county-owned main canyon would expire, and with other dumps filling up, the sanitation district applied for a twenty-five-year renewal. Residents protested and convinced the city planning commission to grant only a temporary permit. For the next three years county officials tried to sway Los Angeles Mayor Tom Bradley to support the use permit, arguing that an alternative dumpsite would be much more expensive for the city. These efforts failed, however, as the city planning commission denied the permit in late 1976, and the Los Angeles City Council rejected the county's final appeal the following year.[41]

The supervisors were deeply disappointed with the denial. Baxter Ward made a motion the same day to ask the county administrative officer to institute a special rubbish tax for Los Angeles city residents to defer the added expenses of transporting rubbish to more distant sites. Peter Schabarum wanted to forbid the city of Los Angeles and its residents from using any other county dump. Mayor Bradley recommended that the city, county, and sanitation district embark on an effort to create a regional plan for it and suggested several courses of action. One was to investigate using one of the canyons adjacent to Mission Canyon, which the developer agreed to make available, but only until it would be needed for his purposes in 1982. This offer was accepted, but the city's consideration of a zoning change to allow another developer to build 500–700 homes on a ridge above Mission Canyon that would require the county to build a road to the development was too much. The supervisors voted to "vigorously" oppose it; Schabarum said it "would be adding insult to injury." But Supervisors Hahn and Edelman were more interested in resolving the entire issue. Hahn wrote to each council member asking them to vote against the new development in the hope that Mission Canyon might be opened. The county tried again in 1981, but the city turned it down again. In January 1982, it closed for good.[42] (See Chapter 9.)

The record of the BOS in dealing with the environment in this era is mixed, most notably in attempts to reduce smog, still a major problem today, and encouraging mass residential development that altered the Eden the supervisors inherited. One example of a change made to the landscape by a county department that seemed to signify a confession of atonement for the sins of the county was the decision the supervisors made regarding planting plastic trees and plants. The controversy arose in 1972, after the Road Department planted a few of them on a median strip on Jefferson Boulevard because they would be located on top of a concrete storm drain with only a few inches under the road surface, allowing little room for roots to grow. This decision had already been implemented on Western Avenue, where artificial plants were interspersed with natural vegetation with little public outcry. The Jefferson Avenue project was different; it generated many phone calls and letters to the supervisors, as well as to metropolitan newspaper editors once the story appeared. "What an indignity to the human spirt," commented one writer to the *Times* after its critical editorial and reporter Jack Smith's humorous take on the situation. Another writer added in the same "Plastic Trees in Tinseltown—Ugh" grouping of letters that, "in the interest of economy, I suggest we have real trees and plastic supervisors." The response of the supervisors, that the artificial plants were better than a barren median, evaporated as a flood of complaints convinced them that the practical decision would not be acceptable. The board voted 5–0 to begin replacing the plastic plants with live plants as soon as the former deteriorated. Nature was victorious in this instance, at least temporarily.[43]

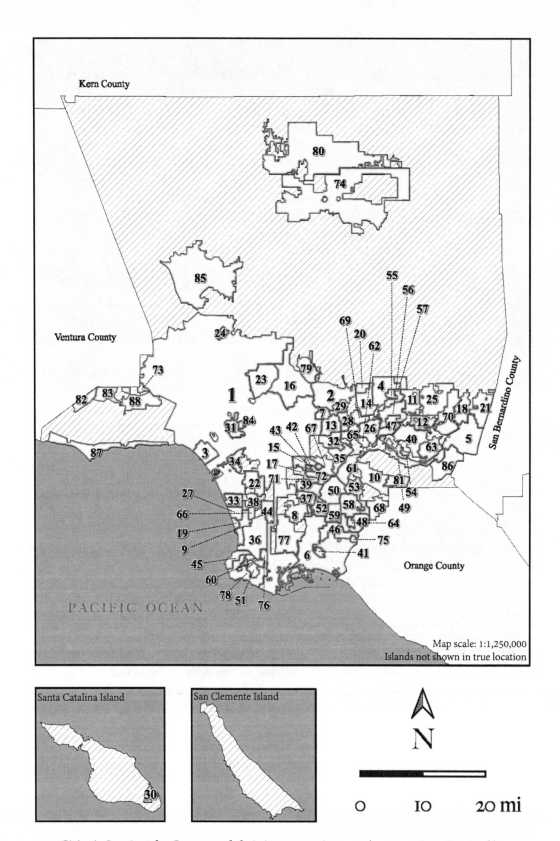

Kern County

Ventura County

San Bernardino County

Orange County

PACIFIC OCEAN

Map scale: 1:1,250,000
Islands not shown in true location

Santa Catalina Island

San Clemente Island

N

0   10   20 mi

Cities in Los Angeles County and their incorporation year (courtesy Ezra Rawitsch).

1. Los Angeles 1850; **2.** Pasadena 1886; **3.** Santa Monica 1886; **4.** Monrovia 1887; **5.** Pomona 1888; **6.** Long Beach (d) 1897; **7.** South Pasadena 1888; **8.** Compton 1888; **9.** Redondo Beach 1892; **10.** Whittier 1898; **11.** Azusa 1898; **12.** Covina 1901; **13.** Alhambra 1903; **14.** Arcadia 1903; **15.** Vernon 1905; **16.** Glendale 1906; **17.** Huntington Park 1906; **18.** La Verne (c) 1906; **19.** Hermosa Beach 1907; **20.** Sierra Madre 1907; **21.** Claremont 1907; **22.** Inglewood 1908; **23.** Burbank 1911; **24.** San Fernando 1911; **25.** Glendora 1911; **26.** El Monte 1912; **27.** Manhattan Beach 1912; **28.** San Gabriel 1913; **29.** San Marino 1913; **30.** Avalon 1913; **31.** Beverly Hills 1914; **32.** Monterey Park 1916; **33.** El Segundo 1917; **34.** Culver City 1917; **35.** Montebello 1920; **36.** Torrance 1921; **37.** Lynwood 1921; **38.** Hawthorne 1922; **39.** South Gate 1923; **40.** West Covina 1923; **41.** Signal Hill 1924; **42.** Maywood 1924; **43.** Bell 1927; **44.** Gardena 1930; **45.** Palos Verdes Estates 1939; **46.** Lakewood 1954; **47.** Baldwin Park 1956; **48.** Cerritos (a) 1956; **49.** La Puente 1956; **50.** Downey 1956; **51.** Rolling Hills 1957; **52.** Paramount 1957; **53.** Santa Fe Springs 1957; **54.** Industry 1957; **55.** Bradbury 1957; **56.** Irwindale 1957; **57.** Duarte 1957; **58.** Norwalk 1957; **59.** Bellflower 1957; **60.** Rolling Hills Estates 1957; **61.** Pico Rivera 1958; **62.** South El Monte 1958; **63.** Walnut 1959; **64.** Artesia 1959; **65.** Rosemead 1959; **66.** Lawndale 1959; **67.** Commerce 1960; **68.** La Mirada (b) 1960; **69.** Temple City 1960; **70.** San Dimas 1960; **71.** Cudahy 1960; **72.** Bell Gardens 1961; **73.** Hidden Hills 1961; **74.** Palmdale 1962; **75.** Hawaiian Gardens 1964; **76.** Lomita 1964; **77.** Carson 1968; **78.** Rancho Palos Verdes 1973; **79.** La Cañada-Flintridge 1976; **80.** Lancaster 1977; **81.** La Habra Heights 1978; **82.** Westlake Village 1981; **83.** Agoura Hills 1982; **84.** West Hollywood 1984; **85.** Santa Clarita 1987; **86.** Diamond Bar 1989; **87.** Malibu 1991; **88.** Calabasas 1991

a. name changed from Dairy Valley in 1966
b. incorporated as Mirada Hills in 1960, changed to La Mirada 1960
c. incorporated as Lordsburg in 1906, changed to La Verne in 1917
d. incorporated in 1888, disincorporated in 1896, incorporated again in 1897

Source: Public Affairs, Executive Office, Los Angeles County website.

3

The County and Its Cities

Seventy-six cities. Plenty room for more.
Seven million people. Open is the door.
Angels we are none, but Angelenos nonetheless.
For we come from the county they call Los Angeles.

"Seventy-Six Cities," music and lyrics by Steve, Paul, and
Ralph Colwell and Cecil Broadhurst

Los Angeles County is probably one of the few counties in the United States that has its own official song. This ditty was composed by brothers Steve, Paul, and Ralph Colwell, and Cecil Broadhurst, while on a tour heading to Southern California by train. It was performed for the first time by the cast of "Sing-Out '65" at a meeting of the Board of Supervisors on September 14, 1965. Board members "were so impressed by the song," that they unanimously declared it the County's official song. Since its adoption, Los Angeles County has added another dozen cities as the population increased from seven million to more than ten million.[1]

The title *Seventy-Six Cities* in 1965 would have been quite different if it had not been for a Los Angeles County innovation in 1954. Prior to that time, there were only forty-five cities incorporated over a span of a century. Ten of them had reached cityhood in the 1920s, a busy decade when a few other communities tried, but failed, and several long-established cities changed course by being annexed to the city of Los Angeles. Reasons for incorporation varied from protecting local resources from control by the county or other cities, to defending the interests of the winter quarters of a circus. Those that disincorporated to become part of Los Angeles city were primarily concerned with a dependable water supply, as well as dissatisfaction with their municipal government. County officials were supposed to remain neutral in the incorporation proceedings while monitoring and ruling on the legal requirements and process, but the supervisors chafed at their loss of sovereignty in the new municipalities. Along with many county employees who might lose their jobs to similar positions in the new cities, they quietly opposed such attempts by the late 1920s. Although residents of many communities expressed dissatisfaction with county government for various reasons, few managed to mount successful campaigns for independence. From 1931 to 1953, only affluent Palos Verdes Estates incorporated.[2]

The dearth of city incorporations after 1930 exacerbated a conflict between the supervisors and some of the older cities in the county, especially Los Angeles. During the Great Depression, the city's mayors and other officials complained that residents of incorporated cities were taxed twice for municipal services; once by the city, and again by the county in forcing those same residents to contribute to the county general fund to pay for services supplied to those living in unincorporated areas. Los Angeles leaders even threatened to secede and form a separate county if the supervisors did not address this inequity. County officials responded that the city calculations were in error and city residents actually received many amenities left out of the city reports. (Additional incorporations might have helped the situation since residents of new cities would have to pay for their own services, which would reduce the county general fund needs for unincorporated areas.) Opposition by regional interests to Los Angeles forming its own county, a political scandal in the city in the late 1930s, and World War II delayed action in that era, but the movement for equalizing tax responsibilities re-emerged by the late 1940s. The California League of Cities pressed the issue in the state legislature, which in 1953 passed the Community Service Area (CSA) law allowing local governments to create multipurpose special districts for residents in unincorporated areas to provide them with specific services paid for by property owners. The first draft of the CSA law was written by Los Angeles County Counsel Harold Kennedy to settle the tax inequity issue, but it was only voluntary for counties. While a few CSAs were created in diverse sections of California, none would be established in Los Angeles County.[3]

The Lakewood Plan

Instead of pursuing CSAs as a solution, Los Angeles County officials moved in a different direction. Since 1908, the county had been contracting with some of its cities to provide services such as municipal tax assessment and collection, libraries, healthcare, animal care, and others offering a cost-effective solution since it already supplied them in unincorporated areas. As Los Angeles County became increasingly urban, additional services were available for contracting. In 1954, the "Lakewood Plan" was created, offering a full menu of county services such as policing, public works, and such to new cities on a contract basis so that these municipalities could achieve independence and limit expenditures and taxes for their residents. It also allowed the supervisors to retain control of county agencies providing those services. This device resulted in the incorporation of most of the thirty-one new cities over the next decade, adding many more county residents paying for their own municipal services. It also spurred complaints regarding county costs charged to the new municipalities and conflicts between contract cities, older cities, and unincorporated areas.[4]

The Lakewood Plan was named after the first contract city, a planned community developed in the early 1950s. The area and its population and tax base were desired by its adjacent neighbor, Long Beach, whose leaders made several attempts to annex it. Lakewood residents who hoped to obtain independence for what would soon become "the largest single-family housing development in the country" consulted Supervisor Herbert Legg for help. Having already discussed the possibility of the county providing many services to the new city, its leaders suggested it to

The development of Lakewood in 1953, the year before its incorporation as Los Angeles County's 46th city (Security Pacific National Bank Collection / Los Angeles Public Library).

Legg informally, and he assisted the group with the change in past county procedure regarding incorporations. With Legg's guidance, the county offered to provide a full range of municipal services for the budding city, an asset that Lakewood promoted in its fights for incorporation and against annexation. In March 1954, the voters of Lakewood approved it by a large margin. Immediately after that, Lakewood "entered into full service contracting and became the first city in the nation to rely entirely on the purchase of all of its basic services from a county."[5]

Several other communities had been contemplating incorporation at the same time as Lakewood (1954), and the latter's success spurred increased action. Baldwin Park (1956) hoped to keep a gravel pit in its orbit, while the leaders of Bellflower (1957) and Bell Gardens (1961) fought to keep gamblers out of their territory. Downey (1956), one of the few created from 1954 to 1964 that did not take full advantage of a multi-service contract, incorporated to provide most services to its residents on its own.[6]

The threat of annexation to one of the older cities in the county was the impetus for the incorporation of several of the other contract cities. Duarte (1957), South El Monte (1958), Rosemead (1959), Walnut (1959), Cudahy (1960), San Dimas (1960) and Hawaiian Gardens (1964) were a few of those that initiated successful campaigns in response to annexation attempts by adjacent cities.[7]

Several contract cities were led to incorporation by local business leaders to protect the interests of their firms as in the older city of Vernon. Dairy Valley (1956), soon to be renamed Cerritos, was created to limit newcomers seeking homes in large subdivisions that would replace dairy operations. Santa Fe Springs (1957) incorporated as industrial leaders campaigned to limit residents and influence municipal policy, although these interests lost some of their desired industrial acreage. Local business representatives led the movement for the City of Commerce (1960), which had a large population of Latinos the proponents hoped would not wish to participate in city governance. And the City of Industry (1957) was created by railroads and manufacturing interests in that area, devising its boundaries to keep out residential voters and control the costs of attendant social services. In order to include the minimum number of residents needed for their proposal, the leaders added the 169 patients and thirty-one employees at the El Encanto Sanitarium. This strategy infuriated Supervisor Kenneth Hahn as it blocked the addition of industry tax resources for the adjacent city of La Puente. Supervisor Legg convinced the rest of the board to follow tradition and approve this proposal since it was in his district.[8]

Class consciousness was also a factor in some of these incorporations. The desire for exclusivity in creating affluent municipalities with minimal taxes and social services was a driving force in the success of Bradbury (1957), Rolling Hills (1957), Rolling Hills Estates (1957), and Hidden Hills (1961), as well as others later. Fear of being annexed by an adjacent city of low-income residents requiring higher taxes for necessary social services made the timing of incorporation even more important for some of them.[9]

Cities chose incorporation for various reasons, and some communities tried to incorporate but failed; a few such as Altadena, on numerous occasions. These included future cities such as Malibu and West Hollywood. Others that tried but failed to gain cityhood in this decade or any other included East Los Angeles, Newhall, and an area called "Hahn" (named after Supervisor Hahn and his family) which fought Hawthorne over annexation attempts in 1960. Most of this area would eventually be swallowed up by other cities.[10]

Hailed by its early proponents as a brilliant invention of the leading urban county in the nation, the Lakewood Plan was touted for its allowance of communities to establish their independence in policymaking and land use, while offering a full range of services, or just a few if desired, carried out by trained county administrators and staff. The sheer number of incorporations of contract cities in its first decade testified to its popularity in Los Angeles County. It quickly spread to other California counties such as neighboring Orange County and even faraway Tulare County by 1961.[11]

The advantages of the Lakewood Plan were obvious for the county and its new cities. Supervisors could retain influence in municipal affairs since the services were provided by county employees and costs were determined by the county. Supervisor Legg was a major figure in the creation of this process, and Supervisor Frank Bonelli was a strong defender of it to avoid the establishment of a "metropolitan supergovernment" that would reduce the power of the supervisors. (See Chapter 6.) Historian Martin Schiesl has noted that the early process was positive in forcing the county to improve its methods in providing services for these cities as the county helped them to finance municipal government in the early stages of incorporation. In addition, a state law in 1955 allowed the cities to collect a uniform sales tax. In 1957, the county created the position of county-city coordinator within the CAO office to monitor the process and maintain cooperation between the county and its new cities.[12]

Critics of the Lakewood Plan soon pointed out its problems. Some saw the "present [1957] incorporation proposals under the Lakewood Plan as a reversal of the trend toward effective county leadership in a metropolitan federation" of local governments (opposed by most of the Los Angeles County supervisors as diluting their power). Some called it "county imperialism" in its retaining control of services in the new cities and continuing the fragmentation of regional governance in creating many more local governments. Others predicted that "the limited size and the lack of a sound tax base also suggest that some of these communities are acting more upon emotion than upon rational consideration of future needs and responsibilities" and would not become self-sufficient, although all of them are still in existence.[13]

Later critics have observed that some Lakewood Plan advocates have used the device to shape the boundaries of their cities to achieve specific goals. One was to draw municipal limits in a manner to form the city as a bastion of wealth and whiteness by keeping out areas inhabited by the disadvantaged and people of color. This tactic would leave poor areas in unincorporated county territory or to be included in less-affluent cities. Other cities were designed to restrict the number of voters, protect industries, and limit social services and attendant taxes. Some suburban cities emerged as middle-class enclaves to avoid higher taxes, a notion that seemed to be proven when they joined the tax revolt of the 1970s as property taxes rose. These were not the advantages the proponents of the Lakewood plan publicized when hailing the innovation.[14]

Other problems with the Lakewood Plan emerged as the cities worked with it. Some municipal officials became dissatisfied with county services, especially the sheriff, fire, and library contracts, and began to drop them. A few even tried to persuade potential contract cities to avoid certain service contracts. The costs established by the county were a constant irritation for contract cities, particularly for sheriff's services. In 1962, city officials argued before the County Grand Jury that the LASD should charge those cities only for the costs of additional service beyond what it would cost if the city was still unincorporated. That issue ended in a compromise, but a later County Grand Jury recommendation in 1969 held that contract cities should pay for *all* direct and indirect costs, as otherwise it would be unfair to the older independent cities that paid for their own police force. This dispute would surface almost every year thereafter as cities added it to their complaints concerning rising taxes based on rising county budgets.[15]

The 1969 investigation was prodded by the older independent cities and indicative of the continuing conflict between those municipalities and the contract cities and county. The independents had given up their crusade against the county to end perceived subsidies for unincorporated areas when the CSA law passed in 1953. But with Lakewood Plan contracts being signed over the following years the older cities deduced that the county still subsidized the newly incorporated areas by keeping contract charges below total costs so that the older cities still paid for some of the costs into the county general fund. In 1961, the older cities formed the

Independent Cities of Los Angeles County to press the issue as a group. Its lobbying came at the same time the county supervisors began to think twice about many more incorporations as a number were in the works in 1963. Early that year the state legislature granted broad powers to the newly established Local Agency Formation Commission (LAFCO), spurring more drives for cityhood. The supervisors decided to limit the creation of more local governments. Los Angeles County's LAFCO surely helped—it approved only three cityhood initiatives in the 1960s and four in the 1970s, while approving many annexations that appeased some communities and neighboring cities hoping to gobble them up. After 1980, seven more cities would incorporate with various amounts of service contracts by 1991 and increasing numbers of contracts were approved for older cities.[16]

Conflicts between county officials and those in independent and contract cities included issues such as who pays for which specific services and how to provide them, the distribution of state gasoline tax revenue, where transit lines should be laid, where to create sanitation, health, sheriff, and other facilities, and other decisions that challenged agreement. County raises for its workers caused major problems for cities that had to negotiate employee salaries with more restricted budgets, especially as county tax rates rose in the 1960s and 1970s. Redevelopment projects in the 1970s that reduced county tax revenues for city improvement projects proved expensive for the county and became almost annual subjects for investigations by the County Grand Jury throughout the 1980s. Some cities proposed projects that involved spaces lacking blighted structures that needed to be replaced; they included a park in Cerritos and an orchard in the City of Industry. In another instance the county was blamed for poor planning and development ordinances for cities in the southeast that required redevelopment in the early 1970s. For some of these cities, incorporation could be an important move to remedy past county mistakes.[17]

As in the county's first century, the county seat was the largest municipality and the most active in contention with county leaders. Relations with Mayor Fletcher Bowron in the early 1950s were generally amiable, except in the areas of smog control and consolidation of duplicate departments. Mayor Norris Poulson also had issues with county smog control, as well as sanitation sites and methods and the Lakewood Plan, which encouraged middle-class flight to new suburban cities and left the central city to the less affluent. The first years of the Samuel Yorty mayoral administration (1961–1973) appeared to be much less contentious than the years following the 1965 Watts Rebellion, when Yorty frequently argued with county officials. He and city council members expressed many disagreements with the county over the management of anti-poverty programs, tax assessment methods, financing a new city library and a current ambulance service, distribution of gasoline tax revenue, maintenance of beaches, sheriff costs charged to contract cities, and other issues. When Los Angeles City Councilman Tom Bradley became mayor in 1973, he immediately tried to establish a better relationship with the county supervisors to settle some issues already mentioned and a few more such as transit and membership in the regional Southern California Association of Governments. Bradley was usually on friendly terms with the Democrats on the BOS, but relations changed after 1980 with the Republican majority.[18]

In two major city battles with the county, Bradley was a central figure. In late 1974 the Los Angeles city attorney filed suit against the county over allegedly illegal provision of services to unincorporated areas financed by the county general fund. This action was one of many taken by the city since the 1930s to force the county to end subsidizing county services by established cities. The county argued that "non-property tax revenues more than offset the costs of such services" during the trial but lost the case. The ruling was overturned in 1983, however, as a state court of appeal ruled the issue moot because of the Proposition 13 tax changes in 1978, and the California Supreme Court dismissed a further city appeal. In a related action in 1977, Los Angeles led a group of independent cities demanding that the county create a single CSA community service area district composed of the 200 unincorporated areas in the county to equalize service charges. The county's LAFCO rejected the plan and the city vs. county trial regarding service cost inequities and the emerging campaign for Proposition 13 in 1978 delayed further action on CSAs.[19]

Another major issue of city-county contention during the Bradley years was redevelopment. The movement of population in and out of the central city area in the 1950s and 1960s spelled an era of decline for the downtown area. In the early 1970s, business leaders became more involved in redeveloping the increasingly blighted area, and the Bradley administration supported the effort to improve the city's economic condition. A Community Redevelopment Agency (CRA) program that would include 255 blocks in the central city was proposed, and then opposed by many factions, especially the county supervisors. As political scientist Raphael Sonenshein noted:

> Under this program, an area of downtown would be declared blighted, and its tax rates would be frozen. The CRA would condemn and purchase property for eventual development. As the tax assessments rose, the "increment" between frozen and real tax rates would be diverted from county coffers into CRA development projects. Thus, downtown renewal would be self-financing, although at a substantial cost to the county treasury.[20]

Despite the opposition, particularly by the county supervisors during an era of rising county tax rates, the plan was adopted with the blessing of business groups and the *Los Angeles Times*. (As one county official noted in comparing it to city complaints about unfairly supporting unincorporated areas, such projects demonstrated how cities could be "guilty of their own tax inequity by the massive use of Community Redevelopment Agencies as mini-tax shelters that are paid for by other taxpayers.") Over the next two decades the supervisors and council member Ernani Bernardi fought the CRA in many instances and occasionally filed suits during the CRA's rocky road to renewal for downtown Los Angeles.[21]

The contention between cities and the county in the first decades after 1950 and later was balanced by cooperation in many instances as these governments frequently worked together for the good of their shared residents. In some cases, they competed for resources and then compromised on solutions that would favor all interested parties. Many mayors and other city officials worked well with the supervisors of their district, especially in the 1950s and early 1960s. Compromises were made on issues such as consolidating health departments and planning transit routes. Amid several conflicts between independent cities, contract cities, and county officials in 1977, the supervisors formed the Los Angeles City-County Consolidation Commission to study and recommend further functional consolidations of the duplicate services of the two large governments. But in the competition for resources and political power between these many entities, agreement could frequently be difficult to achieve.[22]

Breaking Away

The conflicting issues between county government and its cities occasionally reached the point that the cities threatened to secede and form their own county. The city of Los Angeles tried to form a county within its municipal limits during the Great Depression, when city representatives looked for various methods to reduce duplicative costs. City officials and taxpayer groups became especially interested in ending double taxation as residents had to pay city taxes plus county general taxes spent on services in the unincorporated areas. County officials responded that the city's evidence for this did not include some amenities for city residents, that the cost of operating a county would be more than the city's estimated savings, and the separation would be devastating to the remaining area of the present county. Various reports by both entities created in the 1930s, a city political scandal, and World War II delayed any final actions. The issue arose again in the early 1950s, when state legislation offered some relief in expanding special districts to relieve the costs of services for cities and counties. The vast number of municipal incorporations in the 1950s also helped, as residents in former unincorporated areas would have to pay for county services to their cities, reducing some county expenditures.[23]

Los Angeles still was not satisfied, and in 1961 the mayor and city council asked the city administrative officer to report on "the legal steps required to establish separate city and county government of Los Angeles within the present incorporated limits of the City of Los Angeles." The report concluded that in the 1957–1958 fiscal year cities in the county paid a subsidy to unincorporated areas of more than $10.6 million, about half of that from Los Angeles residents. But forming a new county was not the answer. Instead, the city should ask the BOS to establish county service areas in each urbanized unincorporated area so that services would no longer be financed from the county's general fund. This method was the solution recommended by the League of California Cities in the early 1950s, and such entities were created by some California counties, but not in Los Angeles County.[24]

While the supervisors virtually ignored such problems when incorporations flourished in the 1950s, there were stirrings of discontent in the direction of splitting away. Leaders in several cities in the San Gabriel Valley began a movement in 1958 to secede in order to reduce property taxes. The proposed San Gabriel County would include the area from the west Pasadena city limit east to the San Bernardino County line, and from Whittier north to the Kern County line. The early impetus of this movement waned as Supervisor Frank Bonelli fought it and some of the cities included expressed opposition based on the added government costs to be funded. At the same time another movement in the San Fernando Valley aimed to create a new county out of this section of the city of Los Angeles. Its leaders were active for several years but faced both city and county opposition and eventually failed. It did, however, become a precursor for the area's unsuccessful attempt to secede from the city a few decades later.[25]

In the early 1970s, the San Gabriel County movement resurfaced with a new momentum but the same results. The granting of generous pay increases to county employees alarmed taxpayers who would have to pay for them, and city officials who would have to defend their more limited salary offers to city workers. Municipal officers, as well as residents, also complained that the supervisors held lifetime jobs, making them unresponsive to local governments and more concerned with raising taxes to assist their favored interests. A few more cities then moved to the front of the movement, assured of help in the state legislature by state Senator H.L. Richardson of Arcadia. But Pasadena, Whittier, and some smaller cities still opposed it, as it seemed the additional costs would devour the savings. The supervisors fought back with a defense of their responsibility to fund state-mandated services and the help of Assemblyman Frank Lanterman in defeating Richardson's bill to facilitate secession by reducing the number of petition signers and votes needed for approval. This effort was dead by 1972, although some activity, or at least discussion, lasted a couple more years.[26]

A wave of movements for new counties reached the county's shore by the mid–1970s. Talk of creating a new county in the Santa Clarita Valley consisting of Newhall, Saugus, and other communities occurred in 1974, just as another bill circulated in the state legislature that would reduce the number of signatures for petitions to call for a vote. The supervisors were mostly opposed, particularly to the requirement that a commission be appointed to study it and make the final decision, rather than the BOS. The lone dissident was Baxter Ward (in whose district the new county would be formed), who thought that the residents themselves should be able to decide. The BOS majority was also concerned that if the new county was not formed, the expenses of the commission would be paid by the existing county. Despite the protests of the supervisors, the law passed and went into effect on January 1, 1975. With this approval the proponents of "Canyon County" initiated the process.[27]

The mid–1970s witnessed increasing property tax rates to support rising immigration, health care, welfare, and other social services mandated by the state and federal governments, as well as those added by the supervisors that drove up the taxes of county residents. Higher taxes were even more of an affront to those in distant areas, who believed county government was too remote to consider their needs. With the new county formation law in effect in 1975, rebels in the proposed Canyon County and in the South Bay began organizing their campaigns and conducting research to support their objective. The South Bay movement moved slowly, but Canyon County proponents saw steady success, even with the *Los Angeles Times* editorials predicting many problems if the county was created. At the same time Los Angeles County officials examined the costs that the new county residents would have to absorb to continue the same level of services being provided and concluded the tax rate would almost double to meet those standards. The County Citizens'

Economy and Efficiency Commission agreed with this assessment and recommended that the proposal be defeated.[28]

Canyon County leaders would not be swayed. Petitions were signed, and with all prerequisites completed, the supervisors had to put this measure on the November 1976 ballot. The rebels successfully garnered support for the new county in its proposed territory, but opponents managed to convince voters in the rest of the county that the breakaway would negatively affect the remaining residents who would lose too many resources. County firefighters fearing job losses contributed heavily to the opposing campaign, as had county workers opposing city incorporations in the past. The final vote revealed a 55 percent approval by those who would become residents of the new county, but only about 30 percent of voters of the entire county. With this defeat, the five winning candidates for supervisor of the failed county, or "supervisors in exile" as they called themselves, joined other breakaway leaders in seeking a way to again "stand up and face these bureaucratic devils."[29]

While Canyon County organizers carried out their unsuccessful campaign in 1976, secession fever was alive in other areas of Los Angeles County. San Gabriel Valley leaders again began talking of initiating a breakaway, but never carried it through. San Fernando Valley leaders reignited their wish to create a city-county within the city limits, but critics judged it to be too dependent on the rest of the city and the county to survive. Santa Monica city residents proposed a city-county form like San Francisco but failed to get it off the ground. Chumash County consisting of Malibu, Calabasas, and adjacent communities, and Los Cerritos County that would have joined Long Beach and Signal Hill were also proposed, but none witnessed a sustained drive to success. Even a coalition of these groups in 1977 could not help the efforts of any of them.[30]

Two proposed counties located along the Pacific Ocean coastline did reach the election stage, as well as Canyon County again. One of them, Peninsula County, would be composed of Rancho Palos Verdes, Rolling Hills, and Rolling Hills Estates. Leaders from these three affluent cities initiated their campaign in late 1976 and had the financial resources to carry it out. Over the next year they completed all obligations and the proposal appeared on the June 1978 primary ballot. County officials, newspaper editors, and others opposed this new county as an affluent area with gated entrances attempting to escape high taxes and support of social services in the rest of the county, while still taking advantage of the existing county amenities.[31]

Leaders of the other proposed coastline county, South Bay, launched their second campaign in late 1976. This county would be composed of Torrance, El Segundo, Hermosa Beach, Manhattan Beach, Redondo Beach, and Palos Verdes Estates. The breakaway would remove a good portion of the county's western coastline, as well as important oil refineries. The supervisors and the Citizens' Economy and Efficiency Commission opposed it because of the resources it would remove and the fact that it would be too dependent on the existing county. But the leaders diligently collected the needed signatures for it. They also guided the proposal through the county formation hearings in early 1978 and chided Fourth District Supervisor James Hayes for proposing a charter amendment to limit contracts for services to new counties.

The proposal was finally approved for the 1978 primary along with that of Peninsula County.[32]

While these county campaigns moved along, Assemblyman Mike Cullen from Long Beach offered his own plan for creating new counties out of old Los Angeles County. In 1976, he introduced a constitutional amendment bill to create another South Bay County comprised of fourteen cities—the six mentioned above for the county of the same name, as well as Long Beach, Gardena, Compton, Lakewood, Paramount, Lomita, Lawndale, Palos Verdes Peninsula, and parts of Los Angeles City communities of Wilmington and San Pedro. Cullen claimed it was his response to complaints of constituents in his district that Los Angeles County was too large. This proposal became known just after the failure of the initial South Bay County and did not sit well with some of the surprised elected officials of these cities. It would face ample opposition and die in the legislature. In the following year, Cullen introduced a bill calling for an election to determine if Los Angeles County should be divided into two or more counties with the boundaries to be drawn later by a special commission. That bill also faced mounting opposition and died a slow death, while convincing other lawmakers to support a bill approved in 1978 that would make county formation even more difficult.[33]

With Cullen's legislation dead, secessionists turned to their political campaigns to approve their new entities. South Bay and Peninsula leaders were optimistic of victory but had trouble raising funds for their effort. Opponents reminded other Los Angeles County voters that the two new counties would remove important resources and revenue that would have to be replaced by the remaining residents. The specter of Proposition 13 on the same ballot that would reduce property taxes throughout California, further reducing county revenue, eliminated much of the immediacy of creating a haven from high taxes. Still, the South Bay County proposition would receive 73 percent of the votes within its limits, but only 23 percent in the rest of the county. Peninsula County residents would approve theirs by a wide 4–1 margin, but it lost by the same score with other county voters.[34]

One more chance—promoters of Canyon County would try again as they recovered from the 1976 defeat. The proposal faced the same opposition with the tax-cutting Proposition 13 being even more influential since it passed in June and was being implemented. (See Chapter 7.) In the 1978 general election, slightly more voters in Canyon County approved the measure, but it lost by a 2–1 margin in the rest of the county. In the following year the Canyon County Formation Committee dissolved to work on the incorporation of some of its territory as the future city of Santa Clarita.[35]

The 1978 election defeats and Proposition 13 effectively ended the rush to create new counties out of Los Angeles County. With property taxes being reduced and county officials cutting back some services and budgets, residents, particularly those in the suburbs and beyond seemed less interested in rebellion. In addition, the law passed at the same 1978 primary as Proposition 13 vastly increased the number of signatures needed to qualify new county proposals for the ballot. Whether or not county government has been more responsive to distant communities is still open to discussion based on conflicts between those areas and downtown county offices.

Since then, calls for new counties occasionally surface. Examples include a group of San Gabriel Valley city officials discussing the possibility in 1990 as county districts were to be redrawn; an Assembly member proposing the breakaway of the same area in 1995; and another Assembly member offering a bill to allow cities in Los Angeles County to study their situation and form new counties if they chose. So far, no cities have left under these circumstances, which is not to say attempts could not be initiated again.[36]

4

From Watts to Whittier
Boulevard and Beyond

Race relations did not appear as a stated concern of county government upon its conception in 1850. But ever since then this issue has been a problem facing county residents. Discrimination against people of color resulted in violence and segregation throughout the late nineteenth and early twentieth centuries, and county supervisors found themselves forced to address it on numerous occasions. Resistance to discrimination increased during and after World War II as the national Civil Rights movement gained force; rioting in major cities demonstrated that there was a long way to go for the county and the nation. The Los Angeles Watts Rebellion in 1965 and Chicano demonstrations in East Los Angeles in 1970–1971 were emblematic of the frustration of various groups. In addition, the arrival of non-white refugees in the 1970s generated resistance by many long-time residents and various hate groups, sometimes in violence, and required additional health, education, and other services to accommodate them. The treatment of people of color was reflected in the competition of ethno-racial associations of county employees seeking increased representation, benefits, and protection for their members, and in notable cases of several county department heads and others.

The population makeup of Los Angeles County in 1950 mirrored that of the nation for White Americans, who numbered almost 87 percent in both entities. Other groups were further away. Blacks in the county composed about 5.2 percent of the population, compared to 10 percent in the nation as a whole. Latinos numbered almost 7 percent in the county, but only 2.1 percent in the nation. Asian Americans numbered about 1.3 percent in the county, only 0.2 percent nationwide. These percentages in the county changed from 1940, since many Blacks had immigrated to the county for war-related employment, and some Japanese Americans banished to internment camps did not return after the war. By 1960, the White population had decreased to about 81 percent, while African Americans numbered about 8 percent, Latinos moved up to almost 10 percent, and Asian Americans rose to almost 2 percent.[1]

Most all the minority groups had been segregated in different areas until after the war by housing prices and restrictive covenants on real estate that prevented White owners from selling to non–Whites. In 1948, the covenants were ruled unenforceable, but realty associations fought to keep them. When African Americans and other minorities chose to buy homes in previously protected areas, they were met by disapproving White neighbors and sometimes burning crosses and violence. This even happened to singer Nat King Cole, as well as less affluent Blacks. In some cities such as Glendale in the mid–1950s, a "colored person" was not permitted "to live—or even stay overnight" according to Supervisor John Anson Ford. County public housing projects continued to be segregated.[2]

Members of minority groups also faced discrimination in employment, education, and social situations. Poor Mexican Americans were still ostracized from affluent communities, and some juveniles, whether in gangs or not, were castigated as roaming the streets in "rat packs" in the early 1950s. But veterans in that group fared better because of their service during the war. The Asian American situation improved by 1952, when the California Supreme Court struck down the California Alien Land Law so that they could legally own land. However, the memory of fighting Imperial Japan was still in the minds of many Anglos, who continued to discriminate against them. Mas Fukai, the chief deputy for Supervisor Hahn in the late 1980s and early 1990s, recalled his wartime internment and post-war return to Gardena after serving in the U.S. Army as residents spat on him and shops posted signs reading "No Japs Allowed." Like many other Japanese Americans, he quietly rebuilt his life as racism toward his group slowly faded. Blacks continued to experience discrimination in many areas similar, but not as severe, as that in the South.[3]

Three separate instances of discrimination related to Los Angeles County government in the 1950s represent the many more that occurred in this decade. In 1959, Supervisor Hahn, a county member of the Los Angeles Memorial Coliseum Commission, began a crusade to allow Black sportswriters to occupy the press box in the publicly owned Coliseum as White reporters did. Many months later the final decision denied that request with the explanation that Black sportswriters worked for weekly newspapers, and the press box could not even accommodate all writers of daily papers. Another instance followed a BOS decision in 1956 to end tournaments at county golf courses on weekends so that everyone had a chance to play. The request for the decision was made by a minority group, and a complainant wrote to Governor Knight for help in changing it, adding that race had nothing to do with it. Seven years later, the BOS returned to the golf issue when Hahn offered a motion to order the Parks and Recreation Department to investigate discrimination in membership and in vendor contracts on the part of a golf association on county-owned courses. The motion came after a Black federal postmaster was denied membership and resulted in the BOS barring further discrimination in golfing organizations operating at county courses.[4]

Another incident relating to county officials involved an exhibition at the County Museum of History, Science, and Art set to open in October 1951. "Man, and Our Changing World" grew out of a United Nations Educational, Scientific and Cultural Organization conference in Los Angeles. The exhibit explored the relationship of various races through comparisons of bodies, blood, skin, intelligence, and sociological and cultural features to demonstrate the equality of the races and how racial prejudice is learned, not inborn, among other conclusions. These ideas alarmed the museum's board of governors when they previewed it a month before its completion and complained of images depicting the mixing of the races and other components.

They ordered all work to be stopped and demanded that changes be made so that it would be, in their view, more presentable to the public. Word of the stoppage sparked a censorship controversy and backlash by scientists and others, and finally convinced the governors to give up. They warned that the exhibit would cause protests when it finally opened in June 1952; instead, it became one of the most popular ever held at the museum. After a six-month run, it was photographed to circulate at educational institutions for the next few years.[5]

Watts to Whittier Boulevard

The limitations of county and city governments in improving race relations in the 1960s and early 1970s can be seen in the 1965 Watts Rebellion and Chicano riots a few years later. These events followed years of discrimination and the advance of the civil rights crusade in the nation. By 1963, county and city officials and civic leaders were sensitive to rising unrest in the African American community and recent confrontations between Blacks and sheriff's deputies in Birmingham, Alabama. Supervisor Hahn called for a County Human Relations Commission conference on civic leadership "to avert the spread of racial tension and violent demonstrations." Business leaders also demonstrated concern after meeting with county and city law enforcement officials at the same time. The conference, in which Black leaders presented some of their demands, did not produce a definite plan of action, and several peaceful demonstrations followed a ten-day wait-and-see period. By then, an attorney for the NAACP speaking on rising animosity in the treatment of Blacks by the Los Angeles Police Department, noted that it should be resolved "before our city is involved in dangerous incidents." NAACP activist Loren Miller added, "Since everyone expects something to happen, it will." The Human Relations Commission continued to keep the situation under control, and the County Grand Jury began investigating de facto segregation in county public schools.[6]

Over the next year there would be improvements and setbacks for African Americans. In September 1963, the California legislature passed the Rumford Fair Housing Act which prohibited discrimination against people of color in purchasing housing in California. The Civil Rights Act of 1964 outlawed forms of racial discrimination nationwide. Supervisor Hahn hailed these measures, as well as the five-year-old California Fair Employment Practices Act and the county's actions in reducing discrimination over the years, work that helped to avoid the riots and vandalism that afflicted New York, Philadelphia, and other American cities in 1964. But Hahn's celebration would soon expire. Statewide real estate interests fought fair housing and circulated a referendum petition to repeal the Rumford Act. The measure appeared on the November 1964 ballot as Proposition 14. Minority and religious groups opposed it as a threat to restore discrimination. Business organizations and conservatives supported it. The result was another setback for minority groups. Although Proposition 14 would be nullified by the California Supreme Court in 1966, that would be too late to heal the sting of racism already inflicted.[7]

The combination of poor transportation facilities and schools, high unemployment, de facto discrimination in housing and jobs, and frequent confrontations with White police officers finally came to a head on the warm summer evening of August 11, 1965. A California Highway Patrol officer arrested a young Black man for drunk driving in the heavily African American Los Angeles community of Watts, and the crowd witnessing the arrest quickly grew larger. A minor scuffle at the scene escalated into confrontation between White police officers and a much larger group of residents. When the police made more arrests, the crowd began throwing projectiles at White motorists passing through the neighborhood. On the next day, a full-scale rebellion erupted with attendant arson, looting and sniper fire. The violence continued until August 16, when California National Guard troops and local law agencies quelled it. By then, thirty-four persons had died, over a thousand were injured, and almost 4000 had been arrested. Property damage was estimated at $40,000,000 in a scorched area of about 46.5 square miles.[8]

While most of the violence took place within the city's jurisdiction, the county was also involved in responding to it. In fact, Supervisor Hahn ended up in the middle after being informed by the county undersheriff at midnight of the first day that there was a potential riot in the making and could soon become a disaster in county territory. Hahn and one of his aides drove to the location and arrived at 12:45 a.m., when "all hell broke loose." With Hahn's automobile and others stopped, a few

California National Guardsman Lee Benson of the 184th Regiment stands guard in Los Angeles during the 1965 Watts Rebellion (Bud Gray, photographer / Herald Examiner Collection / Los Angeles Public Library).

individuals emerged and began throwing rocks and bricks. Hahn's car was hit several times, the windshield smashed in several places, and he suffered a cut on his neck. He then asked sheriff's deputies and the LAPD to blockade entries into the area. Hahn and his aide were to be driven to his home by a sheriff's deputy, but along the way the deputy was hit by a rock and began to pass out. From the back seat Hahn bolted over the front seat to grab the wheel and steer the car out of harm's way. By 2:30 a.m., they reached a hospital and received treatment for their wounds. Later that morning Hahn attended the BOS meeting and described his experience to the other supervisors.[9]

In the afternoon of the same day, Hahn appeared at a meeting of community leaders and others in Athens Park to discuss a plan to end the violence. Supervisor Debs had asked John Buggs, the executive director of the County Human Relations Commission, to set the community representatives at ease and encourage them to convince those on the streets to stay indoors. The attempt would not end the rioting, however, as it increased. In fact, Hahn was criticized by LAPD Chief William Parker, who mistakenly blamed him for the failure of the meeting. For the duration of the uprising Hahn continued to visit the riot area in his district and confer with Lieutenant Governor Glenn Anderson (Governor Brown was in Greece at the time) regarding issues such as calling in the National Guard, and with city officials.[10]

When the rebellion ceased, state, city, county, and private groups began the effort to rebuild Watts. Governor Brown appointed a special commission chaired by former CIA director John A. McCone that held hearings, analyzed social, economic, and other problems in the riot area, and recommended improvements for educational facilities, job training, and a greater emphasis on crime prevention and stronger community relations between citizens and law enforcement agencies. Although the report released in December received criticism for not going far enough, it did identify major areas for improvement. City government in Los Angeles would have many planning, restoration, redevelopment, and other responsibilities to attend to, and applied for numerous federal and state grants to finance them. The region's Chamber of Commerce appointed a committee of businessmen headed by paint manufacturer Harold C. McClellan to represent private enterprise in the reconstruction work. McClellan led the effort to organize employers to hire and train residents in the curfew area for employment. He obtained funding for this program which placed almost 12,000 African Americans in new jobs by 1967. Private foundations and religious and community organizations also contributed to the effort.[11]

County officials responded to the rioting by temporarily transferring the group guidance (gangs) unit of the County Probation Department to assist the Human Relations Commission. County departments were ordered to cleanup streets and sidewalks in unincorporated areas, and to seek more funding for social services. All county department heads were instructed to report on how they could improve their services in the curfew area. The Human Relations Commission contribution stood out as particularly important as it addressed many of the subjects included in the McCone Commission report. Hahn was immediately concerned with property damage; he lobbied Governor Brown to start an investigation of insurance companies cancelling or raising premiums of policies for damaged properties, and to have the legislature pass a law to allow property taxes already charged on parcels with severely damaged or destroyed buildings to be adjusted, since the owners would not receive government services for them. In December, the board approved increased funding for job training for those on welfare.[12]

The supervisors initiated many building projects completed over the next few years in the Watts area. They included the Martin Luther King, Jr., Hospital (opened in 1971), the acquisition or remodeling of two smaller hospitals and a health center, three welfare buildings, two libraries, a probation office, a municipal traffic court, additions to nine county parks, improvements to roads, and water, sewer, flood control and other infrastructure. The city and school district also completed a few structures in the same area. The Human Relations Commission staff spent many hours working to improve social conditions as fears of another uprising were prevalent, especially at a time of riots in other American cities in 1966–1967. In fact, in November 1966, Hahn led the charge to prevent activist Stokely Carmichael from speaking at a "Black power" rally in the county's Will Rogers Park that Hahn thought might turn into a riot. (The rally did take place, however, and there were no security incidents that day.) And yet with all the county, city, state, federal, and private resources expended in Watts, progress reports a year after the riots by the McCone Commission, by the County Grand Jury in 1967, and by the *Times* in 1967, 1985, 1990, 1995, 2005, and 2015 were usually more negative than positive.[13]

The aftermath of the Watts Rebellion was not lost on another minority group in the county. Residents of Mexican ancestry had also faced high unemployment, poor housing and educational facilities, discrimination on the part of law enforcement and others, and a lack of political power. Cognizant of some of the limited benefits African Americans received after the riots, and rising in proportion to the county population, Latinos began to make their voices heard. In early 1968, Mexican American high school students approached members of the Los Angeles Unified School District to demand changes in educational practices that were rejected. The students responded by walking out of classes and staging sit-ins which became the primary events later known as the "East Los Angeles Blowouts." Further protests focused on issues such as discrimination by the LAPD and LASD and the number of Mexican Americans drafted to serve in U.S. military forces during the Vietnam War. In 1970, the first of several demonstrations took place in unincorporated East Los Angeles. The largest was a National Chicano Moratorium parade on August 29 along Whittier Boulevard, in which thousands protested the war. The peaceful demonstration eventually turned violent when county sheriff's deputies tried to control the crowd. The result included the injury of well over sixty participants, and the death of two protesters and *Los Angeles Times* reporter Ruben Salazar. While covering the story, he took a break in a bar, when a sheriff's deputy shot a tear gas projectile into it that struck and killed Salazar.[14]

There were many conflicting stories and eyewitness accounts of the rioting. Human Relations Commission executive director Herb Carter and several members of his staff attended the parade and rally. After reminding his commissioners that his agency had warned government officials and community leaders of the potential for social unrest in nine areas of the county, including East Los Angeles (as his

Rioting in 1970 following the Chicano Moratorium protest of U.S. involvement in the Vietnam War (*Los Angeles Times* Photographic Archive [Collection 1429], Library Special Collections, Charles E. Young Research Library, UCLA).

agency did for the Watts area two months before that rebellion), he reported that the parade, also attended by many Blacks and Whites, had been peaceful. The ending rally at Laguna Park was also peaceful until later in the afternoon when law enforcement officers moved in, and bottles were thrown at their vehicles. At that point property along Whittier Boulevard was being destroyed, tear gas was dispersed toward the crowd, and Ruben Salazar was killed. Other county officials blamed the riot on "the rhetoric and preachment of militants, the presence of communist outside agitators, and an utter disregard for law and order," he wrote. Defenders of the protesters claimed that deputies, responding to a minor disturbance a block away, used it to forcibly disperse the crowd at the park; the crowd, mostly aggressive youths, fought back. As Carter concluded, the violence marked the end of Mexican Americans accepting further denial of full and equal participation in all aspects of American life. On the local scene, discrimination … and a system of justice which often was unfair in its implementation, have conspired to produce a new generation of Mexican Americans unwilling to wait for the inevitable changes supposedly wrought by the passage of time. For them, the siesta is over, as rightly it should and must be.[15]

The coroner's jury investigating Ruben Salazar's death determined it to be a homicide, but the sheriff's deputy who fired the canister into the bar was not charged with a crime. County supervisors renamed Laguna Park in honor of Salazar and eventually settled a lawsuit with a payment for his family. Several more demonstrations were held in late 1970 and early 1971, ending in further rioting, property damage, and gunshots exchanged, with one death. Finally, protest organizers argued among themselves regarding strategies, and militant action on the streets would be replaced with demonstrations in the county supervisors' board room, where activists and supporters demanded better services and jobs, while Mexican American leaders vied for political office to spur change.[16]

Immigration in the 1970s

In the 1960–1980 period, the population composition of the county changed. The number of White residents would drop by 3 percent of the total in the 1960s and 16 percent in the 1970s. The much smaller African American total would rise 65 percent in the 1960s (to a total of 10.8 percent of the entire population) and 24 percent in the 1970s; it grew much slower in the years after that. The difference would be made up of minorities already in the county and immigrants who entered the country after passage of the Hart-Celler Immigration and Nationality Act of 1965, which allowed many more newcomers from nations around the world. Some of them, especially from Latin America, Asia, and the Pacific Islands, entered the U.S. through Los Angeles, and decided to stay.[17]

The end of the Vietnam War was a major impetus in immigration from Asian nations in this era. When combined with Japanese Americans, Chinese Americans, Pacific Islanders and others from the general area, Asians had comprised less than 2 percent of the total county population in 1960. They more than doubled in the 1960s and almost doubled in the 1970s. The appearance of Vietnamese refugees incited protests throughout the nation and especially in California, where a large number were to be placed by the federal government. Despite a lack of information concerning what was to come, county officials created a task force composed of its departments and an Indo-Chinese Refugee Center to care for them. By 1979, the job seemed overwhelming, as an estimated 100,000 refugees from Vietnam, Laos, and Cambodia had arrived in California; 60 percent of them settled in Los Angeles County. They received help from the county, cities, and private agencies to assimilate and find jobs, with limited financial help from the federal government. The job was finally turned over to the County Office of Refugee Affairs that managed the continuing effort in the 1980s.[18]

Native Americans also increased during the period. From a small community of 1671 in 1950, they were joined by thousands more after 1952, when the Bureau of Indian Affairs initiated a program to move them from reservations to cities. By 1960, there were just over 8000 in the county, and they increased to a total of 48,000 by 1980. In 1976, the supervisors created a Los Angeles County-City Commission on Native Americans with a primary purpose "to attract federal funds to improve the condition" of the county's Indian population. The commission witnessed setbacks over the years in attracting funding to improve the socio-economic condition of the largest population of urban Native Americans in the U.S., but some advances were made in education and other programs.[19]

Latinos, including immigrants from Mexico, Cuba, and Central America, comprised almost 10 percent of county residents in 1960, and grew to over 2 million in

1980. Cuban refugees who fled the 1959 Castro revolution were still being supported to a large extent by the federal government until the mid–1970s. Refugees from El Salvador and Guatemala would arrive in the 1980s to escape revolutions in their own countries. Mexican American citizens in the county received county support as any other citizens did in this era, but those who entered the U.S. without proper documentation faced an array of handicaps.[20]

Since immigration was a national issue, county officials tried on many occasions to compel the federal government to reimburse the county for the costs of welfare and other services. The county counsel filed suit against the United States of America to recover the costs in 1975, as did several other California counties in 1979. Unsuccessful in these attempts, the supervisors tried to limit health and welfare services to undocumented residents on several occasions, although they agreed that undocumented seniors could receive temporary general relief payments if they had lived in the county for at least seven years. While supporting the undocumented to a limited degree, county officials were sued by a legal agency to stop all further expenditures held to be illegal, arguing that such payments could only be paid to American citizens. (The supervisors won that case, even though they had been advised by their county counsel that such payments were not legal.) In addition, Supervisor Hahn wrote to state officials on several occasions for help in standardizing the treatment of the undocumented in all fifty-eight California counties. Amid this confusion in the latter half of the 1970s, the undocumented somehow survived in Los Angeles County. This issue in the next decade would prove to be even more complicated with new supervisors ordering studies to determine whether the undocumented cost the county more in services than they paid in various taxes, and further BOS attempts to limit services.[21]

Race and the County Workforce

Some racial issues reflected the relationship of county leaders and employees. Although several prominent Mexican Americans served as supervisors and other elected county officials from 1850 to 1875, members of any minority group were rarely hired by the county prior to 1950. African Americans mostly served as janitors or nurses, and the first of them to be employed in more prestigious positions stood out: the first Black sheriff's deputy (1899), deputy auditor and deputy assessor (early 1900s), head of the janitor department (by 1918), and a deputy district attorney (1931). Most of the forty-nine Japanese Americans in county employ at the beginning of World War II had been fired or forced to take a leave of absence; few others would join the county workforce into the 1950s. In 1954, the local chapter of the NAACP investigated the status of African Americans in the LASD and reported in a long list of charges that the agency was "guilty of upholding and adhering to deplorable conditions of discrimination and segregation" directed at the sixty-seven Blacks in the department, mostly in jails and the distant Honor Rancho, and in a Black community.[22]

Some of the county supervisors made attempts in the 1950s to reduce racial and religious discrimination in county employment. In 1956, Supervisor Ford proposed the creation of a Fair Employment Practices Commission to "investigate and mediate alleged instances of discrimination in hiring." Supervisor Legg led the opposition of business leaders to this ordinance, defeated by a 3–2 vote. Two years later, Ford brought up the idea again, and asked for a hearing; Legg again led the opposition which tabled the proposal. Supervisor Dorn then introduced a modified version to placate the businesses elite, and he, Ford, and Hahn voted to have the ordinance drafted. At the hearing for this item, leaders of business groups and patriotic societies spoke against it. Some letter writers suggested it was backed by communists; unions opposed it as too watered down; and the county counsel advised that it could only be enforced in unincorporated areas, not in the cities. With that opposition even Dorn would oppose it, and the concept died again. The supervisors did, however, place a charter amendment on the 1958 general election ballot that would ban discrimination in employment by the county of persons "because of race, color, or national origin," and voters passed this measure.[23]

In the 1960s, county officials became more interested in the race and ethnicity of their employees. In 1961, the NAACP again charged the supervisors with discrimination against African Americans, resulting in orders to all department heads to review their procedures and eliminate such bias. In a 1962 board meeting the supervisors asked County Counsel Harold Kennedy how many African American lawyers had applied for positions in his department during his seventeen-year tenure. He replied that only two who passed the Bar were interviewed. (Apparently, they were not hired.) According to Kennedy and Supervisor Bonelli, that was because the department was "one of the finest Legal Departments in the Nation" with "men of outstanding integrity, men who are good Americans and men who are better than average in scholarship." (There was no mention of women in his department.) He went on to report that five years ago he had told Jewish community leaders that there were no members of their faith on the staff, and they should encourage qualified lawyers to be considered; by 1962 there were five on his staff of forty lawyers. In 1963, fearing charges of discrimination in hiring Mexican Americans, the supervisors ordered a report on the issue as they represented only 5 percent of the workforce compared to 24 percent of African Americans. The six-month survey would then be passed on to a committee for further study and delayed action. The county situation would begin to change when employee organizations representing large groups, sometimes in coalitions, became more effective in reducing job discrimination.[24]

County employees active in the campaign to end discrimination in hiring and promotions affecting their minority group created organizations for that purpose by 1970. Their initial activity was apparent in the effort to establish a strong affirmative action program during the 1960s civil rights movement. In 1969, minority workers and community leaders pressured county officials to adopt an administrative code amendment to eliminate all racial barriers in hiring and promotions. An affirmative action committee composed of county management, labor officials, and minority groups was created to assist in the implementation of the program. The BOS also approved Hahn's motion urging unions and contractors to adopt the same policy for the private sector. A month later the board ordered the drafting of new regulations barring discrimination on the part of unions and contractors involved in county public works projects. Before the end of the year, the county personnel director reported significant gains already being made.[25]

Minority workers felt differently. In one instance county library employees complained to the California Fair Employment Practices Committee of bias in hiring in that there were only thirteen African Americans and five with Spanish surnames in a total of 242 professional librarians. Other complaints by employee organizations representing minorities convinced the supervisors in 1971 to create a task force to investigate the results of the program. The final task force report in 1973 was highly critical, especially in the county's recruitment of Mexican Americans and Asians and biased civil service tests, and that minorities and women "are most noticeably lacking in the ranks of top and middle management." The county personnel officer defended his department's work in this effort, but a coalition including employee associations made up of American Indians, Latinos, Asians, and African Americans joined the Women in County Government to lobby for creation of a *permanent* affirmative action commission, as the task force recommended. The CAO responded that it should not be necessary as it would duplicate already established county services. The board did, however, order department heads to submit monthly reports providing information on the race and gender of those hired and promoted.[26]

This decision did not appease groups in the coalition. Several of them sued the county in 1973 based on racial discrimination in employment. The suit and further pressure put on the supervisors moved them to create an Office of Affirmative Action Compliance in 1976, but not the independent commission the groups desired. Over the next several years representatives of the organizations and their allies continued to contact supervisors and department heads about personnel problems affecting their members until the county financial situation in the late 1970s made their requests even more urgent.[27]

"The Coroner to the Stars"

Some of the more publicized conflicts between county officials and employees involving race and ethnicity were reflected in the cases of individuals. The most controversial was that of Dr. Thomas Noguchi. Born and educated in Japan, Noguchi emigrated to the U.S. and served an additional internship and several residencies in Southern California before he became a deputy coroner in Los Angeles County in 1961.[28]

By that time, the coroner's office had survived several controversies for which Coroner Theodore Curphey was blamed in delaying funeral arrangements of the deceased by requiring lengthier autopsies, allowing the illegal removal of "certain organs and tissue sections" without the consent of the family, and mismanaging the office to the point that the supervisors cancelled his trip to Europe to study coroner practices there in 1958 (paid for by the federal government). The BOS became alarmed again in 1961 when the State Board of Funeral Directors and the FBI were investigating charges of collusion between some members of the coroner's staff and private morticians being alerted to potential burials. It turned out that Curphey was secretly aiding the investigation, and the supervisors expressed concern that they were never informed of the probe. In that year, the coroner faced another grand jury investigation of his overruling of a decision of an autopsy surgeon in the case of a high-profile victim. After ten years of controversy, Curphey retired in late 1967.[29]

With the office of coroner open, the BOS looked to civil service rules to find a replacement. The search resulted in a list of the top three qualified applicants, two of whom resided in other states and withdrew when informed they were not acceptable to the USC and UCLA medical schools, so they would not qualify for part-time professorships that Curphey had held. That left Dr. Thomas Noguchi, who also was judged not qualified to teach at the two universities as a professor, although he already held assistant and associate professor positions at USC. Teaching and administrative experience was of supreme importance to the medical schools, so two county supervisors voted against giving the job to Noguchi, while two others voted for him. Officials of the medical schools then invited three pathologists they considered to be qualified to come to Los Angeles to consider the job. The County Employees Association protested that the medical schools wanted to be the "king-maker," and the county counsel ruled that the supervisors would have to vote for either Noguchi or one of the other candidates. Supervisor Debs then joined Hahn and Bonelli in voting for Noguchi and preserving civil service regulations. The vote would eventually be unanimous, and the supervisors placed Noguchi on a six-month probationary period to review his relationship with the medical schools.[30]

Noguchi began his tenure as coroner pledging to improve services, mend his relationship with medical groups, and expand his staff. In June 1968, his employment became permanent, and the supervisors agreed to replace the building for his operation and bring its services up to date. But county support for his office declined by August. A report by the CAO and a *Times* story documented problems in the cramped and understaffed office, many of them present for years. Noguchi's request for twenty more investigators to expedite the process was turned down by the CAO, and USC removed its part-time residents from the office. Noguchi responded that some of the CAO recommendations were superficial, and others could be resolved with more staff and equipment. Over the next six months CAO Hollinger and Noguchi clashed on a few occasions regarding the reorganization of the department, reported threats of resignation by staff members, and additional requests for more resources. An important CAO concern was the charge that Noguchi had merrily danced as he contemplated performing the autopsy of Robert F. Kennedy, who had been assassinated in Los Angeles on the night of the presidential primary in June 1968. (Two respected pathologists defended Noguchi on the Kennedy autopsy.) By February 1969, Hollinger decided to take more drastic action and asked Noguchi to resign, an ultimatum according to the latter.[31]

Noguchi resolved to end this feud by offering his resignation as coroner and "will become a pathologist in the county medical service." But he quickly reversed this decision after his wife wrote to the BOS charging Hollinger with racism in forcing her husband to quit. Noguchi also received "tremendous support from friends who know me well—associates, doctors, investigators and employees in my department." Hahn stated that he had already received telegrams and letters supporting Noguchi and expected a controversial proceeding. On March 4, the supervisors suspended Noguchi pending a report on the CAO charges. Within a week the coroner hired a high-profile attorney, Godfrey Isaac, who raised the racism issue in charging that Noguchi was in the center of a power play between county officials, the medical schools, and other groups. The supervisors did not delay their decision. After hearing a raft of CAO charges which included Noguchi taking drugs and threatening bodily harm to his staff, the board voted 5–0 to dismiss him.[32]

While Noguchi's lawyer and county officials prepared for his civil service hearing and during the proceedings, the coroner's supporters and some media made their opinions known. A *Long Beach Independent Press-Telegram* essay described it as one more example of the county not allowing members of minority groups to manage departments other than that of janitors. An editorial broadcast on KFWB radio criticized Hollinger and the supervisors for publicizing the charges against Noguchi before he had a chance to refute them. Conservative newscaster George Putnam also jumped to Noguchi's defense on his television program in early March. Japanese American newspapers such as *Rafu Shimpo, Kashu Mainichi,* and *Pacific Citizen* printed stories and editorials throughout this period, including full-page statements of Japanese Americans United in the Search for Truth (JUST), which defended Noguchi and castigated county officials, noting that JUST delivered a petition with 7000 signatures to the BOS. Letters critical of the county from JUST, the Japanese American Citizens League, other national organizations, and popular actor George Takei were also received. Clearly, the Japanese American community was highly upset with the county's treatment of Dr. Noguchi, and racism appeared to be the catalyst for it.[33]

The civil service hearings were held in May and June. Hollinger's long list of charges against the coroner included several small items (sloppy files, using too many dishes in autopsies, etc.), to such accusations as taking drugs in excessive quantities, demonstrating psychiatric problems, dancing in anticipation of performing the Kennedy autopsy (a charge soon dropped), and striving to expand his empire by taking over the County Health Department and Public Administrator office, as well as the office of the adjacent Orange County coroner. In addition, it was charged that Noguchi said he would like to see Mayor Yorty's helicopter crash and prayed for an airplane crash into the International Hotel because they would generate publicity for his office, and that he would like to perform an autopsy on Hollinger while the CAO was still alive. Almost eighty witnesses testified in the hearings; Isaac uncovered many conflicts in their testimony, as well as what he charged to be false statements made by four staff members ostensibly to get rid of the coroner. Many of the witnesses also defended Noguchi or admitted that perhaps they were wrong in their earlier statements. The unanimous verdict of the three-member civil service commission cleared Noguchi of all charges, reinstated him as coroner, restored his back pay, and recommended the appointment of another official for the department to handle administrative duties to give Noguchi more time for medical responsibilities, a suggestion Hahn had made earlier. Attorney Isaac added that if the county appealed the decision, "Anyone would have to conclude the county is prejudiced against Japanese Americans."[34]

Dr. Noguchi returned to work immediately and aimed to re-establish his direction of the department. Some of his supporters, including George Takei and the Japanese American Citizens League, urged the supervisors to allow Noguchi to respond to Hollinger's charges (his lawyer did not have him testify), to discharge Hollinger, and to conduct a full investigation of all of those involved in the case. Noguchi did wonder about Hollinger apparently having almighty power with the supervisors, who had no intention of removing the CAO, but the coroner moved on. The supervisors and personnel department assisted in replacing seventeen members of his staff who requested to be transferred to other departments and one who resigned. Hollinger studied the recommendation to add an administrator for the department to allow Noguchi more time for medical work but concluded that it should not be pursued as both Noguchi and the medical association leader opposed it. In 1970, construction of a new building for the coroner was begun, and in the following year a County Grand Jury audit of the internal control and financial records of the department found them to be in good shape.[35]

Controversies involving the coroner's office were sporadic in the 1970s and led to the supervisors adding a budget analyst to handle day-to-day administration of the department. In 1978, Noguchi was accused of covering up the death of a man arrested and held by LASD deputies in jail. He appointed a committee to investigate the case, and both the committee and the district attorney determined there was no foul play. The lawyer for the deceased's family sued the county anyway for $13 million. Also in 1979, the coroner raised protests in declining to order an inquest into the death of a Black woman killed by LAPD officers in a dispute regarding her gas bill. In the following year, the body of a newspaper reporter killed by a motorist and taken to the county morgue took a month to identify, despite the county having information that could have revealed it much earlier. The BOS ordered the coroner and CAO to report on how to improve the identification process.[36]

Nineteen eighty-one would become an even worse year for Noguchi as the seeds of another campaign to remove him as coroner sprouted. In late December, two lengthy stories in the *Times* divulged many problems in the coroner's office, including numerous mistakes in drug testing, failure to perform autopsies in suspicious deaths, and losing vital evidence in the case of a college football star who either committed suicide or was murdered by police in a Signal Hill jail. There were other serious errors affecting law enforcement investigations, trials and insurance settlements, and theft of "jewelry, guns and even gold teeth" at the morgue, along with other charges. Although the articles noted that Noguchi was well-respected as a scientist by his peers, he was portrayed as an egotist who spent a good deal of his time consulting on private outside cases for which he used county resources and was absorbed with cases involving the deaths of celebrities for which he received the title "Coroner to the Stars," as well as his involvement with a popular television show depicting a coroner said to be based on him. Noguchi informed his staff that the criticism included "some untruths and statements taken out of context, but overall the comments about the heavy workload and shortages were positive." A *Times*

editorial appearing the day after the second story disagreed, suggesting that Noguchi might have to be replaced for the department to improve its reputation. On the
next day, the supervisors ordered a full investigation and soon reprimanded Noguchi on the sensationalism of his comments on the deaths of motion picture actors
Natalie Wood and William Holden, both of whom had died one month before the
Times articles appeared.[37]

Over the next two months the CAO and the County Grand Jury conducted
investigations of the coroner's department. At the same time newspaper stories
reported an anonymous letter sent to Hahn describing further problems in the coroner's department, including a mistake in the autopsy of a slain sheriff's deputy. On
March 9, it was reported that Noguchi had been asked to resign by CAO Harry Hufford after the latter's investigation closed. Three of the supervisors agreed, as did a
Times editorial. The board moved slowly in hoping to avoid the embarrassment of a
decade earlier. But by March 25, the BOS finally suspended him, and a month later
voted 4–0 to demote him to "physician specialist" in the department.[38]

In the proceedings before and during the Civil Service Commission hearings,
Noguchi's attorney, Godfrey Isaac, again charged that racial prejudice dominated
the supervisors' actions as "there is no other good reason." But this was not 1969;
the charges were more serious and documented. While Noguchi based much of his
defense on not having enough funding and staff to do an adequate job, one supervisor argued that his was one of the only department budgets that survived cuts based
on dwindling county revenue. Noguchi had reduced support from Asian American
groups, but some African American leaders (including former Supervisor Yvonne
B. Burke) and others who believed the supervisors were being pressured by enter-
tainment figures such as Frank Sinatra and were adamant about the "coroner to the
stars" statements concerning the deaths of movie actors. But mounting evidence
backing the charges and lack of evidence to prove racism limited this support and
helped the county's case. The Civil Service Commission hearing ended in November,
when a hearing officer took the case under submission.[39]

The hearing officer's report made public in the following February raised a controversy with her decision that Noguchi's demotion was not warranted, but his suspension was, since his management of the department was deficient. Reinstatement,
however, would not happen, as the commissioners reversed her recommendation the
following week. Noguchi would be denied a rehearing, and several months later filed
suit to regain his former position. He would lose that trial in 1984, and an appeal in
1986; the California Supreme Court declined to hear an appeal the following year.
He and his lawyer noted that at least the publicity was good for sales of his book *Coroner,* published in 1983, which contained chapters on the deaths of Holden, Wood,
Robert Kennedy, Sharon Tate, Janis Joplin, and others for whom he performed
autopsies. (He also authored *Coroner at Large,* published in 1985, in which he wrote
about the deaths of other well-known figures and referred to himself as the "Detective of Death." In the meantime, Noguchi earned a higher salary in his new position
at the Los Angeles County+USC Medical Center before his retirement in 1999.)[40]

Another case involving an Asian American department head was that of Francis Ching, born in Hawaii of Chinese parents. Ching, the superintendent of the

County Department of Arboreta and Botanic Gardens, was the top candidate for the position of director of the department in late 1969, when the three other candidates failed the civil service exam. But the board of governors of the department decided that they wanted a larger pool of applicants. With that rejection Ching wondered aloud if he might be the victim of racism on the part of the governors. The governors re-opened their search to choose a different candidate with "public relations and social abilities, as well as technical expertise." Ching scored the highest on the exam but was passed over again. By then the supervisors had received many letters of support for Ching, and were no doubt influenced by the recent county debacle with Dr. Noguchi's racism defense. There was also speculation that the two supervisors up for reelection would face "the question of why a member of a minority group had been passed over after finishing first on two civil service exams." The supervisors finally stepped in to resolve the situation and began proceedings to reduce the power of the governors, whose president then resigned. The BOS appointed Ching director, and after discussing the issue with the governors, the supervisors convinced them to accept Ching.[41]

The cases of two African Americans, one a department head, also received media coverage. James Silcott, the county's only Black architect in the 1970s, was demoted in the Engineer/Facilities Department in 1976 and laid off in 1978. During the entire time he claimed to be the victim of discrimination by his department head and staff members, saw his outstanding work evaluations revised, and was assigned to a number to duties such as killing rats in parks. He appealed to the Civil Service Commission, which ordered his reinstatement in 1982, but told him he would have to go to court to have it enforced. He did, and the superior court judge ordered that he be reinstated. With the supervisors and civil service commissioners arguing over who should enforce the ruling and county costs rising, the supervisors ordered an investigation of the ongoing case, further delaying a resolution. Another judge ordered the Engineer-Facilities Department to reinstate Silcott, who returned to work and claimed he faced retaliation and harassment. Yet another judge ruled that the county "admitted in its pleadings that the reason for the demotion and layoff was racial discrimination.... He was laid off because he is Black."[42]

Faced with the continual eroding of their case, plus the fact that Silcott's attorney filed lawsuits for damages in Superior Court and Federal Court, county officials made him an offer: $1.04 million spread over twenty-five years plus retirement to drop all lawsuits and end the case. It took him an hour to decide. He later admitted being frustrated that the perpetrators were not being punished. Supervisor Hahn blasted his four colleagues on the board for allowing the case to drag out to that result, and in not honoring the opinions of the hearing officer and the first judge who upheld the racial discrimination claim. As one of Hahn's deputies reminded him, Silcott was willing to settle his claim in 1980 for reinstatement and $25,000 for his attorney's fees.[43]

The other African American official, Edgar H. Hayes, oversaw the Data Processing Department. In 1987, Hayes claimed that as a county employee since 1959, and one of only three Black department heads, he had been subjected to harassment by CAO Richard Dixon, who transferred his authority and some of his staff to another department without consulting him and denied a salary increase. Hayes then filed a federal court action against the BOS alleging racial and employment discrimination. Dixon arranged for a settlement with Hayes, and they agreed on a $90,000 payment to dismiss the lawsuit. It also included the waiver of a county code stipulation that prohibited the employer of a former county employee to apply for county contracts in the first year of the employee's employment with the company. Although some thought it a bad precedent, the agreement was approved, and the racial discrimination charge was dropped without media attention.[44]

No doubt there were many more individual cases over the years that were not as publicized, and some perhaps not justified. In addition, charges by minority employee organizations were covered more fully as they included large numbers of employees. There were fewer cases based on media and BOS papers as time went on, reflecting the remnants of past race relations in Los Angeles County and the nation.

5

1970s Scandals and County Family Fights

Big Changes Loom in County Government.—*Los Angeles Times*, 1975

The years of the early 1970s through 1980 promised to be an age of change for Los Angeles County government as four of the "Five Little Kings" were replaced. The five county supervisors who held office together from 1958 to mid–1972—the "Board of Eternity" as one observer labeled them—no longer ruled, but their replacements did not substantially alter the ideological direction of governance. In fact, the 1970s witnessed many personal disputes among board members, and a variety of scandals and investigations of elected officials and others afflicted county government at the same time as the Watergate scandal in the nation's capital. Relatively little of a positive nature could be accomplished by the supervisors as the stage was set for possible secession by some cities and a voter revolt against their governance.[1]

In the early 1970s the BOS membership changed tremendously with two deaths, one retirement, and a rare loss in a reelection contest. At the end of the decade an unheard-of mid-term resignation by a supervisor resulted in the appointment of a successor who would hold office for little more than a year. In order, the events included the untimely deaths of Frank Bonelli and Burton Chace in 1972, the defeat of Warren Dorn in the general election that year, the retirement of Ernest Debs in 1974, and the resignation in 1979 of James Hayes.

Frank Bonelli was replaced by Peter F. Schabarum, appointed by Governor Ronald Reagan in March 1972. Born and raised in Los Angeles, Schabarum attended college at the University of California in Berkeley, where he excelled on the football field. After graduation he played professional football from 1951 to 1954, and then started a real estate development company. In 1966 he was elected to the California Assembly and remained there until his appointment as a supervisor. During his tenure on the BOS, he pursued higher offices but failed, and finally retired in 1991. After that he became the father of term limits for state and county officeholders.[2]

The death of Burton Chace of the Fourth District resulted in his replacement by James A. Hayes, a native California lawyer. He served on the Long Beach City Council and as vice-mayor from 1963 to 1966. A moderate Republican, he then was elected to the California Assembly, where he remained until his appointment to the BOS by Governor Reagan in 1972. In 1979, Hayes abruptly resigned from the board and returned to the practice of law and occasional lobbying.[3]

Fifth District Supervisor Warren Dorn's tenure ended in a rare election loss in 1972, defeated by longshot Baxter Ward. Originally from Wisconsin, Ward had been a reporter and local television newscaster until 1969, when he resigned to run for mayor of Los Angeles, as he did again in 1989. He also ran for California governor in 1974. On the BOS Ward would continue to be a crusader and a maverick, always investigating suspected corruption and aggravating his colleagues and other elected county officers and administrators.[4]

In 1974, Ernest Debs retired after thirty-two years of public service. Two city councilmen were the top contenders for his seat on the board. The victor, Edmund D. Edelman, was born in Los Angeles and graduated from UCLA Law School. He served as a staff lawyer for several state agencies and the National Labor Relations Board in the early 1960s. Elected to the Los Angeles City Council in 1965, he represented the Westside then and after his county victory. The liberal Democrat Edelman was the first Jewish supervisor in the twentieth century and would be especially active in issues dealing with social services, the arts, and environmental protection.[5]

When Hayes resigned and disappeared for a short time in 1979, California Governor Jerry Brown replaced him with Yvonne Braithwaite Burke, the first woman and first African American member of the BOS. Burke was a Los Angeles native who received her law degree from USC. She served as a staff member for the McCone Commission after the Watts Rebellion and became the first African American woman elected to the California Assembly in 1966. Four years later she was elected to the U.S. Congress and left in 1978 to run unsuccessfully for attorney general. She served only a short tenure as she lost her election in 1980 but would return to the board in 1992.[6]

County Family Squabbles

Newspaper reporters predicted major changes in county governance in the early 1970s as the composition of the BOS almost completely changed. Of the "Five Little Kings" of the past two decades, only Kenneth Hahn remained. The changes left the board with three Democrats and two Republicans, but not a major change in ideology since Republican Schabarum and Democrat Debs were conservatives, Republican Hayes a moderate, Democrat Hahn a pragmatic liberal, and Democrat Ward a maverick Democrat. From 1972 to 1974, a majority composed of Debs, Schabarum and Hayes opposed Hahn and Ward on many important issues. While the new supervisors promised to bring reforms to board procedures and increasing land developments, only Ward and Hahn would follow it up. When Edelman replaced the retired Debs in late 1974, it seemed that the three Democrats would change the long-standing conservative dominance of the board to a more liberal stance. However, Edelman's appearance had only a limited effect on the ideology of the board; it occurred in the same year as the national Watergate scandal, which cast a negative shroud on government, and the election of California Governor Jerry Brown, whose "era of limits" mantra stressed a reduced state government. By the

Yvonne Braithwaite Burke, the first woman to serve as a Los Angeles County supervisor, is with her family as she is sworn into office by Governor Jerry Brown in June 1979 (Bruce S. Cox, photographer, *Los Angeles Times* Photographic Archive [Collection 1429], Library Special Collections, Charles E. Young Research Library, UCLA).

time Yvonne Burke replaced Hayes in 1979, the fiscal situation in the state and its counties was in a much worse condition.[7]

More important than ideology for the supervisors in this decade was personality, primarily that of former newscaster Baxter Ward, who never let up in his continuing investigations of real and possible scandals. In his first two years on the board, he irritated Debs, Schabarum, and Hayes with his charges of favoritism, accepting campaign contributions from those with business before the BOS, and other conflicts of interest. Ward frequently criticized Debs and especially riled him by regularly walking out of BOS meetings whenever Debs delivered his weekly speech on the positive aspects of county government. Debs was quoted as calling Ward a "jackass" at a meeting Ward did not attend. In the BOS meeting when Debs announced his retirement, Ward said he would miss Debs; the latter replied "Boy, I will miss you, happily." Debs would later win a disability retirement case against the county by claiming stress in his last years in office; he named Ward "as a specific source of aggravation." Ward also clashed with Hayes, especially on contributions by developers, and started an investigation of Hayes using county employees in his 1972 campaign. Although Ward occasionally voted with Schabarum on some issues, the latter usually criticized Ward for his grandstanding and incessant investigations, some involving Schabarum. Hahn, Edelman, and Burke got along much better with Ward than the others.[8]

While Ward was a major problem for three supervisors, others also had their difficulties with colleagues. Hahn was labeled a publicity-seeking politician by many observers, and sometimes egos would collide. His relationship with Schabarum was frequently testy, as he always wanted more funding for his district. Ironically, in 1973 it was reported that Schabarum used county employees to work on his political mailing in violation of county ordinances, and unknowingly awarded the contract for printing the material to Hahn's brother-in-law. In later years Schabarum had little sympathy for Hahn's declining health and blamed him for some of the ills of the county, while Hahn held Schabarum responsible for denying him the rotating chairmanship of the board.[9]

At one budget meeting in 1974, Hahn called out James Hayes for reacting "irrationally and emotionally" to one of Hahn's suggestions, and in another meeting, Hayes called him an "S.O.B." for delaying deliberations when Hayes had to catch a plane for a conference in Hawaii that would begin several days later. Hahn also had to settle a dispute between the director of the Natural History Museum and the president of its Board of Governors in 1978. On the next day, Hayes, a good friend of the museum director, informed the president that his appointment was terminated, and he should not seek assistance from any county supervisor or the county counsel. Hahn, the supervisor overseeing the museum, informed the president that he could only be replaced if his term expired or he resigned, that he should feel free to ask for assistance, and thanked him for his service to the museum for over twenty-three years. Three other supervisors agreed.[10]

Schabarum also fought with Hayes, as he did with most of the others. He also had conflicts with Edelman, on the opposite side of the ideology spectrum, but the two could be friendly some of the time and frequently played tennis together. The quiet Edelman was also on a friendly basis with the others as he was more prone to compromise.[11]

To some extent these relationships, and relations with other county officials and the state and national governments, and issues and events from outside sources would affect county policymaking. Actual county reform, especially relating to the supervisors, was minimal, despite some efforts treated in the next chapter. Many BOS procedures would remain, such as the usual bickering in board meetings, the veil of secrecy in forming and approving policies and contracts, the tradition of each supervisor having the last word in decisions affecting his own district, the "divide by five" method of splitting up funds aimed for specific projects into five equal parts regardless of where they were needed most, and retaining a muddy system of authority for identifying responsibility that confused department heads and others who would be blamed when something went wrong.[12]

The major cause of conflicts between Ward and other supervisors, sometimes even those who generally got along with him, was his incessant investigations of county officials to uncover corruption and mismanagement. Ward's deputies spent more time involved with these probes than the usual county issues, and even encouraged his appointees to dig up dirt on other supervisors, the assessor, and the sheriff. Ward also directed the district attorney and county counsel to conduct investigations that absorbed staff time and resources that could have been devoted to other issues. District Attorney Joseph Busch tangled with Ward on a few occasions; in an early memo Busch noted Ward's lack of civility in communicating. After Busch died in 1975, his spouse won a disability death benefit claim citing his job pressures, especially those brought on by clashes with Ward.[13]

Other elected county officials also had problems getting along. Assessor Philip E. Watson consistently battled with the supervisors, especially Hahn and Ward. Hahn became upset with Watson's proposed state propositions regarding tax assessments and treatment of a Hahn appointee to an assessment appeals board who criticized assessor practices. Ward began to investigate the assessor's office soon after he took office and issued public statements concerning assessment appeals handled by the staff. That pushed Watson to demand evidence for such "inane and frivolous charges" and "either put up or shut up." By 1976, Ward's deputies were busy exploring Watson's operation and found enough questionable dealings to convince the BOS to hire a private investigator who had worked on the Watergate scandal. During the investigation, Watson declared a two-year moratorium on residential property reassessments, which would have reduced county revenue and be unfair to those who had been reassessed the year before. After much confusion, Watson, by then in the hospital after having heart surgery, backed down on the moratorium. At almost the same moment, Ward's expensive private investigator submitted his first report and then a later report with allegations that could not be verified. In the meantime, Watson filed and eventually received a disability retirement claiming his heart ailment was partially brought on by his battles with Ward.[14]

The other elected county official, Sheriff Peter Pitchess, also had a long, negative relationship with Ward, and somewhat less with the other supervisors. It began by early 1973, when Ward announced that the Sheriff's Department harassed the executive editor of a Sacramento news service who wrote critical articles on Pitchess. A month later, Ward released a statement alleging that Debs had been offered a portion of a real estate fee and Hayes was offered a campaign donation from individuals involved in a parcel offered for sale to the county for a sheriff's station in West Hollywood. The news enraged Hayes and Debs, as well as Pitchess, who described Ward as a "third-rate, muckraking, pseudo news reporter." It also set off a search for an opinion on whether a supervisor had the authority to inquire into the policies of the Sheriff's Department and to subpoena the sheriff to attend a BOS meeting, which the county counsel advised in the affirmative. But a district attorney investigation of the sheriff station did not turn up illegalities, and the purchase was eventually consummated.[15]

Ward and Pitchess would be much more engaged in conflict in 1974. In that year, Ward's investigators launched a number of probes focusing on the use of LASD undercover automobiles, a deputy hiding a drug arrest record of the daughter of a county commissioner, the questionable relationship of the LASD with an insurance company, the submission of false mileage claims, installing security devices gratis at the homes of family members and celebrities, and other irregularities. Pitchess responded by withholding personnel and overtime records and telling his deputies to refrain from answering questions unless their supervisor could be present. He also requested the license numbers of the automobiles of Ward's investigators to protect them and sheriff's personnel as harassment incidents increased. The conflict generated animosity on the part of many players, as the other supervisors criticized Ward and the *Times* called for an end to it.[16]

The following year would see further Ward charges of the misuse of LASD helicopters and Pitchess' charge of Ward's involvement in a questionable land deal in Kern County. The feud apparently ended when Ward promised to resign if Pitchess could prove his charge if the sheriff promised to resign if he could not verify it. The CAO determined that the deputies who installed the locks should be punished by the sheriff, but most of the other charges were treated only as problems, not crimes. The CAO also reported a noticeable drop in LASD mileage claims after the abuse became public.[17]

Sheriff Pitchess was perturbed that the other supervisors allowed Ward's investigations and he always criticized their decisions in determining funding for his department. In 1976, he opined that the BOS was "a dismal failure," that the supervisors were only concerned with their own districts and rarely talked to each other. He also endorsed the ballot measure for a county executive who could represent a centralized authority able to increase his budget. But he generally got along with several supervisors at other times. One major exception was his announcement that James Hayes had sold out his Marina del Rey constituents and boat owners by refusing to approve merging the Harbor Patrol with the LASD. Hayes responded by asserting that Pitchess was just having a temper tantrum and didn't care about that issue, and that the BOS vote on it was unanimous.[18]

Unelected county department heads also faced the scrutiny of Ward and other investigators in this era. In fact, three public administrators faced probes in just one decade. Baldo Kristovich faced a district attorney investigation for selling automobiles and other valuables under his authority to friends and relatives, even judges. He was fired by the supervisors in 1971 and eventually convicted of perjury and submitting false evidence. In 1978, another public administrator came under fire for the crime of playing too much backgammon during working hours. Bruce Altman's case involved one of Ward's former deputies, who transferred to Altman's department, and it consumed an incredible amount of BOS time as Ward and Schabarum turned it into a power play. The two supervisors argued and withheld the department's records, but neither emerged as a victor. Ultimately, Altman was banished to a different department. The third public administrator, Gordon Treharne, was the subject of conflict-of-interest charges in 1980, while overseeing the estate of developer Ben Weingart and having himself appointed as a private conservator of the estate. News of Treharne's dual roles sprouted additional charges of irregularities in his office. The district attorney's office investigated but found nothing illegal, and Treharne remained in office.[19]

At the same time as the Kristovich investigation, County Clerk William G. Sharp faced a grand jury probe for mishandling trial evidence in the assassination of Robert F. Kennedy. The County Grand Jury concluded that Sharp was responsible for allowing ballistic items to be improperly stored and parts of documentary exhibits to be removed. The BOS created a special task force to examine the charges that Sharp refuted; only minor problems were discovered. Interest in the Sirhan case would continue, however, as Ward conducted his own investigation in 1974, while coincidently running for governor. In the following year the BOS responded to national interest in the assassination by initiating an investigation that led to hearings and reports by experts. National interest rose again in 1992, based on the opening of previously sequestered LAPD records. None of these efforts have changed the official result.[20]

Three years after the Sharp investigation, Probation Department head Kenneth E. Kirkpatrick was under the spotlight for malfeasance. Kirkpatrick had been blamed for some of the shortcomings in his department in the early 1970s, when Hahn announced that the department failed to follow his own program to reduce juvenile crime. Hahn's office and the *Times* continued to pursue the issue, and the BOS fired him in 1974. Kirkpatrick appealed the dismissal to the Civil Service Commission, which upheld it, but the ruling was overturned. After further appeals in which the rulings moved back and forth, and the ordeal concluded in 1981. Kirkpatrick was officially reinstated and received back pay for those seven years.[21]

Another department head faced dismissal in the early 1970s and did not fare as well as Kirkpatrick. County Marshal Timothy Sperl was the subject of a district attorney investigation initiated after Ward received reports that Sperl's staff had been working on Hayes's 1972 election campaign while on county time. Hahn then asked Sperl for more information on the use of his staff in lobbying legislators in Sacramento and providing transportation and security at private parties for them. The County Grand Jury investigated the charges, and in January 1975, indicted Sperl on eight felonies, including embezzlement of public funds and grand theft in assigning deputies to lobby for

Los Angeles County Coroner Thomas Noguchi presents diagrams of Robert Kennedy's wounds during a 1974 investigation of Kennedy's assassination (Joe Kennedy, Photographer, *Los Angeles Times* Photographic Archive [Collection 1429], Library Special Collections, Charles E. Young Research Library, UCLA).

the department and to chauffeur Hayes for three months during his campaign, and conspiracy to obstruct justice in covering it up by altering and destroying county records. Sperl was convicted of four of the charges. Two of his top deputies were fired by the acting marshal, and Sperl was fired by the municipal court judges who hired him. Hayes, a central figure in Sperl's downfall, escaped prosecution, despite Ward's continuing attempts to have him indicted for accepting political favors.[22]

County commissioners also came under fire at various times. They included Regional Planning Commissioner Owen Lewis, whose reappointment by Schabarum was denied due to a conflict of interest. This decision was a departure from the usual BOS tradition of allowing each supervisor to appoint and reappoint their own choices for commissions and committees. In this case, Schabarum was livid that all four of his colleagues would vote against him, and it might have affected his relationship with the two who remained on the board after the 1980 election. Other regional planning commissioners were being chauffeured to and from their meetings under the surveillance of Ward's investigators that year as Ward wanted to end that benefit.[23]

The supervisors even argued with county judges in the 1970s, especially over travel expenses regarding lobbying. The first such conflict occurred in 1961, when the BOS adamantly opposed the lobbying of Superior Court judges in Sacramento on seven bills the supervisors opposed. The issue emerged again in 1976, when Municipal Court Presiding Judge Joseph Grillo asked for more funding for his courts. In August, he requested travel funds for himself and another judge to speak in a legislative hearing in support of a bill to increase the number of judges in his court. The BOS opposed the bill and the request, so the CAO declined it. Grillo then issued a court order mandating the county to provide tickets for flights to Sacramento, which the county counsel advised would be illegal. When a member of the county auditor staff denied it, Grillo instructed a court bailiff to arrest him for contempt of court and sentenced him to two days in jail. He was allowed to leave his cell that afternoon and Grillo withdrew the contempt order several days later.[24]

After at least sixteen stories in the *Times*, including several negative editorials, a censuring by the Los Angeles County Bar Association, and failure to be reelected as presiding judge by his colleagues, Grillo sued the supervisors for the travel expense. He also claimed the experience adversely affected his health. The BOS asked him to drop his suit, and again rejected his claim. In March 1977, Grillo won his case and the county declined to appeal it. Later that year Grillo received a disability retirement based on stress. The arrested auditor also applied for a disability benefit since the arrest caused stress for him.[25]

Lobbying by judges surfaced again in 1978, when the twenty-four judicial districts of the County Municipal Court hired two private legal firms to research and lobby in the interest of the court after the judges heard of possible deep budget cuts if Proposition 13 was approved. (On Proposition 13 see Chapter 7.) In meetings with the county counsel and supervisor deputies, the judges believed that the county admitted that it must pay for private counsel since the county counsel represented the county in any legal conflict. Each of the districts then paid a portion of the legal fees from their own budgets and requested payment of the remaining fees from the county auditor. He declined since the supervisors had not approved them before-hand. The judges then filed suit to have the county make the payments. Hahn called for the auditor to end payments to the private attorneys hired by the judges and col-lect the unauthorized funds already received by the legal firms, so the firms sued the county for their fees. The conflict continued until May 1980, when a Superior Court judge from San Diego County ruled in favor of the judges.[26]

Other Scandals

Besides BOS feuds and Ward's investigations of county officials, other scan-dals surfaced involving the county workforce and its contractors in the tumultuous 1970s. Ward and his investigators were extremely busy at the time, especially in 1973 and 1974, and then tapered off as they transferred to other departments and finally stopped with the Watson fiasco in 1977. During those years, Ward's investigators had some success and many failures as they were discovered raiding the desks of county employees, spying on top county officials, and removing county documents. In addi-tion to the probes already mentioned, Ward's team investigated the rise in the con-tract price from $5.5 million to over $55.7 million demanded by the architectural firm that designed and built an addition to the Rancho Los Amigos medical facil-ity. The additional costs occurred when county officials requested changes while the project was already underway and feared upsetting the supervisors since the firm was a major political donor to several of them. Other than revealing that a deputy of Schabarum (and of Bonelli before him) had accepted personal favors from the firm but would not be charged in this instance, no one was held responsible for the mon-strous overcharge.[27]

Other Ward investigations included a probe of four architectural firms which contributed to the supervisors and received contracts before approval by a review board, for which the County Grand Jury found no evidence of criminal actions; investigations of hospital staff forging doctor signatures to obtain drugs at the LAC+USC hospital (formerly County General), and of its doctors claiming too many hours on timesheets; an ambulance chasing ring operating at the same hospital also involving one of Debs' deputies that was initially reported by the *Times,* and at least ten other investigations of the activities of county officials and employees.[28]

As previously noted, the County Grand Jury conducted several investigations and audits of possible mismanagement and criminal activity in county government in the 1970s. They included probes of judicial misconduct in furnishing bail bonds in 1972; on contracts awarded by the Purchasing Department in 1973 and 1978; a criti-cal audit of problems in the Mechanical Department in 1977; and several more.[29]

Major newspapers inspired several investigations and carried out some of them. A series of *Times* stories launched the second probe of the coroner's depart-ment under Dr. Thomas Noguchi that ended with his demotion. (See Chapter 4.) In 1980, the paper printed a story on the questioning of one of Schabarum's depu-ties accused of giving an official county decal to Kenneth Bianchi, who applied it to his windshield to help him appear as an undercover policeman when he abducted victims to assist "Hillside Strangler" Angelo Buono. The Schabarum deputy was also questioned about attending parties provided by Buono and Bianchi featuring teen-age prostitutes and the attendance of a Schabarum appointee to the Highway Safety Commission. As a result, the commissioner resigned, an investigation of the deputy began, and Sheriff Pitchess called on Schabarum, who knew of the decal and parties a year earlier, to resign. An angry BOS voted to end the distribution of decals and badges to anyone other than safety personnel but would later restore some of the badges. At the same time, Schabarum suspended another one of his deputies for allegedly pressuring a federally funded agency in the county to hire his girlfriend and then convincing Schabarum to cut off funding for the agency after she was fired because of her job performance. A month later the district attorney staff cleared the deputy and continued to investigate charges that the poverty agency supplied young women "and 'wined and dined' supervisor's deputies in return for unspeci-fied favors." The charges of frequent parties and women supplied to deputies could not be verified, but the agency's contracts with the county were canceled anyway.[30]

As can be seen from the above, the 1970s were a trying time for county gov-ernance as officials waded through scandals and personal conflicts while trying to address other important issues such as rising tax rates, gasoline shortages and air pollution. In an era of increasing distrust of public servants at the federal, state, and local levels, these investigations based on real and false evidence, along with others not mentioned here, certainly contributed to that distrust.

1970s County Elections

Supervisorial elections in the 1970s were almost identical to that of the 1950s and 1960s in that incumbents rarely lost. In this decade it happened twice for different reasons. Most followed the 1970 pattern of incumbents winning in the primary and avoiding a general election run-off. Kenneth Hahn, a White politician in a minority district, would demonstrate the power of an incumbent who took good care of his constituents by winning all three of his primaries with over 80 percent of the vote.

In 1972, the benefit of incumbency was a plus for Schabarum and Hayes, both appointed to their positions after the deaths of their predecessors. Schabarum won a close race in the primary, and Hahn again easily defeated William C. Taylor, a Com-munist Party USA official, as Hahn constantly reminded voters. Hayes, who had the endorsement of his predecessor, Burton Chace, would face Los Angeles City Coun-cilman Marvin Braude in the general election. Braude was endorsed by the *Times* and county social workers, and stressed environmental issues, and he pledged his support to Hayes after the latter's victory.[31]

Fifth District incumbent Warren Dorn barely ran ahead of television news-caster Baxter Ward in the primary, and the two faced off in the general election. During the campaign, Ward accused Dorn of multiple shortcomings, especially of favoring wealthy developers and failing to reduce smog. The campaign turned into a mudslinging affair as Ward brought up the fact that Dorn had been arrested for petty theft in 1946, while Dorn pointed out the ties of Ward's father-in-law to organized crime, which ended at least when he died in 1959. The Ward campaign was heavily overspent by Dorn's wealthy treasury. Ward defeated Dorn in a close election, when reporter Bill Boyarsky concluded that "deaths and the election ended the alliance of Dorn, Chace, Bonelli, and Debs, who had run the board for sixteen years. Hahn was usually the dissenter." The *Times* editors expected substantial reforms to be enacted but were much too optimistic.[32]

The initial stages of the 1974 election promised another attempt at reforming county governance. In late 1973, Los Angeles City Councilmen Edmund Edelman and John Ferraro considered a run for Debs' Third District seat. Edelman decided to go for it just before Debs announced he would retire at the end of his term. Ferraro and eventually eight others then entered the race, with Debs endorsing Ferraro and the AFL-CIO and the *Times* backing Edelman. Ferraro was considered the favorite of business, while Edelman was a liberal reformer, both good friends on the city council. In the primary Edelman came in first and Ferraro second, and in the general election Edelman easily defeated Ferraro. Meanwhile, Schabarum defeated his two opponents with a landslide of votes in his first reelection bid.[33]

The next supervisorial election in 1976 was more typical of supervisor contests. Ward, Hayes, and Hahn had no serious competition, so they won in the primary. Hahn defeated an African American businessman, who would run against him three times and never receive more than 9 percent of the vote, and a feminist and member of the Socialist Workers Party in this contest.[34]

The 1978 election had the same result. Edelman faced a few opponents, including a political activist with the Coalition for Economic Survival. But none of them had a hefty treasury, and he garnered 74 percent of the vote. Schabarum did face one strong candidate who collected 28 percent in the First District, but the incumbent was victorious with 56 percent.[35]

The 1980 election would be different. While Hahn again emerged as victor in the primary with almost 90 percent of the vote, two other incumbents would meet defeat. In this year Schabarum found his opportunity to change the ideological makeup of the board by financing a conservative challenger. Ward and Burke faced several opponents in the primary and defeated almost all of them. In the general election, former Assemblyman Michael Antonovich, who had received the endorsement of soon-to-be President Ronald Reagan, raised funds to dominate the campaign in which Ward accepted only small donations, Antonovich won with 55 percent of the vote. The contest was not as civil for Yvonne Burke in her first election. Her opponent, conservative Deane Dana, was financially supported by Schabarum to add another Republican to the board. Dana's staff made sure to stress Burke's race and liberal ideology in a mostly White, conservative district, and he would easily defeat her in the general election.[36]

Law and Order

When Sheriff Peter Pitchess wasn't fighting with the supervisors over tight budgets and Ward's allegations, he was dealing with a variety of issues including contract cities protesting LASD charges for patrol services and resistance to women being assigned to patrol duty in 1972. He also assisted in the settlement of a lawsuit involving a $19 million criminal records filing system he convinced the supervisors to purchase that was not installed correctly and the manufacturer then sued the county for ruining its reputation. (The suit was settled, not in the county's favor.) In another issue involving records, the county public defender brought an action against the LASD in 1977 for destroying citizen complaints against deputies just one month after a judge found that similar records shredded by the LAPD could have been helpful to attorneys defending those charged with resisting arrest or assaulting an officer.[37]

In addition, Pitchess and his deputies had to fight crime, from simple "morality" offenses the supervisors wanted to end, to more complex and violent crimes committed by organized criminals and even youngsters. Before 1970, the BOS had been active in suppressing various morals issues such as topless waitresses serving customers in bars, various forms of gambling, and pornography. Bars and restaurants were regulated to some extent by the County Public Welfare Commission, which issued licenses for such establishments. In 1975, an ordinance prohibiting nudity in county parks and on county beaches was passed. And in 1977 and 1978, the county turned to zoning restrictions to eliminate sex-oriented businesses in unincorporated Lennox and a district adjacent to Whittier.[38]

More serious crimes included the usual violent and non-violent felonies, some of them attributed to organized crime figures and groups. Organized crime in Los Angeles County and California was prevalent and under surveillance by law enforcement agencies. Hahn became especially interested after being informed by Pitchess of the "very real danger" of the current connection between organized crime and the game of backgammon. In 1975, Hahn's motion in a BOS meeting to have Pitchess submit information on the danger was approved, and the sheriff forwarded the report on "the ever-persistent threat of increased Organized Crime influence" the following year. Within weeks the supervisors requested Pitchess and others to report on Hahn's plan to expand the county Delinquency and Crime Commission into a larger citizen's crime commission. Despite his past revelations of this activity, Pitchess believed crime commissions were failures, created by citizens because of the "inability or unwillingness on the part of official government processes to respond to serious crime." That was not the case in Los Angeles County, he believed, as "a coalition of effective, professional law enforcement, a concerned citizenry, and honest public officials has been successful in keeping organized crime in this community to a minimum." Two years later Hahn reminded Pitchess of this statement after reading an LASD report on organized crime and noting that it clearly demonstrated a "real threat to the community." In 1980, the district attorney informed the BOS that racketeering cases against five local La Cosa Nostra leaders had been dismissed in a Los Angeles federal court. And in 1983, the LASD compiled a report requested by the BOS on the status of organized crime in the county, which also included important gangs. Clearly, organized crime was still alive in Los Angeles County.[39]

The Sheriff's Department also operated the county jails, almost always overcrowded and rife with violent jailers and inmates. Pitchess reported some of the problems to Hahn in 1974, informing him that the Hall of Justice jail and administrative building was literally falling apart, with large chunks of concrete falling off upper floors and damaging automobiles parked below. In January 1975, the ACLU sued the county because of overcrowding and "intolerable conditions" at the Men's Central Jail. Referred to as the Rutherford Decision named for one of the inmates, this case would be extended for decades as the U.S. Department of Justice inspected the jail occasionally and the LASD and ACLU agreed to mitigation measures. The conditions improved but overcrowding continued over decades as the inmate population increased. A 1978 race riot at the county's Wayside Honor Rancho pointed to another growing problem in incarceration.[40]

Other county correctional facilities also experienced problems in the 1970s. Another suit by the ACLU in 1973 focused on inmate complaints at the Sybil Brand Institute for Women, including violation of constitutional rights and privacy. Juvenile Halls under the jurisdiction of the Probation Department were also under scrutiny. Central Juvenile Hall, while under investigation by the U.S. Department of Justice, was judged to be substandard in many ways in a suit filed by the Western Center on Law and Poverty in 1975. The suit asked for a permanent injunction against the county subjecting juveniles to the conditions listed in the suit or to close, and a preliminary injunction was issued. Conditions there had no doubt been exacerbated by the 1971 earthquake that damaged the Sylmar Juvenile Hall in the San Fernando Valley, and many of the latter's inmates had to be transferred to Central Juvenile Hall. In the same year the BOS began to make plans for the replacement of the Sylmar facility, which led to disagreement over whether it should be rebuilt at its former capacity of 411 beds, or if a more modern approach in building two smaller juvenile facilities should be approved. The debate continued for several years before the hall was rebuilt and finally opened in 1978.[41]

The substandard conditions in juvenile halls exacerbated racial conflict and violence for juveniles already engaging in more serious crimes. In 1971, the Probation Department reported that juvenile crime dropped with the help of its programs stressing rehabilitation. But by the following year it was on the increase, especially by gang members. LAPD Chief Ed Davis attributed the crisis in the juvenile justice system to inaction on the part of the BOS, and the board declared a crackdown on hard-core crime in 1973. In late 1975, Sheriff Pitchess initiated a new war on juvenile crime and gang activity in East Los Angeles and South Los Angeles with the help of the Probation Department, district attorney, and the courts. Some progress was made, but not enough to reduce the crime rate. By 1980, Acting Probation Department head Kenneth Fare called for an overhaul of California's juvenile justice system with tougher sentences and other reforms to stem the increase, especially in Los Angeles County. The call for reform failed, as evidenced by increasing juvenile crime amid fewer jobs and more gangs in the 1980s.[42]

Brutality and Shootings

The LASD on patrol could be a welcome sight to county residents, many of whom expressed their thanks for a job well done to the supervisors. And even though the supervisors, especially Baxter Ward, had their conflicts with Sheriff Pitchess, the BOS worked with the LASD in efforts to reduce crime and improve law enforcement practices. At times supervisors acknowledged the efforts of sheriff's deputies in the field, as well as higher ranking officers such as the commanders in charge of jail facilities who Edelman thanked in 1978 for their efforts at equal treatment of gay men and lesbians. But law enforcement in the 1970s was a difficult task in a metropolitan area such as Los Angeles. There were many complaints from those encountering deputies whose conduct was unwelcomed. Hahn's papers contain many of them, some for racism expressed by deputies in a district containing many people of color. Not all the charges could be verified, but the sheer number is certainly serious, especially considering Pitchess's efforts to destroy official complaint documents to protect his deputies.[43]

Individual incidents regarding LASD abuse included complaints of the treatment of arrestees at the Firestone Station jail in 1973, the mishandling of striking workers in Paramount, and abuse charges made against the "Lynwood 6" at the LASD Station. Another complaint was made by a mother in Alhambra of deputy arrogance and mistreatment faced by her son in a county jail, noting that she had been a "right-winger" but now would become an activist. A more broadcasted incident involved Henry Vasquez, a county employee recently accepted for training to become a marshal. Vasquez witnessed the brutal beating by deputies of a neighbor suspected of assaulting a deputy while arresting him in a domestic dispute in 1979. Vasquez stated that he raised his voice to object to the treatment and was then thrown to the ground and kicked by deputies who arrested *him* for assaulting a deputy. Pitchess defended his deputies, but the district attorney's office dropped the charges. A month after he testified in a BOS hearing about the confrontation, Vasquez was removed from the eligibility list for the marshal job. When the supervisors found out about the alleged retaliation, they investigated it; almost suddenly Vasquez returned to the eligibility list. As a result of the two beatings, Vasquez helped to form the Southeast Community for Justice to fight police abuse.[44]

The 1979 hearings in which Vasquez testified had been called by Edelman after numerous complaints about LASD and LAPD abuse and brutality. Edelman had already called for hearings into police shootings and killings by the city's LAPD in 1977. At that time the LAPD was considered to have a loose policy in using deadly force compared to other law enforcement agencies in the county, while the LASD had the most restrictive of the entire group. Edelman wanted to know if county agencies besides the district attorney could be of more help in investigating the shootings. The police chief and the sheriff considered the hearings a waste of time and showed little interest. District Attorney John Van de Kamp proposed adding fifteen investigators to his Special Investigations Divisions; other speakers recommended independent investigations instead. The result reflected the differences of opinion and the possible costs of delayed actions for over several years.[45]

Major shootings and trials in 1979 stirred interest in new investigations of the use of deadly force, this time regarding the LASD. These would follow the well-publicized incident in which Eula Love was shot eight times and killed by two LAPD officers, when she threatened to hurl a knife at them while disputing a gas bill.

In one LASD case, a deputy sheriff went to trial on a charge of firing into the rear portion of a vehicle passing by a large party and striking a passenger in the back. Assistant District Attorney Johnnie Cochran believed the deputy was "guilty as all hell," but that the judge in the trial did not want to convict an officer and found him not guilty. At about the same time, another deputy shot and killed a Good Samaritan who came to the rescue of an elderly neighbor who had just been assaulted in West Hollywood. The supervisors immediately ordered an investigation, and an irate Sheriff Pitchess castigated them and the district attorney for making charges without enough facts. In the following March, the deputy was cleared of an honest mistake and no charges were filed. Soon after the Good Samaritan killing, the sheriff agreed to allow deputy district attorneys to "roll out" to scenes of police killings to aid investigations, a procedure Pitchess earlier opposed, and would later oppose again. The BOS approved it in October 1979.[46]

With this information on these incidents and non-lethal charges of brutality leveled against the LASD, Edelman conducted hearings on police abuse and asked for an LASD report on the accusations. Pitchess addressed the charges and defended his deputies and Undersheriff Sherman Block appeared in a hearing and denied any "pattern of violence" on the part of the LASD. He refused to answer questions regarding individual complaints and downplayed them, stressing the "ever increasing level of violence in our community." Representatives of minority groups considered some of his further testimony as racist, but violent crime did increase in the county, particularly in minority areas where conflicts with deputies were more common. Little positive action resulted from these hearings at the time.[47]

Expanding Social Services

Los Angeles County social services in the 1970s would see an expansion of programs for an increasing number of clients. The Great Depression had altered the previous program which relied heavily on state government and local charities to aid indigents as the state increased its involvement and the New Deal federal government created new relief programs such as aid for those physically unable to work and social security for senior citizens. Counties still had to provide support for those able to work and increasing administrative costs to implement the various programs. With the rising population and influx of residents from other states to Los Angeles County in the late 1930s, welfare costs rose to over 40 percent of the overall county budget by 1940. As a result of the postwar recession and return of those in military service, the figure rose to over 60 percent of the budget by 1950. Fortunately for the county, the percentage would decrease as the national economy improved and the federal government picked up more of the tab.[48]

During the 1950s, the nation's energized economy saw a drop and then a modest rise in total spending on welfare in the county. Criticism of the welfare program included stories about those on relief purchasing television sets, the rising costs of food for indigents, the duplication of government efforts to administer welfare programs, and Hahn's initiative to prevent those persons owning land from receiving welfare grants. In the 1960s, the costs escalated more rapidly as the population increased and new federal programs required local administration and larger staffs. The BOS searched for ways to reduce the welfare budget, including forcing able-bodied recipients to replace Mexican nationals who had worked in the recently ended bracero program (labor unions and farmers objected), demanding tighter controls in issuing checks to prevent duplicates and counterfeits, supporting a Community Work and Training Program to find jobs for recipients, and continuing to protest limitations of federal funding. In addition, the supervisors demanded more welfare funds from the state legislature and hoped the state would take over support of the entire system. There were also calls for welfare reform by the County Grand Jury in that decade, along with new federal revenue generated by the War of Poverty.[49]

In 1966, the supervisors decided to reorganize their welfare apparatus by dividing the Charities Department into four separate units; one of them, the Bureau of Public Assistance, would become the Department of Public Social Services (DPSS). Hailed by the supervisors as a method to streamline administration, it aimed to create tighter restraints and insure more local control in decision making. This change, however, did not solve welfare problems. The federal government continued to cut some funding and created new regulations requiring more county workers, and the U.S. Supreme Court issued a ruling in 1969 that relaxed the residency rule for recipients who could receive benefits sooner. As a result, the supervisors joined those in other counties calling for a march on Sacramento to demand more funding, but the state would not provide it. In December, more than 300 shouting welfare recipients protested at a BOS meeting demanding a special Christmas grant for food and other necessities. The board adjourned and walked out in the middle of it.[50]

From 1965 to 1970, welfare costs in Los Angeles County doubled, and in late 1970, the supervisors called on President Nixon, Congress, and the state legislature to "lift the burden of welfare administration from the taxpayers of Los Angeles County." By early 1971, the number of residents of other states who moved to California after the U.S. Supreme Court outlawed the state's five-year residency requirement had bloated the welfare rolls by over 100,000 persons, half of them residing in Los Angeles County, according to Hahn. He called on Congress to amend the U.S. Constitution to establish uniform benefits in all fifty states. In March, the supervisors unanimously called on Congress to take over welfare programs and administer them in the same manner as Social Security. State government added to the problem, when Governor Ronald Reagan proposed major budget cuts for counties that would increase welfare costs; in 1971, his "welfare reforms" would do the same.[51]

The number of persons on welfare in March 1971, would prove to be the all-time high for the period to 1977 as the situation improved over the next few years, despite the national recession. All California counties were aided by the federal government's takeover of administering three of its aid programs, relieving counties of some staff and other costs. Federal revenue-sharing begun in 1972 supplied counties with funding for items such as welfare and other social services, some of it passed on to private delegate agencies.[52]

Despite the opportunities, many problems faced by the supervisors and the

DPSS and its clients raised the total costs of welfare to a new high in 1977, before settling down. One major cause was the ending of federal programs to support Cuban and Indochinese refugees. Another was the attempt of the Social Security Administration to remove undocumented persons from the three programs it had taken over in 1973. These moves would add more recipients to the county welfare rolls; for the latter group it would last until they could make their immigration status permanent. In fact, the confused situation regarding the federal, state, and county policies on undocumented immigrants qualifying for welfare would complicate the program throughout the 1970s and later. The 1973 County Grand Jury recommended that all recipients should prove their citizenship or legal entry to the U.S., and in 1975, the DPSS director informed the BOS that 99 percent of immigrants did prove it by showing their green cards. The supervisors frequently argued over whether the undocumented should receive benefits but agreed unanimously to seek federal and state support for the blind, aged, or disabled among them.[53]

Newspaper accounts of welfare fraud also highlighted the loss of welfare funds and reduced taxpayer confidence in the program. Several described scandals involving "welfare queens" and other recipients accused of scamming the system. More irritating to some taxpayers was fraud by county employees which occasionally appeared as clerks and social workers manipulated the procedures to embezzle funds. There were also reports that county employees received welfare checks, which might have left one wondering if they inaccurately reported their income or if their salaries were really that low. In 1977, out of the approximately 127,000 employees of the county and its larger cities, there were 1820 on the welfare rolls; 198 received payments they were not entitled to, and their case was referred to the district attorney for possible prosecution.[54]

In addition, the supervisors had to face angry crowds in their meeting room as groups of recipients and advocates protested decisions regarding shifting funds to other issues, low or no raises as the cost of living rose, and other changes. Sheriff's deputies had to be called in several times to remove protesters. After the fifth such protest at consecutive meetings in 1971, a county social worker leading the protest was removed with three others and fired for insubordination. The lack of child support payments also became a problem as the county had to make up for it with additional support for children. And corruption in various social services agencies receiving federal funds and monitored by another county department added to staff responsibilities of other county units in supplying the services.[55]

The county also worked with other government entities in providing welfare-related support and myriad social services to county residents through private non-profit agencies. One such agency was the Economic and Youth Opportunities Agency of Los Angeles (EYOA), created in 1964 as a successor to an earlier federal anti-poverty program that fell victim to competition between minority groups, local government officials, and residents. The new agency was intended to address juvenile delinquency and unemployment with programs aimed at education, probation, and other services. It was governed by a joint powers' agreement between the supervisors and the county schools department, the city mayor and council and the city school district. From its inception just before the Watts Rebellion, the EYOA was wracked with racial and political turmoil. Financed mostly by the federal government early on, a proposal to have the county assume 50 percent of the costs of the program and concerns about the election of the board of directors spurred the BOS to threaten pulling out of the program in early 1966. Charges of inflated salaries of EYOA executives, mismanagement and further bickering among EYOA directors and government officials, and a walkout by disgruntled staff members resulted in the county and city threatening to pull out of the of the joint powers agreement.[56]

Instead, the government units reorganized the EYOA in 1972 as the Greater Los Angeles Community Action Agency (GLACAA) committed to the same goals as the EYOA. Unfortunately, GLACAA suffered from the same shortcomings as its predecessors, with racial competition and conflict, mismanagement of funding and poor administration. It was also the victim of the withdrawal of some federal funding in 1973, forced to rely on the support of the smaller treasuries of the county and city of Los Angeles. After two years in operation, the County Grand Jury examined it and its distribution of funds to its delegate agencies and found a few problems that led to city and county audits. The county audit found "extensive management short-comings" and both audits recommended that GLACAA be dissolved. In June 1977, the embattled director resigned; a month later county and city contributions were curtailed but not completely stopped. In 1977, the federal government began its own investigation and verified the earlier findings. City leaders finally decided to withdraw support and the county followed suit in 1978. GLACAA officially shut down after its story appeared on the television program *60 Minutes;* its responsibilities were transferred to city and county departments. In its short lifetime the GLACAA staff did have some success with finding jobs for their clients and providing other services amid the administrative chaos.[57]

In the 1970s, the county also supported a growing number of community organizations that supplied a variety of social services to residents in low-income areas with federal grant money administered by the county's Department of Community Development. An increasing number of these agencies came under investigation by county and federal auditors for mismanagement and corruption (at least twenty between 1977 and 1982). U.S. authorities would disallow certain expenses prohibited in the contracts, forcing the county to seek reimbursement for the expenditures already made. In some cases, officials of the agencies were investigated for criminal offenses. Conflicts of interest, nepotism, bloated salaries for staff, overspending on goods and services, purchasing goods (sometimes luxury items) for personal use, and links to the underworld were some of the charges, as well as bringing guns to meetings to intimidate agency directors. Some of the agencies would eventually be cleared of the charges, others terminated when grant money disappeared, all to the embarrassment of the BOS and county officials overseeing them. Many were in Schabarum's First District, including one in which one of his deputies was charged with influencing the supervisor in ending the agency's contract, and another in which the agency's staff helped another Schabarum deputy in a campaign for the California Assembly.[58]

The East Los Angeles Community Union (TELACU) was the most successful of such agencies in promoting jobs and economic development in its area. It became snared in an investigation due to its handling of federal grants and political campaigning for its favorite politicians and would be suspended by the BOS and city of Los Angeles in 1982 after a series of articles and editorials in the *Times*. This organization did not dissolve, however, and eventually transformed itself from a non-profit to a successful private corporation as it is today.[59]

As the Final Report of the Los Angeles County Grand Jury concluded near the end of this very tumultuous decade in which many personality conflicts among the supervisors and other county officials played a role:

In 1979 Los Angeles County stands strong but bruised and troubled on a middle ground between contesting forces within and outside the County.... In the governance of the people of Los Angeles County, as elsewhere, the test of success is cost-effectiveness only in part. A computer or an economist can check on this. The more important test, evaluated only by discerning human judgement, is success in social, educational, esthetic, and ethical effectiveness. Do the County and its four-score cities provide for each resident ever improving opportunities for a livable environment, health, safety, job security, instruction, culture, self-respect, and justice? The answer is an appraisal of the state of the county.[60]

6

Reforming the County Government Structure

Politics 101, ladies and gentlemen, never give away your power.—Mark Ridley-Thomas, 2015

The era since World War II has witnessed may attempts to reform the structure and operation of government in Los Angeles County in major and minor ways. Some involved merging county departments for improved administration and consolidating county agencies with those of cities to avoid duplication of services. Others embraced expanding the membership of the board of supervisors and creating an elected executive as reformers hoped to improve citizen representation and bureaucratic administration. The 1970s saw many efforts toward the latter changes, mostly unsuccessful, as some supervisors continued to oppose reforms that would limit their political power.[1]

In 1950, the structure and process of county government was like that of 1852, when the Board of Supervisors was first established. The county charter, which became effective in 1913, created a few changes, but not in overall governance. There were no checks and balances as in national, state, and city governments; supervisors still held legislative and executive powers, as well as some quasi-judicial review.

Calls for a more modern and efficient county government in the Great Depression decade of the 1930s, as well as the threat of the city of Los Angeles forming its own county, resulted in a major effort on the part of the regional elite and political reformers to alter the county structure. The Committee on Governmental Simplification created to study the problem concluded that the county was still the logical unit for largely metropolitan functions; that cities should retain sovereignty in more local matters. In addition, the committee recommended that the BOS should be expanded to fifteen members to better represent all residents; a county manager should be appointed as an administrative executive; densely populated areas in the unincorporated areas should be incorporated as cities and residents should pay higher taxes for services as they did not pay city taxes; and made several other recommendations. The supervisors resisted losing some of their power to additional members and a county executive, and they declined to put these proposals on a county ballot. They did, however, add a county administrative officer (CAO) to assist them in budget and other functions in 1938.[2]

After World War II, demands for a more efficient and representative government increased, occasionally at the request of some supervisors. The 1951 County Grand Jury foreman related to the supervisors that his group's audit found a "substantial amount of blundering, waste, and dilatory tactics on the part of county officials and county employees" due in large part to the limitations of the antiquated county charter. Grand jurors also pointed out in many annual reports that changes were needed. The 1958 jury charged that the situation was so serious that "the republican form of government traditional in America has broken down in Los Angeles County." Fourteen years later, another grand jury found county government to be "inefficient" and "unwieldy," "run by stodgy, ineffective supervisors and policed by potentially intimidating law enforcement agencies." Grand jurors in other years expressed similar criticisms. The Citizens' Economy and Efficiency Commission, whose members were appointed by the supervisors, almost annually called for major reforms in county structure and process since 1965. Metropolitan newspapers frequently editorialized for reforms and a more unified local government; even neighborhood newspapers chimed in with editorial concerns about county inaction, inefficiency, and corruption.[3]

Despite these critics and major blue-ribbon committees created in the 1950s and 1960s (to be discussed later in this chapter), reforms would be few and far between. Supervisors might have supported the creation of such important bodies, but rarely followed their advice, and frequently opposed any change in the system. In 1952, Supervisor John Anson Ford, usually a reformer, led the opposition to a grand jury call for a modern county charter. A Los Angeles Metropolitan Area Government Study Commission composed of 165 members was formed in 1958 to reorganize county government, but little came of it. Baxter Ward's frequent muckraking investigations of alleged and real misconduct after 1972 did little to bring major reforms, which he actually opposed on occasion. Some supervisors might have supported a particular reform or two but would fail to vote to put others on the ballot for county residents to decide. Overall, the supervisors usually tried to improve government while retaining their own power. They were not the tyrants as described by their opponents, but certainly failed modernizers in most major cases in the immediate post–World War II era.[4]

"Metropolitanism" and Regionalism vs. Local Control

One of the far-reaching reforms involving the Los Angeles County government structure after World War II was the intrusion of metropolitan agencies that usurped some of the power of the supervisors in decision making. The county already operated under some control by the federal and state governments, but during the Cold War 1950s, an opposition to federal agencies and influential professional organizations labeled it "A Socialist Scheme to Destroy Local Self-Government." In this thinking, local elected offices were weakened by dictatorial experts who managed large, centralized governments, and destroyed the individual rights of Americans. Some charged that the scheme was being carried out at 1313 East 60th Street in Chicago, a building on the campus of the University of Chicago. Twenty-two national organizations had their main offices there and were thought to comprise an invisible government controlling America. The opposition spread throughout the nation, as even California politicians such as Alan Cranston and Donald Jackson warned of its influence.[5]

In Southern California, Hamilton Beamish was an avid fan of the conspiracy theory and defended it in newspapers and a letter to Supervisor Ford in 1958. The primary local exponent was Jo Hindman, an Inglewood housewife who wrote several articles about it for the *American Mercury*. She also defended it in debates, including several with historian Henry Steele Commager on issues inspired by a National Library Association program to encourage lectures she considered to have "a socialist slant." She occasionally appeared at BOS meetings to offer her advice and criticism for appointing a charter revision committee and adopting the Lakewood Plan to create "skeleton" cities. Despite her views, city officials in the county joined the supervisors in discussing various plans to modify and create joint local agencies with related tasks, and the BOS established a committee to study the county charter and recommend improvements.[6]

Interest in metropolitan government in Los Angeles County was spurred by a sixteen-volume study of local government published by the John Randolph Haynes and Dora Haynes Foundation in the early 1950s, covering both the integration and centralization of functions and possibilities of regional rather than local administration. In addition, movements to strengthen metropolitan authority in Miami, Cleveland, St. Louis, Nashville, and other urban centers also supported the concept in the 1950s and early 1960s. In fact, the Los Angeles Chamber of Commerce sponsored a symposium on the topic in 1958, in which speakers from Toronto and Dade County, Florida, were invited to present the experience of their governments. By 1961, the California Governor's Commission on Metropolitan Area Problems advocated the creation of multipurpose districts (rather than single purpose units like the County Air Pollution Control District) to address issues of regional concern. The *Times* also began to support the concept late in that decade, while many community papers still opposed the idea. Although the county supervisors appointed a 165-member commission to study the idea in 1958, they expressed little enthusiasm in reducing their own power. The board joined the League of California Cities in supporting local home rule in controlling vice in 1962, and, for the most part, avoided regional compacts on important issues.[7]

Change would come by 1965, when the federal government required the creation of Councils of Government (COG) organizations in urbanized areas to coordinate and plan regional transportation projects and make sure that federal funding was being spent properly. In 1963, a proposed plan to include ten counties in southern and central California raised the fear of local officials that it would put the south under the domination of a state agency. Those officials took control and organized the Southern California Association of Governments (SCAG) to include only the counties of Los Angeles, Orange, San Bernardino, Riverside, and Ventura, along with seventy-one of the 154 incorporated cities within them. SCAG would aid the local governments in transportation and other issues involving more than one county as a planning and advisory body without any enforcement powers; local control would not be limited, and governments could withdraw if they wished. Federal requirements stipulated that COGs must represent at least 75 percent of the population of the region or risk losing federal grants for many different purposes.[8]

The latter requirement imposed an immediate problem in that Los Angeles County and the city of Los Angeles decided not to join SCAG. Since more than 25 percent of the SCAG population base was in the county, none of the member governments could receive federal grants. That revelation, as well as the fact that the county was already in the midst of losing a major parks grant, forced the supervisors and city officials to rethink their strategy for retaining local control, which would not be lost anyway since local government officials were the SCAG directors. The BOS held out until January 1966, when the supervisors conducted a hearing in which almost 200 speakers, mostly women led by Jo Hindman, opposed it, calling SCAG a "Federal blackjack." Fearing they had no choice in the matter, Hahn, Dorn, and Chace voted to join SCAG, while Bonelli and Debs opposed it. Bonelli refused to give up and created a plan to make the county itself a planning agency that would include the city of Los Angeles, which still held out for a smaller, more urban region. His intransigence caused a stir in a BOS meeting when he accused the three supportive voters of approving membership in SCAG only to win federal contracts. Dorn called it a lie, and a verbal clash ensued. The discussion ended with Hahn declaring that SCAG was not "as some would have us believe, some sort of Communist plot conceived by some mysterious New York–Chicago axis." Bonelli recommended changing SCAG by eliminating its staff, so that member dues would no longer be required. The BOS approved the plan in concept and sent a request to each city in the county asking for support. The plan would not fly, however, and after more lobbying, the city of Los Angeles finally joined. With a $100,000 grant from the federal government, along with its regular budget based on member fees, SCAG began its planning operation in 1967. Within two years it created a regional program including a data system, land use inventories, population and housing surveys, an airport study, and other research, as well as approving hundreds of various federal grants for projects of its members.[9]

While SCAG performed its research, its critics thought it too passive in making decisions. Some city officials believed SCAG should be reconstituted with more power in regional issues. Other critics, chief among them the Los Angeles County BOS, thought it had not been highly effective. In March 1971, the BOS was informed that a state legislator was proposing a new regional agency to control smog that would replace the units of six counties, and Los Angeles County would have to pay 70 percent of the costs. With that news the BOS voted unanimously to withdraw from SCAG at the end of the fiscal year and go it alone. But after newspaper editorials, letters from various officials supporting SCAG, and finally the failure of the smog agency bill, the supervisors decided to remain with SCAG on a month-to-month basis.[10]

In the early 1970s, while Los Angeles Mayor Tom Bradley encouraged African American elected officials to get involved in regional governance, Los Angeles County supervisors continued to oppose SCAG and attempted to break free from it. Pete Schabarum, who initially supported regional agencies, joined Hahn, who also favored them in his early years, as the two most vocal critics. Both Hahn and Schabarum, along with Debs and Ward, feared that SCAG was acquiring too much authority in determining transit route selection, and the BOS eventually sued the federal government to limit SCAG's power in that undertaking. The supervisors also asked President Nixon to suspend SCAG's review of applications for federal grants for human services programs. In 1974, the supervisors' fear of a SCAG "supergovernment" probably increased when they were informed that a bill in the California Assembly would turn SCAG into a "mandatory statutory agency" that would "ultimately be amended to include taxing powers." To the relief of the supervisors, the bill eventually died.[11]

In 1975, the newest supervisor, Edmund Edelman, joined James Hayes as defenders of SCAG. In fact, Hayes was the chairman of the SCAG executive committee that year, when a new transit plan to reduce driving and smog reached completion. But Schabarum and Hahn, with their parochial outlook in viewing "regional government as a foul conspiracy," were in their "annual snit" in threatening to bail out. During the summer, Schabarum recommended changes in the SCAG boundaries and participation in its decisions, the first opposed by other counties, the latter opposed by most cities. After these failed, CAO Harry Hufford was asked to report on the merits or demerits of continued participation in SCAG, along with possible alternatives, and recommended that the county continue its membership. In 1977, Schabarum offered a motion to support Ventura County's quest to pull out of SCAG and set a precedence for Los Angeles County. He also proposed that the county's SCAG dues that year be withheld until the agency resolved several concerns regarding representation and voting. CAO Hufford later reported that SCAG had taken such actions and should be paid the dues. The decade would end with Los Angeles County opposing an ambitious SCAG plan to build a huge island in San Pedro Bay to accommodate an international airport, and the fight continued.[12]

While the supervisors tangled with SCAG in the 1970s, they acquired another regional agency with which to contend. As these agencies became more common, the supervisors feared that the state legislature was about to create one to reduce air pollution that would usurp local control. Amid increasing criticism of the county's Air Pollution Control District in 1975, they joined three nearby counties in forming the Southern California Air Pollution Control District (SCAPCD). But fear of Los Angeles County control of the unit led to the formation of the South Coast Air Quality Management District (SCAQMD) over which Los Angeles had limited influence. Beginning in 1977, the supervisors would engage in conflicts with the SCAQMD over dues, territory, leadership, and other issues. (See Chapters 2 and 9.)[13]

In addition, agencies representing the entire state such as the California Air Resources Board would add to further encroachment on the power of county officials. A new one in the mid–1970s, the California Coastal Commission, would play a major role in municipal incorporations and development along the coastline in that decade and after. Conflict with this agency became so intense that the supervisors requested a grand jury investigation of it in 1980 because of reports of the commissioners accepting funds from developers. In the following year, the state legislature refused to accept any of the county's recommendations for appointees to the commission; three of the nominees were members of the conservative BOS majority. (For more on the Coastal Commission see Chapter 9.)[14]

County Government Consolidation

Two major issues clearly define the efforts of the supervisors to reform the shape and operation of county government in these years. One involved the waste and confusion of duplicate agencies. The other was altering the structure of governance since 1852 consisting of five supervisors acting as a legislative, executive, and quasi-judicial branch with no checks and balances like the federal, state, and city forms. (Think of it as five U.S. presidents and no Congress, or Congress without a president.)

Prior to World War II, there were few attempts at consolidating county departments, agencies, commissions, and offices as the bureaucracy grew to provide additional services for more county residents. During the war two units were re-joined in 1944 as the Parks and the Recreation Department. After the war the supervisors began to expand various government services for a booming population in unincorporated areas and contract cities; they found it expedient to merge departments, when possible, to reduce administrative costs and duplication of effort within their jurisdiction.[15]

Some of the successful mergers after 1950 included the County Surveyor being folded into the County Engineer Department in 1955; the latter then combined with the flood control and road units as the Public Works Department in 1984. The Department of Health Services consisted of the Health, Hospital, Mental Health, and County Veterinarian offices by 1973–1974. Urban Affairs and Community Development joined for a short time in 1976. In 1982, the Housing Authority and Redevelopment Agency were consolidated with the Community Development Department as the Community Development Commission. The Beaches and Small Craft Harbor departments merged as Beaches and Harbors in 1982–1983. These were only a few of the mergers in the 1980s and early 1990s.[16]

Two mergers of the county courts operations were finally settled after long conflicts between supervisors and county judges. Recommendations by the County Grand Jury and Citizens' Efficiency and Economy Commission had supported the motions of several supervisors since the 1960s to merge the Office of County Marshal into the Sheriff's Department, since the duties were similar, and sheriff's deputies already served court documents and acted as bailiffs for the Superior Courts. But Municipal Court judges, for whom the marshals worked, argued that the jobs were not identical. The judges lobbied state legislators and others while Supervisor Hayes, assisted in his political campaign by County Marshal Speryl and staff, opposed any change. Even a 1980 plebiscite in which two-thirds of county voters supported the merger was of no immediate help. The contest dragged on until 1993, when the supervisors finally forced the merger amid many complaints by the judges.[17]

The Superior and Municipal Court judges also became involved in the long crusade for a consolidation of the courts championed by Kenneth Hahn since the late

1950s. Hahn sought unification of those two and the remaining justice courts to make the justice system more efficient and economical. He composed numerous press releases and motions extolling this objective over the decades. A 1998 state ballot proposition passed a year after Hahn's death finally paved the way for the merger in 2000.

Beyond theses victories for department consolidations lay a few that never made it.

These attempts met with opposition from department heads, staff members and supporters who feared the downfall of their favorite agency. Larger consolidations that never materialized included Supervisor Kenneth Hahn's idea in 1973 "to reorganize the 54 various departments into nine agencies," and Supervisor Michael Antonovich's "eventual goal" of having "the departments consolidated in fifteen 'super' departments." (No ideological conflict here, as these were the views of a liberal and a conservative.)[18]

City and County Consolidations

Besides rationalizing changes within county government, its leadership also worked with officials in its larger cities, mostly Los Angeles, the county seat. Since the early twentieth century, the county had provided contract services such as tax collection, library, and health facilities. The 1954 Lakewood Plan accelerated the availability and use of such contracts, particularly with new and smaller cities that found it more convenient and economical to pay for such services. Another method was to consolidate city and county functions to avoid duplication of effort and expenditures; this was carried out primarily with the largest city in the county.

In the late 1930s and 1940s, city and county representatives attempted to consolidate their health departments, which provided some of the same services to city residents. But the negotiations failed due mostly to deciding which entity would provide the service. The population increase and rising taxes after 1950 spurred more interest in eliminating duplicate services as newspaper editors and business leaders prodded government officials to act. In 1954, the supervisors and city council members created a Local Government Consolidation Study Committee to identify possible mergers. After four years of study, the committee determined that a complete unification of the two health departments would not save money and instead recommended a plan in which both would still exist, defeating the purpose of consolidation.[19]

The city-county consolidation committee faded out of existence in the following year when a plan to merge city and county jails considered by the County Grand Jury in 1956 was being negotiated. In 1961, it was generally approved by city and county leaders, including LAPD Chief William Parker and Sheriff Peter Pitchess. The county acquired one city jail by 1964, with another still being studied. In that year, the supervisors requested a report on the status of city-county consolidation and the CAO described several mergers considered successful to various degrees, those currently in the works, and some that could be initiated.[20]

The year of 1964 would also be the year of a major success in this campaign. City and county leaders had been re-examining the possibility of consolidating their health departments. In late 1962, officials of both entities formed a committee to compose a plan to complete the merger. It was supported by most of the supervisors, by Mayor Sam Yorty, and by council members in the affluent city districts. In opposition were council members in low-income districts led by Gilbert Lindsay (a former deputy of Supervisor Hahn), who feared the loss of jobs of city workers, Supervisors Hahn and Chace, and a few city health officials. At the same time, a bill being considered in the state legislature would compel counties to subsidize cities with their own health departments, which could help merger opponents and spur cities such as Long Beach and Pasadena to demand subsidies as well. (Supervisors Chace and Dorn, both former city officials from Long Beach and Pasadena respectively, joined with Hahn supporting the bill.) Amid this conflict and defeat of the bill, the supervisors finally approved the merger, as did the city council in 1964.[21]

With this victory for consolidation the *Times* predicted many more possibilities and provided a list of services beyond municipal borders, including parks, airports, law enforcement, planning, and traffic control. But progress moved slowly. When Tom Bradley took office as mayor of Los Angeles in 1973, he made consolidation a priority in early meetings with the supervisors and agreed on creating a blue-ribbon commission to study the issue. The *Times* pointed out that many studies had already been done and it was time for action. Hahn responded with ideas for the five supervisors and five council members to appoint one person each to work together to advance consolidation. Supervisor Edmund Edelman's motion to create a Los Angeles City-County Consolidation Commission was approved in 1977. These efforts led to more studies but few victories. In 1974–1975 the city and county agreed to county operation of city beaches. Over the same years efforts to consolidate the LASD and LAPD ended after disagreements on how much it might save and who would direct it; a 1974 idea of merging the libraries was nixed by the supervisors because the county operation was decentralized compared to the city's central library; a proposed merger of airports in 1974 failed; and a merger of city and county fire departments in 1980–81 concluded that it could not be done "due to political realities" and funding. Since 1980, large-scale consolidations of city and county services have been considered, but not accomplished.[22]

Complete Consolidation

When Supervisor Edelman proposed a City-County Consolidation Commission in 1977, he believed that this group would recommend individual mergers of services that would eventually merge the entire city and county into one governmental unit such as the city/county of San Francisco and other metropolitan centers. Similar ideas were over a hundred years old. In 1861, a bill proposed to consolidate Los Angeles city and county was introduced in the California Senate, but never became law. In the 1930s and after, the city of Los Angeles proposed the transformation of itself into a county to provide all services offered by both governmental units. During World War II, Supervisor John Anson Ford proposed a borough system of county government that would consolidate many services on a large scale while allowing local governments to provide a few services in municipalities. This idea was rejected by small cities that feared the takeover by a distant power center. A borough system within the county similar to Ford's idea was floated in 1955–1956 but failed in the general election. By the 1960s, the *Los Angeles Times* began proselytizing for expanded regional governance and the "consolidation of services in a 'federation' of regional authorities or in a multi-purpose agency," citing Portland as a good example. All of these and other "solutions" faced opposition from those who feared the loss of local control and additional taxes they believed to be necessary to support a new and powerful government agency headed by members of the political elite. Efforts of the advocates of increased regional governance, however, would continue. (See Chapters 8 and 9.)[23]

Expansion of the BOS and Addition of a County Executive

Structural change to the top rungs of county government has been a major issue throughout the twentieth century and still is, as it impacts apportionment, representation, and the process of county governance. State legislation can call for such changes, although they are decided in local actions. In this process, the BOS decides, or is forced to decide, which proposals will be put on the ballot, and voters make the final decisions on structure if allowed by the supervisors. In many cases there has been opposition on the part of most supervisors refusing to relinquish their power to additional colleagues or a strong executive.

As mentioned earlier, Los Angeles County government in 1950 was virtually the same as in 1852, when the BOS was established for California counties. The five supervisors were both the legislative and executive branches of government and held some judicial review powers. There was no elected executive such as a mayor who could provide a balance of power and oversee the administrative affairs of county departments and other units. The other elected officials—sheriff, assessor, and district attorney—directed their own departments subject to budget decisions of the supervisors. The 1913 county charter changed some of the features of the original system but left the powers of the supervisors intact.[24]

In the next two decades, two attempts at reform were initiated, but neither resulted in major change. A charter amendment to expand the board from five to seven members reached the ballot in 1926 but lacked campaign support. A mid-1930s movement for change included, among other features, expansion of the BOS to fifteen members and the addition of an appointed county manager to assist the supervisors with the annual budget and perform other administrative duties. Both charter amendment proposals were opposed by the supervisors and never offered as ballot measures. The BOS did create an appointed county administrative officer in 1938, but this officer would work for the board, not as an independent executive.[25]

Calls for changes in the county government structure in the 1950s and 1960s became more numerous. In fact, the BOS meeting room in the Hall of

Administration under construction in the 1950s was designed to accommodate nine chairs for nine supervisors, testimony to the prevalence of thoughts of possible changes in their number. Civic organizations, blue ribbon committees, the County Grand Jury, and major newspapers, among others, called for expanding the board and creating an independent, elected county administrator. Supervisor Hahn began campaigning for these changes in the early 1950s and would continue throughout his forty years in office. His motion to expand the board to nine members began in 1956, but he could not convince his colleagues to put it on the ballot. Supervisors Ford, Chace and Legg thought it would end in more debate and less work; Jessup claimed it would be more appropriate in remote areas. The board instead decided to have the CAO consult with experts regarding possible changes to the charter that might be needed.[26]

The CAO study dragged on many months until newly elected Supervisor Warren Dorn proposed in 1957 that a study commission be appointed to examine these two issues and others that called for changes to the county charter. The motion lost as only Dorn and Hahn voted for it. However, Ford, who judged the charter to be "of superior quality" that made it possible for the county to be an "amazingly efficient" form of local government, eventually changed his mind. Although he still believed a larger board would slow down the process and lead to vote trading and logrolling, he joined Dorn and Hahn in Dorn's second attempt to create a charter study committee.[27]

The nine-member (later ten-member) charter study committee headed by Henry Reining, Jr., Dean of the School of Public Administration at USC, included Frank R. Seaver, one of the freeholders who composed the 1913 Los Angeles County Charter. The group began their work in October 1957 and submitted a report in the following summer. The members found the existing charter to be simple and flexible but recommended several amendments to meet the changes in population and conditions over the last forty-five years. These amendments included the enlargement of the BOS to eleven members for better representation; the appointment (not election) of a county manager who would have more power than the current CAO position created by ordinance instead of being included in the charter; the assessor and sheriff to be appointed, rather than elected, to professionalize administration; and several other changes, one of which would encourage fair job consideration for minority workers.[28]

Many of the committee's recommendations were in line with the concurrent study of the 1958 County Grand Jury and supported by the *Examiner* and the *Times*, among others, but not the supervisors. Upon presentation of the report to the board, several supervisors immediately expressed reservations to accepting all of them. Ford opposed board expansion to eleven but might support seven, and opposed removing his deputies from civil service, but favored the appointed assessor and sheriff. Chace, Hahn and Bonelli adamantly opposed board expansion, the county manager, and the appointment of assessor and sheriff. Warren Dorn cast the only vote for board expansion to eleven and the county manager. Soon after the vote, he lobbied his colleagues to change their view, or he would ask for an election of county freeholders to alter or replace the entire charter. After further consideration, the board decided to place seven charter amendments on the November ballot that did not include a county manager in the charter. Board expansion impinging on the supervisors' power was also left out.[29]

The fight for a larger board was not over, however. In early 1959, the impetus for the larger board and the county manager office reappeared and faced the same BOS opposition. Bonelli was especially adamant and received ample support in his district, an area experiencing many incorporation attempts that would limit supervisorial control. In a long BOS meeting with many speakers, Dorn tried to resurrect board expansion, but to no avail. Additional attempts to get it on the ballot that year in an even smaller addition of seven could not surpass the supervisors' concern with their own positions.[30]

Reform momentum re-emerged in the early 1960s with a more ideological slant on the Reining results. In late 1961, the supervisors were prodded to appoint a new charter study committee to review the Reining committee report and make recommendations deemed necessary "for the improvement of the County charter." The twenty-five-member committee hand-picked by the supervisors spent four months studying the charter and the previous report. The committee concluded that the board be expanded to seven members, and the office of chief administrative officer be included in the charter. The board expansion proposal was supported by the League of Women Voters and other groups and opposed by the influential Los Angeles Chamber of Commerce directors, who approved of the county manager plan and other proposals. This time three supervisors—Dorn, Bonelli, and Debs—voted to put the expansion plan on the ballot with four other amendments, but not the county manager. With little campaign support the two additional supervisor seats failed by a margin of 2–1.[31]

Through the rest of the 1960s, calls for BOS expansion and a county executive received less attention. In 1964, the supervisors created the County Citizens' Efficiency and Economy Committee (later becoming a commission) composed mostly of business leaders to study all components of county government, including its basic structure, and recommend changes. After two years of study, the committee made various suggestions, such as consolidating some departments and giving more authority to top officials. A.C. Rubel, the committee chair, pointed out that the burden of accountability to residents for the five supervisors was too much, and the CAO and department heads needed clearer lines of authority to relieve the supervisors of some details of daily governing. However, the addition of more supervisors or a stronger administrator had not been mentioned—yet.[32]

Supervisor Hahn tried to partially address that omission in 1969, when he proposed that the county counsel prepare a charter amendment to increase the board from five to seven members, eventually to eleven by 2005. Bonelli led the attack on this proposal, arguing that it would be too costly to add two more members and their staffs, and that residents in the county's cities were already represented by mayors and city councils, as well as the supervisors. Chace joined the opposition, but Dorn and Debs voted with Hahn to order the amendment drafted. The *Times* found the action to be encouraging but lamented that an amendment for a county executive could not be included, since Hahn postponed it for the time being. As the editorial opined, "Los Angeles has a generally good government despite the present system. Board reforms could make it that much better."[33]

The 1970s would prove to be a much more active decade for the pursuit of board expansion and a county executive. The County Grand Jury was especially concerned with these two issues as it recommended a larger board and a strong county executive in its final reports of 1970, 1972, 1973–1974, and 1975–1976. The Citizens' Efficiency and Economy Commission examined the issues in 1970, 1972, 1973, 1974, and 1976, and either recommended expansion and a strong executive, or its members split on several occasions. The *Times* editors and other major newspapers were also wholly supportive, along with the League of Women Voters and other civic groups. African American leaders and County Federation of Labor officials spoke out for it in the 1970s, stressing its benefits for Blacks and Latinos if members of those groups could win elections to the new offices.[34]

But strong support did not result in victory. In July 1970, the supervisors considered whether to place Hahn's board expansion plan and several other charter changes on the ballot. Hahn and Debs favored expansion, but Bonelli and Chace again panned it. Dorn, who then opposed it, considered approving it to give voters the final decision; in the end he voted no. A proposal of the Citizens' Economy and Efficiency Commission for an appointed county executive was approved. The only "no" vote came from Hahn, who wanted an elected executive instead. Hahn would later oppose the idea, charging that it would establish an executive "with almost dictatorial powers to run the County," a spoils system, and increased taxes. Ironically, Hahn's argument would be turned against him in later years when an elected executive was proposed. The voters agreed with him this time and voted against it.[35]

In 1971, pressure from outsiders was applied to expand board membership. State Senator Mervyn Dymally introduced a bill in the California Legislature that would require one supervisor for each one million residents in each county, a bill that would only apply to Los Angeles County at the time because of its population. The *Times* editorialized that it was one of several attempts to expand the board to accommodate members of minority groups and provide better representation with which the editors agreed. However, the paper also pointed out that it could only be done by a charter amendment voted by residents and was thus unconstitutional. Most supervisors agreed, and Dorn demanded that Governor Reagan veto the bill. The same threat from the legislature came in 1975 and was also killed in a collision with the California constitution.[36]

Hahn returned to his quest for more supervisors to be added gradually through 2005 and an elected county executive in 1972, with his motion for charter amendments to be prepared for both proposals to be placed on the November ballot. His argument for the additional supervisors was the usual request for better representation, and for an elected county executive to fill the need for checks and balances. He added that this position had been increasing in counties throughout out the nation, and that Vice President Spiro Agnew had once held the post in Baltimore County, Maryland. The full board ordered a hearing on these proposals, and eventually voted 3–2 to leave them off the ballot. Five other proposed charter amendments survived.[37]

Hahn would not give up easily, and in the following year he tried again. This time his motion called for preparation of draft amendments for several reforms including BOS expansion and an elected county mayor (the same position as executive), as well as additional civil service commissioners, consolidation of some functions, and other changes to garner more support from his colleagues by adding their favorites. This motion passed unanimously. Hahn immediately began proselytizing for the elected mayor, writing to the editors of metropolitan papers that residents surely would understand the need for a strong separation of power in government as apparent in the current hearings on the national Watergate scandal. The 1973 County Grand Jury endorsed the board expansion and county executive addition, as did the Citizens' Economy and Efficiency Commission. Most of the board seemed more interested in consolidating their power over county department heads, however, and declined to approve expansion and an executive for the ballot.[38]

In 1974, the trend continued as Hahn offered yet another motion for board expansion to seven and an elected county executive but was rebuffed. A week later Pete Schabarum proposed an appointed county executive by charter amendment. Hahn then tried again for expansion and the board decided to refer both to the Citizens' Economy and Efficiency Commission. The members of the latter divided on the executive issue and decided to wait until the supervisors made a recommendation on expansion. Hahn promoted expansion, but his colleagues voted him down. He and Schabarum argued in the *Times* about whether an elected or appointed executive was best; the supervisors voted against putting it on the ballot in any form.[39]

Hahn would not give up. In late January 1975, he submitted yet another motion calling for the establishment of a charter study commission of fifteen members to modernize county government, paying special attention to expanding the board of supervisors and adding an elected county executive, as well as other reforms. In what might be considered a surprise, the supervisors voted unanimously for the study. Coincidentally, it occurred on the very same day of the announcement that a private organization was about to embark on its own major study of county government that had grown too large for its present operation governed by the five supervisors. The *Times* editorial screamed "There's Hope at Last," and Hahn eventually withdrew his motion in favor of the new major attempt at reform.[40]

The Public Commission on County Government

The excitement of *Times* editors regarding the new group of reformers taking over was based on the past actions of most of the supervisors, who religiously guarded their power. But the times were changing. The fervor of county reform was exacerbated by Baxter Ward's many investigations of county scandals and the election of reformer Edmund Edelman. It was also shared by attorneys of major law firms who decided in 1974 that county government needed to be modernized and that their leaders should spearhead a program to that end. In that year, the Los Angeles County Bar Association proposed an independent study of county government "by an interdisciplinary committee of highly esteemed citizens" to identify problems and solutions. These attorneys, as well as business leaders, academics, and members of the League of Women Voters, the Urban League, and organized labor formed the Public Commission on County Government, an elite civic group that would oversee the study and provide for its financing. Future U.S. Secretary of State Warren Christopher, then president of the County Bar Association, would guide the early planning of the project.[41]

Financial support for the commission would come in the form of a generous research grant from the John Randolph Haynes and Dora Haynes Foundation, the oldest general-purpose philanthropy in Los Angeles. Foundation trustees would monitor progress of the program and even suggested a few ideas to commission members. In fact, the trustees were so devoted to this study as one of many projects examining local government, that they chose it to commemorate the fiftieth anniversary of the foundation's creation in 1926. With funding assured, Christopher announced the launching of the project in January 1975. Dean Harold Williams of the UCLA Graduate School of Management and Seth Hufstedler, a former president of the California State Bar Association, were selected as co-chairmen of the commission. Edward K. Hamilton, a visiting professor of public management at the Stanford University Graduate School of Business, as well as well as a deputy mayor of New York City earlier, served as the executive director.[42]

The commission staff began work on the project in February, and soon the supervisors began offering support. Hayes pledged his help in that month, and Edelman expressed his support in March, as did a *Times* editorial. In the same month Hahn, who was initially skeptical of the bar proposal, dropped his plans for a separate charter study. Two months later he spoke to the group regarding the power of the supervisors and need for an executive branch. In fact, he even admitted that he would be interested in running for elected county executive, as was speculated by reporters in 1973. By early May, there were rumors that Schabarum, who now approved of the election rather than appointment of the executive, might pursue that office. Baxter Ward also expressed some support, although, as with Hayes, that would not last very long.[43]

For the rest of 1975, the commission research staff, which then included USC Professor Francine F. Rabinovitz and future Southern California politics expert Steven P. Erie, among others, conducted hearings and performed other research. They produced four studies specifically on the county's law enforcement, health services, and road departments, and a major examination of the county's overall governance and decision-making process. These studies were technical in nature and aimed to change the process of government to make the services more efficient. Both the strengths and weaknesses of these operations were noted. One of the negatives was the "divide by five" practice of the supervisors in determining the amount of funding to spend on various issues as being equal for each district, regardless of where the funding and services were needed most.[44]

By February 1976, the studies had been made available and the final report—*To Serve Seven Million*—was distributed. The report focused primarily on governance, but also included specific problems related to the General Plan lawsuit, county relations with cities, street sweeping costs, "ritualistic" supervisor meetings conducted in secrecy which limited public comment, and so forth. The major recommendations regarding governance included the need for the board of supervisors to expand to nine members and for the creation of an elected county executive officer to handle administrative affairs and represent the county with one face in negotiating with the state and federal governments. These two goals would establish a clear separation between legislative and executive powers and functions. The proposals certainly were not new as they had been suggested many times; coming from this important commission they acquired increased prominence.[45]

The Haynes Foundation trustees were so proud of the Public Commission's work that they approved another more limited grant to finance a program to educate the public to its merits. Most of the supervisors, however, did not receive the final report in the same manner. Hayes and Ward opposed the major recommendations. Only Edelman fully embraced all of it. Schabarum would not accept the elected county executive proposal as presented, but perhaps a specific charter amendment. And Hahn supported some of the concepts in the report but was disturbed with what he perceived to be its highly critical nature. At the first formal discussion of the proposals on February 19, Hahn, Edelman and Schabarum allowed Hayes and Ward to rip the county executive and board expansion proposals for three hours regarding costs and executive power. Some of these criticisms were probably used by one of Ward's constituents in a phone call to Edelman's office in which she exclaimed: "We've got enough high-paid crooks and damn fools as it is."[46]

The Public Commission on County Government leaders pressed on. They appeared before the supervisors to explain the rationale behind their proposals. At the first meeting they were supported by Asa Call, the local dean of conservative Republican political activists and a major player in state and national election campaigns; but it was opposed by former Supervisor John Anson Ford on board expansion. After several such hearings, the BOS delayed action to further study the proposals, to the dismay of the *Times* and commission leaders who wanted it on the June primary ballot. Finally, after a long period of reading charter amendments for both measures, Ward decided to let the voters decide, and both were placed on the November ballot.[47]

In the election campaign for both proposals the supervisors lined up where they had been. Hayes and Ward opposed both and were two of the three individuals who wrote the opposing ballot arguments. Edelman and Hahn supported both. Schabarum supported the elected county executive, but not expansion of the board to nine. Supervisor involvement included speeches, letters to the editor, and debates: Edelman and Ward debated at a political party meeting in the San Fernando Valley in early October, and Hahn and Hayes squared off at Town Hall a few days later. Of the major newspapers, the *Times* continued to support both and worked with proponents, while the *Herald Examiner* opposed both as too costly and complicating government even more. In October, a study of the Citizens' Economy and Efficiency Commission appeared, revealing its support for the elected executive, but divided on board expansion. Civic and tax groups worked with their usual allies.[48]

Unfortunately for the Public Commission and other county reformers, the election occurred at an inopportune moment for major change. Increasing demands for reduced taxes which would generate a major revolt in the near future and continuing reports of government scandals resulting in a lack of faith in government took their toll. The limited campaign of the reformers was also an important element in the loss. The county executive met defeat with 42.8 percent in favor; board expansion received the approval of only 35.4 percent of the electorate. But the reformers would not stop after this defeat. As the president of the Haynes Foundation wrote to the new Bar Association president early in December, "Supervisors Hayes and Ward emphasized the additional burdens the enactment of [Propositions] A and B would impose on the taxpayers ignoring the ultimate benefits to be derived from such legislation, and thus exploiting the public antipathy toward higher taxes."[49]

Although the elected county executive measure lost, it did win more than four of every ten county voters, and in 1978, Hahn proposed that it be considered yet again. It also attracted the attention of the concurrent County Grand Jury as it had for many of the past few years. In the final report released in June, the grand jurors concluded that the supervisors should put the executive issue (but not board expansion) on the November ballot. The members pointed out a noticeable "lack of accountability at all levels of county government" that led to "citizen unrest" as evidenced in recent political initiatives, county secession movements, and the low morale of county department heads and other employees working in a situation devoid of strong leadership. With the publication of this report Hahn announced his support for the County Grand Jury and went into action. After some study and heated discussions among the supervisors, a charter amendment would be drafted for the executive that made only a few changes to the 1976 version, including a statement that the cost of this change would be no more than the present cost of the supervisors and CAO performing that function. Hahn convinced Edelman and Schabarum to vote with him to place it on the ballot.[50]

As opposed to the 1976 reform effort, the 1978 proponents of change formed a coalition to organize and fund the election campaign. The League of Women Voters, California Common Cause, Los Angeles Area Chamber of Commerce, Los Angeles County Bar Association, and other groups and individuals worked with Hahn and Edelman to pass Proposition C, as it appeared on the ballot. The noted political management firm Braun & Company was hired to aide this "County Taxpayer's Coalition" with strategy and media assistance. The *Times* once again supported the proposal with editorials and sympathetic stories, one of them lauding the executive form as in the government of King County, Washington, as a model. (The paper did, however, publish opinion essays criticizing the concept.) Other newspapers such as the *Herald Examiner, Torrance Daily Breeze, Santa Monica Evening Outlook*, and *Valley News*, all four of which had opposed the elected executive in 1976, changed their opinions and supported it this time. Radio and television stations also broadcasted editorials in its favor.[51]

The opposition to Proposition C comprised a loose assortment of individuals and tax reduction groups. Maurice Chez, former chair of the Citizens' Economy and Efficiency Commission, wrote one opinion piece in the *Times* opposing it. But Baxter Ward was the most obvious speaker as he campaigned against it and wrote the opposition ballot argument with James Hayes and Los Angeles City Council member Ernani Bernardi. Ward even proposed limiting the total number of present supervisor deputies to remove one of the major attributes of the plan in that the executive's staff would acquire some of these deputies as a means of keeping over-all costs the same. The most significant barrier to victory for the reformers, however, was the June tax revolt which convinced many voters that additional government was always expensive and probably not needed in the year of the passage of Cali-fornia's Proposition 13 tax limitations (see next chapter). Other county ballot pro-posals such as contracting out some functions to private firms when less expensive, and revisions to the civil service system that could reduce expenditures and per-haps taxes to fund them, passed easily. The county executive proposal did garner a larger percentage of votes than in 1976, but voters were still not convinced that it was necessary.[52]

After the 1978 election, other issues impinged on the structural reform impulse. The Citizens' Economy and Efficiency Commission, which had supported the elected county executive and board expansion in the past, delivered its report "Challenge for the 1980s: Can We Govern Ourselves?" in January 1979. The report included many recommendations for the improvement of the structure of county government, but no mention of a larger board or an elected executive. And in June 1980, Schaba-rum called on his colleagues to help him put an amendment for creation of a county mayor (elected executive) on the ballot that year. He made this call in a publicized speech before the Pomona Lions Club in which he described county government "as a 'rudderless ship'" and offered critical remarks about each of his four colleagues. His proposal went nowhere with the rest of the supervisors.[53]

The desire for change in the county structure did not die. In fact, the crusade for a county executive and additional supervisors would grow in the next decades and appear on ballots in the early 1990s and 2000s. (See Chapters 10, 11, and 12.) At this writing, these reforms still seem to be objectives in each California legislative ses-sion, but nowhere closer to be adopted than in the past.

7

Taxpayer Revolts

Vote yes on Proposition 13 and send Sacramento a message that you are willing to surrender home rule in exchange for financial dependence on the state.—*Los Angeles Times* editorial, 1978

This looks like a real turn of the tide against public-sector imperialism.
—Norman Macrae, *San Francisco Chronicle*, 1979

Expanding county budget items and rising property taxes to pay for them in the 1970s exacerbated earlier taxpayer protests and efforts to limit rising property assessments and tax rates.[1] By that decade, several crusades by anti-tax activists resulted in a few failed tax reduction initiatives until the passage of Proposition 13 in 1978. This measure had a profound effect on state and local government in California. It reduced property tax revenue, limited future efforts to raise taxes, and curtailed government services over the next few years. It also changed the relationship between counties and the state, as counties lost some of their "home rule" independence. In addition, rising taxes during this decade of recession also spurred residents of many communities in the county to campaign for municipal incorporation or even a new county to control their own land use and service delivery needs as has been addressed in Chapter 3.

Rising county budgets and property taxes were a problem long before the 1978 victory of California's landmark Proposition 13. In the era of the Great Depression and World War II, representatives of taxpayer groups and individual protesters appearing in Board of Supervisors budget hearings were loudly vocal about lowering property taxes and ending county services they thought too expensive or unnecessary. The BOS and business and civic groups responded with the creation of committees to study the situation and recommend solutions, but these groups moved slowly. Threats of taxpayer strikes occurred several times and setting tax rates could be a trying time for the supervisors and the assessor.[2]

The years after 1950 were no different. In fact, that year started with complaints of a huge projected increase in the county budget requiring a higher tax rate. The supervisors justified the increase because of the expansion of the population, raises for county employees, and additional state and federal mandates, while protesters demanded reductions to lower their taxes. The supervisors did cut a significant amount of funds from possible additions to the budget, but the final amount necessitated a record tax rate to balance the books. That year's budget process would be like those of the following years of the decade. Protests would continue, some as letters to the supervisors and even the governor. At one event, a 1957 demonstration in the Memorial Coliseum, Supervisor Hahn defended the BOS unconvincingly, and a Citizens Committee for Fair Taxation vowed to recall the county assessor from office. Some critics pointed out that tax bills always seemed to decrease in an election year, "and then soar to new heights between times," while the supervisors blamed state legislators for adding new service mandates without additional revenue.[3]

The 1960s would experience a similar pattern. The supervisors began 1960, an election year, with a promise to reduce the tax rate, which surprised the assessor, who noted that it would take a large reassessment of property values based on the same rate to balance the budget. The assessor and the supervisors were right, as the final tax rate was slightly below that of the previous year. But that was because much heftier reassessments multiplied by that rate meant that taxes paid would rise to support a larger county budget. The result was obvious to residents; groups in communities complained of unfair assessments and lobbied the supervisors and state legislators to revise the process. Protests continued with activists forming a Property Taxpayers Council in 1961 to pursue reforms.[4]

The lobbying of taxpayer groups with support of county officials throughout the state was instrumental in the creation of appointed tax appeals boards to hear requests for changes in the assessments of individual parcels formerly done by the supervisors. The proposed constitutional amendment appeared on the 1962 general election ballot. The supervisors endorsed it, no doubt relieved to pass this job on to someone else, but Assessor John Quinn opposed it because of its possible costs. The measure, which only applied to counties with more than 400,000 residents, passed handily. The supervisors created two such boards in 1963, and the number of annual appeals rose to almost 6000 by 1966. The process worked so well that Supervisor Hahn recommended it as a model for a state review board to investigate possible underassessments of parcels belonging to large corporations and industries in the state.[5]

Although relieved of hearing assessment appeals, the supervisors still had to cope with property taxes by approving the tax rate percentage necessary to multiply the total assessments to support the final budget. As costs of additional services rose, so did the budget and the protests of those having to pay for it. The board approved a new record budget in 1962; 1963 was about the same. But 1964 saw an uproar as the supervisors blamed the assessor for low reassessments resulting in a high tax rate; the assessor blamed them for a skyrocketing budget. As a result, an unlikely tax rebel emerged to remind them to slash the proposed budget. Mike Rubino, a beer truck driver from Alhambra, called for a meeting at San Gabriel High School Auditorium for those in the area who wished to protest their recent tax bill. The 1500 residents who attended expressed their disgust to Supervisor Bonelli and a representative of the assessor. Rubino then planned a demonstration at the BOS meeting a week later and brought almost 5000 protesters with him in buses. Unfortunately for the protesters, the supervisors attended a County Supervisors Association of California convention in Palm Springs that day. But four of them returned early to face Rubino and others who did show up to harangue the supervisors as the sources of their discontent. On the following Monday, 500 protestors stormed the

Hall of Administration and filed 8000 petitions protesting high assessments. Rubino continued to represent his group and planned further protests in 1966. In referring to Proposition 13 many years later, he claimed that "we lit the fuse on the bomb Jarvis made explode."[6]

Despite Rubino's activism, little was being done to lower taxes. Tax appeals boards began to hear reassessment challenges and representatives of other tax groups continued to speak at BOS budget hearings, but tax relief was difficult to achieve. The supervisors tried to limit additional costs such as employee salaries and benefits and new services after the County Grand Jury judged the costs to be too high, but some interest groups fought to retain or expand programs already in existence. In 1967, Hahn asked Governor Reagan to authorize the state legislature currently in special session to pass laws needed to overhaul California's property tax structure. With other major issues to deal with during this session, however, property taxes would have to wait.[7]

Another major element in county taxes in the 1960s was the addition of a new assessor.

With John Quinn retiring in 1962, economist Philip E. Watson defeated a department veteran and five others in the primary election, and a Los Angeles city councilman in the runoff that year. Four years later he was reelected in the primary, easily defeating Communist Party organizer Dorothy Ray Healey and all other challengers. In those years he tangled with other county officials on many occasions, as when he proposed suing the state for more tax funding and was stopped by the county counsel. He later argued with the supervisors over his estimate of the reassessment of property in 1963. That led the BOS to grossly underestimate the tax rate, and to Watson's refusal to appear before the board to defend himself. In 1966, he appeared before the County Grand Jury to address charges of special treatment for some taxpayers during a state investigation of all California assessors following a San Francisco scandal. In late November, he was indicted on three counts of receiving bribes, which he claimed to be contributions to his reelection campaign. Fortunately for Watson, his attorney was the same one who defended Supervisor Herbert Legg after his indictment in 1955 and acquittal in 1956. By May 1967, all three charges against Watson had been dismissed. In the following two months, Supervisor Dorn charged him with favoritism in assessments and tried to appoint a citizen's group to investigate but could not obtain a majority vote for the motion. These conflicts between the assessor and the supervisors would escalate in the 1970s, after Baxter Ward took office and until Watson finally retired. (See Chapter 5.)[8]

Watson's most notable endeavors in these years were two California ballot propositions, both referred to as the "Watson Initiative." The first came in 1968 and would have set property taxes to 1 percent of assessed value and limit the amount of bonds that could be issued by a taxing authority such as the county. The proposal would eliminate property tax revenue for schools and welfare services which would require other unidentified funding. The Los Angeles County supervisors initially supported it in April, but gradually realized it would have a serious negative effect on county revenue. In fact, the BOS even blasted Watson for spending thousands of county funds on the campaign for his measure after he claimed it was being done with volunteers. The BOS, as well as Orange County supervisors, the *Times*, the Chamber of Commerce, and other groups throughout the state opposed it as a gift to major landowners that would cripple government services and force higher taxes on homeowners. With the added opposition of Governor Reagan and Democratic leader Jess Unruh, the proposition was handily defeated.[9]

One of the groups supporting Watson's initiative was the United Organizations of Taxpayers headed by retired businessman Howard Jarvis. He had run unsuccessfully for mayor of Los Angeles several times, and for the U.S. Senate in the Republican primary in 1962. By 1968, he attended BOS budget hearings each year to protest high taxes and commanded a group of volunteers without money or tax expertise to gather signatures for a tax reduction initiative on the state ballot. At first, he criticized Watson for a conflict of interest in using county resources for his own initiative. Eventually, Jarvis supported the Watson proposal, since he could not gather enough signatures for his own. After the defeat, he ran for a slot on the state board of equalization in 1970 but lost again. In 1971, he and Watson began working on their next property tax reform initiatives. Jarvis's organization could not obtain the necessary number of signatures, so Jarvis joined forces with Watson again.[10]

Watson's 1972 initiative would limit property taxes to 1.75 percent of market value or sales. Consumer and corporate taxes would substantially increase, but not nearly enough to make up the difference as it would create an estimated deficit of over $1 billion for state and local governments. His major financial backers included large landowners—farming companies, land developers, and such, who had the most to gain. The opposition included Governor Reagan and many other state officials, university presidents, business and labor leaders, and other community activists. They hired the Braun & Company political consultants to handle the campaign, stressing the message that it would increase taxes and cut funding for education and other government services. The BOS finally opposed the "cruel hoax" only days before the election; it lost by a 34 percent to 66 percent margin.[11]

Jarvis and Watson would both try again with similar petitions in 1976, but neither collected enough signatures. In 1977, when Jarvis ran for mayor of Los Angeles a second time, they decided to combine their efforts with Paul Gann in northern California. But they split up that year due to personal rivalries and the fact that Watson was busy fighting with the county supervisors and about to retire. Jarvis and Gann would continue the effort that would lead to the placing of a constitutional amendment limiting property taxes on the 1978 ballot that would become Proposition 13.[12]

The impetus in the 1970s for property tax initiatives grew increasingly important throughout the decade. In 1970, the Los Angeles County supervisors again requested that the governor call a special session of the legislature to consider tax reform legislation. Two years later they asked Governor Reagan and state legislators to enact a complete overhaul to counter further tax initiatives they believed would disrupt state and local services, and to support the tax reform program of the County Supervisors Association of California. Reagan did respond to some of these entreaties in 1973, when he sponsored Proposition 1, which would limit state expenditures and property tax rates, eliminate some personal income taxes, and require state funding for any new programs to be carried out by local governments.

Tax reform organizations such as that of Howard Jarvis and various state officials supported it, but many civic groups countered that as written it would just create new local taxes for low- and middle-income residents. The Los Angeles County CAO advised the supervisors to oppose the measure for the same reasons, and the board agreed. The proposal did better than the Watson initiatives, but still met rejection.[13]

Meanwhile, the supervisors debated reductions in expenditures as annual taxes rose. In 1972, Hahn suggested that they eliminate budget items to support local tourism and building clubhouses at county golf courses, and to halt increased benefits for department managers. Additional Hahn proposals included paying for capital projects from federal revenue-sharing funds rather than the general fund which would result in reduced funding for community organizations that received the money and cutting $50 million from the proposed 1974–1975 budget by eliminating non-critical capital projects and 2 percent of county personnel. He requested that the assessor, other county officials, and the County Citizens Economy and Efficiency Commission review assessment procedures and recommend how to reduce the tax burden on homeowners and senior citizens for state legislators and the governor to carry out. These attempted solutions made hardly a dent in the tax monolith at the time, as the county tax roll and rate increased with more federal and state service mandates. The budget and tax rate reached an all-time high in 1974 and would rise again the following year.[14]

Fiscal calamity in New York City in late 1975 sparked a more urgent campaign to address rising taxes and budgets. In October, that city almost declared bankruptcy, sending shockwaves throughout the nation and other parts of the world. The Los Angeles County BOS immediately asked the County Citizens' Economy and Efficiency Commission to review the New York crisis and suggest preventative recommendations "to safeguard Los Angeles County from a similar disaster." The commission responded with the first of several reports documenting structural and operational problems with county administration, noting that several other major American cities "have also been operating on the brink of financial disaster in recent years," and Los Angeles County is "moving rapidly toward a serious fiscal crisis." Coincidentally, the report appeared at the time the supervisors were delaying action on placing on the ballot the proposals put forth by the Public Commission on County Government, which addressed some of the report's recommendations. (See Chapter 6.)[15]

The supervisors made initial stabs at reducing expenditures during the 1976 budget hearings, which exhibited the usual features of them demanding equal fund distributions in each of the five districts of protesters appearing to fight for cuts or continued funding, and of the CAO advising further cuts. Eventually, the supervisors approved eliminating funds for capital projects and hundreds of employees. The latter included 111 jobs in the Assessor's office, which would delay reassessments, meaning fewer valuation increases so less county revenue and a higher tax rate. In August, 900 protesters forced the reopening of budget hearings and the cutting and adding of funds continued as unions tried to delay layoffs. The supervisors finally approved an underfunded, and possibly illegal, budget. Just before tax bills were mailed in October, tax reform leaders such as Howard Jarvis urged revolts and recalls of county officials, but the enthusiasm soon died down.[16]

In 1977, the supervisors continued to look for solutions to their income and revenue problems. A hiring freeze and limits on raises and benefits, restrictions on department spending, and other controls reduced the county workforce by 4000 in the 1976–1977 budget year and kept some related costs from rising. The supervisors also cut the size of their own staffs to help. Two of them even offered their own (unsuccessful) property tax proposals: Baxter Ward's proposal of a split-roll feature to tax homeowners at a lower rate was judged to help those who needed it least; James Hayes's California initiative would slash property taxes by 70 percent and prohibit counties from being forced to assume the cost of any mandated programs, leaving those to the state and federal governments. Near the end of the year CAO Harry Hufford estimated that county finances were in much better shape, with only a $33 million budget deficit because of service reductions and elimination of over 9 percent of county jobs. At the same time, conservative Supervisor Schabarum became chairman of the BOS and promised to continue cutting taxes and county employees.[17]

By then, however, it was too late. State legislators had made several attempts at cutting property taxes during the year but produced nothing. In fact, the announcements that state employee pensions skyrocketed, and county pensions were also in the red and would require additional funding, made the immediate situation even worse. Along with continuing inflation and distrust of government since the Watergate scandal, Howard Jarvis and his associates would finally get their tax reduction initiative on the state primary ballot in June 1978. As political scientist Gary J. Miller has observed, the recession and building boom pause in the 1970s drove up housing prices for baby boomer families fleeing to the suburbs and seeking more amenities; and older residents, particularly those retired on fixed incomes, watched their taxes grow and their egg nest decline. Both groups looked more positively to a major change in their fortunes about to happen.[18]

Proposition 13

The year of 1978 opened with the Jarvis-Gann initiative approved for the ballot, and the state legislature and local governments in California in defensive mode. If approved by the voters Proposition 13 would limit property taxes to 1 percent of assessed value based on 1975 values, cap annual increases at 2 percent, and allow reassessments at full market value when the property changed owners. It was estimated that the cut in state property taxes would reach almost 60 percent with no plan to replace that revenue, and it also required a two-thirds vote to pass future taxes. Having done little to address rising property taxes over the decade, the legislature quickly passed the Behr proposal, which became Proposition 8, to compete with 13. Proposition 8 would cut property taxes 30 percent for homeowners only, double the tax credit for renters, give additional relief to the elderly on fixed incomes, and limit future government expenditures. The latter proposal would have much less impact on local governments and was endorsed by many of them, including Los Angeles County, as well as the County Supervisors of California Association. Those same organizations opposed Proposition 13, as did the League of Women Voters of California, League of California Cities, California Common Cause, the California Taxpayers Association, California State Employees Association, the AFL-CIO, future California Republican governors George Deukmejian and Pete Wilson, and business groups such as the California Retailors Association and Los Angeles Area Chamber of Commerce, among others. Additional individuals supporting Proposition 8 rather than 13 included Governor Jerry Brown, Supervisors Hahn and Edelman, and Los Angeles Mayor Tom Bradley, all considered by tax reform populist Jarvis to be symbols of "big government."[19]

Los Angeles County officials began planning early to address both proposals. In January, the BOS ordered a CAO study of Proposition 13 effects on residents and hearings the following month. CAO Hufford concluded that it would "provide a windfall for the wealthy and for business" as it would cut county tax revenue by 58 percent, requiring layoffs and reduced services with no requirement that the savings be passed on to renters. In March, Supervisor Edelman initiated his frequent public appearances in opposition to Proposition 13 when he debated Howard Jarvis on the merits and drawbacks (as the two interpreted them) of the "Landlords' Enrichment Act," as the *Times* called it, since Jarvis also headed the Los Angeles Apartment Owners Association. Later that month the supervisors ordered Hufford to prepare his usual budget and two more: one based on Proposition 13 passing, and one for Proposition 8.[20]

In April, the *Times* reported that County Assessor Alexander Pope endorsed Proposition 8 and not Proposition 13, that Jarvis admitted his creation needed further work, and that Moody's rating service had suspended its rating on California bonds until after the election. The County Citizens' Economy and Efficiency Commission released a statement advising a no vote on Proposition 13 as it was not real tax reform. Hufford presented his estimated budget for Proposition 8, which included some cuts and the possibility of a slightly lower tax rate, but it depended on property reassessments and other contingencies. Although the supervisors had not received Hufford's Proposition 13 budget details, the majority had already made up their minds about that "pig in a poke," as Ward labeled it. When Schabarum called for a vote to endorse Proposition 13, Hahn, Edelman, and Ward voted no, while Schabarum and Hayes voted in the affirmative.[21]

On May 2, Hufford presented his Proposition 13 budget to the supervisors. They would be in for a shock. Even with several assumed revenue sources added, the county's budget would be slashed by over $1 billion. That would require about 36,000 layoffs (almost half of the county full-time workforce), the closure of four hospitals, 69 percent of municipal courts eliminated, a cut of 71 percent of funding for parks, 58 percent for fire stations, 73 percent for libraries, over 33 percent for the Sheriff's Department, and the closure of museums and other cultural institutions, as well as leaving all departments with depleted staffs. The county credit rating would certainly drop, and all services would be affected. The document would become known as the "Doomsday Budget" by critics who accused county officials of grossly exaggerating to scare residents into voting against Proposition 13. It has been noted that in April the two tax proposals were running neck and neck in popularity, but by mid–May, after the Doomsday Budget received abundant media coverage, Proposition 13 had moved far out in front. If the publicity was intended to scare voters away from Proposition 13, it certainly had the opposite effect.[22]

The Doomsday Budget also spurred two supervisors to step up their campaign to defeat Proposition 13. Edelman and his chief deputy tried to convince officials of cities with county contracts that their services contracts might end or increase in price, that their redevelopment projects and revenue-sharing funds would be jeopardized, and that most county subsidies for various programs would be curtailed. Hahn offered a motion to cancel contracts with community social services groups, instruct the county engineer to send notices to owners of buildings leased to the county that the leases would be cancelled, and to arrange to transfer patients to private hospitals. He wanted the county public defender to negotiate with the Bar Association to have private lawyers volunteer their time to defend the accused who couldn't afford it, and for the county to look into ending medical school subsidies at hospitals. One deputy thought Hahn seemed to be trying to scare various special interests into opposing Proposition 13 but didn't go far enough. Near the end of May, Hahn even moved that the assessor be directed to send out notices that residential (not commercial) property-tax assessments would be frozen that year; newspaper editors suggested it might be a way to shift the blame for higher taxes from the BOS to the assessor. (At a conference twenty-five years later, Assessor Pope said he didn't send the notices out, and Edelman could not recall if they did, as at that time "we were swirling around in a sea of, I think, confusion.")[23]

Apparently, these moves did not have as much effect on voters as did the Doomsday Budget. Proposition 13 was victorious in Los Angeles County, as well as in most of the rest of the state, with almost 65 percent of the total vote (less than the two-thirds vote it required to change it or create new taxes). Proposition 13 was especially popular in the suburbs and with the single-family homeowners who lived there. Only three counties—San Francisco, Kern and Yolo—voted against Proposition 13 and for Proposition 8. (San Francisco County had a high percentage of renters who would have benefited by Proposition 8.) As the *Times* reported, the election was heard throughout the nation—the "Second Boston Tea Party" according to the *New York Times*—and Howard Jarvis prepared to spread his campaign to other states. Meanwhile, Los Angeles and other California counties and cities would have to cope with less.[24]

The Aftermath

The initial response of Los Angeles County officials to the passage of Proposition 13 was to begin reducing expenditures and seek help from Sacramento. The county auditor reported a cash flow problem that would leave the county's general fund empty by July 13. The County Museum of Art's Museum Associates support organization filed the first of the many lawsuits challenging Proposition 13, and

Howard Jarvis and his supporters celebrate the victory of Proposition 13 in 1978 (Mike Meadows, photographer. *Los Angeles Times* Photographers Archive [Collection 1429], Library Special Collections, Charles E. Young Research Library, UCLA).

Supervisor Hahn proposed a motion to allow such governing boards of the county cultural institutions or other private support groups to operate them. He also proposed that the top 100 corporations in California be asked to donate part of their Proposition 13 savings to support cultural and recreational programs, while admission fees for the museums and additional user fees were established or raised. Layoffs of some employees, especially in the flood control and library departments dependent on property taxes began, and the supervisors ordered a freeze on hiring, raises, and promotions. Four libraries closed and services in others reduced; two health centers and three neighborhood service centers closed; three district attorney offices were shuttered and some of its units reduced; three LASD detention camps and one probation camp for juveniles closed; and capital projects were deferred. Cities in the county also faced major reductions, as Vernon had to lay off seventeen of its twenty-two firefighters. In addition, the amount of the budget subject to local control of the supervisors dwindled from 40 percent in 1977 to 14 percent, with the state and federal governments controlling decisions on the remainder.[25]

Most of the above cuts were made even though California counties would receive a windfall of surplus funds the state held for such emergencies. Los Angeles County received a $580 million reprieve, although the bailout would still leave the county with a 15 to 20 percent budget shortfall requiring service reductions and layoffs. The supervisors knew that the state surplus would not last forever, that "California is on Borrowed Time," according to Edelman. They pledged to continue lobbying the state and federal governments for more funding and proposed procedures to simplify the administration of services to avoid duplication and waste. The County Citizens' Economy and Efficiency Commission decided to rely on private funding rather than its county support. And Governor Brown appointed a commission to study the structure and operation of state and local governments and propose reforms. In the private sector, a Citizens Permanent Committee on the Recall of Public Officials formed to pursue the removal of politicians who proposed new taxes.[26]

By September, however, the situation markedly improved. The state added another $100 million in surplus funds, and with the savings already produced the county budget for the fiscal year almost reverted to its pre–Proposition 13 level with a need for only 343 layoffs. Libraries and flood control might still be hit hard since those services were funded by special districts, not the county's general fund. That conundrum would be settled in the following year. By February 1979, the surplus funds encouraged Hufford to propose salary increases for the workforce averaging 4.5 percent, and up to 15 percent for some department heads (13 percent for himself). Although there had not been any increases for several years, the amounts proposed for top officials raised protests in many quarters, especially in the state legislature. Since the passage of another bailout bill for 1979 to 1980 was delayed until July, the raises would have to wait, and some would be reduced based on federal guidelines responding to the national economic situation. (Sheriff Peter Pitchess asked Edelman to continue negotiating with his sheriff's deputies in the interim; Edelman replied, "I don't think you understand the meaning of the words 'bail out.'") During that year, the supervisors added several additional fees for county services, which incurred the wrath of Jarvis, who claimed those fees were really taxes and threatened to begin a new initiative campaign to terminate efforts to implement new taxes without a vote.[27]

The continuing search for new revenue by the supervisors played into the hands of tax reformers who placed several more initiative measures on the ballot. After their victory in 1978, Howard Jarvis and Paul Gann had a falling out, and in the following year Gann sponsored an initiative to limit state and local government spending and return surpluses to taxpayers. This Proposition 13 also won approval with 76 percent of the votes. Jarvis then returned with another initiative in 1980 to cut personal income taxes by 50 percent and eliminate business inventory taxes. The opponents of Proposition 9 (labeled Jarvis II) called it an irresponsible scheme to benefit the wealthy that would cause chaos in the state; it failed. (The BOS split 2–2 on endorsing this proposal in an election year.) Jarvis returned in June 1982 with a proposal to adjust income tax brackets to the Consumer Price Index which would reduce state revenue; this one succeeded. In 1984, Jarvis and Gann hooked up again and presented Proposition 36, intended to prohibit further taxes, and provide refunds on downward reassessments. Opponents charged it was unfair to new businesses, jeopardized public education and opened new loopholes in the tax laws, convincing voters to reject it. In spite the defeats, Jarvis and Gann would remain active in state tax proposals.[28]

California surplus funds were depleted by 1981, and the state, feeling the pinch of Proposition 13, reduced support for local governments. Cities and counties continued to lobby state legislators and the governor for more tax revenue from other sources such as a tippler tax and give local governments more discretion in spending. But little could be accomplished when the state had its own limitations. Los Angeles County also limited budgets and expenditures, such as reducing the number of employees between 1975 to 1983 by almost 10,000 positions and established new user fees which improved its financial situation. In 1984, thanks to the national economy improving with federal deficit spending, the county's budget did not suffer major cuts. In fact, there would be no layoffs that year and the supervisors could argue over how high of a raise to give top county managers (the conservative Schabarum favored those as high as 16.5 percent, but only 5.5 percent for the rank and file). Not all counties would be as fortunate as Los Angeles, however, as a County Supervisors Association of California report noted in 1985 that half of the state's counties were "in serious financial trouble with no immediate remedies in sight." Things would get worse in a few years when the economy was again in dire straits.[29]

The Legacy of Proposition 13 in California and Los Angeles County

In the four decades since the landmark passage of Proposition 13 there have been many retrospective articles, policy studies, books and conferences examining its impact on state and local government, mostly focusing on its positive and negative features. While it did have a major benefit for property owners in the state in 1978 by reducing their taxes and keeping the rise at a low and consistent level thereafter, experts have also identified its drawbacks as even Howard Jarvis once admitted that it was not perfect. The value of homes purchased later would be assessed at the current market value, rather than the assessment of an identical house owned by a neighbor since 1978, a seemingly unfair situation that has been held legal by the courts. Commercial property owned by for-profit businesses did not change hands as often as residences, so reassessments based on sales of property have not occurred as often. Renters paid part of their landlords' property taxes in monthly rental payments but were not guaranteed a discount based on tax cuts. Other drawbacks, such as loopholes that aided businesses and wealthy descendants of 1978 property owners, appeared over time, some corrected, some not. And while it also drew attention to California's ancient financial system and other administrative problems, fundamental change in those areas have still not come about. Calls for a split-roll process in which commercial property is assessed periodically at its current market value have been suggested since before Proposition 13 was even placed on the ballot (Edelman called for it in October 1977),[30] but proposals in the legislature have not gone very far until recently (a failure in 2020). In these years many observers have called Proposition 13 the "third rail" of California politics (in a comparison to the electrified rail on rapid transit systems) as it is so popular that politicians are reluctant to tamper with it.[31]

The failure of the state legislature to enact any major tax reform in the 1970s before Proposition 13 was placed on the ballot was the major impetus to approve the measure, and those directly affected by rising taxes in an era of recession and distrust of government were its prime supporters. Its passage would also affect other types of taxes, such as those on retail sales, and additional and higher fees for services. State legislators and administrators would have to be more cognizant of their decisions that could increase spending without revenue to offset it. And many of the worst fears expressed by opponents during the campaign never came about as governments responded to reduced income. As political scientist Raphael Sonenshein and other scholars have noted, Proposition 13 also gave California Republicans an important political issue to contend with Democrats, even as some Republican leaders initially opposed it. On the national level the tax revolt would spread to other states as politicians embraced it, and Ronald Reagan would take advantage of it in his campaign for the presidency in 1980.[32]

Proposition 13 had a profound impact on local governments in California such as Los Angeles County. Besides draining some funding for services and reducing workforces that carried out state and federal mandates, as well as decreasing support for non-mandated services, the efforts to address the change led to a shift in budget decision making as the state acquired more power in fiscal policies at the expense of counties and cities. Los Angeles County supervisors would lose some of their "home rule" discretionary power because of the change, although they still have tremendous power in the roles they play in determining land use and social services, as well as other issues they control in the nation's most populous county. And because of the availability of a significant state surplus of funds for the first few years after 1978, the county was not as restricted in spending as feared just prior to the passage of Proposition 13. The actual results of the measure would be felt in the 1980s, when surplus funding ended, and especially during the 1990s recession and again in the first decade of the 2000s.[33]

8

The Decade of the "Solid Three"

The first ten months of 1980 had not been good ones for Supervisor Pete Schabarum, the lone conservative Republican on the BOS. He was in the minority in voting on many county issues, and embarrassed when the other four supervisors rejected the reappointment of a commissioner he had chosen. He contemplated a run for governor of California at the time, but that went nowhere. One of his aides was involved in a possible sex scandal and inappropriate bullying of a contractor organization; another aide was tied to the sensational Hillside Strangler murders by supplying official county decals to one of the killers.

On the other hand, things were also looking up for Schabarum. The 1960s social and political unrest was followed by a conservative trend evident in the 1978 Proposition 13 taxpayer revolt against rising taxes in California and the nation. Along with growing criticism of President Jimmy Carter's administration, the former conservative governor of California, Ronald Reagan, was elected president in November 1980. In Southern California, conservatives were well organized and successful. Schabarum contributed to the campaign of one of the two Republicans running for Los Angeles County supervisor that year, and those two candidates rode the conservative trend to victory. Schabarum assumed he would now control the BOS and reduce the size of county government. Despite many efforts of the "Solid Three," county government grew larger and more expensive.[1]

In the 1980s, three of the supervisors on the board in the past decade continued to hold office: liberals Kenneth Hahn and Edmund Edelman, and conservative Pete Schabarum. The ideological composition of the board would change, however, as two conservatives joined Schabarum as a bloc that would not be quite as solid as some critics predicted. One of the newcomers, New York City native Deane Dana, moved to California with his wife during his military service. He then was hired as an executive in the Pacific Bell Telephone Company and became active in local Republican Party politics in Long Beach. A moderate conservative without any experience in government, he defeated Fourth District Supervisor Yvonne B. Burke in 1980. On the board this Reaganite usually voted with the conservative bloc, but occasionally joined the liberals when expedient for him to do so.[2]

The other newcomer was Michael Dennis Antonovich in the Fifth District. A native of Los Angeles, Antonovich taught government and history classes at a local high school. In 1972, he was elected to the California Assembly and served until

1978, when he lost in the contest for the state's lieutenant-governor. Two years later, he defeated Baxter Ward in the Reagan landslide. Antonovich was a more doctrinaire conservative than Dana and Schabarum. He served as chairman of the state Republican Party when he ran for U.S. Senator in 1986 but lost in the primary.[3]

County Elections in the 1980s

The 1980 general election was different for the supervisors than earlier contests in that the races for two of the seats were competitive. Hahn was again victorious in the primary with almost 90 percent of the vote, but two other incumbents would meet defeat. Baxter Ward and Yvonne Burke faced several opponents in the primary and defeated all of them, while Schabarum's favorites moved on to the general election. In that contest, Antonovich received the endorsement of soon-to-be President Ronald Reagan; the challenger won with 55 percent of the vote. For Yvonne Burke, the general election campaign would be much less civil. Schabarum saw it as an opportunity to change the board majority, so he financed the campaign of Deane Dana. During the campaign, Dana's staff was sure to point out Burke's stand on school busing, then a major issue, as Dana's fliers seemed to darken the color of her skin. It might have been enough to make a difference as Dana defeated her.[4]

In 1982, Schabarum, who "enjoyed the heck out of last year" as leader of the conservative majority, and Edelman ran again with huge bankrolls for their campaigns. Both won easily in the primary, as did Sheriff Sherman Block, who had little opposition. The race for assessor included incumbent liberal Alexander Pope, businessman Steven Weeks, and several others. Schabarum loaned $25,000 to Weeks, the favorite of the conservatives, but was not enough to boost Weeks as Pope won handily in the primary.[5]

The 1984 contest would be more contentious. Schabarum broke the BOS tradition of not interfering in the campaigns of other supervisors by trying to convince an African American Republican in the Reagan administration who grew up in the Second District to run against Hahn. The potential candidate finally declined, and just hearing the news of Schabarum's scheme convinced Hahn to contribute some unneeded funds to the opponents of Dana and Antonovich. (Hahn won in the primary with 86.84 percent of the vote.) Assessor Alexander Pope joined the fray in Dana's district and was endorsed by Hahn, the *Herald Examiner*, the *Sentinel*, and organized labor, among others. Dana had been collecting large donations from developers and portrayed himself as a moderate on rent control and other issues; he even tried to link Jesse Jackson to his campaign by including a photo of the civil rights leader in campaign mailers. Antonovich also had amassed a large campaign chest and faced three opponents, none of whom had half as much funds as he did. Both Dana and Antonovich would make good use of their treasuries to win reelection in the June primary. In the race for district attorney incumbent Robert Philibosian, originally appointed by the conservatives, faced Los Angeles City Attorney Ira Reiner, and made enough mistakes to allow Reiner, supported by Democrats and a Black-Jewish alliance, to win in the primary.[6]

In the 1986 election, Schabarum ran unopposed. Edelman had three challengers: a conservative mechanical engineer, a Socialist garment worker, and a stripper named Venus de Milo. None of them received many votes in the primary, so Edelman did not have to continue the effort in the general election. Sheriff Block had only token opposition and was easily reelected again in the primary. In the race for assessor, former Assemblyman Jim Keysor, and Deputy County Assessor John Lynch, moved on to the general election, with Lynch victorious and off to a controversial tenure.[7]

The 1988 election was another complicated contest, especially for Hahn. This would be his tenth election since 1952, and it had been noted over the last decade that his continuing success blocked opportunities of young Black candidates in the county's heavily minority Second District. In January 1987, he suffered a stroke and several seizures following it. Speculation emerged that he might not run again. In fact, several Black religious leaders urged Hahn not to run because of his health, while liberal leaders opined that if he were reelected and had to leave office early, Governor Deukmejian would appoint a Republican replacement. Newspapers that usually endorsed him, including the *Torrance Daily Breeze* and *Herald Examiner,* favored a Black candidate, Southern California Association of Governments official Gil Smith. But the *Sentinel,* the *Times* and other papers stuck with Hahn, who won in the primary with 84.21 percent of the vote.[8]

At the same time, Dana and Antonovich stood for reelection. Dana again presented himself as a moderate, which helped in gaining the endorsement of unions, the *Times,* and the *Herald Examiner.* He faced two weak challengers, so instead of spending from his huge treasury he loaned much of it to his son in an unsuccessful quest for a seat in the Assembly. Dana was still able to win easily in the primary. Antonovich had a rougher go of it, even though he had plenty of funds from developers. He would face Don Wallace, a Los Angeles Fire Department captain endorsed by the *Herald Examiner* and the *Times,* five others, and his old nemesis, Baxter Ward. During the primary campaign Antonovich also faced angry homeowners and activists in a backlash against his support of massive development and spent over $1 million to Ward's less than $1000 but could not win it. So Antonovich fought Ward even harder, enlisting his father to seek campaign funds by aligning Ward with the "Hollywood radical types, the local liberal activists, the extreme environmentalists, and the gay and lesbian activists as well." Antonovich again spent freely, and the *Times* made no endorsement, although its editors noted that Antonovich was worse than Ward. Aided by the large turnout in a presidential general election, Antonovich won by a seven-to-two margin.[9]

In the other 1988 race for an elected county official, District Attorney Ira Reiner faced three opponents. Criticized for constantly seeking publicity and measuring all his decisions by their political ramifications, the *Times* found him to be generally efficient and the most qualified of those on the ballot. He would win easily in the primary.[10]

One of the supervisorial contests in 1990 was rejected as it came amid a redistricting conflict that was not resolved until early 1991. (See Chapter 10.) In the other race, Edelman easily rode to victory, as usual, in the primary. The county-wide elections of sheriff and assessor were not affected by redistricting. In the case of the former office, Sheriff Sherman Block was thought to be a shoo-in, but found himself in the center of an LASD scandal in which ten deputies were indicted for stealing seized drug money. He was opposed by a detective, the cousin of former sheriff Eugene Biscailuz. The scandal and other factors convinced the *Times* editors to avoid making an endorsement, concluding that the LASD needed reform. But incumbency again had its advantage as Block defeated Biscailuz handily. Seven candidates vied for the assessor position, including the embattled incumbent, John Lynch, and several members of his staff. The *Times* would endorse one of them other than the incumbent, but a different deputy would come in second to Lynch. In a further upset, Kenneth P. Hahn, unrelated to the supervisor but whose name probably helped, was victorious.[11]

A New Board Majority

After the first of the 1980s elections, the two additions to the board would join Schabarum, finally in command after spending eight years in the minority. An acolyte of Ronald Reagan, who appointed him to the board, Schabarum supported Proposition 13 and most other conservative issues. He was ambitious and hoped but failed to be elected California governor in 1982, to be appointed to President Reagan's cabinet, to be chosen as Secretary of Transportation for President Bush in 1988, and appointed state treasurer in 1988. His desire to win at all costs was displayed in a softball game played by county employees in 1986, when the former pro football player rounded third base and headed home, where he slammed into the waiting catcher with the ball. The catcher—a 135 lb., fifty-year-old grandmother—was flattened, but still held on to the ball as the supervisor was called out and a brief brawl ensued. Such behavior was part of his personality, which was well known to reporters and associates. No doubt it was a factor in his arguments with his two conservative compadres on the board, causing rifts in the majority.[12]

When the two victorious Republicans prepared to take office with Schabarum, their opponents worried that liberal achievements in the past would soon be erased. One union leader predicted that Schabarum "has already been fitted with his crown and promises to be more obnoxious than ever," expecting "confrontation with these three reactionaries on the board who may now feel they have a mandate to take on public employees." This premonition of conflict on labor and other county issues would prove correct to a large degree. The two new supervisors quickly replaced the deputies of their defeated opponents and selected those with similar political beliefs. Many county decisions would result 3–2, as they frequently voted as a bloc. The 3–2 votes would come on issues such as supporting an amendment to the U.S. constitution to make English the official language of the nation and blocking a liberal-backed motion to declare Martin Luther King, Jr.'s, birthday a county holiday. Motions limiting the power of labor unions and services for undocumented residents, restricting health and other budget allotments for the disadvantaged, protecting public safety departments, and for many other purposes would win on the conservative/liberal vote.[13]

In 1986, one of Edelman's deputies informed him of a newspaper reporter investigating three current items being advanced by the conservatives to gain more control over the county bureaucracy that the two liberals probably would not support. One was putting on the ballot a charter amendment that would remove the top three levels of county managers from civil service protection if they agreed to compete for performance bonuses, and to deny civil service status to new employees in those ranks. Another would give the conservatives more control over all departments with Schabarum's motion to abolish chairmanships in which each supervisor was assigned to oversee one-fifth of county departments as the first supervisor to handle problems. This change from tradition would limit the liberals' involvement in individual departments, since managers would have to address the entire board without first consulting a single supervisor who might be the most knowledgeable on a certain issue. Both motions were approved, but the latter would eventually be dropped.[14]

The third item was Dana's successful motion for a study of the merits of an appointed assessor. All fifty-eight county assessors in California were elective, but the duties of the office had changed since Proposition 13, and there were a few appointed assessors in other states. In the past, reformers had recommended the appointed assessor, when the conservative supervisors opposed it. The *Times* endorsed it in 1973 and 1978; and the current assessor, Alexander Pope, supported it in 1984. But 1986 would be different due to fears that the three conservatives would appoint an assessor to follow their instructions. Edelman, Hahn, and their 1978 adversary Howard Jarvis signed the ballot arguments against it. Pope would reverse his prior approval, and the *Times*, other newspapers, and radio and television stations editorialized against it. This time the conservatives lost with the defeat of the charter amendment.[15]

Their candidate, however, was eventually victorious. John Lynch, who refused to pay for his candidate statement in the sample ballot, was accused of intimidating a co-worker who displayed a bumper sticker for an opponent on his automobile. One week after Lynch took office, he refused to admit auditors to continue a routine audit, sparking a long feud with the county auditor. In November 1987, he was accused of assaulting one of his employees and then firing his chief deputy over a personality difference. Lynch's additional personnel problems with his staff and other county officials and criticism from the County Grand Jury sparked opposition to his next election in 1990. In that contest other Los Angeles city officials joined Edelman, the *Times*, and the widow of former assessor Phil Watson in endorsing Kenneth P. Hahn, an appraiser in the assessor's office, who won in a close race with the incumbent.[16]

As many issues will demonstrate, the conservatives were not always united, especially when considering personalities and self-interest. Only one year after the conservative takeover, Schabarum and Antonovich disagreed over the former's motion to repeal a 1979 ordinance requiring fire-resistant roofing on all new homes in unincorporated areas. Antonovich's district suffered from recent fires, and Schabarum wanted to keep housing costs down in his less flammable bailiwick. In 1981, they argued over Antonovich's attempt to name Sheriff Pitchess's successor without Schabarum's approval. In 1982, Schabarum refused to approve Dana's motion to oppose the appointment of liberal Cruz Reynoso, the first Latino appointed to the California Supreme Court; he did not know Reynoso "from a bale of hay," so he would not vote either for or against him. In the next year Dana split from his partners by introducing a successful motion to create a holiday dedicated to Martin Luther King, Jr., the same as he had opposed in 1981, but now favored when trying to change his image to a moderate. By 1984—election year for Dana and Antonovich—it was apparent that the conservatives were no longer the "Solid Three" as a *Times* story described the change to "Every Man for Himself." Schabarum and Antonovich argued with each other in budget deliberations, and Dana joined the liberals in opposing state Proposition 41, which would cut health and welfare funds for the poor. By 1989, the arguing would continue to the point that Dana and Antonovich, who argued with each other, would eventually be ready to sacrifice an unreliable Schabarum to keep a dependable Republican majority. (See Chapter 10.)[17]

Besides occasionally battling with his conservative colleagues, Schabarum was more frequently feuding with the liberals. He occasionally played tennis with Edelman in the 1970s, but with control of the majority he ended the games in the 1980s. He vowed to end the tradition of the chairman not scheduling the vote on an item if an interested supervisor could not be present, as Edelman had just done to him, and he generated newspaper quotes criticizing Edelman by that time. Schabarum's feud with Hahn since the 1970s was even more serious, as the former had a dartboard in his office with a photo of Hahn on the target. With the votes of most of the supervisors, Schabarum consistently denied Hahn the annual chairmanship of the BOS, a largely symbolic office with some control of BOS. In 1981, Hahn protested state Senator John Schmitz's public statement calling for a military coup in the U.S. if President Reagan's economic policies could not be passed by Congress. A few months later, Hahn submitted a motion that Schmitz should be censored for that opinion, and it was approved, to the disappointment of Schabarum, who supported it when Schmitz initially uttered it. In 1988, just one year after Hahn's stroke, Schabarum blasted him in a shouting match during a BOS meeting, when welfare workers packed it to protest low allotments. These incidents were only a few of many. Schabarum also feuded with CAO Richard Dixon on many occasions after the power of the CAO was strengthened following Proposition 13, and that of the supervisors reduced.[18]

In a few cases the two liberals also split on various issues. Edelman tried to cooperate with the conservatives in the early 1980s, to the dismay of progressives who opposed him in elections. But on many issues, he joined Hahn, and in certain cases he might be the only dissenting vote. This most notably occurred in 1988, when Hahn joined the three conservatives in opposing Edelman's motion to provide bleach kits for needles to prevent drug users from spreading AIDS. The *Herald Examiner* castigated the "Four Blind Mice" as being "blinded by the politics of self-righteousness" for such a cruel decision, while Edelman, whose district included many gay men, was heralded for his stand. But most of the time the two liberals agreed in principle on issues and usually voted together.[19]

The "New Federalism" and State Relations

When the conservatives took over control of the BOS they looked to their hero, President Ronald Reagan, for guidance in downsizing county government and acquiring additional federal funding for federal mandates. When the president visited Los Angeles in 1982, they went out of their way to honor him and plead for more money for social services and federal takeover of costs for undocumented residents. Dana used the occasion to promote his meeting with the president to discuss Reagan's New Federalism program granting more local control. Schabarum appeared on the front page of the county newsletter shaking hands with Reagan, and all five supervisors appeared with Reagan on a later page. (Just after Reagan departed, Schabarum ordered his aides to grab the chair the president sat in at a function in the Music Center, take it up to his office, and put a plaque on it.) Schabarum also offered a motion in 1984, approved 3–2, to support the president's call for a balanced federal budget and presidential line-item veto opposed by Los Angeles newspaper editors and others as hamstringing the government in emergencies and used mostly to cut funding for social services. And in 1986, Schabarum offered a motion praising Reagan as a state, national, and world leader, and moved that the CAO should order the county's legislative representative in Washington to seek a law to rename the Angeles National Forest as the Reagan National Forest. The motion was approved 4–0, but the name change never happened.[20]

Despite these tributes to the president, the conservatives did not get all they asked for. Reagan wanted to trim his own budget, which restricted funding for federal mandates for welfare and healthcare, and, of course, all funding came with strings attached. Revenue sharing funding ended in 1986. In the same year, Congress passed an amnesty program for some immigrants, but not enough funding to pay for the added expenses. Federal housing and other programs assisted in some issues, but not as much as the supervisors had hoped.[21]

In their relationship with state officials the three conservatives expected a more congenial partnership by 1982, when former Long Beach Assemblyman George Deukmejian was elected California governor. In the past few years, Governor Jerry Brown and the Democratic majority in the legislature had dueled with the BOS over spending in the post–Proposition 13 era. To change that relationship with Deukmejian, the conservative majority reached out to the new governor for more funding by appointing Deukmejian's ally, Robert Philibosian, as district attorney after John Van de Kamp's election as state attorney general in late 1982. In the following year they appointed former Republican legislator Paul Priolo as a county lobbyist. Priolo's employment for one year resulted in mixed reviews and charges of a conflict of interest as he also represented a candy manufacturer when the supervisors tried to establish a sales tax on candy. In 1985, the conservatives hired Deukmejian's controversial former finance director as a lobbyist on a one-year contract.[22]

These appointments and their friendly relationship gained little help from the governor. Antonovich did have Deukmejian's support in his election as vice-president (and then president) of the California Republican Party in 1983. But the 1980s were a trying time for state government as well as the county, and

Deukmejian had fifty-seven other counties and the state apparatus to contend with. All California counties pleaded in unison for fewer cuts in state funding in 1985. In 1987, Hahn criticized the governor's deep cuts in health and education. In 1988, he complained the late state budget that delayed the county's budget resulted in short-term solutions to complicated issues as the supervisors gambled on the amounts of state funding for its mandates. Clearly, the BOS lobbying efforts did not work very well for Los Angeles County.[23]

While Democrats in the legislature were still on good terms with the two Democratic supervisors, the former did not get along well with the conservative majority. The legislators were particularly upset that Schabarum and Hayes had supported Proposition 13 and then asked for more funding for salaries, parks, and other amenities while planning cuts in social services for the poor. Tempers flared occasionally as a group of twenty-one legislators apologized to the supervisors in 1981 for the "expletive-laden criticism" by one of their number after the BOS cuts to health centers and the Martin Luther King, Jr., Hospital. In that same year, another legislator saw all five supervisors meeting with state officials in Sacramento and asked the district attorney of that county to investigate it as a violation of the Brown Act prohibiting secret meetings. By 1987, enough state legislators wrote directly to county department heads suggesting changes in their management, that Schabarum offered a successful motion to have the CAO recommend how to treat such letters that he considered to be undue pressure from those who voted on funding needed by the departments.[24]

In the 1980s, the BOS continued to contest state government in trying to protect local control usurped by state-created regional agencies. This was particularly true for its relationship with the Southern California Association of Governments (SCAG), which continued its planning function, and the South Coast Air Quality Management District (SCAQMD). The BOS was not alone in this endeavor, as several cities in Orange County boycotted SCAG over the years and Ventura County tried to pull out of it in 1977 and 1992. Los Angeles County made many attempts to end paying dues to SCAG after becoming a member. The county supervisors would have the same relationship with SCAQMD, especially when one of its conservative supervisors was on the board in the late 1980s. And the BOS would officially oppose any state legislation aimed at creating "another unnecessary layer of review," as Schabarum described it in 1985. (See Chapters 6 and 9 for more on SCAG and SCAQMD.)[25]

A major regional threat to BOS power appeared in 1988, with the publication of *LA2000: A City of the Future*, the final report of a 150-member committee formed by Mayor Tom Bradley and composed of business, academic, and community leaders. The committee examined regional resources and problems such as crime, housing, smog, and transportation, and surveyed residents for their attitudes on those issues. The major recommendations of the report included the need for two new regional agencies with the power to manage growth and improve environmental quality. After the report circulated, the 2000 Partnership was formed as a private, non-profit group of civic and business leaders to pursue regional governance in Southern California. The group was only active for a few years, but its reports generated more interest in regional governance by state legislators.[26]

As it turned out, Assembly Speaker Willie L. Brown, Jr., had already ordered a study of conflicting governing bodies "fighting over the same dollars" in a "crazy-quilt" service delivery system. Starting in 1989, five bills to advance regional governance were introduced. One offered by Brown in January 1990, would establish seven regional commissions in the state representing various numbers of counties with broad power in major issues. Los Angeles County would be included in one of them with five adjacent or nearby counties, and the new commissions would replace agencies such as SCAG and SCAQMD. The plan was hailed by the 2000 Partnership and others to reduce pollution and sprawl, but the County Supervisors Association of California and individual counties and cities opposed all these bills as dilutions of their authority. All five bills died in committees, but four of them appeared again the following year. They met a clash of interests as counties, cities, SCAG, developers, the new state Republican administration, and the Democratic legislature had different agendas. By early 1992, the regional bills were dead, and the BOS was back in the saddle again.[27]

The Sixth Supervisor

The county faced consistent funding shortfalls in the years before and after Proposition 13 in 1978, and the county administrative officer (CAO) played a major role in addressing the fiscal calamities. He was often labeled the county's "sixth supervisor" by media reporters and analysts because of his political power and influence over other county officials. In one newspaper story the CAO of the moment was described as "the Man with the Clout," and "the county's dispenser of officially and supposedly nonpolitical information," who had to "steer a middle course between the opposing factions" of the BOS. As one scholar opined, "although the CAO is subordinate to the Board, that person can carve a position for himself that rivals the position of Board members." The power of the CAO depended on his managerial skills in dealing with department heads, his role as gatekeeper for the supervisors and processor of information they needed, his creation and control of annual budgets, and his ability to acquire at least three of the five votes to approve or reject supervisorial motions.[28]

Three administrators served as CAOs during the reign of the BOS majority in the 1980s. The first, Harry L. Hufford, graduated from UCLA with a B.A., from USC with an M.S., and Loyola Law School. He began working for the county in 1953 and served in several departments until his appointment as county CAO in 1974. Hufford was in the position in 1978, when the passage of Proposition 13 resulted in the change of budgeting as CAOs had to rely more on limiting spending instead of raising more tax revenue to balance budgets. He left the office to join a law firm in 1985 and returned in 1993, for almost nine months as interim CAO.[29]

James C. Hankla succeeded Hufford in February 1985. Hankla was a resident of Long Beach who received his M.A. degree in Public Administration from California State University at Los Angeles. He worked for the City of Long Beach in several positions for almost 20 years before moving to Virginia in 1980 to work in a private real estate marketing firm and in municipal financing for several cities. He returned to California and in 1982, was appointed by the county supervisors as executive director of the Community Development Commission and then chosen CAO as the favorite of the conservative majority. He would serve for only two years, resigning partially because of the structural limitations of his office and the opportunity to be hired as city manager of Long Beach.[30]

Richard B. Dixon replaced Hankla in March 1987. He had graduated from Pomona College and did graduate work at UCLA. He started to work for the county in 1958 and eventually moved to the CAO office, where he became the county budget officer. In 1984, he was appointed county treasurer-tax collector, and then as CAO. Over the next several years he would fight many battles with Schabarum and later Gloria Molina, both of whom thought he was trying to accumulate too much power for himself. Dixon was finally forced out of his office by the supervisors in 1993, and soon hired as a consultant for the county retirement association.[31]

All three of these CAOs had different conceptions of their positions and different experiences with the members of the BOS. Hufford thought of himself as allowing democracy in the bureaucracy by letting department heads go directly to supervisors with their issues, as many had done in the past. He could rankle the majority, as he did in 1983, by recommending an across-the-board budget cut that would affect their favored public safety departments as much as social services. Hankla demanded managerial control of the bureaucracy rather than competition with the supervisors and resigned partially because he could not acquire such power. Dixon got along well with most supervisors as he worked hard to increase benefits for them and was more interested in building his own personal power.[32]

For all three of these CAOs, budgets were the major problem in the decade. As mentioned in Chapter 7, the national economic downturn of the 1970s and Proposition 13 severely restricted county budgets after 1978, although bailout funds from the state became available in the first few years. Hufford's term after 1978 mostly consisted of planning staff and service cuts until the state came to the rescue. The crisis seemed to improve in 1984, but federal cuts during the Reagan years and more state cuts led to Hankla's recommendation for cuts again in 1986. Dixon would face major state reductions in 1988 and proposed more cuts in the approved 1989–1990 budget. Not all proposed cuts in the decade were made, as CAOs always seemed to discover additional funds at the last minute. And appeasing at least three of the supervisors who had their own priorities, while also fulfilling state and federal mandates, was an annual challenge. Unfortunately, the situation would become even worse in the 1990s, when at one point the county teetered toward bankruptcy.[33]

Contracting Out

The 1980s were trying times for many county employees as the BOS majority and other officials limited their numbers through attrition and layoffs. The relationship between county management and labor in the 1950s was described by Supervisor John Anson Ford as genial; it was a "nice, family business," according to a former union leader. That changed to adversarial with several strikes by county workers in the 1960s. The next decade was less contentious, as Pete Schabarum single-handedly tried to restrict employee gains. But threats of layoffs after Proposition 13 passed in 1978 limited union demands for raises and benefits.[34]

In December 1980, the new BOS majority began taking steps to implement their program to reduce county expenditures and the power of unions. Shortly after the conservatives took charge, Schabarum stated in his first speech that the new majority would be "intent on breaking the old board's 'alliance with union bosses' and forming a new 'partnership with business.'" Over the decade the three conservatives clashed with unions in changing county provisions dealing with labor, striving to outlaw strikes and other work stoppages, and encouraging and rewarding other county officials in limiting workforce initiatives and reducing the size of government as the Reagan administration pledged at the national level.[35]

County social workers picket a BOS meeting in 1966 during the first strike by county employees (*Los Angeles Times* Photographic Archive [Collection 1429], Library Special Collections, Charles E. Young Research Library, UCLA).

One of the most controversial achievements claimed by the conservative supervisors regarding labor in the 1980s was contracting out county projects to private businesses. Proponents claimed that contracting out saved funds by hiring firms that would be more efficient and competitive when compared to government. In the post–Proposition 13 era, this method was also popular with taxpayers demanding further budget cuts. The program would not be that simple, however, as contractors were profit-driven and limited wages and benefits of their workers; some lowballed their price to win the contract and raised it after they started the project. The replaced county workers had to be retrained for other jobs or laid off, requiring further county assistance. Like most local governments, the Los Angeles County experience in the 1980s and after would be a mixed blessing.[36]

Prior to 1978, the county depended on a few contracts awarded to firms for specific services that could not be performed by its workforce or had to be done in remote locations. In fact, the county was more of a contractor itself as it offered several services such as libraries and health facilities to its cities since the early 1900s, accelerating them after the creation of the Lakewood Plan in 1954. In 1974, the BOS approved Schabarum's motion to place a charter amendment on the ballot to allow for county contracting of cost-effective services beyond the few situations allowed in the charter. He claimed it would save money and affect less than 40 percent of county workers, none of them laid off, which, of course, questioned the savings. Opposed by unions and the *Times*, the measure met defeat. Four years later, he submitted virtually the same proposal, and with Howard Jarvis, fresh from his Proposition 13 victory, the two led the charge in a landslide victory. In the next several years the process experienced problems documented in a County Grand Jury audit noting overstated claims of savings, and that 95 percent of layoffs were Blacks or Latinos, as well as scandals involving mismanagement by social services agencies under contract.[37]

When the conservative majority took over, the program continued to grow, and though it might have been successful in some instances, it would experience many more problems. The conservatives had the votes to approve the contracts, while the two liberals opposed some because of the human costs, especially for low-paid minorities. The 1983–1984 County Grand Jury ordered another audit of the program—by a private contractor—that found problems with assessing the costs resulting in the county paying even more; in a lack of oversight by county management; and other shortcomings. A 1983 California Assembly hearing on contracting out noted criticism of the Los Angeles County program regarding overstated savings and its impact on minority employees. The state's Little Hoover Commission reiterated the exaggerated savings charges three months later. In the meantime, Schabarum and Hahn argued the cases for and against the program leading to changes made by the CAO and a BOS policy of no layoffs to protect minorities and women. Others criticized the work of many contractors as slipshod since their low-paid temporary workers had no loyalty to the county.[38]

In the second half of the 1980s, the board majority assisted by CAO Richard Dixon tried to strengthen the program and BOS control, while the liberals resisted. In late 1986, Schabarum proposed a charter amendment that would remove the requirement for private contracts to be cost effective, which deleted its basic attribute; it finally passed in 1988. The BOS asked the Citizens' Economy and Efficiency Commission to analyze the program in 1987; the final report, criticized for its private sector view of local government efficiency and for lack of evidence, called for more contracting and made a few recommendations. The Los Angeles Taxpayers Association commissioned a study of contracting in the county and city of Los Angeles, and its final report called for more contracting estimated to save the county $300 million and the city $400 million. Union leaders opposed it immediately and spurred a lengthy *Times* article noting that private firms accounted for a small percentage of the overall county budget, that it did not reduce waste, and it hurt workers.[39]

In the meantime, CAO Richard Dixon proposed several measures to enhance management of the program. In March 1987, he informed department heads that they no longer needed to get his approval of contract solicitation documents prior to soliciting bids. This would streamline the process, but also reduce oversight as required by the original ordinance. In 1988, he proudly informed the BOS that the county had saved $147.7 million in contracting out, a figure that would be contested by the county auditor and by unions on several occasions. Dixon also reported that he had completed a study demonstrating that minority- and women-owned businesses could be assured the opportunity for competing for major contracts. That would turn out to be an overstatement in the next several years.[40]

There would also be many studies and examples demonstrating the negative features of the program. The 1986–1987 County Grand Jury commissioned yet another audit of the program by a private firm, resulting in a long list of recommendations to improve lax contract preparation and oversight of services. Several publicized setbacks for the program were also reported. In one 1987 case, a private security firm contract would not be renewed because of "performance deficiencies" and the costs of changing firms would add to the contract. In the 1980s, the county had to defend itself against lawsuits filed by 250 residents after a Malibu landslide destroyed their homes. Short of enough lawyers to handle it, the BOS had to contract with private attorneys, and chose one of the most expensive firms in Los Angeles, costing the county $35 million for the homeowners and several million more for its contracted private lawyers. In the same year, the BOS refused to rescind an $80 million contract with a private firm for its vehicle fleet maintenance after the firm was named in a federal investigation of fraud in a military contract. The conservatives defended the contractor, while Hahn called it "the biggest turkey the county has gotten into." The firm survived the federal investigation, but within months was accused of shoddy work and many long delays affecting county services. In November 1989, the firm asked for an additional $2.8 million for its contract, citing more vehicles to service than originally thought. That would raise the annual price to be much more costly than if county workers would have done it; eventually the county settled on a lower amount.[41]

By the summer of 1989, county unions were lobbying for an investigation to determine whether contracting out was cost effective. Hahn brought it to the BOS in a motion to have the entire program since 1979 examined by the County Grand Jury. A *Times* opinion piece on privatization describing it as a "Blunt Weapon Against

Minorities" appeared at the same time. Three months later, a survey revealed that eighty-one workers in one contracted company did not receive health insurance, and of fifty-four who needed medical attention, forty-one obtained it at a county health facility. Clearly, some of the drawbacks of contracting out, as well as the positive features, were still in evidence as the arguments for and against it moved back and forth. The debate would continue in the 1990s, as Supervisor Gloria Molina led efforts to ensure that minority- and women-owned businesses enjoyed full access to the county's contracting program, and that contractors be required to provide health insurance for their workers. The county continued its contracting program with various shortcomings and successes.[42]

Law and Order

The first major change for the LASD in the 1980s was the retirement of Sheriff Peter Pitchess, who held that office since 1958. In December 1981, he announced his impending departure before his term would end the following year. He recommended that the BOS appoint Undersheriff Sherman Block as acting sheriff; Block could then use that title in the coming June primary. Antonovich suggested the appointment be made right away, but Schabarum, who had been feuding with Pitchess for several years, refused to reveal his position. Anxious to make the appointment but leery of offending the leader of the conservative majority, Antonovich decided to wait for Schabarum to join him in early January. The acting sheriff, a native of Chicago, had been with the department for twenty-six years and undersheriff since 1975.[43]

Over the decade, the LASD continued to enforce the law in unincorporated areas and in many contract cities and cooperated with others. In a major impetus to fight organized crime in the county, the LASD worked with the district attorney, LAPD, and other cities, as well as state and federal agencies such as the FBI and IRS. A 1983 LASD report on organized crime in the county noted that members of "traditional" groups from the east coast and Midwest such as the Mafia still operated various rackets along with local gangs. Gang activity was growing so rapidly by 1988, that Supervisor Hahn asked Governor Deukmejian "to immediately declare a State of Emergency in Los Angeles County" and order the California National Guard "to assist local law enforcement in battling gang violence in the County." Hahn called Los Angeles County the "gang capital of America" and asked Sheriff Block to hold a summit to recommend ways to reduce it and find jobs for gang members. Gangs were also heavily involved in the illegal drug trade that spurred efforts to stop it. Earlier in the decade the supervisors approved additional expenditures for a gang peace project. On the subject of sex crimes in 1986, Schabarum recommended that the offenders be castrated, and chided the media for "going bonkers" with the story.[44]

Attempts to control "morality" activities such as distribution of material considered offensive to some also required law enforcement resources. The County Commission for Women, created in 1975 to work toward equality of the sexes, advocated a ban on sexist videos, which Edelman opposed because of First Amendment considerations. In 1985, the commission drafted an ordinance to restrict pornography. After reviewing it, the county counsel and CAO determined that it would be preempted by state law and unconstitutional as a similar Indianapolis ordinance had been ruled by the U.S. Supreme Court. The county counsel suggested two alternative options, one based on a Los Angeles city ordinance being considered. The County Obscenity and Pornography Commission did not take an official stand on the ordinance, but in a straw vote the result was ten members opposed and two abstentions, with no approvals. Despite these warnings, the supervisors persisted, while representatives of the ACLU and a Feminist Anti-Censorship Taskforce protested BOS approval. In June, the supervisors rejected the restrictive ordinance and voted in favor of two others that were much weaker.[45]

The next step for the Women's Commission would be to see that the two watered-down ordinances passed, which they did in July 1985, and then request that the supervisors appoint a blue-ribbon task force on the subject. While some newspapers still criticized the Women's Commission and the BOS for continuing to advance it, including editorials noting the commissioners condemned motion pictures they had never seen, the BOS approved of the task force proposal in October. The task force presented its recommendations for a stronger ordinance in July 1986, and the County Obscenity and Pornography Commission continued its efforts to do the same after agreeing to comment on a report by a federal commission on pornography headed by Attorney General Meese. Over the next year the commission and task force studied the Meese report and made recommendations, while Roman Catholic Archbishop Roger Mahony led a crusade against X-rated movies and the supervisors agreed to form yet another task force for that particular purpose. The *Times* editorialized that many citizens abhorred pornography, but again warned the supervisors on censorship. And the crusade continued.[46]

Once individuals were arrested for a crime, they became a problem for the county while awaiting trial and if convicted, since the jails were always overcrowded. The Rutherford lawsuit by the ACLU continued to require monitoring of county jails. The Department of Justice (DOJ) inspected the Men's Central Jail in 1985, finding it to be improved, but still overcrowded, violating the civil rights of inmates. That spurred Hahn to request that a $200 million bond for jail construction be prepared for the June 1986 ballot. The DOJ also examined the conditions at the county's juvenile halls, of which one of the inspectors found them to be "the worst I've ever visited in any major metropolitan area in America," despite the county's efforts to improve them. Sheriff Block set some of the blame for jail overcrowding on the courts allowing too many procedures that delayed trials and sentencing. Block's method of reducing overcrowding was releasing prisoners early, a common solution for sheriffs in the nineteenth and early-twentieth centuries, and again in the 2000s. By late 1986, Hahn could report that the county had made great strides in reducing the number of inmates through early release and transferring many to state and other county facilities. More help for the problem was Hahn's successful 1986 bond measure that supplied funds for jail expansion, the price of which grew to $325 million by early 1989. The supervisors had few options, however, at a time that new state requirements raised the prices for all counties. In August, the board approved a $600 million plan

Men's Central Jail inmates bed down in a chapel due to overcrowding in 1987 (Robert Gabriel, photographer, *Los Angeles Times* Photographic Archive [Collection 1429], Library Special Collections, Charles E. Young Research Library, UCLA).

for several jail facilities in the system, including expansion of the downtown Men's Central Jail, opposed by the neighboring Latino and Asian communities.[47]

Within the walls of county jails and outside of them were many complaints of abuse and brutality by sheriff's deputies, although perhaps fewer that in the previous decade. The reports usually involved residents in racial and ethnic minority communities. These included abuse of Japanese Americans in 1984, of a deputy beating a Latino that same year, and of a cover up of LASD abuse of African Americans in

1985. The later 1980s would reveal newspaper stories of an FBI investigation of deputies burning crosses in an area of the men's jail where Blacks were incarcerated (two deputies were dismissed), and a three-year compilation of citizen claims against the LASD for abuse and brutality that cost the county $8.5 million. In 1989, the county was also being sued by citizens in the vicinity of the Lynwood Station in a federal class-action suit documenting brutality and racism on the part of some deputies in a clique called the "Vikings," whose members adopted gang-related expressions in their "tattoos, graffiti-spraying, street jargon, and hand signs." In the same year, the sheriff suspended eighteen deputies under investigation for running a drug theft ring and moved others out of their unit. Sheriff Block would end a year of scandal and thirty-seven LASD shootings deploring the negative features.[48]

Health and Social Services

The struggling national economy in the 1980s, with cuts in federal and state funding after Proposition 13 affected all California counties. In Los Angeles County, the conservative majority responded by reducing funding for rising health and welfare costs for the less fortunate. In 1981, they argued with the liberals on cutting $265 million in funding for general relief recipients. Over the next several years the staff of the Department of Public Social Services (DPSS) was reduced, several of its offices closed, and complicated applications for relief kept some applicants from being able to fill them out. In 1983, the supervisors proposed several new programs to reduce the number of recipients, but the DPSS chief warned that recent court decisions might block them. One was Schabarum's suggestion to force recipients to enlist in the U.S. armed forces. Many would be disqualified for age and physical reasons, and one radio station editorial pointed out that involuntary servitude was a violation of their civil rights. Another idea was workfare, which required recipients to accept jobs to pay for some of their aid. This project failed when the number of those who applied overwhelmed the staff capabilities. A workfare program operating on a private contract would finally be implemented in 1988.[49]

Negative publicity relating to the DPSS handling of relief also cast suspicion on how the county spent tax funds. They included reports of fraud and theft by county workers, and of aid being distributed to a Russian spy recently arrested by the FBI. The DPSS chief was congratulated by a federal official in 1985 for the department's outstanding contribution to national error reduction efforts in the federal AFDC program; by 1989, the DPSS error rate jumped to the second highest in California. An audit in that year revealed that for eighteen months, the county had overpaid some recipients a total of $121 million and shortchanged others $25.4 million.[50]

Additional problems for the DPSS included changing state and federal regulations regarding welfare payments to undocumented residents, which had continued since the 1970s. The conservatives tried to limit any increases and ordered more studies of whether the undocumented cost more than they paid in taxes. Two of the conservatives voted for a small increase in general relief in 1985, but the three avoided any serious additions until forced by a lawsuit and threats of more suits. While the

Demonstrators protesting healthcare budget cuts outside of a Board of Supervisors hearing in 1981 (Fitzgerald Whitney, photographer, *Los Angeles Times* Photographic Archive [Collection 1429], Library Special Collections, Charles E. Young Research Library, UCLA).

supervisors searched for other methods to reduce the costs, Hahn proposed that the state take over all general relief costs since Los Angeles County handled 52.8 percent of those cases but had only 31 percent of the state population. He repeated it with a BOS motion in 1990, when one California county faced bankruptcy.[51]

The difficult economic times and 1980s welfare policies also had a profound impact on homelessness in major urban centers like Los Angeles. President Reagan's tax cuts, state and county budget cuts, and the shortage of affordable housing in Los Angeles County saw the number of homeless increasing both downtown and in the suburbs. Counties and cities slowly responded to the problem, but early in 1982 Dana led a limited effort to create a task force of county officials to find surplus county buildings and food for those living outside and in their vehicles. A County-wide Task Force on the Homeless was created to include representatives of community organizations as well. Hahn championed a board resolution to ask the federal and state governments to improve conditions for the homeless mentally ill. As Hahn noted, their numbers increased through "Greyhound Therapy," whereby communities throughout the nation arrested vagrants and gave them a one-way bus ticket out, especially to Los Angeles. Two court rulings finally forced the county and city to act. The county had to pay more to house them, and the city was enjoined from LAPD sweeps of Skid Row and harassing them.[52]

In early 1985, the County Grand Jury asked the BOS for more help for the homeless. The grand jurors determined the homeless situation to be a disaster that needed emergency help; the *Times* called it a "shameful fumble" on the part of the supervisors. Later, the CAO reported on state and federal assistance and resources to help, and the Countywide Task Force offered twenty-three recommendations for improvements. Hahn wrote to Mayor Bradley suggesting the city and county work together to build homeless shelters. But this entreaty was unsuccessful, as Dana and Antonovich opposed cooperation that might reflect well on Bradley, thought to be getting ready to again oppose their favorite, Governor Deukmejian, in his reelection bid. In October 1985, poverty law firms and the ACLU sued the county over relief grants for the homeless; Edelman and Hahn agreed with the plaintiffs as the BOS continued to disagree on this issue.[53]

Early 1987 saw a bit of progress as Antonovich followed the efforts of Hahn and Edelman to create a joint city-county program to build shelters. But cooperation ended by the summer, when the city sued the county for not paying its "fair share" of homeless aid, and Antonovich threated a counter suit. In 1988, Edelman made another attempt to establish a city-county task force on homelessness, but Dana organized opposition against it. A year later, Edelman again joined forces with Bradley to create a pilot program to link existing programs for the homeless in the Skid Row area. The program, funded with Edelman's and Hahn's district discretionary money and a matching grant from the city, had no support from the three conservatives. The differences between the latter and the city would continue to throttle efforts to help the homeless into the 1990s, when new representatives of the two governments arrived.[54]

Health services fared as bad as welfare in the 1980s, as most supervisors were more apt to protect other county services when budgets were tight. Moderate cuts in aid for mental and physical treatment, hospitals, and health centers in the late 1970s were severe by 1981. In that year, the BOS majority voted to close nine health clinics and several hospital units and end all non-emergency health aid for undocumented residents, a decision blocked by the courts. While the county faced a $75 million cut in health services, Schabarum promoted a $20 million bond measure to finance a comprehensive health center in his district. Just after the board slashed budget funding for services at the Martin Luther King, Jr., Hospital, located in a heavily minority area, and lost $5 million in state funds as legislators protested the 9 percent raises given to county workers, Antonovich received approval for a search to purchase an existing hospital in his district. By the end of the year, the California Supreme Court ordered the reinstatement of 233 laid off health workers, to the consternation of the three conservatives, and the CAO found enough funding to end further layoffs.[55]

The situation did not improve much in the following year. Two state legislators representing Latino districts proposed a bill that would transfer authority over county health services from the supervisors to a Los Angeles County Health Authority administered by five members appointed by state officials. (Fortunately for the supervisors, this bill died in the state senate.) In June, the board majority sought to curtail health costs by approving a pilot program to require poor, uninsured residents to pay a $700 cash deposit for care at the Los Angeles County+USC Hospital if they refused to sign up for Medi-Cal, the program for the poor. (Refusal could lead to deportation of the undocumented.) The board also studied the possibility of privatizing health jobs. In late 1983, Dana and Antonovich supported new and expensive health facilities in their districts after voting for massive healthcare cuts mostly in minority communities. And, not coincidentally, 1984 was an election year for both.[56]

Funding problems for health services in the 1980s and after were exacerbated by the growing AIDS virus, first clinically observed in Los Angeles, New York, and San Francisco in 1981. In the next several years the virus spread rapidly, especially to young gay men, and became an expensive service for centers like Los Angeles County, where treatment of its victims could take a prolonged period of hospital care and some care givers were unwilling to care for fear of infection. By 1985, over 900 cases had been reported in the county, over half of them resulting in death. The virus also spread to minority communities, as well as to drug users sharing infected needles. Local government response was slow, as the major result was the Los Angeles City/County AIDS Task Force created by Mayor Bradley and Supervisor Edelman in 1984. Edelman's district included heavily gay West Hollywood, and he took the lead in organizing hearings by the task force to plan a strategy, to unify private agencies such as the Gay and Lesbian Services Center in support and educational efforts and raise funding for more county health services for victims.[57]

Edelman and Bradley planned these efforts in the first year of the task force. But the county's effort was limited in relation to the enormity of the problem, so much so that an AIDS Advisory Committee appointed by the state legislature voted to give the Los Angeles share of funding for AIDS public education to private groups rather than the County Department of Health Services. The decision followed and would be followed by actions of supervisors who demonstrated an aversion to protecting gays and drug users. Antonovich, Dana and Hahn ordered the withdrawal of a pamphlet for junkies on how to avoid AIDS financed by city and county funds. Schabarum attacked a "privately funded, sexually explicit AIDS prevention pamphlet" for gays as "hard-core pornographic trash," and then, by a 4–1 vote, won a review of $1 million in county contracts with gay organizations that put the funding in jeopardy. The *Times* criticized Schabarum, while the chair of the city-county task force pointed out the "squeamishness of elected officials, especially in Los Angeles," and refuted the claim that the county had spent a large amount on AIDS education. In October, Schabarum proposed closing gay bathhouses as had been done in New York City, and the BOS voted 4–1 to approve an ordinance for it. In November, Antonovich recommended that gays should become heterosexual in their "own best interest" as a solution to the epidemic. Clearly, four of the supervisors had personal difficulties in dealing with this critical issue.[58]

In 1986, U.S. Surgeon General Everett Koop called for more educational efforts to combat AIDS. The supervisors responded with funding to support a pilot program initiated by gays to pursue safe sex practices. In the following year, the BOS also formed a new AIDS Commission to replace the informal city-county task force. But some county officials would continue to oppose the efforts. Several members of the County Obscenity and Pornography Commission raised an uproar in a meeting regarding a gay educational brochure with graphic language that upset a few members. At about the same time, Antonovich and Schabarum blocked the county's acceptance of a $20 million federal grant for AIDS education for minorities after the ACLU sued the county over lack of such support. In 1989, two county commissions complained to the BOS that AIDS funds had been spent too slowly and services were disproportionately concentrated in White rather than minority communities. In that year and 1990, AIDS activists in groups such as ACT UP/LA would increase their protests in disrupting BOS meetings; after one of them, Schabarum claimed that "the average person does not care about AIDS funding," and he received many calls and letters about it. The supervisors did increase funding to some extent, but not enough to stem the virus. In March 1991, *Times* reporter Bill Boyarsky opined that it was up to the new liberal BOS to make a difference in a disease that had taken 7,787 lives in the county since 1981.[59]

A major change in county social services in the 1980s was the creation of an improved system for taking care of children, although it faced numerous problems in its implementation. In the early years of the decade there were increasing instances of child abuse in Los Angeles County; the 1982–1983 County Grand Jury reported that the DPSS Child Abuse unit could not keep up with them and asked the BOS for help. After a five-part television news series reviewed some of the problems, Supervisor Edelman followed that advice in acquiring BOS approval for more funding for the unit and more BOS involvement in improving it. Edelman also proposed establishing a single county department combining the Adoptions Department with children's units in the DPSS and Probation Department.[60]

In September 1983, the issue exploded when reports of children at the McMartin Preschool in the South Bay might have been molested by its staff, leading to the arrests of seven teachers and administrators and bizarre stories related by the children to interviewers. The founder of the school and the son of the administrator were eventually tried before a jury that deadlocked in 1990, and the son was tried again with the same result. In the meantime, the case received national attention focusing on the inconsistent stories of the children and the methods of the interviewers leading them. "McMartin mania," as one falsely accused mother called it, was prevalent throughout the nation, as several other schools became scenes of similar witch hunts.[61]

In the early months of "McMartin mania" Edelman presented his idea for a Department of Children's Services to the BOS. With further lobbying of his colleagues, along with television appearances and letters to community activists, he pushed it through in April 1984, with only Schabarum's no vote. After this victory, the organization of the department began with resistance from the DPSS fearing a cut in state funding. Despite many hurdles, Edelman and his staff had the department going by December.[62]

While the department originated with the best of intentions, it would suffer over the next decades from internal, external, and county-induced problems that limited success. In 1985, the first director quickly fell out of favor with some members of the commission that oversaw her department by barring them from making unannounced visits to inspect facilities, her lack of recruitment and training, and delays in licensing foster homes. There were also complaints from representatives of non-profit agencies, her insults regarding Edelman and his staff behind their backs, and interviews with her staff based on her direction of the department. After six months on the job, the BOS announced her "separation from County service effective immediately." At the same time Schabarum and one of his deputies reportedly tried to get rid of Edelman's appointee to the commission to appease the director before her release. By the end of the year, a new director for the department took over.[63]

Rather than getting better after the above events, the department faced more obstacles. In 1989, the *Herald Examiner* printed a seven-part "Throwaway Children" series describing the plight of children who died while in county custody, resulting in a hearing in the state legislature. Reports of abuse were so common that legislators considered taking over the department. In 1990, the union representing the department's social workers hoped to have the director replaced, and a story appeared that a department supervisor was being investigated for child molestation. Antonovich called for a reorganization of the department and replacement of this director and his top lieutenants. CAO Dixon took over as acting director and a major overhaul began. The reforms were lauded by some critics, but further problems would develop that would reveal critical shortcomings in the 2010s.[64]

So, the "Solid Three" supervisors could be ideologically united in many issues in the 1980s, but the bloc was not as solid as some observers believed. Especially late in the decade, they turned on each other more often than earlier. They did accomplish some of their objectives such as contracting out services to private enterprise but could not reduce the size of the county budget and the workforce or the number of its services; state and federal mandates demanded more, even though additional funding would not always be available.

9

Development Unchained

Residential and business developments in the unincorporated areas declined somewhat in the 1970s with the national recession and court rejection of Los Angeles County's General Plan limiting project approvals. With final acceptance of the General Plan in 1980, the county's Regional Planning Commission made up for lost time with its pro-developer agenda. Most of the new development took place in the north and west areas of the county, some of it passed against the advice of the department staff because of environmental concerns. But development was a private initiative issue for the three conservative supervisors, who received generous campaign contributions from interested developers. Although they faced opposition from environmental groups, the slow-growth movement, and residents who moved to incorporate their communities to thwart unlimited sprawl, a considerable number of residential subdivisions were approved. Increased development also brought more pollution in the air, waterways, and the coastline, as well as conflicts with cities over locations for landfills and toxic dumpsites.

The "Solid Three" conservative supervisors in the 1980s were much more pro-growth and development than their two liberal colleagues, although the latter were not anti-growth. Their districts were much more urbanized than the other three, so they had to accommodate apartment and commercial builders more than suburban subdividers. The effort to please developers was evident in such cases as delaying incorporations of new cities so that the developers could have the county approve their projects that neighbors opposed and influencing county planners to appease the builders. Deane Dana and Pete Schabarum even admitted that the county's task is to "assist individuals in the use of their land," rather than to protect the public's interest.[1]

Evidence of the appreciation of developers for their three favorite supervisors appeared in a long article in the *L.A. Weekly* newspaper in 1985. Based on county and state planning and campaign contribution records, the authors found that between 1980 and 1985, the three conservatives received almost $860,500 from the top twenty developers, while the two liberals received about $66,500. Schabarum, the leader of the "Solid Three" and an old pro at both football and organizing such contributions, received a good portion of the funds, as did Michael Antonovich, whose district was the site for the much of it. Dana, who represented a swath of the coastline, received the largest share, as he provided the necessary third vote for projects elsewhere. Both Dana and Antonovich would relax some of their defense of developments in election years when district residents protested the projects. Schabarum never seemed to mind, since his campaign treasury assured easy victories.[2]

The BOS was aided in its efforts by the Regional Planning Commission (RPC), consisting mostly of developers, realtors, and others associated with development. The RPC had always been considered pro-development, and its members were occasionally accused of conflict of interest. Most members in the early 1980s were also associated with development and sympathetic to the supervisors who appointed them; one even proudly admitted his pro-development prejudice. In fact, the *L.A. Weekly* study reported that the RPC approved 90 percent of all projects it considered; of the 10 percent it rejected, the BOS approved 90 percent of them on appeal.[3]

The Regional Planning Department also played a role in land use based on development, although limited by reduced funding in the 1980s. The agency had been made a department to put it under the control of the BOS, rather than the RPC, so supervisors could exert influence to please favored developers. Dana had a geologist removed from a project when the applicant, one of Dana's major contributors, complained that his conclusions did not favor the project. A planner who had raised questions about shady projects in the City of Industry and then pointed out problems with a heliport license was fired and then reinstated by the Civil Service Commission. When the department director with a reputation for following directives of the conservative supervisors strayed from that path, he was replaced with a new director who heard from Schabarum's RPC appointee that he was going to "be working for Pete." He also heard that Schabarum received planning information much faster than other supervisors. With BOS interference and staff losses during the budget-cutting 1980s, it was no wonder that department morale was low, and some projects might not be carefully scrutinized.[4]

Another player in the development process was the Local Agency Formation Commission (LAFCO) for Los Angeles County. Created in 1963, the commission's five members included two county supervisors. Before 1986, it was thought to be under the control of Schabarum and other supervisors, but by then its membership grew to seven, with two supervisors, three city officials, and two non-government members. It also came under scrutiny by newspapers and reformers who demanded changes in its powers and its process of issuing denials of cityhood to please Schabarum and developers.[5]

Resistance to this status quo would bring changes in the second half of the decade. Regional agencies continued to operate and in many cases affected development projects in the county: the Southern California Association of Governments issued several major planning documents that could influence the size and shape of projects; the South Coast Air Quality Management District and the California Air Resources Board issued directives to reduce increasing air pollution from more subdivisions and industrial structures; the California Coastal Commission limited development along the coast; and other state and regional agencies were responsible for other facets of the changes to the landscape, air, and water. The slow-growth movement of the late 1980s saw an increase in protests against excessive development as the movement's leaders, environmental groups, state lawmakers, city officials, and residents fought to limit growth. This was particularly noticeable in

Antonovich's Fifth District, where many of his voters living in cities protested when development in adjacent open areas threatened to impinge on their settings and lifestyle. Courts became even busier in these years with lawsuits and other legal matters relating to continuing development. As the *Times* editorialized in 1998, "county planning" was considered an oxymoron in such major undertakings, especially for massive projects.[6]

Incorporation as a Response to Development

The 1980s were years of tremendous residential development in the areas under county control. Unincorporated communities responded to the resulting environmental changes by organizing cityhood movements so that they could make land use decisions on their own, usually to keep growth to a sustainable limit. Incorporation activity was particularly strong in the Fifth District, the site of plenty of open land. On the western extreme bordering Ventura County, a master plan community of the 1960s straddled the county line, its northern portion added to Thousand Oaks when it became a city in 1964. The Los Angeles County portion grew as an affluent community opposed to major change and incorporated as Westlake Village in 1981. In the same year, the adjacent community of Agoura Hills tried to incorporate with Calabasas but was disallowed as infeasible. In the following year, however, Agoura Hills cityhood campaigners made it the county's eighty-third city in November 1982.[7]

Another incorporation in the Fifth District began in the Santa Clarita area which had failed twice to form a new county in the 1970s. After the second defeat, community leaders decided to create a new city to block further attempts by the BOS to allow unrestrained development. Progress lagged, but the campaign picked up in 1986, when a group of dissidents started a recall drive against Supervisor Antonovich, citing his approval of too much dense development and heavy grading of the hills. In 1987, cityhood proponents submitted their petitions, and during the LAFCO hearing a number of developers and their lobbyists asked for their properties to be left out of the proposed city limits; LAFCO accommodated them by deleting about 50 percent of the proposed property. By then, Schabarum entered the controversy by trying to delay LAFCO approval to save the county over $4 million in services for the new city. He was also accused by state Senator Ed Davis of helping the developers who opposed it, rather than remaining neutral as a member of LAFCO, especially since this was not even in his district. But Hahn, Antonovich, and Edelman voted to set the election. On November 2, the residents of Newhall, Saugus, Valencia, Canyon Country, and parts in between voted for cityhood, established two weeks later.[8]

Back to Calabasas: The 1981 proposal to incorporate with Agoura Hills was not acceptable, so community leaders of Calabasas proposed incorporation in 1987. As with Santa Clarita, Sen. Davis informed Supervisor Edelman that Schabarum favored developers in this instance and should be removed from LAFCO. In this "Davis-Schabarum feud" the senator claimed Schabarum inflated the price of incorporation while Davis had already introduced a bill in the state legislature to help balance the proposed city's budget so that it could be approved by LAFCO. Also, like Santa Clarita, developers wanted their properties left out of the new city and persisted in lobbying LAFCO. Schabarum continued to block progress as cityhood backers sued LAFCO for denying approval. After further negotiations with the county and developers, the cityhood advocates agreed to a compromise, and incorporation became effective in 1991.[9]

The road to cityhood took even longer for the coastal community of Malibu, located along the Pacific Ocean and into the hillsides in District 4. The impetus for incorporation was avoiding the expensive construction of a sewer system and the massive development that would follow it. In 1960, Supervisor Burton Chace tried to replace the many septic tanks in the area with a county sewer system paid for by residents in a sewer district which could result in approval of a slew of proposed residential subdivisions. The residents fought several bond measures to finance the sewer in which major developers contributed heavily to the bond campaign; all of them failed by large numbers.[10]

After Chace's death in 1972, and during the moratorium on development in the later 1970s, the county backed off on the sewer issue. With Deane Dana's takeover of the Fourth District the impetus to help developers returned. By 1985, county engineers planned a massive sewer system that would accommodate tremendous development, paid for by present residents. County officials argued that it was necessary because septic tanks leaked sewage into the ocean, posing a health risk, and had already resulted in a serious landslide. At almost the same time as the announcement of the project, the county plan for Malibu that would include 11,000 new dwellings was rejected by the California Coastal Commission. In the following year Assemblyman Tom Hayden and state Senator Gary K. Hart joined the fray in aiding the opposition as most supervisors tried to delay cityhood advocates until the sewer issue could be resolved. Schabarum was again active in another supervisor's district, and CAO Dixon warned the supervisors that the county could be liable for further land slippage if the sewer was not built. Compromises approved by the supervisors were offered to reduce the cost of the sewer to almost half, but the opposition remained adamant as the cost rose because of county mistakes.[11]

The situation changed in 1989, when the Coastal Commission denied the county's alternate plan for the sewer system. The BOS then delayed action on setting a date for the cityhood election until after the Coastal Commission reviewed the sewer proposal again, and the supervisors twice ignored a judge's ruling to set the date. In the June election, incorporation passed by a wide margin, so the supervisors delayed the date of incorporation until the sewer could be started. When the Coastal Commission denied the county appeal, the official incorporation date became March 28, 1991. Conflict between the BOS and Malibu leaders continued in several issues, but eventually were settled, and after a state mandate to reduce pollution into the ocean, Malibu finally began building a sewer system for its civic center in 2015.[12]

On the county's eastern fringe, Diamond Bar also incorporated to stop rapid development after two decades of Supervisors Bonelli and Schabarum favoring developers. Originally established in the 1960s as a master-planned community by one of Bonelli's major contributors, the property was sold to several developers in the 1970s. The master plan was soon discarded, and residential subdivisions followed. Schabarum monitored its progress after that, working with an advisory council to placate residents and developers and opposing attempts at incorporation to keep it under county control. By the late 1980s, dissidents organized a cityhood campaign to limit rampant development and related traffic problems; it was finally successful in 1989.[13]

The incorporation of West Hollywood in 1984 reflected previous county development rather than involving new structures in an open landscape. It was spearheaded by gays demanding civil rights and elderly residents wanting to retain rent control in a district containing many apartments. Cityhood advocates raised funds for a preliminary study, and LAFCO finally approved it in May 1984. With support of the supervisors for an election set in November, landlords who had opposed it suddenly pressured the BOS to extend the rent control ordinance as a means of removing that issue during the election. The three conservatives, all ideologically opposed to the principle of rent control, approved the extension; it made no difference as the cityhood measure passed. Three weeks later the city council chose a gay mayor, and passed an ordinance banning discrimination against gays, and a law that rolled back rents.[14]

Several attempts of other communities to incorporate failed for various reasons. Residents of another coastal community, Marina del Rey, was denied since the county owned most of the proposed city. Unincorporated East Los Angeles tried several times but could not generate enough revenue to support it. In the eastern portion of the county, Hacienda Heights proponents considered incorporation three times, but failed to win enough votes.[15]

Development Outside the Cities

The 1980s also saw many conflicts with developments in unincorporated areas that did not become cities (besides those mentioned above), especially in the Santa Monica Mountains. In the prior decade much of the area became a national recreation area protected by the federal government, although large swaths were still privately owned. In 1979, the Santa Monica Mountains Conservancy (SMMC) was created as a state agency to purchase available land in Los Angeles and Ventura counties to prevent development in the mountains and add to the park for recreation. The SMMC received funding from federal, state, and local governments, and its success always depended on the fluctuation of that support.[16]

At the start of the federal government's land acquisition program and creation of the SMMC, local Congressman Anthony Beilenson asked Los Angeles County officials to establish a moratorium on subdivision approvals and building permits to prevent additional development that would drive up land prices. The Regional Planning Commissioners were leery of its legality or flat out against it, and a sympathetic Supervisor Edelman admitted that he would not have the support of his BOS colleagues. Those views would not change after the conservative majority took over and reviewed the proposed county growth plan for Malibu–Santa Monica Mountains in late 1981. After hearings in which property owners and environmentalists presented their cases, a decision had to be made quickly since an emergency ordinance controlling development would expire, and the planning chief predicted the BOS could expect a "deluge" of requests from developers. Rather than accept the plan, the three conservatives voted to approve an interim plan that reduced the projected population and included changes recommended by Antonovich and Dana, who represented the two affected districts.[17]

The Malibu–Santa Monica Mountains Area Plan was revised in early 1982, followed by RPC hearings. The new version was developer-oriented, giving more weight to property owners than protection of the environment. The plan would increase housing densities and weaken restrictions on properties that already had access to water and sewer lines. Opponents saw too many possibilities of using the document for piecemeal zoning in the future. In anticipation of the BOS decision in December, several groups in Malibu and the mountains joined forces as the Santa Monica Mountains and Coastal Alliance to defend both areas from overdevelopment. This alliance would be countered by the established Concerned Citizens for Property Rights Inc., which claimed to represent small property owners aligned with the three conservative supervisors. Led by those three, the BOS approved the plan with a few modifications for the Malibu area and little change for the mountains.[18]

The BOS decision preceded a lawsuit filed by the Monte Nido Valley Property Owners Association against the county for allowing major development in the Santa Monica Mountains based on the density in the plan allowing too much urban expansion. It was followed by a BOS request to Interior Secretary James Watt asking for federal funding for new land purchases in the Santa Monica Mountains. Watts's response indicated a lack of funds in the budget "as the need to curtail excessive Federal spending continues to be of paramount importance." With that denial, the supervisors continued to allow a significant amount of development in the Santa Monicas over the next decade.[19]

In approving developments in the Santa Monica Mountains and elsewhere, the county sacrificed important natural resources that in most cases could not be replaced. Chief among them were native oak trees and other flora and fauna. The destruction of native oak trees became a major issue in the San Fernando Valley and Santa Monica Mountains by the late 1970s, so much so that the BOS approved an emergency ordinance in 1979 limiting it in unincorporated areas. After two years of study, a permanent ordinance was adopted, a compromise between developers and environmentalists that limited removal of oaks larger than eight inches in diameter. The ordinance was made permanent in 1982, but lacked enforcement, as the County RPC approved proposals such as a site near Newhall that would allow the destruction of 336 oaks in 1986, and so many others involving hundreds of native oaks that Edelman's appointee to the commission advised that a stronger ordinance was necessary. The ordinance was strengthened in 1986, but the destruction continued, such as the removal of more than 1000 trees for a site in pre-cityhood Calabasas in 1991, with many more oaks destroyed to make way for landfills and subdivisions in the 1990s.[20]

The research for a new County General Plan in the late 1970s included a 1976 study by expert scientists that identified sixty-one Significant Ecological Areas (SEAs) that should be protected as much as possible from incompatible development. The chosen SEAs ranged from "austere desert buttes and ancient oak savannas to deep canyons, coastal dunes, and wetlands ... selected for their value as habitat and migration corridors for wildlife, or as strongholds for threatened plants, birds and other animals." In addition, a Significant Ecological Area Technical Advisory Committee (SEATAC) was formed to review projects impinging on SEAs and advise county planners on how they would be affected.[21]

In 1990, two articles in the *Times* challenged the county's treatment of SEAs. They concluded that SEAs had been "nibbled by development" and were increasingly under pressure from more of it, that county planners did not keep track of them and treated them inconsistently, that the BOS majority was more concerned with appeasing developers, and that conflicts of interest on the part of SEATAC members limited its effectiveness. The planning department director responded that the articles gave incomplete or misleading impressions implying that the county neglected SEAs, and that the SEATAC conflicts of interest resulted in only one meeting cancelation. Budget restraints limited monitoring and county acquisition of the land, he noted, and some projects interpreted as concessions to developers were actually compromises to protect the resources. In addition, only thirty-eight of the SEAs were in unincorporated areas, with twenty-three of them in cities where the county had no jurisdiction.[22]

Some of the information in both the articles and the response were a bit exaggerated and surprising, since the author of the articles spent time with the department planners in doing his research. Some of the county-monitored SEAs did see approved reductions of the resources, and at least one major development in an SEA area where many native oak trees would be removed had already been approved by the RPC. Edelman requested that a study be done soon to effectively protect the SEAs and joined a supervisor in adjacent Ventura County to promote his idea in both counties. Edelman's plan included a full-time biologist to monitor the SEAs and developer fees to help fund it. The RPC would not go as far as Edelman recommended, but a new BOS majority was more inclined to accept it. In 1992, the SEATAC asked the commission and the BOS to adopt a new policy to require developers who degraded an SEA to acquire and preserve a replacement site. These changes would not end further controversies regarding SEAs, but they certainly slowed down the process of allowing such destruction to take place.[23]

More Development, More Air Pollution

Increased development brought more people, so more vehicles, more barbeques, more industrial smoke, and a continuation of unhealthful, eye-burning smog. In all California counties, two agencies were tasked with reducing major sources of it. In Los Angeles County, the California State Air Resources Board (CARB) was responsible for motor vehicle exhausts since the 1960s, and for overall state standards; the South Coast Air Quality Management District (SCAQMD) controlled stationary sources. The Southern California Association of Governments (SCAG) also played a role in its regional planning research and reports, especially related to transportation.

In the latter half of the 1970s, CARB was headed by Chairman Tom Quinn, a politically active administrator who engaged in several controversies with agencies in Southern California. Described as an aggressive leader, he soon stepped on the toes of regional officials in requiring steel plants and oil companies to reduce pollution. In his criticism of the SCAQMD he accused it of lax enforcement and called for a grand jury investigation. Quinn's "press releases and off-the-cuff barbs designed to sting" embarrassed industry leaders and local smog officials until he was replaced in 1979.[24]

As mentioned in Chapter 2, by 1977 the smog agency in Los Angeles County was the SCAQMD. The Los Angeles County supervisors were not happy about the creation of this agency. Hahn claimed that all regional agencies had been failures and this one would require Los Angeles County to pay 73 percent of the agency budget. Ward thought the proper agency for this task was CARB, which could enforce it on a state-wide basis. In fact, the supervisors decided to exit SCAQMD and refused to fund it. That move did not set well with the state attorney general and environmental groups threatening to sue the county. The attorney general did sue the county, and the California Supreme Court ordered the supervisors to pay up.[25]

The SCAQMD had a rocky beginning. City and public members of the board of directors opposed funding from sources such as the motor vehicle tax partially distributed to cities and supported property tax sources that would be paid by counties. The County Grand Jury, which had already criticized the former county agency for lax enforcement, pointed out that Supervisors Schabarum and Hayes, who served on the board in 1978, rarely attended any of its meetings. Also in that year, the SCAQMD and SCAG completed the first draft of a master plan for the next five years to reduce air pollution in the district based on a list of 125 tactics. The plan circulated to major polluters and state and local officials, among many others, one of whom panned it as another attempt to "restructure the lifestyle of California citizens." The CARB staff criticized it by recommending even stronger controls, to the point that SCAG directors "vehemently" opposed it, fearing it would usurp too much of "local government's role." The CARB review prodded even Schabarum to support the less restrictive SCAQMD plan finally approved after a compromise was reached by CARB, SCAG, and SCAQMD.[26]

On one of the issues raised by the anti-smog agencies in response to federal Environmental Protection Agency (EPA) demands, Hahn took the lead in opposing the requirement for annual inspections of automobile emissions and possible repairs. In 1979, he fought against a law requiring annual smog inspections, arguing that the law would hurt disadvantaged drivers who could not afford the inspection. He took a stance directly opposite of his liberal colleague, Ed Edelman, who became a leader of the forces supporting the law to reduce smog and avoid EPA reductions in federal funding. The reluctant state legislature eventually passed it after the EPA announced the withholding of highway and sewage treatment funds for six urban areas in California. But Hahn did not give up, as he called for the repeal of the "116 million a year rip-off." He even forwarded to Edelman a letter from one of his constituents, a widow and senior citizen dependent on Social Security who just had her twenty-four-year-old Ford repaired and couldn't afford the $50 smog inspection fee, but it didn't change Edelman's stand on reducing smog and avoiding a cutoff of federal funding.[27]

In the early 1980s, the supervisors were involved in other issues related to air pollution and the agencies responsible for cleaning it up. Territorial disputes between CARB and SCAQMD were notable, and state legislators searched for ways to restructure the latter to improve relations. Conflicts among SCAQMD directors also became a problem. Two supervisors sought the help of President Reagan, in motions approved by the BOS; Antonovich asked him to prohibit the EPA "from adopting an extreme interpretation" of the Clean Air Act, and Dana requested the president to continue the county's share of 1983 Federal Highway funding while the county moved forward to comply with Clean Air standards. These years revealed a lot of activity, but few positive results.[28]

On a more positive note, in 1982 Hahn issued a statement based on reports that Prince Philip of Great Britain had been warned that Los Angeles was too smoggy for horse-riding endurance events scheduled for the coming 1984 Olympic Games and recommended moving them to San Diego County. "If the smog is too bad for the horses, what about the athletes?" Hahn asked. Although he would never be appointed as a director of SCAQMD, he asked its officials to work with other agencies to create contingency plans for reducing smog during the Olympics. In the month before the games, after nineteen straight days of smog alerts, he called an emergency summit of business leaders of some 4000 firms to cut air pollution beyond CARB standards. Most had already begun implementing their own plans; when combined with temporary programs of the city of Los Angeles, SCAQMD, and other agencies, the air was much better than usual and a model for further smog reduction.[29]

The later 1980s saw even more criticism of SCAQMD. An EPA and CARB audit released in February 1987, found a few problems that needed to be addressed, but overall improvement since 1981. A week later a Congressional hearing in Los Angeles was highly critical, as Congressman Henry A. Waxman, who based his statements on the audit, charged that the SCAQMD "had lost control" and "undermined the federal program designed to prevent new industrial pollution sources from worsening air quality in Southern California." Critics such as the *Times* still complained that much more needed to be done. Another newspaper in May reported results of a study that included evaluations of the agency's top fourteen directors which gave nine of them a failing grade on votes for various clean air measures.[30]

The criticism in early 1987 led to changes embodied in a state law approved later in the year despite opposition from the California Chamber of Commerce and various business associations, the building and trucking industries, and the majorities of county supervisors of Los Angeles, Orange, Riverside and San Bernardino. The law would grant more enforcement power to SCAQMD to create new transportation and stationary source programs and to prohibit past directors or staff members from representing businesses seeking contracts for five years after they left the agency. The law also reduced the number of directors from fourteen to eleven, all of whom would be appointed or reappointed with the intention of removing those considered to be "lethargic." That would include one of the supervisors from Los Angeles County, and Antonovich was selected by his colleagues to represent Los Angeles County. Committed to protecting the interests of businesses and residents while considering anti-pollution measures, he would begin his long tenure on the board by vowing that "progress cannot be made at the expense of industry."[31]

Water Supply and Pollution

The increasing need for water supply and distribution in Los Angeles County during the 1980s was generally handled by water districts and municipal agencies such as the Los Angeles Department of Water and Power (LADWP) by obtaining it from the state system, by water wholesalers such as the Metropolitan Water District of Southern California, and through local groundwater sources. The county supervisors were directors of several small waterworks districts and concerned with making sure that enough water was available, and that water pollution was cleaned up to protect public health. Since the region is prone to periods of heavy rains and drought, the BOS has been involved in flood control efforts since the 1880s, and in ensuring a necessary supply of water since the early 1900s. Flood control is the responsibility of a county special district governed by the supervisors and has been funded heavily by the federal government.[32]

Since 1950, the supervisors supported the major California initiatives to make more water available, including the 1960s State Water Project and California Aqueduct bringing water from the north, and the Peripheral Canal project, approved in 1980, but repealed two years later. While Arizona planned to take its share of Colorado River water that Southern California had been receiving, Supervisor Hahn initiated a campaign to replace the water that would no longer be available by 1985. In 1981, he resurrected his idea based on a study in 1963 (begun after several drought years) to build a pipeline from the Columbia and Snake Rivers in the Northwest to Los Angeles by way of Lake Mead on the Colorado River. Much of the water in these rivers flowed to the Pacific Ocean and was considered a waste by Hahn and others who had little understanding of its importance and volume. Hahn wrote to Department of the Interior Secretary James Watt and the local Chamber of Commerce and convinced the other supervisors to join him in trying to drum up support for the project, while also campaigning against the repeal of the Peripheral Canal project. He failed in both efforts.[33]

The later 1980s were dry years, when interest in water supply resurfaced. The 1988–1989 County Grand Jury sponsored a study of city and county water reclamation during the drought and found little being done. The report appeared at the same time as Congressman Esteban Torres's call for an investigation of the EPA cleanup of the San Gabriel Groundwater Basin, where sixty wells had been shut down because of contamination. In June 1990, Supervisor Edelman spearheaded the creation of a Los Angeles County Water Advisory Commission to make recommendations involving water supply. In that same year the *Times* reported that Ventura County supervisors were contemplating a suggestion to tow an iceberg from Antarctica to increase the water supply during the current drought.[34]

The latter idea coincided with Hahn's revival of his quest for river water from the Northwest. In May 1990, he sent letters to many government officials in Washington, Oregon, and four other states, as well as to California legislators and newspapers, describing his project and asking for support. The *Times* called it impractical. Response in the Northwest was more extreme, as some officials interpreted it as Hahn implying it was their duty to supply Los Angeles with water. A Washington state senator replied that "THERE IS NO EXCESS WATER IN THE COLUMBIA RIVER!" He also suggested rationing the "water going into all those swimming pools," and informed Hahn that Seattle also rationed water and it was needed for salmon spawning in the river. A Northwest journalist thought it would be a good idea to send water to California if that would keep Californians from moving up to the Northwest. And an Idaho official replied that it would happen "only over my dead body." Clearly the idea was not received well, and since a federal law required six states to approve such a transfer, it was not going to happen. In the 1990s, the County Grand Jury would frequently study water supply solutions as dry years disappeared and returned.[35]

The county was also concerned with pollution of fresh water in rivers and streams, partially caused by increased residential and industrial development. A larger problem was pollution of salt water in the Santa Monica Bay fed by toxic waste over decades. The crisis surfaced in early 1985, when a television program and newspapers reported scientific results of investigations revealing the levels of DDT and PCB dumped into the bay and off Santa Catalina Island over the last fifty years. The news became an immediate scare, particularly since fisherman devoured fish that had consumed DDT, a toxic substance that had been banned years earlier. Assembly member Tom Hayden began an investigation to determine how state and local agencies, including the State Department of Health Services, which was reported to have known about it for twelve years, the Los Angeles Water Quality Control Board, and county sanitation districts neglected the conditions, and why county health officials failed to inspect the area to gauge the health risks. Hayden pressed county officials to respond quickly, especially in warning fishermen of the dangers.[36]

Cleaning up the toxic material would be a time-consuming process for the EPA, the state, and the county, all of which had a role. Hayden introduced several bills in the legislature as a state response, and the EPA went after some of the major polluters to pay for the process. In 1990, the county approved a $12 million settlement with the federal and state government for the sanitation districts allowing tons of toxic waste to be dumped since the late 1940s. The cleanup was not completely over, as more DDT was found by scientists in the San Pedro Bay and off the Palos Verdes Peninsula in 1991 as it was stirred up. In the early 1990s, the County Department of Health Services (DHS) monitored the bay for health risks related to the dumping, sewage spills and storm runoff pollution.[37]

In the year the toxic waste problem appeared, another environmental threat attacked the Santa Monica Bay. In mid–1985, a lawsuit by an environmental group against the city of Los Angeles for dumping partially treated sewage with toxic chemicals into the Santa Monica Bay was about to end. As it turned out, the city had been avoiding the full treatment required by the federal Clean Water Act since its passage in 1972. Combined with the news of the toxic waste dumped there by industries approved by the county and state agencies, the threat to health became more severe. In July, Assembly member Hayden reported city raw sewage overflows at Ballona Creek entering the ocean, and he asked county and state agencies to investigate. City sanitation engineers had already begun planning improvements, while a state water agency started to issue fines for the overflows and a few more spillages occurred. By the end of the year, the city had a program to repair the entire system and begin full treatment of sewage. It only took a court order, embarrassment, and a $625,000 fine for violating the federal Clean Water Act to move the project along.[38]

While the city began repairing its system, the supervisors requested state hearings on the overflows, which Schabarum blamed on Mayor Bradley, at the time running for governor against Schabarum's Republican ally, incumbent George Deukmejian. But federal officials blamed the spills on both the city and county, which did not fully treat its sewage and pumped it through old pipes into the bay in violation of federal standards. In 1988, Hayden accused the county of dragging its feet on hazardous waste cleanup as the county sanitation district requested its third waiver in nine years to delay full treatment of its sewage. He noted that at the 1986 hearings, Dana testified it was obvious that the city was responsible for the sewage mess; two years later, after the city had surpassed the county in sewage treatment, county leadership was the problem in delaying the cleanup. In 1989, the County Public Works director continued to monitor the upgrade of the city's Hyperion system, as he had been instructed by Dana in 1987, and he reported that the most recent overflow of raw sewage was caused by a power failure at a county pumping plant.[39]

Waste: Solid and Hazardous

The 1980s witnessed the continuation of the 1970s county and Los Angeles city feud regarding the siting of solid waste dumps which would affect land, air, and water in the county, especially as residential development escalated. (See Chapter 2.) In 1981, Supervisor Schabarum threatened to close all county landfills to the city if the latter did not allow county waste to be dumped in Mission Canyon on land owned by the county, which needed a city permit for dumping. With the county's Palos Verdes dump full and closing in 1981, and Mission Canyon closed by the city in early 1982, the situation turned into a waste crisis. Extending the life of the Puente Hills landfill exclusively for county waste would help, while the supervisors looked into creating a county-wide sanitation authority to survey possible dumpsites.[40]

In 1985, the state entered the controversy as Governor Deukmejian vetoed the city's proposal to circumvent disposal planning and the California Waste Management Board demanded that the county complete its long-stalled waste management plan. The supervisor majority held out for permission to use three county-owned canyons in the city for solid waste disposal and refused to approve the plan until the city surrendered. The city and county then resorted to negotiating over the use of the canyons. Schabarum would try to expedite it by requesting that the plan for the Spadra waste-to-energy plant in his district be shelved until each area of the county handled its own waste, as he estimated that landfills in his district received 60 percent of the county's trash. In September 1987, he would conjure the image of the current New York City garbage barge bound for an ocean dump in ridiculing a Los Angeles city investigation of shipping its garbage to Guatemala. Shortly thereafter, Mayor Bradley complained to the County Grand Jury that the county was not leading the way in its solid waste responsibilities, while Edelman tried to forge a compromise. The city then put pressure on the county by informing the supervisors of it terminating the county's license to provide access to the Scholl Canyon landfill in Glendale.[41]

Nineteen eighty-eight would finally see a break in the feud after release of the county's Solid Waste Management Action Plan, which described the crisis. Dana and Antonovich, both amid reelection campaigns, joined Edelman in compromising with the city. The three agreed to a plan for a new site for a county-city landfill in Elsmere Canyon. In the following year the county examined ten proposals for shipping some of its waste by rail to remote desert areas of Southern California and Arizona, although only one site would eventually be necessary. In addition, passage of the state's Integrated Waste Management Act of 1989 promised to reduce the need for landfill by mandating a recycling program for many materials. Some disagreements between supervisors and Mayor Bradley and the city council persisted in the early 1990s, but progress continued as the city and county compromised and the waste crisis finally ended.[42]

Another issue for county sanitation officials was how to treat and where to store hazardous waste. The problem ranged from the leakage of gases from closed or closing landfills and private industrial facilities, preventing toxic waste from poisoning underground drinking water sources and sewers, and convincing residents to allow such facilities in their vicinity, to illegal dumping of waste in non-approved areas. The 1980–1981 County Grand Jury made a special note in their final report to point out the problems of dealing with hazardous waste and reminded the supervisors that it was their responsibility to plan to resolve the growing problem.[43]

This decade of hazardous waste treatment began before the 1980 election in which Supervisor Baxter Ward was deposed. In August he heard on a television news broadcast that residents in the vicinity of the Capri Pumping Service east of downtown Los Angeles were at risk of health hazards. Ward took the director of the County DHS to the site the following morning to inspect it; state and county investigations commenced. Soil samples of nearby homes exhibited high levels of toxic penetration, and the unsafe storage of toxic industrial waste on the site resulted in a notice of abatement. It was then revealed that one Los Angeles city agency had been trying to shut down the facility for two years, while another allowed it to continue operation on the basis that this minority-owned business employed residents of the surrounding area. The county health investigation indicated that mitigation measures needed to be taken immediately, but the owner delayed action. By late 1980, the city took responsibility for cleaning the adjacent properties. The project was not completed until August 1982, after the state spent $250,000 removing cyanide and the owner finally removed all hazardous waste and storage materials.[44]

In 1980, the County DHS also investigated a solid waste and hazardous landfill leaking gasses in Monterey Park. The department ordered the owner to devise a system for controlling methane and vinyl chloride gas migration implemented in the next two years. It was not effective enough to prevent further protests from city residents and a second lawsuit filed by the neighboring city of Montebello in 1983. Within one year the landfill was closed, and still belching gas, its toxic liquid waste trucked to a site in Kern County. One EPA official predicted that it would "soon qualify as a federal superfund site." It did, as the EPA took over cleanup partially funded by companies that had contributed to the problem over many years.[45]

In 1981, the issue became more explosive when a toxic dump site already being cleaned up as a federal "superfund" project in Santa Fe Springs erupted into explosions and fires. Located in an industrial area with nearby oil and other flammable substances, as well as residential properties beyond, the sounds could be heard all the way to Seal Beach; over 2000 people had to be evacuated. The county asked the federal government to provide money for a quicker cleanup, and the EPA responded with funding and supervision of the project while the property owner and the lessee who stored chemicals there sued each other over which one would pay for some of the liability. Eventually, the paint company that owned the chemicals took responsibility for the rest of the cleanup.[46]

By 1983, seven other hazardous dumpsites in the county had been identified by the EPA, and the supervisors directed the DHS to report on health problems there every month and for the district attorney to take whatever legal action was necessary to clean them up. State officials then scheduled the seven for cleanup. In the following year methane gas detected at the BKK landfill in West Covina led to the permanent shutdown of the only remaining toxic waste treatment facility in the county, forcing its hazardous waste to be taken to the dump in Kern County. Meanwhile, SCAG proposed the creation of a Southern California Waste Management Authority composed of seven counties and the cities of Los Angeles and San Diego. Membership was voluntary, and not all invitees would participate. Ever the mavericks in joining regional agencies if not mandated, the Los Angeles County supervisors decided to go their own way.[47]

In late 1989, the *Los Angeles Times* published a special report on the state of the Southern California environment. The report contained segments with the views of experts and short essays evaluating the air, ground water, coastline, ocean, wildlife, resources, waste, health, and energy components of the landscape, waterscape, air, and other features that described the plight of the counties in the region. As the report began: "Southern California mirrors the nation's environmental problems, and the future holds both peril and promise." The 1990s would be the "Decade of Decision—a time when Southern Californians must choose between reclaiming the best of nature or squandering what remains." The quotes aptly describe the situation in Los Angeles County as well, as the 1980s took a toll on the environment with massive residential and industrial development covering the landscape, loss of flora and fauna, and continued pollution of the air and water. Demands on the environment increased and resources dwindled, but to be sure, many residents still believed that the situation could change for the better in the 1990s.[48]

10

"Fiefdoms Under Fire"

Redistricting is a game in which territories containing people with certain political proclivities and ethnic identifications are arranged to benefit one interest or another.—J. Morgan Kousser, *Colorblind Injustice*

The three-year period of "Fiefdoms Under Fire"[1] (1988–1991) saw a legal assault on the Board of Supervisors to counter the board's redistricting methods in the past that restricted the election of minority candidates. The lawsuit by the federal Department of Justice (DOJ), the American Civil Liberties Union (ACLU), and the Mexican American Legal Defense and Education Fund (MALDEF) was one of many Voting Rights Act struggles in the United States, including an earlier contest in the city of Los Angeles and later cases in various cities throughout Los Angeles County. As court actions in the 1988–1991 contest played out, calls for a larger BOS, as well as an elected executive, were proposed, but initially rejected. In this redistricting case the issue revolved around who is represented, as well as how many voters should be represented by a single supervisor.

One of the most important accomplishments of the civil rights movement in the 1960s was the Voting Rights Act of 1965. This legislation emerged after suppression of African American voting had been prevalent for a century, and protests were being met with violence in the states of the old Confederacy. President Lyndon Johnson pressed for a law that would put an end to discriminatory methods of preventing citizens from registering to vote and then voting, and to back it with federal enforcement. A divided Congress finally passed the Voting Rights Act, and Johnson signed it in August 1965. Over the next several decades, amendments were added to address diluting the voting strength of minorities by gerrymandering political districts and favoring majority groups with at-large elections, rather by districts. The law has been the basis for hundreds of legal actions in states, counties, and cities initiated by the federal government and minority groups, sometimes successful, sometimes not. It is still invoked in voting cases throughout the nation, as well as in recent contests in Los Angeles County cities that retained the at-large voting process.[2]

It is not coincidental that the California Senate was reapportioned at the same time to guarantee the "one man, one vote" principle that formed the basis for voting rights in the 1960s. Before 1965, the Golden State's legislature followed the federal plan which included a lower house based on population and a smaller upper house based on the number of its units, in this case counties. This meant that Los Angeles County, with over six million residents, had only one state senator, while three rural counties in northern California with a total of just over 14,000 residents shared one senator. For years political leaders in urban areas complained of this inequality, and in the early 1960s, Assemblyman (and future Los Angeles County supervisor) Frank Bonelli and others led an unsuccessful fight in the legislature and in state initiatives. After a 1964 U.S. Supreme Court ruling that both houses must be based on population, Governor Edmund G. Brown, Sr., and the legislature approved a law to change the composition of the state senate in 1965, the same year the Voting Rights Act passed. Almost suddenly, Los Angeles County included the home districts of fourteen of the forty state senators.[3]

Voting Dilution in the City of Angels

Since passage of the Voting Rights Act, the Department of Justice has prosecuted hundreds of cases accusing cities and counties of restricting voting by minority groups. Many of these entities are in the Deep South, although some, like New York and Chicago in the 1980s, could be found in the northern and western states. One of the latter, the city of Los Angeles, was named in a federal lawsuit in late 1985. At that time, the Reagan administration's DOJ faced criticism for working to dismantle federal protections against discrimination, DOJ officials determined that Los Angeles officeholders had discriminated against Latinos in revising city council districts in 1982 based on the 1980 census. Mayor Tom Bradley, the city clerk, and thirteen city council members were accused of violating the Voting Rights Act and producing a plan that retained virtually the same district boundaries as the Latino portion of the city population rose to 27 percent by 1980. Not a single Latino was elected to the city council in the 1985 primary and general elections (one had served from 1949 to 1962, and a few Latinos had been on the council before 1885). The DOJ was prodded to file the lawsuit by Latino political figures, particularly California Assemblyman Richard Alatorre, who chaired the elections and reapportionment committee. A 1983 report of the California Advisory Committee to the U.S. Civil Rights Commission that criticized the city redistricting plan provided documentation for the allegations.[4]

The timing of the November 1985 lawsuit was interesting, since Art Snyder, the city councilman of the Latino-majority Fourteenth District, resigned that year and would be replaced by Alatorre, who won the election two weeks after the lawsuit was filed. In addition, the DOJ lawsuit was interpreted by many, including Latinos, as a Reagan administration tactic to embarrass Los Angeles city Democrats, primarily Mayor Tom Bradley, then believed to be planning to run for California governor in the next year as he had in 1982. Further, Alatorre was chosen to head the council committee to review the district boundaries, possibly to approve of them for his new colleagues, who would eventually decide not to fight the suit after the city initially opposed it. Latino legal experts hoped to join in the lawsuit, since they did not trust the city or the Reagan DOJ. In March 1986, the local chapter of the NAACP announced that it would also join the lawsuit as its members feared the downtown district of an African American council member would be transferred to Alatorre in the process. Clearly there was much confusion regarding the legal and political jockeying at the time.[5]

In defense of the city's position on the matter, David Cunningham, an African American council member, argued that the city was not "anti–Latino" in contesting the lawsuit. In a *Times* editorial page response to an earlier editorial, he asserted that "people of this city do not vote because of a candidate's ethnicity; they vote *regardless* of it." He asked, "How else do you explain a four-term Black mayor in a city with less than 20 percent of the Black population?" He also noted the repeated election of Art Snyder in a district that was about 70 percent Latino, and the elections of several other council members of various ethnicities in districts in which they were in the minority.[6]

Instead of fighting the suit, the city council unanimously agreed to create new district boundaries to settle it. Alatorre devised boundaries that penalized several of his colleagues, but appeased others; the council approved it in July. Mayor Bradley vetoed it, however, as it might hurt the only Asian member of the council who happened to be Bradley's ally in the gubernatorial election year. As the result of a compromise, Bradley signed a revised plan and the issue bounced back to the court and then to opposition from the council over the election schedule. A revised plan that might create an additional Latino seat in the San Fernando Valley after the incumbent died was met with heavy protest and the veto of Bradley, which was quickly overridden. The final plan was accepted by a federal judge, and the DOJ lawsuit dismissed. As a result, in 1987, Assemblywoman Gloria Molina became the first Latina ever elected to the city council in a district that was modified in the redistricting process.[7]

Redistricting in Los Angeles County

The 1913 Los Angeles County charter allowed county supervisors to change the boundaries of their districts at *almost any time;* since the 1960s, California counties have been required to reapportion their districts to equalize population after every federal decennial census. As historian J. Morgan Kousser has written, in the 1950s and 1960s, the supervisors modified their district boundaries in 1953, 1955, 1959, 1963, and 1965 based on population estimates. The 1953 redistricting, the first since 1935, was aimed to result in a population of about 500,000 in each of the five districts. In 1959, recently elected supervisor Ernest Debs orchestrated a trade to obtain some affluent territory in Burton Chace's district, a transaction Kenneth Hahn claimed was done in "a cloak and dagger style" that did not equalize the five districts. (There was speculation that Debs did so to obtain more White voters to counter the popularity of his past and future rival Edward Roybal in the East Los Angeles portion of Debs' district.) The 1963 redistricting followed a different pattern. After over a year of secret discussions, no one was allowed to see the map or report on the proposed boundary revisions, or to speak for or against them at the public meeting. The approval process took only five minutes to keep "all five members happy" by avoiding protests of "property owners, the county's seventy-four cities or civic groups."

Gloria Molina (center) celebrates her election to the Los Angeles City Council following a redistricting court case in 1987. By the end of this chapter, she will be a Los Angeles County supervisor elected in 1991 after a county redistricting case (Patrick Downs, photographer, *Los Angeles Times* Photographic Archive [Collection 1429], Library Special Collections, Charles E. Young Research Library, UCLA).

Redistricting was accomplished in 1965, following a California Supreme Court decision ordering Santa Clara County to better equalize its population or voter registration. In this instance, there was still a degree of secrecy and more transfers of population between districts as Debs acquired more White voters in the San Fernando Valley and a few in other areas.[8]

The 1971 redistricting procedure was the first to be mandated in the year after a federal census. In this case the entire process appeared to be more transparent to appease critics such as the League of Women Voters and newspaper editors, as well as possible government agency scrutiny. However, the supervisors and their appointees still controlled the entire proceedings. Territory had to be moved from the heavily populated First and Fifth Districts to the more central Second, Third and Fourth; the Third District of Supervisor Debs moved further into the San Fernando Valley. Five years later the supervisors acted on another Voting Rights Act issue when they voted 3–2 to file suit against the federal government to challenge the validity of the 1975 amendments that mandated multilingual ballots to recover the costs of producing them. In contrast to their redistricting successes, this effort failed.[9]

In 1981, the supervisors initiated another redistricting effort based on the 1980 census. Again, they set out to protect their fiefdoms after a change in the ideological composition of the board. The three Republicans worked to retain their conservative and partisan majority and force a liberal Democrat to be eventually replaced by a liberal member of the rising Latino minority. This would be the first redistricting of the county in which minority groups played an important role.

The process started with each supervisor appointing a member of the district boundary committee charged with submitting maps of possible district composition. Unsurprisingly, the supervisors chose individuals who would protect their interests—three former chief deputies, a local politician, and a state Republican Party strategist. This group of four males and one female, all of them White, stood out as antithetical to the changing state and federal criteria in drawing district lines. Following the protests of Latino groups, five more members were added—all members of a minority, three of them former supervisor deputies. At the same time the BOS created a fund for minority groups to pay for the use of the computer system of the Rose Institute at the Claremont Colleges in drawing the lines that might increase minority influence.[10]

One group that took advantage of the computer fund, the Californios for Fair Representation, sought to increase the political power of Latinos as they comprised 28 percent of the county population by 1980. At the end of July 1981, the group submitted a map aimed to concentrate the Latino population in two districts to eventually elect Latino supervisors in both. The plan would divide the San Fernando Valley into three supervisorial districts, as well as moving some of the more affluent areas out of Edelman's Third District, which included heavily Latino East Los Angeles. The result would raise the Latino population in the Third District to 50 percent, and in Schabarum's First District to 42 percent. This plan was endorsed by leaders of the Black community but considered much too radical for all five supervisors and their representatives, who virtually ignored it. In fact, members of the Californios for Fair Representation later claimed that they were almost shut out of the process after that. They could not document what transpired in boundary committee meetings because audio tapes of the meetings were unavailable—the county tape recorder broke down during the first meeting and was never replaced.[11]

In the meantime, Republican strategists submitted several maps that would limit the Latino population within Schabarum's district and locate 50.2 percent of it in Edelman's. The change would also put some pockets of Democratic strength in Republican districts into the liberal Second and Third districts. This would include moving heavily Black Compton to Hahn's district because Deane Dana wanted to be rid of it; that city voted almost 96 percent for Yvonne Burke in 1980. By late August, a Republican plan opposed by the Californios for Fair Representation that included these and other changes was recommended by the boundary committee for BOS approval. Since the proposal required the votes of four of the five supervisors, there was little chance that the two liberals, who had the most to lose, would support it. As the state-mandated deadline for approving any plan approached, the conservatives felt pressure to compromise to keep the decision from being made by a committee composed of the liberal district attorney, liberal assessor, and Sheriff Pitchess, then feuding with Schabarum. When the supervisors returned from their vacations in September, they had to face a demonstration at one of their meetings orchestrated by the Californios for Fair Representation and behind-the-scenes arguments with colleagues and staff. On the final day of the deadline, the supervisors disappeared from their meeting in pairs to bargain and alter district lines to avoid violating the Brown Act, which prohibited secret deliberations of a majority. By the end of the day, a new plan was unanimously approved with few residents affected by the boundary changes. As Schabarum observed, "If you like the old boundaries, you're going to love these."[12]

Supervisors Edelman and Hahn declared victory over the Republican majority after redistricting was completed; a leader of the Californios for Fair Representation took solace in not losing any influence in Schabarum's district. But in the end, this episode would be just one more effort by the supervisors to protect their jobs and ideology. Minority groups were used by both sides to advance supervisorial objectives or reject political attacks. The 1981 conflict did not change the supervisors' views on the Voting Rights Act of 1965 itself, which had been amended to include consideration of minority communities in redistricting. In 1982, the board voted unanimously to urge the U.S. Senate to extend the act for another twenty-five years. A few years later, some of the supervisors would probably regret that vote.[13]

Garza v. Los Angeles County Board of Supervisors

The next time the Los Angeles County supervisors faced a redistricting challenge came sooner than they planned. Following the successful 1985–1986 suit against the city of Los Angeles, MALDEF lawyers focused their continuing redistricting efforts on the county, where they believed gerrymandering to limit Latino influence to be even more egregious. MALDEF and other groups convinced DOJ administrators to initiate an investigation, and in February 1988, DOJ officials informed the county that they would begin the probe of the 1981 redistricting process. The DOJ then notified the county in May that it planned to file a suit based on the Voting Rights Act, charging that the county discriminated against Latinos by spreading them throughout several districts to dilute their influence. A month later the county counsel and CAO met with DOJ officials to negotiate a settlement. The DOJ presented a map indicating that a Latino majority supervisorial district could be formed and granted the county additional time to explore the possibility of creating such a district.[14]

While some county officials tried to form a Latino district, the supervisors expressed other responses to the possible federal lawsuit. Schabarum charged that the lawsuit was "racist" in favoring one group, and he was no doubt disappointed that the Reagan administration, to which he thought he was politically allied, had initiated it. (Some observers believed that Republicans filed the suit to gain the support of Latinos in the coming presidential election for George H.W. Bush.) Schabarum also accused Hahn and even Dana of conspiring to create boundaries that would not favor him. Antonovich claimed that it was "un–American" for any group to seek racially oriented representation and compared one possible solution to it to the current sectarian strife in Beirut, Lebanon. As a *Daily News* editorial noted, it might be "contrary to the American ideal of equality before the law—to make reapportionment decisions based on race." However, the supervisors "didn't act very color-blind when they took such pains in 1981 to prevent the Latino community from becoming a significant force in supervisorial elections. Having played the racial redistricting game themselves, they have no right to complain when they are caught at it."[15]

Hahn responded by resurrecting his idea of expanding the board of supervisors to seven, with at least one seat planned for Latinos. Although expansion had been defeated many times in the past, major newspapers joined in supporting it for completion after the 1990 census. (Some also included the addition of an elected county executive at the same time.) But the three conservatives on the board argued that it would be too costly and add a larger and unneeded bureaucracy. Edelman voted for expansion to seven, as he always had, and Dana indicated he might favor adding two districts to end the lawsuit. The need for board expansion to settle the lawsuit would reappear in editorials over the next two years; it was introduced as a state constitutional amendment in 1989, this time for nine members, but would not be carried to fruition.[16]

While the supervisors debated actions they could initiate, the DOJ demanded progress in July, giving the county ten days to produce a new district map. When that period expired, MALDEF, supported by a coalition of Latino groups, filed a class action complaint for violation of voting rights in the U.S. District Court and asked the DOJ to file its suit. At the same time, the local chapter of the ACLU filed a similar suit. Lawyers for both MALDEF and the ACLU feared that the DOJ would not act because of pressure from the conservative BOS majority with close ties to Reagan administration. Apparently, the latter relationship was not that close, as the DOJ filed suit two weeks later. All three suits were eventually joined.[17]

The county response to the DOJ suit was the same as its response to MALDEF and the ACLU. County lawyers argued that a district containing 50 percent or more Latino voters could not be created because of the large numbers of undocumented adults and people under the voting age. Schabarum also pointed out that claims in the suits that there had never been a Latino elected to the board of supervisors were false because his grandmother was "a full-blooded Mexican." (Beyond that stretch, he was correct, since seventeen Mexican Americans served as a supervisor from 1852 to 1876.) County officials also studied the maps provided by the plaintiffs and concluded that such a majority Latino district could not be formed. DOJ officials contended that such a district could be formed, and the lawsuit could be amicably settled. Newspaper editorials advised such a settlement, as opposed to a long court case that would be an expensive waste of taxpayer money. But Mayor Tom Bradley and other elected officials continued to support the suit. The conservative majority on the board decided to fight this "nuisance suit," as Antonovich called it, and the county's fees paid to hired lawyers began to take a toll.[18]

Over the next year the lawyers for both sides conducted well over 100 depositions from those associated with the 1981 redistricting effort. It seemed more than a coincidence that all five supervisors and their top deputies had trouble recalling the details of their actions and could be of little help. County staff members had better memories, as one of them recalled that the supervisors met in groups of only two (three at one time would constitute a quorum and violate a state secrecy law) on the day of the approval; all five supervisors could not recall these get-togethers. Letters found as part of the discovery process included one in 1981 from Dana to Schabarum and Antonovich advising the hiring of an expert on redistricting who would protect them in case a Latino district had to be formed. Although U.S. District Judge David V. Kenyon originally set a trial date of August 8, the sheer volume of the depositions and provision of hundreds of thousands of county documents delayed research, moving the new trial date to January 2, 1990.[19]

Toward the end of 1989, a rift appeared in the conservative majority that could lead to a settlement. In October, the DOJ presented a map which would create a Latino district in the Third District and force Edelman into Dana's domain (supervisors were required to reside in their district). A month later the supervisors replied with a map that would carve a Latino district from the First and Third Districts, assuming the absent Schabarum might not run for reelection in 1990. MALDEF then offered a new map that would make Schabarum's district 70 percent Latino with 47 percent of them registered voters. The supervisors countered in mid–December by approving Dana's plan that was similar to MALDEF's in making Schabarum's district heavily Latino. The 3–2 vote, with Dana joining the liberals, signaled a split among the conservatives. Schabarum was livid, informing the media, "So much for that conservative majority you folks are always talking about," and threatening to contact GOP leaders throughout the state to be aware of Dana's treason. The threats apparently worked; Dana's independence quickly vanished as Schabarum fought back. When MALDEF rejected Dana's plan and left its own, endorsed by the DOJ and ACLU, on the table, Dana backed down and Schabarum led the 3–2 vote to oppose it. Talks between the opposing sides broke down and Schabarum asked a federal official to protect his interests in the case "as a Hispanic individual" by making him an intervenor in the event of "political assault" by the plaintiffs or his colleagues on the BOS that might reduce his chances in a future election.[20]

The redistricting trial lasted over three months. County officials and their staff members, redistricting experts, historians, and others were questioned based on their depositions regarding the 1981 redistricting process, and many of the former continued to exhibit "selective amnesia" regarding the events of that year. The county's hired lawyer tried to make the case that a majority Latino district could not have been created in 1981 because there were not enough registered Latinos of voting age to form a cohesive district; that many Latino residents did not have U.S. citizenship; that Latinos were not a monolithic community as they came from a number of countries in Latin America; and that they were spread throughout the county, rather than in one area, as was more prevalent with minorities in the Deep South. The lawyers for the plaintiffs were confident of their presentation that the supervisors conspired to save their fiefdoms, and several attempts at a settlement were made. In one of them, MALDEF raised the possibility of the judge expanding the board to nine members as a solution, but the judge questioned his own authority to add new supervisors. In two instances the supervisors were asked to settle, once by several Latino political leaders backed by a large group of supporters. They reminded the board that Schabarum might not be running for reelection and a compromise seemed to be in order. But Schabarum sluffed off the Latino appearance as a media event, while Antonovich admitted that the issue was not about Latino voting but about ideological control of the BOS. Ideology and resistance to change demanded that a compromise would not be accepted by the three conservatives, while the liberals still hoped for a settlement.[21]

After thirty-eight days of testimony and five days of closing arguments, the trial ended on April 10. On June 4, Kenyon announced his ruling in favor of the plaintiffs. The BOS redistricting in 1981 continued to fragment the Latino population, he decided, but it was not because of racism on the part of the supervisors. "They acted primarily with the objective of protecting and preserving the incumbencies of the five Supervisors or their political allies." (In other words, it would save their jobs and the ideological status of the present board.) With that, the supervisors had to design a new redistricting plan to help a Latino win a seat on the board. Kenyon also recommended that the supervisors consider expanding the board to avoid further discrimination. Hahn proclaimed that he would immediately offer a motion before the supervisors to expand the board to seven for the November election. Schabarum observed that he still believed that district boundaries "should not be based on ethnic factors." Antonovich described the ruling as a "joy ride of judicial activism." The disappointed conservatives voted 3–0 to appeal the ruling. Yolanda Garza, an East Los Angeles chemical engineer, MALDEF activist, and lead plaintiff of the lawsuit, was especially satisfied with the outcome as she responded: "For my family, for my community, for my own self-worth I wanted to do something." "Now I can go back and tell my community that it made a difference."[22]

Since Schabarum did not run for reelection, it was believed that the supervisors would allow his district to be modified to become the Latino district Judge Kenyon required. But with Schabarum still on the board, it was possible that the three conservatives could carve the Latino district from Edelman's territory as they attempted to do in 1981. This would prove to be the case as the conservatives, who were given a deadline by Kenyon, created a map that would make Edelman's district 74 percent Latino. The conservatives had already rejected the maps submitted by MALDEF and the ACLU as plans "written by liberal zealots looking to turn the Board of Supervisors into a rubberstamp for their philosophy" as Antonovich described one of them. The new map the conservatives delivered to Kenyon at his deadline favored their own districts. A *Times* editorial labeled the process an "Outrageous Back-Room Deal" in which the new Latino district with absurd boundaries would still contain Edelman, "a popular, well-financed incumbent" who would be "difficult for any challenger to unseat." In addition, the conservatives voted secretly to immediately pay a law firm $500,000 to represent a "third-party citizen" to appeal the Kenyon ruling all the way to the U.S. Supreme Court if necessary. Schabarum designated himself as that "third-party citizen," and if the agreement posed a conflict of interest for the law firm, the money would go directly to Schabarum to hire the lawyer of his choice. The *Times* suggested that those who carried out this "cynical, secretive, ruthlessly self-interested raid on public funds" should be recalled from office.[23]

The county plan also alarmed African American leaders who found it discriminatory as it lumped affluent Beverly Hills in the same district as Hollywood and the

Black community of Watts. Hahn charged it would reduce Black influence in his district, and both he and Edelman decided to hire private counsel to defend themselves. After further consideration, Kenyon ruled the county plan to be "nonsensical" and approved a new map by MALDEF and the ACLU. This one located a 71 percent majority of Latinos in Schabarum's First District, 51 percent of them registered voters. It also changed the district from 50 percent Democratic to 66.5 percent, and only 23.3 percent Republican, which must have raised Schabarum's hackles. In addition, Beverly Hills and Hollywood would remain in Edelman's Third District.[24]

At this point the *Garza* case began to move through the appeals process. The U.S. Ninth Circuit Court of Appeals initially ordered a stay of the redistricting implementation several days after Kenyon's decision. The ruling pleased the conservative supervisors who had pursued the appeal, but not for long. In early November, the appeals court upheld Kenyon's ruling, although one of the three judges questioned the use of an entire population within a district as opposed to the number of registered voters as the measure of minority voting strength, a feature that the county lawyers had questioned during the trial. As this issue had been prominent in other voting rights cases, the judge thought it violated the "one man, one vote" concept attached to the Voting Rights Act of 1965 amendments. However, the other two judges, like Judge Kenyon, saw no conflict with this measurement. In January 1991, the U.S. Supreme Court rejected the county's final appeal without comment. "Well, the Board of Supervisors today ran out of courts," observed one of the lawyers for the plaintiffs.[25]

The long county redistricting process had finally ended, and it was time to begin the next decennial census redistricting required by state law. This one would be different in that there were new characters involved and more possibilities of additional supervisorial districts to consider. In addition, the county would be required to obtain a DOJ preclearance of any proposed changes in the voting process for supervisors over the next eleven years to avoid features not approved in the *Garza* decision. But the next election would not be as complex as the last since there would be no court case to complicate it. And the county would not have to pay almost $13 million in lawyer fees again as it did in the *Garza* case.[26]

Garza and the 1990 and 1991 County Elections

The 1990 redistricting decision had a profound effect on the Los Angeles County election that year and the next. In December 1988, Schabarum revealed in an interview that he might not run for reelection in 1990. Having just been informed that he would not be appointed Secretary of Transportation by President George H.W. Bush, he acknowledged weariness after seventeen years on the BOS and said he would think about it and "see how the mop flops" on the possibility of retiring. With the redistricting suit already in full gear and his bailiwick being considered as the potential Latino majority district, the admission of this possibility would affect political strategies regarding the 1990 election by both sides of the redistricting issue. Throughout the next year Schabarum let the mop flop and said nothing more about retiring, even as one of his conservative colleagues recommended that his First District become the Latino district.[27]

As the filing deadline for candidacy for the 1990 election approached early that year, Schabarum delayed his decision until almost the last minute. This occasion was welcomed by potential Latino candidates, but they would have little time to decide on whether to run in the district that had yet to be modified. It also infuriated Antonovich, who complained that the surprise announcement left little time for possible Republican candidates to decide. Within five days ten candidates filed to run. They included Sarah Flores, Schabarum's deputy for many years, whom he snubbed for Superior Court Judge Gregory O'Brien; former Congressman Jim Lloyd; and a few local city officials, among others. Three of the group were Latinos and three others African Americans. Antonovich and Dana made their final break with Schabarum as they supported Flores, a conservative Republican, as did Sheriff Block.[28]

With the primary only a few months away, the campaign started immediately with Schabarum funneling some of his past political contributions to O'Brien, and Antonovich and Dana contributing to the Flores effort. O'Brien was accused of hiring questionable consultants by the major San Gabriel Valley newspaper, which endorsed Jim Lloyd, the former Democrat turned Republican. The *Times* endorsed Flores and Ed Edelman, who did not bother to conduct a campaign and would win easily again.[29]

The campaign in the First District received a shock after Judge Kenyon delivered his ruling in the redistricting suit just one day before the June 5 primary. Kenyon's decision left the candidates uncertain as to whether they lived within the boundaries of what would become the modified district. The *Garza* plaintiffs even asked the judge to throw out the next day's election.

The contest proceeded, however, and Flores won with about 35 percent of the vote. The turnout, a record low, might have been partially due to the uncertainty of the legality of the First District contest. The results were touted by conservatives who said that a Latino could win an election in that district without having to change it as the court demanded. It should be noted, however, that the three Latinos in the contest received a total of less than 40 percent of the vote, while the other contestants garnered a majority of 60 percent.[30]

Despite protests by the victorious Sarah Flores, on the same day that Judge Kenyon accepted the new MALDEF/ACLU map of the First District, he voided the primary results and ordered a November primary for this district using the new map. This map moved the homes of Flores and second-place candidate O'Brien to the Fifth District, but Kenyon waived the residency rule in case his decision might be appealed. (If the rule stood and either of the two won the election, they would be required to move into it.) Flores would run again in the primary that was eventually pushed back to January 1991, but O'Brien dropped out long before then.[31]

Antonovich and Dana continued to support Flores in large part to increase the chances that the *Garza* decision would be overturned on appeal based on her June victory. Antonovich even suggested that she be appointed by Governor Deukmejian to replace Schabarum when his term ended in December so she could be considered the incumbent in the primary. Schabarum had other ideas, however, as he moved out of his home and into a condominium located in the new First District. That would allow him to legally remain in office since his term was extended until a successor could take office in the following year. Antonovich then asked the governor to investigate Schabarum's residency, but the governor's office referred that decision to the federal court as it related to the redistricting case. Schabarum would remain a supervisor until the end of February 1991.[32]

Kenyon's August ruling spurred activity among Latino community leaders to find a consensus candidate among the several who had already expressed interest. The leading contenders, Democrats all, included U.S. Representatives Edward Roybal and Esteban Torres, and Los Angeles City Council members Richard Alatorre and Gloria Molina. In November, the prospective candidates began to announce their candidacy to run against Flores. The first one, Gloria Molina, won her Los Angeles City Council seat in 1987, after the city's settlement of its own redistricting case. State Senator Art Torres joined the race days later, Rep. Matthew Martinez followed the next day (and dropped out early), and state Senator Charles Calderon announced a few days after. In addition, several other candidates filed to run, including some who were in the June primary, and—of all people—Pete Schabarum, who did not actually run a campaign. With only ten weeks until the primary, the candidates had to work quickly. Molina gained the support of Edward Roybal and Esteban Torres, both of whom decided not to run, and the Mexican American Political Association, while Art Torres received the endorsement of Mayor Tom Bradley, Supervisor Hahn, SEIU Local 660, and the Sierra Club. Supervisors Dana and Antonovich endorsed Flores again, and Edelman and Schabarum remained neutral.[33]

Gloria Molina and Art Torres finished first and second in the primary and moved on to the general election. Flores came in third with 21 percent of the vote and would soon become a deputy for Antonovich as she then lived in his district. She endorsed Torres, as did Calderon, who finished fourth. The *Times* endorsed Molina, believed to be the candidate who could change things. In the brief period to the general election, both Molina and Torres appeared as similar liberal Democrats, and this campaign, like the primary, was a personal contest rather than one based on the issues. In the end, Molina defeated Torres with 55 percent of the vote, and became the first woman *elected* to the Los Angeles County Board of Supervisors since its creation in 1852 and the first Latino/a elected in the twentieth century. To be sure, without the Voting Rights Act of 1965 and the *Garza* decision, it is doubtful that these major changes would have occurred in the year they did.[34]

11

Another Change
in Leadership

The 1991 special election following the *Garza* decision placed Gloria Molina on the Board of Supervisors and changed its composition to three liberals and two conservatives. The change could be noticeable at times in the 1990s, but not always. Molina was fiercely independent, while Kenneth Hahn and Ed Edelman retired in 1992 and 1994. Three other supervisors joined or re-joined the board in the decade to keep the liberals in the majority. But there would not be a major difference in overall budgeting as the national recession and other limitations precluded expansion of county services. In 1995, fears of bankruptcy loomed amid massive cuts planned for health services until a federal bailout saved the day. Riots in the streets of Los Angeles erupted again in 1992, revealing the lack of attention to inequality since the 1965 uprising. Amid these problems and many more, the county's position improved by the end of the century.

As noted in Chapter 1, Los Angeles County became a major West Coast defense center during World War II with the infusion of federal funds to establish military installations and contracts to arms manufacturers. After the war, manufacturing plants also produced consumer durable goods aimed at markets near and distant; the metropolitan area soon ranked first in industrial production in the nation.[1]

Over the next several decades the regional economy would change as a national recession, global competition, and banking and petroleum crises, among other factors, combined to reduce the number of industrial firms in the county and manufacturing employment. With the end of the Cold War, a reduction in federal defense spending in the early 1990s eliminated jobs in military support and aerospace, the county's chief industry. Funding the county depended on for decades was reduced, and it forced reliance on conversions of old installations and on other industries. In this national and local economic predicament, county officials had to meet their responsibilities in the 1990s and into the early 2000s.[2]

The Board of Supervisors

The 1990s saw a major turnover in the BOS as Michael Antonovich was the only supervisor to serve the entire decade. With the retirements of Pete Schabarum, Kenneth Hahn, Edmund Edelman, and Deane Dana, three new supervisors and the return of one former supervisor would change the ideological composition of the board. Personalities and other issues, however, could be more important factors in many decisions made in these years.

The first newcomer, Gloria Molina, won the 1991 special election to replace Schabarum in the First District. Molina was a Los Angeles native, a teacher, and a political activist involved in social welfare agencies and served in the U.S. Department of Health and Human Services. In 1982, she won election to the California Assembly, and five years later would be elected to the Los Angeles City Council. She served as a supervisor until reaching the end of her term limit in 2014.[3]

Kenneth Hahn announced his retirement in early 1992, and African American politicians in the Second District began campaigns to succeed him. The victor would be Yvonne Braithwaite Burke, who served on the BOS in 1979–1980. After her defeat in 1980, Burke returned to her law practice and participation in the activities of various local, state, and national organizations. These included the Regents of the University of California, and as chair of the Los Angeles Federal Reserve Bank. In 1992, she ran for office again; her victory that year marked the beginning of her second term that would last until her retirement in 2008.[4]

Ed Edelman retired from his Third District seat in 1994, and it would be occupied by another Westsider, Zev Yaroslavsky. A Los Angeles native, Yaroslavsky had been a Democratic political activist since before his graduation from UCLA. He then became the executive director of the Council on Soviet Jewry. In 1975, he won the Los Angeles City Council seat vacated by Edelman when the latter joined the BOS. Yaroslavsky was a longshot running against a City Hall favorite, but he won and served until his election to the BOS. He remained there until termed out of office in 2014.[5]

Deane Dana decided to retire from his Fourth District seat in 1996, and immediately endorsed his chief deputy, Donald Knabe, for the job. Born in Illinois, Knabe moved to California and settled in Cerritos, where he started a business. He also became involved in politics and was appointed chief deputy by Dana in 1982. While in that position he served as a Cerritos city council member and mayor in the 1980s and ran unsuccessfully for the California state Senate in 1988. A favorite with the coastal business establishment, he was termed out of office in 2016.[6]

County Elections

As mentioned in Chapter 10, the 1990 election was modified because of the Voting Rights Act decision and resulting change in supervisorial districts. Ed Edelman was reelected for the last time in the primary along with Sheriff Sherman Block, but a challenger, Kenneth P. Hahn (no relation to the supervisor), defeated the incumbent assessor in the general election. Since the First District boundaries were changed, the results of the first primary were thrown out and a new primary held, and Gloria Molina was eventually elected.

By April 1991, it was apparent that Hahn would not run again due to his declining health. Before the end of the year, state Senator Diane Watson and former

Supervisor Yvonne Burke, both African Americans, decided to run in this heavily minority district. During the campaign, Hahn endorsed Burke, while the *Times* endorsed Watson because of her "go-get-em style," although the editors thought Burke more than capable. Watson came in first the primary, but Burke won in the general election. After that Watson called for a recount and then filed suit against Burke for election improprieties, but the suit was thrown out because of lack of evidence.[7]

In the two other supervisorial contests, both Antonovich and Dana initially faced six challengers. Antonovich had little trouble with his mostly unknown opposition and used his large campaign fund well to win in the primary. Dana had two better-known opponents; one of them, Gordana Swanson, was a Rapid Transit District commissioner he fired when he first assumed office. The well-funded Dana was forced into a runoff with Swanson and changed his caretaker image. Spending over $2.5 million, a record at that time for a supervisorial race which came to about $9 per vote, he defeated Swanson.[8]

In the race for county district attorney, incumbent Ira Reiner faced four major challengers. One was Gilbert Garcetti, former head of the D.A. Special Investigations Division which probed allegations of police brutality in the early 1980s. As Reiner's chief deputy, Garcetti was demoted as some observers believed because of his "high-profile personality." Reiner, a "media hound" himself, had been embarrassed in several highly publicized court losses by his prosecutors, and had a difficult task in defending his record. With a late infusion of funding from family and friends, Garcetti came in first in the primary. Sparks between the two began immediately but did not last long. In September, Reiner suddenly quit the race, claiming he did not want to go negative. But his many well-known losses and personality contributed to his downfall, and Garcetti had the momentum. On election day, Reiner's name still appeared on the ballot, but Garcetti received 82 percent of the votes.[9]

The 1994 election was less complicated. Edelman was retiring with Molina up for reelection along with Sheriff Block and Assessor Hahn. In the primary, Molina ran unopposed; Block had five opponents; Hahn had fifteen opponents; and Los Angeles City Councilman Zev Yaroslavsky faced three other candidates for Edelman's seat. After relatively quiet primary campaigns, Molina, Block, Hahn and Yaroslavsky all received over 50 percent of the votes for their office and were elected.[10]

1996 was another election year for two supervisors and the first for a new one. Antonovich faced only one opponent, who barely campaigned and raised less than $500 to Antonovich's $900,000; the incumbent won with 74 percent of the vote. Early that year Yvonne Burke survived an attempt to recall her by a movie extra critical of her votes on layoffs of county employees and cuts in welfare payments. The recall leader did not oppose her in the election as he had in 1992, nor did anyone else, so she was reelected in the primary. Dana had announced his retirement and anointed his chief deputy, Donald Knabe, as his successor. Knabe would compete with five others, including Gordana Swanson, Dana's major opponent in 1992. Although Knabe was well-funded for the campaign, he could not round up enough votes to avoid a runoff with Swanson. During the general election campaign, Knabe continued to receive contributions from Dana, developers, and several county employee unions, while Swanson used loans from her husband and herself, and donations from a few others, totaling less than one-fifth of Knabe's treasury. He used his funds well and won in a landslide.[11]

The other county official pursuing reelection in 1996 was District Attorney Gil Garcetti. After his office's surprising loss in the O.J. Simpson double murder trial, Garcetti became vulnerable to criticism from many quarters. He had a large treasury at the time, but also five major opponents. He received the backing of Sheriff Block, the *Daily News*, and several other newspapers. His political consultants warned that he would only attract a quarter of the primary vote, but he received 37.5 percent to 21.4 percent for second-place John Lynch, a deputy district attorney who spent little in comparison to his boss. In the general election campaign Lynch continued to focus on Garcetti's losses. The close vote took two weeks to complete; Garcetti was finally declared the winner by less than 5000 votes out of the total of 2.2 million.[12]

The 1998 contest was the usual for supervisors, but not for the Sheriff. Gloria Molina had no opposition, while Zev Yaroslavsky had three minor opponents; both incumbents were endorsed by the *Times* and won easily in the primary. Assessor Hahn also won in the primary. Sheriff Sherman Block would run again and face three current and former members of his department, including Chief Lee Baca. By that time Block's health had become an issue, along with the many problems the department faced over the decade, enough that the *Times* failed to endorse him for the first time. Instead, the paper backed retired Chief William A. Baker, the only African American in the race. Baca made mistakes in the campaign but managed to win enough votes to join Block in the November runoff. In the next few months Block seemed to be gaining support until late October, when the sheriff died after surgery to remove a massive blood clot in his brain. His name remained on the ballot, and Baca defeated his deceased opponent with 61 percent of the vote.[13]

Finally, in the year of the millennium, only one office was interesting in county elections. Supervisors Burke, Knabe, and Antonovich ran unopposed, all of them reelected in the primary. Rick Auerbach, appointed interim county assessor that year when Kenneth P. Hahn retired, defeated fifteen other candidates. District Attorney Gil Garcetti again faced one of his assistants for the position and was saddled with the LAPD Rampart scandal, among others, as another embarrassment for him and his department. Again, the *Times* endorsed his major opponent, this time Steve Cooley, who ran slightly ahead in the primary. In the general election Cooley did much better, winning with over 63 percent of the vote.[14]

The BOS in the 1990s

With the departure of Pete Schabarum in early 1991, local observers anticipated a major change in the ideological outlook of the board with a liberal majority. One reporter wondered if Chairman Ed Edelman would take advantage of his "Chance to Shine" as the board's new leader. Others thought the mild-mannered Edelman might not be up to the challenge, and with Hahn in declining health, the winner of the First District election would assume control. Edelman did take the helm, but the 1990s would be an era in which the board members would not be in as much ideological conflict as in the previous decade. Although four of the five supervisors, along with the CAO, sheriff, assessor, and district attorney would be replaced, sometimes more than once, there was not a major revolution in priorities since the county lacked adequate funding to assume new programs or even support most established services at previous levels.[15]

One reason for the limits of liberal power was that the three of them did not always get along, a problem shared by the "Solid Three" conservatives in the late 1980s. A good portion of that can be attributed to Molina's personality. Early on she resurrected her Los Angeles City Council reputation as an independent member with an abrasive style in public settings. Some observers admired her for shaking up the old system and demanding accountability. Her style, however, was well-known, as those present at BOS meetings noted her intensity in grilling county department heads for information. One of them fainted at a meeting; a co-worker listened to another meeting and heard Molina "verbally and publicly castrate" the county counsel. She also tended to dominate conversations, so much so that in 1993, Chairwoman Burke passed a motion to limit the speaking time of supervisors after one of Molina's long statements which included cutting off Dana when he tried to ask a question. Liberals did not always work well together in the 1990s.[16]

Like her predecessor, Pete Schabarum, Molina also jousted with CAO Dixon, who initiated several actions approved by the rest of the supervisors that primarily served top county officials and their departments. Dixon continued to increase his political power and improving the lot of his five bosses would certainly help. He might have been an able administrator, as some supervisors and others believed, but his frequent programs intended to increase benefits for top management during lean economic times did not go over very well with state legislators, who had to hear of the county's dismal predicament when the supervisors asked for financial help.[17]

Molina's feud with Dixon began before she even took office. In March 1991, she asked Hahn and Edelman to delay a vote on Dixon's plan to raise salaries for BOS chief deputies by up to 28 percent and giving the CAO more power in that area. The item was finally put off until after she took office. In May, Dixon proposed a plan to give monthly professional development stipends to all county judges, elected officials, and department heads that could be spent on personal computers or whatever else they wished. The supervisors, except for Molina, approved the program one week after making budget cuts in almost all county departments; Molina asserted that it would make them look self-serving to state legislators whom they lobbied for more funding at the same time. During budget discussions, she brought up the issue again and convinced her colleagues to extend the benefit only to judges. In August, Dixon proposed to give $3 million in bonuses for selected county managers in his annual performance-based pay program, this just after the board had approved a budget with no raises for county employees. An irate Molina had not been informed of it; she publicly scolded Dixon and convinced the board to suspend the plan for several years.[18]

The $3 million in suspended bonuses included $2000–$2500 to five members of Dixon's staff for an "outstanding performance" in the 1991 redecorating of

Dixon's offices. That project was to have cost about $2 million, but the supervisors found out that it had ballooned to over $6 million; $8.8 million according to the auditor-controller. The cost of the elaborate furniture rose to more than 95 percent of that originally reported to the supervisors. According to a grand jury audit, the project was not included as a capital item in the county budget, and Dixon had destroyed most office files related to it. In the same month came reports that the supervisors had spent over $32.5 million to staff their offices and for travel, community social service organizations, and other expenses such as elaborate furniture, crystal ceremonial gifts, speech writers, Dana's $74,000 armored car, and bullet-proof desk blotters they could use as a shield in case of an attack during a public meeting. Since the items did not appear in a budget, the supervisors and Dixon could order what they wanted and would get it. Dixon, who should have kept track of such expenditures, "said he wonders if anyone cares how much each supervisor spends." Molina certainly did, especially when county services for the disadvantaged faced reductions.[19]

In addition to these instances, Molina also contested Dixon on his plan to expand the transportation allowance for hundreds of county managers that could be added to their retirement base; hiring several consultants to raise money for the health department, but spent more for office rental, furniture, and so forth than they brought in, and then rewarded them with raises for their work; and giving raises to seventy members of his staff and himself for which he did not seek county approval, while calling for pay cuts and layoffs of other employees.[20]

At the same time, Dixon was also being criticized for many of his actions in newspaper editorials, and by the County Grand Jury and others as amassing too much power. In January 1992, Molina had enough, suggesting to Dixon that he should resign, especially after "your devious and unethical handling" of a recent item on the BOS agenda. She even provided a long list of his actions to justify her demand. Dixon decided not to leave at that time. But six months later, after the grand jury audit and other problems in the first half of 1992, Dana, facing reelection, urged him to quit. Dixon agreed that he would step down "in the best interests of the county." In February 1993, he informed the BOS of his impending departure and provided a list of his key accomplishments, none of which included his actions noted above. Eight months later he was hired as a consultant to the county retirement agency; Molina responded with a recommendation that the county file a lawsuit to stop it.[21]

Besides jousting with Dixon in the early 1990s, Molina also tried to reform the process of county governance to improve transparency in decision making and equality in the treatment of its clients. Her various reforms would not always be shared by the others. In early 1992, she proposed a "comprehensive governmental reform" package including ethics and conflict of interest rules regarding the receipt of gifts and other gratuities by county employees, and lobbyist registration and regulations as required by federal, state, and local government, along with an elected county executive and the expansion of the BOS, the latter already being set for a vote in the primary election that year. She offered a motion for the county counsel to draft ballot language for the package, but her colleagues found it to be too much to consider, and they merely received and filed it.[22]

Molina did not give up, however. Having been on a city council committee to create an ethics ordinance, she was aware of the reticence of office holders to limit their relationships with donors, and she persisted with both the ethics and the lobbyist measures. She proposed a separate ethics ordinance, but the other supervisors determined that it only copied a state law. Her idea for the lobbyist ordinance was surprisingly introduced by Antonovich, spurring Molina to respond, "I hope this means a new direction for this man and the board." But the Antonovich proposal was a watered-down version of Molina's and had little effect on lobbying.[23]

With the addition of Yvonne Burke on the BOS in December 1992, things began to change. In that month, the actions of two of Dana's deputies acting as his alternates on the Metropolitan Transportation Authority (MTA) board of directors in voting a large MTA contract for one of his major contributors spurred Molina to revive her ethics and lobbyist reforms. Burke was sympathetic as she had tried to have the county counsel draft a similar lobbying ordinance in 1980. In early 1993, Molina introduced her much tougher lobbying ordinance; with Burke's support it passed by a 3–2 vote. It would certainly come in handy just a few weeks later, when it was revealed that a firm employed by the county to lobby for it at City Hall also represented private clients doing business with the county. Molina's ethics reform idea for county employees eventually succeeded, as a county code like the state penal code would be strengthened in a few more years.[24]

In addition, Molina was active in improving gender equality on county commissions as she had while on the city council. Her 1991 motion passed with only one dissenting vote. She also worked with Mayor Tom Bradley as directors of the Los Angeles County Transportation Commission (later MTA) in improving its policies regarding contracts awarded to businesses owned by minorities and women, and with Burke on establishing equal rights for women competing for county contracts.[25]

As will be seen, there were other issues that Molina contested with her colleagues; sometimes with an individual, sometimes with the two conservatives, sometimes with the liberals, and occasionally with all four of them. Some conflicts were not based on ideology, as she also joined conservatives in some votes. When Molina first ran for the office of supervisor, some newspaper editors supported her because they believed she would shake up an institution that needed change. They would not be disappointed.

The Almost Changing County Structure

Gloria Molina's recommendations to improve the BOS process were based to a large degree on those offered by the Public Commission on County Government in 1976. The BOS also considered changes to the structure of county governance in the 1990s; most of them failed.

The expansion of the BOS and creation of an elected county executive came up many times after unsuccessful elections in the 1970s and calls for them during the 1980s. In 1991, the subject arose with redistricting necessary to respond to the 1990 federal census. The committee determining the new district boundaries first studied adding two more seats, but the *Garza* plaintiffs and Molina objected that it would dilute the newly established influence of Latinos. Some newspaper editors agreed, pointing out that most of the supervisors were merely trying to save their own jobs and limit Latino representation to just Molina. Hearings on the seven-member BOS also demonstrated that the plan might not be accepted by the Department of Justice based on the *Garza* decision. In June 1991, a survey done for the Los Angeles County Bar Association that included questions about BOS expansion and adding a county executive concluded that expansion might pass in an election, but the county executive measure was doubtful.[26]

By January 1992, the boundary committee added a nine-member BOS to its considerations. It would likely consist of two Latino districts, one African American district, one combined-minority district, and five possibly White districts. At the same time Edelman began his campaign for an elected county executive, hoping to have both measures approved on the same ballot. The two measures were considered by the BOS along with Molina's reform package including ethics and lobbyist registration ordinances. None were approved at that meeting, as other supervisors added their own preferences and filed the motions after Molina left the meeting. The BOS later considered the measures again, and that time Molina withdrew her demand for an ethics ordinance as a last chance to save the others. The BOS voted to put BOS expansion to seven and to nine along with the elected county executive on the ballot, with expansion dependent on the passage of the executive. (Edelman asserted that a larger BOS without an executive would only make county government more complicated and subject to special interest control.)[27]

During the campaign for the reforms, editorials recommending that CAO Dixon should resign probably influenced how some voters perceived the proposed county executive. Edelman led the effort for it, directed by a paid public relations firm and joined by Common Cause and the League of Women Voters, among others. Antonovich and Dana signed the ballot arguments against both the executive and board expansion to nine, and the supervisors withdrew the expansion to seven measure as it might have triggered another voting rights lawsuit. Howard Jarvis's tax reform organization opposed both as a waste of taxpayer money, and MALDEF opposed the executive as it would reduce the recently acquired power of minority supervisors. Newspapers split on the subject, with the metropolitans generally for both measures. As in the campaign for the two in 1976, both were easily defeated. The BOS would remain at five, although the concurrent addition of an African American to replace Hahn did bring some change.[28]

County reform met defeat, but it did not die. In 1996, the California Constitution Revision Commission recommended structural changes such as a more powerful executive. The Los Angeles County Grand Jury followed it by urging the BOS to put a strong executive initiative on the ballot, although the board declined. In 1999, state Senator Richard Polanco proposed a bill for a state ballot initiative for Los Angeles County voters to expand the BOS to nine after several Latino legislators protested some of the board's decisions. Yaroslavsky took advantage of the timing by submitting a motion to have the county counsel draft two ordinances to place board expansion and an elected county executive on the November 2000 ballot.

Antonovich was the lone opponent. The *Times* again supported the two reforms, although its editors noted that a possible reason for the state legislators to propose it was "to increase their options for future elective office."[29]

Molina abstained from voting on the motion because of her concern that pushing it too hastily would result in another failure. She and Burke offered a motion to have the BOS create a commission like the 1974–1976 Public Commission on Los Angeles County Government to thoroughly analyze the issues. The motion was opposed by various groups as holding up the process and diluting the influence of minority groups; it would be defeated by Yaroslavsky and the two conservatives.[30]

The first few months of 2000 saw further actions by Polanco to introduce new complications such as term limits for county officials, and the BOS once again considered creating a commission to study county reform. The BOS followed the progress of Polanco's bill and tried to head it off by putting an expansion measure on the November ballot, but not the county executive proposal. The *Times* agreed with Yaroslavsky that expansion should not be considered without the executive and opposed the proposition. So did the two conservatives, who helped to fund the opposition, arguing it was too costly and just a future job opportunity for Polanco. Molina and Burke, county unions, and some minority and civic reform groups supported it, but it was crushed 64 percent to 36 percent.[31]

Since 2000, interest in these county reforms still arise locally and in Sacramento. In 2007 the supervisors transformed the County Administrative Officer position into the County Executive Officer, but the CEO was still appointive, not elected, and only ceded limited additional power. In 2015, the BOS repealed all but the title of the officer in scaling back its power to the previous decentralized structure. The 2015–2016 County Grand Jury analyzed the position and recommended that the BOS create an independent elected executive, as well as expanding the BOS to at least eleven members to better represent county residents and spend less time on administrative matters. None of that has happened. In Sacramento, a state senator proposed a constitutional amendment to require all counties of two million or more residents to expand their BOS to seven members. The *Times* and former supervisor Yaroslavsky both opposed it without a county executive. That effort failed, as did another attempt two years later.[32]

Although the number of supervisors has remained the same, their length in office changed, as term limits would eventually overhaul membership on the BOS. Pete Schabarum was the chief source behind it. He started with state legislators, many of them his political opponents during his supervisorial tenure. In late 1989, he led the movement to limit the terms of state legislators and other elected officers. His state constitutional amendment initiative passed easily with the support of business leaders and tax reform groups in the 1990 general election. At the same time, he threatened to go after his BOS colleagues, claiming he would get a state legislator to introduce a bill to limit Los Angeles County supervisors to only two four-year terms. He filed two proposals for two terms for the supervisors of large counties, and limits for U.S. Senators and Congress members from California. The proposal regarding the federal positions would be unconstitutional, since the state had no authority to restrict federal elections, and Schabarum would eventually drop both.[33]

At the end of the decade another group funded by Schabarum began an initiative effort to change the Los Angeles County charter to restrict supervisors to two terms. While the signatures were being collected, state Senator Polanco proposed that it be added to his quest for expansion of the board. He pulled it from his bill when the supervisors agreed to put the expansion issue on the ballot. In July 2000, Schabarum informed his former colleagues that his petition would receive enough signatures to be placed on the ballot and asked them to include the charter amendment proposal on the November election ballot. Before enough signatures could be verified, however, the County Registrar-Recorder revealed that there were not enough of them submitted by the legal deadline. The petition sponsors filed suit, arguing that the county overestimated the number of signatures needed. The judge agreed, and by August 2001, the BOS compromised with the initiative proponents by agreeing to place two charter amendments on the March 2002 ballot, one to limit supervisors to three four-year terms, and one to limit supervisors plus the elected sheriff, assessor, and district attorney to three terms.[34]

The addition of the three other elected officials raised another complication. All three opposed it and were supported by the county counsel and a labor lawyer who argued that only a state constitutional amendment could revise the length of the terms of those county officials. Sheriff Baca then sued to have both measures taken off the March 2002 ballot. He would lose that suit and an appeal, and despite newspaper editorials opposing the concept, both measures passed easily. Baca would file another suit in 2003 to remove the sheriff and would win his case the following year. The assessor and district attorney would join him two years later by winning theirs. In 2012, Antonovich proposed a ballot measure to stretch term limits for the supervisors for eight more years. But only he and Knabe voted for it; Yaroslavsky vehemently opposed it and Molina and Mark Ridley-Thomas abstained.[35]

Law and Order

As one LASD publication notes, the decade of the 1990s was a roller coaster of a ride for the department, with some positive achievements and many scandals and setbacks. The decade began with Sheriff Block coming out of a troubling year which included the LASD failure to prevent the shooting of some innocent citizens, the dismissal of two deputies after burning a cross in front of Black inmates at the county jail, and the suspension of eighteen deputies involved in an investigation of the theft of almost $1.5 million in seized drug money. Ten of them were indicted by a federal grand jury for the theft in 1990, and the scandal dragged on with eight more suspended and the final group of defendants convicted in 1992. Also, in 1990, newspapers reported a settlement of a lawsuit filed by lawyers for six African American jail inmates beaten by sheriff's deputies in 1986, a suit for which the BOS approved a $175,000 payment; and one in 1991 of a retired deputy whistleblower suing the LASD for being forced to retire because of his critical comments on LASD tactics. Clearly, the LASD image was not a bright one at this time and would not get better in the immediate future.[36]

The Kolts Report

In March 1991, the televised beating of an African American by LAPD officers resulted in the arrest of four of them, and the creation of an appointed commission headed by former U.S. Secretary of State Warren Christopher to investigate police racism and brutality. In August of that year, a sheriff's deputy shot and killed a nineteen-year-old Latino at a housing project in East Los Angeles. In the same month two LASD deputies in a larger group shot an African American nine times in the back, and two other young men were shot and killed by deputies. These killings and several others that year spurred demands from elected officials and activists for an independent investigation of deadly force by the LASD. Sheriff Block initially prevented any outside probe but did agree to appear at a BOS hearing in which he admitted the employment of rogue deputies as the Christopher Commission had identified rogue LAPD officers. He then appointed an investigative committee of prominent civic leaders which he would head. After continuing complaints, a *Times* story reporting that the LASD had cost the county over $32 million in excessive force lawsuits over the last four years, and word that the federal Commission on Civil Rights might conduct its own investigation, the BOS decided to act. Edelman, Hahn, and Molina voted to hire a special counsel to conduct an independent probe. They chose retired Superior Court Judge James G. Kolts, who started work in late 1991.[37]

The Kolts Commission, as it is referred to, carried out its investigation with fewer resources than the Christopher Commission, but was able to analyze a wide variety of issues related to deputies and the use of excessive force. The final report contained chapters on handling complaints, recruiting and affirmative action, hiring, stress management, and community-oriented policing, as well as officer-involved shootings and tracking the use of force. Interviews, LASD reports, and records of arrests and other incidents comprised some of the many sources used by the researchers; a long list of recommendations would be the result.[38]

One chapter of the report dealt with racist LASD "deputy gangs," like the Vikings at the Lynwood Station accused of violations of civil rights, personal injuries, property damage, and wrongful deaths of nearby residents. The victims sued the county and won an $8 million settlement in 1996. Members of the LASD cliques sported tattoos and adopted other images like gang members, as well as their hand signs and jargon. They had been known to exist for two decades, usually in minority communities, and seemed to increase in number after 1990. The commission report concluded that "the issue of deputy gangs is inflammatory and should not be allowed to fester." The groups should be broken up, and "gang-like behavior" should be punished severely.[39]

The Kolts Commission produced its report in July 1992. Critics such as the ACLU and other civil liberties advocates charged that the recommendations did not go far enough; the district attorney's office complained it was inadequate; and the president of the union representing deputies claimed the statistics used in the study to be inaccurate and the entire report flawed. Sheriff Block initially embraced the spirit of the report, and then observed that it was wrong about the sixty-two unidentified problem deputies, but he would make sure that all complaints were addressed. In October, his office issued a response to the report, addressing all 180 recommendations: 137 had already been implemented or were in process; nineteen required significant fiscal resources of over $4 million or legislative action and were still being studied; and the department did not plan to implement the remaining twenty-four.[40]

Kolts and his staff did not agree with the progress made on many items listed by Block and were deeply concerned with those the department did not intend to implement. In discussions with LASD leaders, many of the differences were resolved. But Kolts was particularly concerned that the response claimed that the bias of his own staff had determined the problems and solutions when most of his conclusions were based on interviews with LASD personnel. He also disagreed with the sheriff's recommendation against a citizen commission composed of civilians and professionals being created to audit the department's progress in reducing excessive force and urged the supervisors do so. Kolts and Block compromised in agreeing that the LASD would fully cooperate with the Kolts staff in making periodic audits of department progress and that a board of retired judges would be appointed by the supervisors to review citizen complaints of excessive force. The BOS approved this compromise, to the disappointment of civil rights advocates, who wanted the citizen commission instead. It also provided that an ombudsman would be hired to ensure that citizen complaints were handled, and that Merrick Bobb, the general counsel for the Kolts staff, would monitor LASD compliance with the recommendations every six months.[41]

Over the next two decades, Bobb and his staff completed thirty-one semi-annual reports on LASD progress in reducing excessive force, as well as special reports to the BOS. Some of them were positive, some negative. During the remaining years of Sheriff Block's tenure, there appeared to be a good relationship between Bobb and the department. But it reportedly deteriorated under the leadership of Sheriff Lee Baca and his top aide, Paul Tanaka (a former Viking), when the reports became more critical. In 2014, Bobb filed his last report and retired just as many critical newspaper stories on a major LASD jail scandal appeared.[42]

Speaking of jails, as the LASD publication noted, "For as long as the Los Angeles Sheriff's Department has been in existence, the one consistent problem with which the sheriff has had to contend is jail crowding." During the 1990s that would be back and forth. The Men's Central Jail continued to be monitored by the U.S. Department of Justice (DOJ) as a result of the Rutherford Decision and experienced a rash of inmate escapes until the Twin Towers facility opened in early 1997. Besides escapes, over a thousand inmates were released early because of budget restrictions, and thirty-five were released accidentally in 1995–1996. Conversely, the BOS had to approve a settlement for inmates who had been held past their release dates due to errors. In addition, the LASD would have to deal with the Kolts Report recommendation to stop assigning jail duty to new recruits as their initial experience dealing with gang violence and brutality.[43]

The jail issue and reports of waste in the LASD operation, which included a $200,000 emergency purchase for cookies, spurred the BOS to request a state audit of the department that resulted in recommendations to improve its financial situation. In 1997, Assemblyman Antonio Villaraigosa called for state oversight of the LASD budget. The county budget picture had improved, however, so there were demands for raises for deputies. After Lee Baca's election in 1998, he promised to "raise hell" in fighting for more funding for the department, but soon lost some credibility when criticized for using a patrol helicopter for his own schedule and purchasing an expensive jet to replace a 1978 Cessna belonging to the LASD. In late 2000, he announced his ambitious plans to restructure the LASD over thirty years; expand education opportunities for jail inmates, build more stations, and other projects at a cost of $1 billion. A reduction in the county budget in the 2000s would limit that agenda.[44]

The office of the district attorney also kept busy in the 1990s, primarily in opening and closing specific units as its budget fluctuated. In that decade, Ira Reiner and Gil Garcetti and their staff focused much of their attention on high-profile cases involving celebrities, law enforcement officers, and others receiving publicity such as the last McMartin Pre-School trial, the killings of the Menendez brothers' parents, and those of Rodney King precipitating the 1992 urban uprising, and O.J. Simpson. As noted earlier, the media attention to these trials had much to do with the defeat of incumbent district attorneys in 1992 and 2000. Besides its prosecution staff, district attorney units were also involved in issues such as reduction of domestic abuse, enforcing child support payments, and challenging gang members, all of which continued after 2000.[45]

Tight Budgets

The early 1990s were lean years for county finances. With the national recession and the downsizing of the aerospace industry and the military presence in California, federal and state funding for local government was reduced considerably. More immigration in the 1980s, restraints on taxing opportunities imposed by state initiatives, and shifts in state funding previously made to counties exacerbated budget shortages and reduced services. In Los Angeles County the situation was made worse by the many actions of the CAO and BOS in approving various programs to increase the salaries and benefits of county management at the expense of services to constituents. These programs raised the ire of state legislators when the supervisors traveled to Sacramento to ask for additional funding and faced the same cold reception as they had after the board approved hefty salary raises while receiving a state bailout to address Proposition 13 reductions.[46]

The county survived the 1990 budget year, although with many cuts due to prior spending and a reduced state budget. The 1991 budget would also be limited. New Supervisor Gloria Molina recommend adding $39.3 million to it for services she considered important, while suggesting work furloughs for some employees, cutting management salaries and bonuses, and items to increase county revenue. There would be some cuts that year, but CAO Dixon replaced them with his expensive office renovations and perks for management mentioned earlier. In October, he informed all department heads that 1992 would be an extremely tight year and to begin to act immediately.[47]

Dixon's warning would prove accurate. As the economy worsened, the county needed to make major cuts for a massive shortfall. The initial approved budget included $176 million in cuts, mostly closures of facilities and layoffs, based on optimistic hopes for an adequate state contribution that never happened. A raft of new fees had to be created, and departments faced major reductions. In late September, the supervisors solved their deficit by deferring $200 million in employee pay and benefit increases to the following year and refinancing some county debt to be paid later. The compromise was approved by four supervisors who saw no other way to save services and avoid layoffs and would be defended jointly by the surprising duo of Molina and Antonovich. The lone dissenter, Ed Edelman, feared it to be the road to bankruptcy.[48]

The budget situation for the following year looked even worse. Dixon estimated the shortfall to be $750 million to $1 billion. In March 1993, interim CAO Harry Hufford recommended a 25 percent slash in services after Governor Wilson proposed moving property tax revenue for the counties to schools, spurring Antonovich to suggest the county withhold its property taxes from the state. Hufford's list of cuts included closures of some fire and sheriff's stations, probation camps, and all health centers, and a reduction of 9536 positions. The BOS approved cuts to most programs, but especially health and welfare, along with about 2000 layoffs in late July. Over the next two months the legislature found more funding for the county, the unions agreed to forego raises to avoid layoffs, and the CAO suddenly found another $125 million in savings after union negotiations had been completed.[49]

In early 1994, the supervisors heard that the county was in a much worse financial predicament of their own making. Borrowing millions over the last two years created a $1 billion debt coming due soon. New CAO Sally Reed searched for opportunities to balance the budget. Like most other department heads, the sheriff and district attorney complained of possible reductions, and county workers protested with sickouts. Reed predicted a 38 percent overall cut would be needed; she targeted the LASD, parks, and libraries. The BOS borrowed more money to pay off debts and raised their estimates of tax revenue to balance spending.[50]

The supervisors might have given more thought to some of their budget juggling when it was announced in late 1994 that adjacent Orange County had just declared bankruptcy. The Orange County treasurer had put taxpayer funds in a pool that included those of cities and other government agencies in the county and used them to invest in high-yield bonds and other instruments and borrowed money using the bonds as collateral. When the interest rate did not change as he expected, his $20.6 billion pool declined in value and the state assumed management of that county's financial affairs. Los Angeles County supervisors already worried about possible bankruptcy as it had been in the news since December 1. On that day, the county assessor and tax collector assured them that Los Angeles County's investment process was not like that of Orange County, that "we have no such concerns for our portfolio," so they had nothing to worry about.[51]

Or so they wished. Several weeks later the auditor-controller announced that the state would reimburse some funds to the county later than he had assumed, so the county might run out of cash by late March. The supervisors began looking for possible cuts, adopted a hiring freeze, and called for a blue-ribbon budget task force to propose a long-range plan to resolve it. In May, the supervisors made their annual pilgrimage to Washington, D.C., with the sheriff and district attorney to lobby for federal money. In June, Wall Street put the county on warning, and Yaroslavsky raised an alarm that the shortfall was then at $1.2 billion; he even mentioned the word "bankruptcy" if the supervisors were not successful. CAO Reed proposed a budget calling for the elimination of 18,255 jobs, which would be fought by county unions. The board approved the cuts except for the health department, and Sheriff Block threatened a lawsuit while District Attorney Garcetti refused to cut his staff. In the meantime, the 1994–1995 County Grand Jury, an Emergency Coalition of county unions, and the State's Legislative Analyst Office produced studies of various aspects of the problem with recommendations that centered on the need to raise more revenue and reduce costs, few of which could help much in the present situation.[52]

In July 1995, a judge refused to halt 1400 county layoffs. Unions staged protests and sickouts and sued the county. Molina and Yaroslavsky took another trip to Washington, D.C., to lobby President Clinton. In early August, the BOS voted for deep cuts if the state or federal governments did not help; the state did, but not nearly enough. So, the BOS considered new taxes and bonds at the same time Moody's downgraded the county's credit rating which could make the interest unbearable. By mid–August, a bill had been introduced in the legislature to take control of the county's finances, and a county finance officer informed the board that if a judge blocked the cuts approved by the BOS, the county would be insolvent by October 1.[53]

County officials had recently arranged to send out 5200 layoff notices in mid–September when informed that a tentative agreement had been worked out with the federal government to provide a $364 million rescue package for the county's health system. While on a trip through Southern California, President Clinton announced the agreement, and praised the proposal that would move the county close to less expensive means of care in health clinics. In bailing out the Department of Health Services (DHS), the measure went a long way in solving some of the county's fiscal problems, although not all of them. Some health workers were still laid off, and other cuts would be made elsewhere.[54]

Despite the federal bailout, CAO Sally Reed still predicted a $1 billion shortfall for the 1996–1997 budget. A few temporary solutions cut that amount in half, but Reed identified more cuts that would have to be made if nothing changed. (She would not be around to see the ongoing effort to reduce expenses as she became increasingly frustrated in dealing with the supervisors and unions and left to take a pay cut in becoming the head of the state Department of Motor Vehicles in 1996.) Molina and Antonovich suggested raising more revenue by tapping the county retirement fund; the BOS had just borrowed money from it to pay off its debt the year before. Amid these negative developments the county did improve its financial position as the national economy became more robust, and the budget was approved in June. A few layoffs would still occur later in the year, and a state audit recommended additional actions to meet possible financial uncertainties.[55]

By late 2000, five years after the county's brush with bankruptcy, the supervisors faced a $31 million budget surplus. The two conservatives hoped to expand some services, while the three liberals decided to save it in case of a change in the economy. In that year that a budget expert predicted that the county could still face bankruptcy if there was another recession. And there would be trouble in 2002. The CAO faced that calamity with a proposal to make cuts to the LASD, welfare, probation, health, mental health, and library programs, with the elimination of over 2000 vacant positions but no layoffs. Reserve funds in the health and other departments would help to cushion the impact of state funding cuts, tax shortfalls, and increased costs in operations. That recession would last another two years but would not be as bad as the 1990s.[56]

The Healthcare Crisis

The main component of Los Angeles County's budget problems in the 1990s centered in the Department of Health Services (DHS), including its aging hospitals. As the county faced annual shortfalls for most of the decade, the DHS was a consistent target for cuts. Many of its employees were slated for furloughs or layoffs when growing expenditures such as medical malpractice claims sapped resources, and long delays for indigent patients spurred lawsuits aimed at improving services. The problems increased as the DHS budget faced cuts in funding for mandated services over those years.[57]

In early 1995, the CAO predicted layoffs and recommended the closure of Los Angeles County+USC Hospital (LAC+USC) if there was no alternative. In July, the county's appointed Health Crisis Task Force concluded that current efforts did not meet the needs of the population because of misplaced priorities with emphasis on care in hospitals rather than outpatient care. The task force also recommended closing LAC+USC along with other cuts and changes to save the health care infrastructure from permanent damage. The situation deteriorated so much that the DHS planned to cut services for the mentally ill, while the supervisors voted to close twenty-eight of thirty-nine community health centers and all six regional health centers by the end of August. In September, it looked as though the entire healthcare system would collapse. However, the county Health Crisis Task Force headed by Burt Margolin, its anointed czar, arrived in Washington, D.C., and worked out the deal for the $364 million federal bailout with a pledge to switch to less-expensive outpatient care. A much smaller deficit remained, but the DHS structural deficit would not be solved for a few years.[58]

Another major problem based on the county's budget calamities was the effect on the supervisors in dealing with the county's oldest extant hospital. The LAC+USC Hospital, built in the 1920s and early '30s, had been considered for renovation since 1964, and a few studies and construction drawings had been done, all put on hold for various reasons. The 1994 Northridge earthquake, which damaged the building significantly, spurred immediate action in approving the project with requested funding from the Federal Emergency Management Agency (FEMA). The hospital would have to remain open since the county's fiscal disaster in 1995 reduced major activity on the project as county funds dwindled, and federal help was not enough.[59]

Planning continued, however, and several studies estimated how many beds it should include. The two most important studies recommended 788 beds or 750–780 beds, and the DHS decided on the 750 figures. In 1997, Molina, whose district included the hospital, led a campaign for 750 beds, enlisting the aid of elected officials, medical professionals, and community organizations; many of the individuals would appear to speak at BOS hearings and to lobby the BOS. The other four supervisors favored fewer beds. Antonovich informed one private hospital administrator that he believed a 391 alternative was needed because of the current surplus of beds in hospitals throughout the county; that it would save the county $70 million per year compared to the 750-bed plan; and that it would satisfy the agreement with the federal government to downsize hospital care and focus on less expensive care in clinics. The other two liberal supervisors preferred 600 beds as the maximum number, as did a *Times* editorial, based on similar arguments and how much they thought the federal government would help. Both Burke and Yaroslavsky offered the motion for 600 beds to decide the issue. The final 4–1 vote favored 600, or 500 if enough state funding could not be added.[60]

Defeated on this issue by her fellow liberals and the conservatives, Molina did not give up. In July 1998, she distributed a booklet consisting of studies and arguments for the 750-bed facility to arouse interest in changing the BOS decision. At the same time, her ally, state Senator (and future supervisor) Hilda Solis, introduced a bill to force the issue by requiring that the hospital should be able to accommodate 750 beds, but only staff for 600 patients for the time being. Yaroslavsky, Knabe, and Antonovich opposed it as stepping on local control, and the latter convinced Governor Wilson to veto the bill. In the following year Molina tried to re-open the issue but failed, and angrily accused the other supervisors of racism, since the hospital was in a largely Latino community. That charge brought a critical editorial in the *Times*, and she eventually apologized. After the controversy subsided, the hospital finally opened in 2008 to accommodate 600 beds.[61]

The 1990s deficit also delayed improvements to the Harbor-UCLA Medical Center in Torrance and heightened the recent animosity between Molina and Burke. In 2000, Burke wanted to start renovations on the hospital that had been planned for a decade. Molina was perturbed that Burke expected to fund it, since she had opposed the LAC+USC Medical Center replacement. Knabe, whose district included the hospital, agreed with Burke, since funding had already been spent on planning. Molina, still simmering because of the 750-bed issue, was joined by Antonovich, who complained that funding for hospital projects in his district had been canceled or delayed. So, Burke's project would be delayed, but eventually the renovations for Harbor-UCLA were completed, and the BOS split on the issue (liberal + conservative v. conservative+ liberal with Yaroslavsky in the middle) would end.[62]

Race and Riots

Almost three decades after the Watts Rebellion in 1965, another uprising occurred in Los Angeles that pushed Los Angeles city and county governments to face some of the social problems within their midst. During that time span, newspapers made periodic assessments every five or ten years to determine what improvements had been made in the low-income areas of South Los Angeles based on prevailing views of the major problems identified in various studies and government reports. Those assessments usually concluded that little had been done to ameliorate the challenges faced by residents.[63] In fact, as the Los Angeles County and City Human Relations Commissions noted in 1985, "We cannot emphasize too strongly the critical nature of the problems described in this report and the implications of continued inaction. We should not have to wait for a second Los Angeles riot to erupt to bring these problems to serious public attention."[64]

In the early 1990s, the continuing socio-economic conditions in South Los Angeles were exacerbated by the national recession causing increased unemployment, which followed a period of competition for jobs in the area between African Americans and the increasing Latino population. Members of both groups faced mistreatment by the LAPD in the city of Los Angeles and the LASD in unincorporated areas of the county which would soon be documented by two government commissions mentioned earlier in this chapter. For some Blacks, the presence in their neighborhood of Asian American storeowners reminded them of the lack of opportunity compared to those of a different race. All these factors laid the foundation for another rebellion that would be different in some respects from Watts.[65]

Several incidents in 1991 would eventually spark the uprising. In March, an African American, Rodney King, was pulled over by the LAPD after a high-speed chase and beaten severely by officers, all of it caught on videotape by a local resident. The video would appear on television frequently, and four officers were arrested on charges of brutality. In the same month, a Black teenager was killed by a Korean storeowner after a scuffle in the store. The storeowner received a sentence of five years of probation by a White judge, which raised protests in the Black community. In August, an LASD deputy killed a Latino in an East Los Angeles housing project and set off a four-hour melee with 300 residents. These were the most publicized incidents of police violence that year.[66]

The first trial of the four officers who beat Rodney King concluded in April 1992 with a verdict by an all-White jury of not guilty for all four on all charges. By then, residents throughout the U.S. had seen the film of the beating, and African Americans and others in Los Angeles were stunned. Just after 6 p.m. that day crowds at Florence and Normandie began attacking vehicles and their White occupants, dragging Reginald Denny out of his truck, and severely beating him in a news clip seen often that night. Protesters at the LAPD headquarters torched a parking kiosk, and smashed windows and glass doors at the nearby County Hall of Justice and Criminal Courts Building. Smoke and fires could be seen in many parts of Los Angeles County as buildings were looted and torched. Both the City of Los Angeles and the county declared a local emergency as the rioting spread to over a dozen cities, including Compton, Hollywood, Long Beach, and Pomona. By the next day, Latinos had joined the looting, making it a multiethnic uprising. The National Guard was called in to help law enforcement, and President Bush ordered U.S. troops to assist. The violence finally subsided, and the city and county curfews were lifted on May 4.[67]

As a result of the rebellion, sixty people died, according to the county coroner, and over 2300 were injured. A RAND Corporation study stated that almost 10,000 persons were arrested, 51 percent of them Latino and 36 percent African American, which led a RAND criminologist to conclude that "This was clearly not a Black riot. It was a minority riot." Almost 1600 buildings had been damaged, 613 of which had to be demolished, with over $780 million in estimated damage. Long-term job losses as a result were estimated to be 11,500.[68]

The county response to this urban uprising involved safety measures during the violence and recovery programs after the curfews were lifted. The latter included the DHS keeping health centers open and investigating health hazards throughout the county; relaxing some rules for distributing financial aid to victims and providing advice for help from social agencies; applying for federal emergency grants for gang enforcement teams and many other programs to restore peace and safety; and other initiatives to serve victims and restore county services. In addition, Supervisor Edelman led the effort to work with news directors to review media coverage of the riots partially blamed for exacerbating the violence. He revived the effort late in the year to avoid such coverage after the second trial of the four officers by the federal government on charges of civil rights violations regarding the Rodney King beating.

Burning buildings on Vermont Avenue during the 1992 uprising in Los Angeles (Gary Leonard, photographer / Los Angeles Photographers Photo Collection / Los Angeles Public Library.)

Edelman also helped plan the county program to prepare for another civil uprising if the officers were again found innocent, and county officials created a strategy to be ready with a two-hour warning to be given by the judge in the case when the jury reached its verdict. The plan would not be necessary, however, since two of the officers were convicted, the other two acquitted.[69]

The 1992 uprising generated a multitude of studies and essays on its causes and possible solutions soon after the curfew was lifted; it became a laboratory for social scientists. It also spurred a private agency organized by Mayor Tom Bradley soon after to rebuild the damaged structures and reinvigorate the curfew area with private investment. Headed by 1984 Los Angeles Olympics director Peter Ueberroth, Rebuild L.A. had an impressive board of directors representing major corporations, civic organizations, minorities, and other groups, and began its work in June. While it achieved some success in raising funds for reconstruction and adding jobs, its direction was not always clear, so progress lagged. Ueberroth resigned as its leader a year later, although he stayed on the shrinking board of directors, who downsized their agenda. In 1996, Rebuild L.A. began plans to close shop in the following year as originally planned.[70]

Since the end of the 1992 uprising, the *Los Angeles Times* has printed stories on its legacy; like the Watts Rebellion the updates usually come every five or ten years— 1997, 2002, 2007, 2012, and 2017. Most of the stories are like the last: many people think it will happen again, there is still disparity of opportunity, and some lots of former buildings are still vacant. The 1990s also witnessed further county government involvement in racial and ethnic issues such as the BOS support of Proposition 187 in 1994 and opposition to Proposition 209 in 1996, among many other decisions. And the larger issue of race relations continues as evidenced in annual reports on hate crimes and hate groups in the county produced by the County Human Relations Commission, the work of human relations agencies in other cities in the county, the number of opinion pieces on race and segregation in metropolitan newspapers, and the ever-growing number of studies by social scientists.[71]

On February 18, 2000, and most of the rest of that year, Los Angeles County officials and employees celebrated the county's 150th birthday. Events took place in many county facilities, especially the museums and the County Fair, as well as other venues. A parade on Wilshire Boulevard was scheduled, along with a special celebration planned at Dodger Stadium, where Lenny Kravitz, the Goo Goo Dolls and other entertainers would perform at a "Wango Tango" concert. Of course, many 150th birthday souvenirs (keychains, a clock, birthday caps, candy jars, etc.) were available at reasonable prices at the County Store in the Hall of Administration. Fortunately, the events occurred at a good time for the county's financial position, as proceeds from the merchandise were not necessary to balance the budget.[72]

12

Los Angeles County Government
in the New Millennium

Since 2000, Los Angeles County government has wrestled with many of the same problems it has faced in the past with mixed results. Continued budget cuts to health services limited care for low-income residents; brutality and the operation of county jails by the Sheriff's Department led to Sheriff Lee Baca's departure in 2014; and the indictment of the county assessor in 2012 and evidence of malfeasance in cities in the county are reminiscent of past corruption. Scandals in county foster care, probation, and other departments have raised the ire of supervisors and residents and are more evidence of mismanagement and poor oversight. In these two decades the membership of the BOS and the offices of assessor and sheriff have been completely changed, but some of the old problems remain. Conversely, more recent improvements in the direction of jail incarceration and other issues speak to further reform efforts in addressing some of the shortcomings of county governance.

As the period from 2000 to 2020 is still fresh and lacking distance from which to judge it, and necessary historical sources are not yet available, this chapter will briefly review, not analyze, some of the important events and trends to suggest continuity and change with the county's past.

The Changing Board of Supervisors

From 2000 to 2020, the entire membership of the BOS changed. Yvonne B. Burke in the Second District was succeeded by Mark Ridley-Thomas, a former Los Angeles City Councilman and member of the California Assembly and state Senate, who would be termed out in 2020. He was replaced in 2020 by state Senator Holly Mitchell, a former Assembly member and director of a social services agency, who changed the board late that year to all women supervisors.[1]

Gloria Molina in the First District and Zev Yaroslavsky in the Third District would be termed out in 2014. Hilda Solis, a former member of the California Assembly and state Senate, and the U.S. Congress, as well as U.S. Secretary of Labor since 2009, replaced Molina. Yaroslavsky was succeeded by Sheila James Kuehl, a former television actress who had also served in the California Assembly and state Senate.[2]

Two more supervisors were termed out of office in 2016. Don Knabe in the Fourth District was followed by Janice Kay Hahn, daughter of Supervisor Kenneth

192

Hahn, and a former member of the Los Angeles City Council and U.S. Congress. After thirty-six years in office, Michael Antonovich of the Fifth District was succeeded by Kathryn Barger, his chief deputy for fifteen years.[3]

The supervisors in office in the early 2000s continued to share some differences based on their personalities. Antonovich and Knabe would get along well as they had similar political interests. The three liberals were not as copasetic. Molina continued arguing with her colleagues and grilling county department heads (see Chapter 11). She and Yaroslavsky carried over some of their personal differences from their years together on the Los Angeles City Council and then on the BOS. However, the two joined in many initiatives as they frequently became frustrated with the operation of county government. Burke was more even-tempered. Ridley-Thomas had to spend time getting to know his four colleagues who had been on the board for well over a decade and tried to get along with all of them. The addition of Solis and Kuehl seemed to improve personal relationships of the supervisors, and the further addition of Hahn and Barger has taken it even further.[4]

Ideological similarities and differences have continued to be as loose. The two conservatives, Antonovich and Knabe, voted the same on most issues, although Knabe joined the three liberals on occasion, as did Dana before him. The three liberals would generally vote together on social services issues, although on some votes Yaroslavsky would side with the two conservatives; on even fewer votes Molina would join Antonovich, and in rare cases Burke and Yaroslavsky would join the conservatives in opposition to Molina. Since most BOS votes are determined before their meetings, most decisions are recorded as 5–0, although Solis, Kuehl and Ridley-Thomas voted together against the conservatives in some controversial issues. Since 2016, most votes have been 5–0 (or 4–0–1 if there were absences or abstentions) with a few opposing votes by Kuehl and the more conservative Barger.[5]

Regarding the structure of county government, most supervisors after 2000 usually opposed any calls for reform by the County Grand Jury, civic groups, and newspapers. After many failed attempts to expand the number of supervisors to improve representation, the supervisors opposed attempts by state legislators to force the issue. In 2007, the supervisors partially modernized the CAO position as the County Executive Officer, but the CEO was still appointive, not elected. In 2015, the later BOS repealed all but the title of that officer.[6]

The BOS also fought against outside attempts to redistrict the county after decennial U.S. census projects were completed. Burke was especially concerned that her district might be reconfigured so that there would no longer be an African American on the board. In 2001, the supervisors protected their districts in opposition to Latino groups hoping to create a district for another Latino on the board. In 2011, the process started again, with Molina presenting a plan to add a Latino majority seat in Yaroslavsky's district (supported by Latinos), Ridley-Thomas's plan to add a Latino seat in Knabe's district (supported by a coalition of ethnic groups), and Knabe's plan to preserve the status quo. The winner, of course, was the latter plan encompassing a few minor changes.[7]

The 2011 redistricting drama was followed by a change in the California Voting Rights Act that spurred activists to change representation in cities from at-large elections to districts. The activity also spurred state legislators to consider the Los Angeles County process and produced a bill creating a fourteen-member independent redistricting commission to modify supervisorial boundaries designed to prevent BOS gerrymandering of the past. The *Times* and a Latino redistricting consultant pointed out problems with the bill, but Governor Brown signed it without comment.[8]

Since 2000, the BOS has had several occasions to revisit calls for the appointment of other county elected officials based on the actions of those currently holding the positions. In 2012, County Assessor John Noguez was arrested and accused of bribery and conspiracy in taking payoffs to assist a representative of wealthy property owners in manipulating their tax assessments. Noguez refused to resign and continued to receive his salary until his tenure ended. The scandal generated recommendations that the office of assessor should be filled by an appointed expert, but no action resulted. The Noguez case was dropped in 2020 but could be initiated again.[9]

Another elected official, Sheriff Lee Baca, encountered criticism at the same time because of the LASD scandal in treating jail inmates. He became enmeshed because of his participation and would eventually be convicted of obstruction of justice and lying to federal agents and prosecutors (see below). Calls for the appointment of the sheriff were heard, some demanding both the assessor and sheriff be appointed. These opinions followed county-sponsored investigations since the final report of the Reining Charter Study Committee in 1958, but neither office have been changed to appointive.[10]

Besides the ideological and personal attributes of the post–2000 supervisors, as well as changes or attempted changes to the structure of county government, they also coped with major events and decisions occurring in California, the United States, and even the rest of the world which affected local policies and actions. The 2003 recall of Governor Gray Davis and his replacement, Arnold Schwarzenegger, a stronger Democratic legislature, and the state's economic fall and rise have affected funding and other issues for counties since then. National politics, violence related to hate groups, the 2008 recession, and the initiatives of the Trump administration have also affected many county policies. And the rise of international terrorism with al-Qaeda and the September 11, 2001, attacks, the Iraq and Afghanistan wars, and ISIS atrocities and the COVID-19 pandemic throughout the globe have made their mark in local security precautions and immigration, among other issues.[11]

Law and Order

Since 2000, there have been many additions made to LASD infrastructure and new programs to improve training of deputies, the treatment of jail inmates and other facets of preserving order. There have also been scandals involving members of the LASD which reflected badly on many top officials and deputies. A few of these include the deputies unloading 120 rounds of ammunition in a Compton residential area in which one deputy shot another one; seven members of a secret LASD "gang" known as the Jump Out Boys being fired for celebrating police shootings;

and a sergeant claiming he had been threatened at gun point by a member of another LASD clique. In 2009, it was admitted that the LASD had trouble hiring new recruits as it had to accept many that it would have been rejected in the past, according to the Office of Independent Review, created in 2001 to analyze citizen complaints. Other issues involved large settlement payouts by the county resulting from detectives withholding evidence proving the innocence of a defendant, of deputies planting illegal drugs on innocent residents; and of jailors accused of brutality.[12]

Sheriff Baca, a smart and politically ambitious administrator, was respected as a leader in law enforcement in the early 2000s. But many of his actions were not as positive. He became known for taking care of his political supporters, and as a "Sheriff to the Stars" with the favorable treatment his deputies supplied to celebrities. It was revealed that Baca launched an expensive investigation for one of his "Baca's Favored Few" in Beverly Hills, located outside of his jurisdiction. The state attorney general initiated at least two investigations of Baca; one regarding his support unit of businessmen who financed his political campaigns. In 2014, a television news station reported that he hired four field deputies, some of whom received more than $100,000 annually and a county car but did virtually nothing for the county.[13]

Baca's retirement in the same year came when his role in the department's major jail scandal was about to overtake him. Reports of civilians witnessing deputy brutality in 2011 and other actions spurred county and federal investigations that convinced jailors to admit brutality that top LASD officials overlooked. Federal officials began an investigation without informing Baca, and his top aides tried to obstruct the probe. Over the next three years eighteen deputies and their superiors were arrested and tried on charges such as inmate abuse, smuggling contraband into cells (in one case in a burrito), obstructing justice, and impeding a federal investigation. Most would be convicted and sentenced to various terms of incarceration.[14]

By 2015, it was Baca's turn. He and his chief assistant were indicted for participating in some of the crimes. In his second trial the jury convicted him of three felonies, and he was sentenced to three years in prison (not county jail). His downfall would lead to the appointment of an interim sheriff, the 2014 election of Sheriff Jim McDonnell, and the creation of an oversight commission for the department. More calls for reforms of the LASD jail operation continued, as did reports of the activities of a growing number of LASD "gang" cliques. In late 2018, a new sheriff was elected, and it did not take long for the BOS to challenge his early decisions protecting his favorites. Sheriff Alex Villanueva's many conflicts in his power struggle with the BOS and other county officials include his disputes with individual supervisors and the CEO, as well as noncooperation with the County Counsel and Inspector General. His department would also see more LASD shootings of minority residents and criticism of their handling of local protests during the national response to the death of George Floyd by police in Minnesota in 2020. By the end of that year, the supervisors were searching for a method to remove him from office. In early 2021, the California attorney general ordered a civil rights investigation of the LASD, "an agency beset by allegations of deputy misconduct, controversial shootings, and resistance to oversight from Sheriff Alex Villanueva."[15]

In the meantime, LASD deputies and supervisors continued to do their jobs as the department served the county's unincorporated areas and many of its cities by contract. In another department responsible for public safety, District Attorney Steve Cooley declined to run again in 2012, and Chief Deputy D.A. Jackie Lacey won election in that year. Both administrations have been lauded for their work, but also criticized for rejecting many of the cases filed against LASD and LAPD officers. (This issue played a role in Lacey's defeat by George Gascón in 2020.) Like the LASD, the Probation Department experienced misconduct scandals created by some of its officers during the post–2000 period. In fact, the department was placed under federal oversight twice for several years each for various scandals involving staff misdeeds and abuse of juveniles; the BOS finally established an oversight commission for it.[16]

Health and Social Services

Some of the county's most important services are those that aid disadvantaged residents who need assistance with basic human needs, such as healthcare, financial aid, housing, and the protection of children in dire circumstances. As mentioned in Chapter 11, the Los Angeles County Health system teetered on the verge of collapse in 1995 because of the county's financial situation. With the help of a federal bailout, the Department of Health Services (DHS) survived that threat but faced continued problems after 2000. While the LAC+USC Hospital was rebuilt and opened in 2008, the MLK-Drew Hospital was forced to shut down in 2007 because of recurring mismanagement and malpractice problems jeopardizing accreditation and federal funding. The closure put a strain on county medical services until it reopened in 2015.[17]

The financial situation would improve, however, with DHS restructuring and the help of the federal government, a tobacco industry lawsuit, and county voters. Along with the 1995 bailout funds, the Clinton administration granted a five-year Medicaid waiver renewed in 2000, saving the DHS millions. The county's lawsuit against tobacco companies (as part of a suit involving forty-five states) resulted in a settlement in which the county would receive $2.8 billion over 25 years beginning in 2000. Zev Yaroslavsky's ballot proposal to add a parcel tax on property to raise funds for trauma centers was approved by more than the two-thirds majority needed in 2002. These additions to DHS funding helped to ease future reforms as the DHS adjusted to the increase in patients because of the Patient Protection and Affordable Care Act and many more challenges, including the COVID-19 pandemic addressed by the County Public Health Department. The virus and its variants took over 28,000 lives in the county by early 2022, as well as generating various conflicts among county leaders on who should address it and with residents on the rules and demands ordered by the BOS.[18]

County welfare services followed earlier changes made by the state and federal governments. In 1988, California created the Greater Avenues for Independence (GAIN), a welfare to-work program for its counties, which BOS put under the supervision of a private contractor. In the 1990s, GAIN garnered praise for its efficiency but criticism for placing its clients mainly in low-paying jobs.[19]

In 1996, the federal government ended its welfare program for families (AFDC) and created a more limited replacement for which it supplied funds to the states. Fortunately for many recipients, the national economy improved by the end of the 1990s, so more jobs became available. After 2000, the situation became worse for some in Department of Social Services (DPSS) programs as the poverty gap in Los Angeles widened; state aid declined during the late 2000s recession, and eventually improved.[20]

Serving some of the homeless in Los Angeles County is also one of the services of the DPSS. After the conflict between the city and county governments in addressing this issue in the 1980s, several committees were formed to deal with it until the Los Angeles Homeless Services Authority (LAHSA) was established as a city-county joint powers agency in 1993. It was not very successful in stemming the tide of homeless during the recession of the early 1990s, having limited power and funds. By 2005, LAHSA operations were described by the County Grand Jury as being in "serious disarray." The number of homeless in the county at that time was estimated by the *Times* editors to be 88,000, the most in the nation.[21]

In the following decade, the situation improved in better economic times but rose again to about 57,000 in 2017. Progress has been slow in finding housing for the homeless, although both the city and county of Los Angeles approved major ballot measures in 2016 and 2017 to expand funding for the program. Legal problems involved with business property owners and advocates of those in homeless encampments regarding cleanup and enforcement plans, and disputes with other residents regarding the siting of housing for the homeless still have a long way to go, as the number of homeless rose to about 60,000 by mid–2019.[22]

The Department of Children and Families Services (DCFS–Families was added by 1994) had seen years of chaos since its creation in 1984. Protecting children required the cooperation of staff in several county departments to report warning signs of abuse by adults, and communication was not always timely or complete. Social workers on the staff sometimes had difficulty in analyzing each case, and they always seemed to be assigned too many clients at the same time. Cases of child abuse and problems with private care agencies and foster parents climbed in the 1990s, and scandals involving children attracted immediate media notice and calls for investigation. Several department heads were forced out or resigned before 2000 because of these scandals.[23]

The post–2000 decades were no different. Newspapers reported in 2000 that the foster program was in disarray after the deaths of several children under the county's care, and that one private agency had been misspending government funds as the state and county tried to shut it down. In 2002, the state performed an audit that pointed out some of its problems. In 2009, the supervisors were "shocked" to hear that fourteen children under county care had died the year before; still others would die later that year. In 2010 and 2011, articles and editorials in the *Times* revealed more problems with foster care and more deaths of children.[24]

After further criticism from the state on BOS oversight of the DCFS, the department faced its worst nightmare in May 2013, when an eight-year-old boy died after being tortured and abused by his mother and her boyfriend. Department social workers had been informed of the ongoing abuse by several witnesses, and there had been six investigations, but they decided not to remove him. Four social workers were then accused of felony child abuse and other charges by ignoring repeated abuse. They were eventually cleared over a year after the death of another young boy, who suffered from abuse by his mother's boyfriend after the DCFS and LASD had been alerted. Meanwhile, more problems surfaced in the DCFS operation as the supervisors and other county officials worked to reform the department.[25]

Cities and Transit

The relationship between county officials and members of city governments during these years appeared to be generally cooperative, although they were in competition in some issues, especially when it came to revenue to finance their operations. Since the county supplied services to many of its cities under contract, there continued to be disagreement on what those services should cost, both between county and city officials and between the supervisors and the sheriff. The supervisors continued to be concerned with redevelopment projects in the cities that restricted county tax revenue and would fight many of those projects until Governor Brown ended that program in 2012, because of frequent abuses in the past, many of them in Los Angeles County.[26]

Government corruption in the county's cities also became a chief concern for the supervisors. A *Times* story in 2003 revealed that several cities in the southeast portion of the county had experienced corruption. The epidemic would continue in many of them as well as in cities further east and west. Most consisted of individual city officials charged with fraud and accepting bribes in investigations by the FBI and state and local agencies.[27]

The most serious scandal occurred in Bell, a working-class city, where the city manager, his assistant, the police chief, and all members of the city council were charged with various crimes after a series of *Times* articles appeared in 2010. Reporters found that the city manager earned almost $800,000 per year plus many perks; his assistant's salary was over $376,000, and the chief of police made almost 50 percent more than the county sheriff and LAPD chief. Part-time Bell City Council members were paid over $100,000 for their work and never questioned the amount. These revelations, as well as reports of city loans made to the officials, spurred protests, pay cuts, lawsuits, a recall election, and an investigation that sent most of them to trial. All except the police chief (forced out of his position) would be convicted of various charges; the city manager received a twelve-year sentence plus almost three years in a federal prison for tax fraud. His assistant (noted for her "Pigs get Fat" emails regarding their salaries) got more than eleven years. And the council members received shorter sentences based on their participation. The five-year ordeal led to many reforms and lawsuits; it certainly put Bell on the map.[28]

City representatives in the county were also involved in rapid transit planning and operation along with the supervisors. In 1964, the legislature created the Southern California Rapid Transit District (RTD) to take over that responsibility, with a board of directors that included city officials and the supervisors. This agency was not very successful, and in 1977, the Los Angeles County Transportation Commission (LACTC) consisting of all five supervisors and several city appointees took over planning and funding duties while the RTD handled the operation. Supervisor Kenneth Hahn led the political campaign in 1980 to pass Proposition A, which called for a sales tax increase to fund a rail rapid transit system and reduce RTD bus fares. The winning measure followed several failed proposals in the 1970s and would supply funds for rapid transit for many years.[29]

Success in creating rapid transit would not occur rapidly, but it did occur, as the RTD and LACTC directors and managers argued throughout the 1980s, mostly feuding over issues such as the type of transit to be built, where routes would be located among possible city options, and how cities should use their funds. Financing was also a challenge as the Reagan administration opposed many calls for federal contributions. In 1987, while the county supervisors complained of the actions of other directors, the County Grand Jury blamed the supervisors for the LACTC-RTD woes and left it to them to make changes. In the same year there were more calls for major changes in the administration of the two contending agencies. As the feud continued in late 1988, Mayor Tom Bradley suggested a compromise in which clear lines of authority would be agreed to by both, and the supervisors approved it. Disagreement continued, and eleven months later, Hahn asked the director of County Beaches and Harbors to locate a small yacht, put the general managers of the RTD and LACTC on it, and "take them out to sea near Catalina and anchor them there until they work out the differences between their two agencies."[30]

Despite the decade-long feud, the first rapid transit route, the Blue Line, opened for riders in 1990, and another tax measure to support the system won voter approval that year. But the feud lingered until the two agencies finally merged as the Los Angeles County Metropolitan Transportation Authority (MTA, or Metro) in 1993. The MTA bus and rail system was headed by thirteen directors including the five county supervisors and eight representatives of cities. During the 1990s, three additional lines were begun and finished amid several investigations by federal authorities of corruption, cost overruns, construction problems, conflicts of interest regarding contractors, questionable loans for directors, and various lawsuits by contractors. The Bus Riders Union protested, and the Los Angeles office of the NAACP filed a suit charging racism based on fare hikes in low-income areas that was finally settled in 1995. All of this occurred with the agency frequently in debt, some seven billion dollars in 1998.[31]

In the post 2000 years, the MTA has not seen the same type of corruption charges aimed at its leadership as in the past. However, it has still faced criticism of some of its decisions based on fare hikes, purchasing expensive new rail cars and buses, more strikes by its drivers and mechanics, and the location plans for subways, among other issues. A 2008 federal audit criticized the MTA for civil rights violations in eliminating some of its lines. In fact, more than one critic opined that rapid bus transit, rather than fixed rail, made better sense in Los Angeles because of its experience with transportation changes.[32]

On the other hand, the MTA has survived much of that criticism in the last two decades and moved ahead with planning and building its system. Since 2000, it has completed two additional major lines and two new busways and expanded the bus system and other services with additional projects in the works. With the *Times* supporting it as needed for future transit, along with business leaders and organized labor, the agency won ballot measures in 2008 and 2016 to permanently increase the county sales tax to pay for maintenance and new projects. The 2016 measure received approval by more than 71 percent of county voters, testimony that MTA's public is still willing to support it, despite more criticism and a decline in ridership and a fluctuation in its services.[33]

Responses to the Trump Administration

One of the most powerful outside influences on some decisions made by Los Angeles County government since late 2016 has been the Trump administration and its initiatives affecting everyday life for county and U.S. residents. In sync with the efforts of California and some other states to reject or limit those federal actions, the Democrats on the BOS, and frequently the lone moderate Republican, voted on occasions to address federal changes that could affect the entire nation.

The county BOS began to oppose Trump's plans just two weeks after the new supervisors took office as the majority voted to defend beneficiaries of the Deferred Action for Childhood Arrivals (DACA) program considered to be at risk for deportation. Since then, the BOS approved resolutions and calls for action by state officials and state representatives in Congress to again defend undocumented immigrants residing in the U.S., as well as forcing the end of the ban on the immigration of Muslims; to oppose federal cuts in housing programs, a national healthcare proposal to replace Obamacare, and the separation of children from their parents crossing the southern U.S. border; and to support the Paris Climate Agreement and net neutrality. The supervisors also supported lawsuits against the federal government filed by the California attorney general, as well as endorsing suits filed by other states.[34]

Within the county itself, the BOS voted to limit cooperation with Immigration and Customs Enforcement officers in county jails and support the state sanctuary law, even when the sheriff opposed it. The board also approved additional funds for immigration lawyers and rejected EPA efforts to relax air pollution standards in the county. Criticism of the president himself would follow, especially concerning the actions of national and more local hate groups he neglected to condemn. These decisions and others mentioned above certainly put the BOS in the mainstream of California discontent with the initiatives of the Trump administration. The election of President Joe Biden in late 2020 has certainly changed the relationship of the county and federal governments since then.[35]

As mentioned in the introduction, this book is not an encyclopedia of county history since 1950. Many county issues have not been considered, even though the research for this book included them, because of their sheer number. This chapter has focused on some of the more important issues and actions in the post 2000 decades, all of which will need some time to place in a more comprehensive overall context. Much of it is still being played out at this time, and all of it is subject to change with future historical analysis and interpretation.

Epilogue

Since World War II and much earlier, Los Angeles County has been a leading urban county in the U.S. For better or worse, and in many ways, it could be a guide to success and pitfalls for other modern counties with large urban populations demanding new services and amenities and working with state and federal governments creating new mandates and changing financial support.

In the post-war years, the county experienced economic prosperity and population influx during the Cold War fears in the 1950s; civil rights demands by several groups and a full-scale urban rebellion in the 1960s, along with protests against the war in Vietnam; the national Watergate scandal and improprieties of county officials casting suspicion on governments at all levels; the taxpayer revolt against rising levies and attempts of communities to split off and form new counties in the 1970s; the Reagan administration decade of promised government downsizing but actually growing government in the nation and county in the 1980s; and the national recession, almost bankruptcy, and another urban uprising in the 1990s. In the new millennium, wars and recessions, continued social inequality and civil rights restraints, and other local, state, national, and international conditions, trends, and events have had their effect on county government and residents throughout the nation.

In guiding Los Angeles County through this maze, its leaders have had to establish policies and make decisions as a group which, like other governmental boards, included members that certainly did not agree on all issues. This is apparent in the major themes that run through the post–1950 decades. The personalities of the supervisors were different, some more forward than others based on their attitudes and temperaments. Their ideologies sometimes grouped them in cliques opposing other cliques, especially in the 1980s, although personalities could limit the effectiveness of the majority seemingly in control. The structure of county government preserved and limited the power of county leaders and the process of government administration; attempts to alter it demonstrate how board members defined their power in relation to ideals considered to make them more representative of and more responsive to their constituents. And the many, many "outside" forces, such as lobbying by local city officials and interest groups, demands of higher levels of government, environmental threats and changes, and national and international events and issues also played a role in decision making.

Like the "Courthouse Crowd" before them, the Titans of Temple Street after 1950 faced many of these restraints while trying to keep the county ship on an even keel. They certainly had many problems in doing so as they allowed massive residential development, which is especially apparent during wildfires and with major traffic congestion and have failed on occasion in their oversight of county agencies such as the sheriff, probation, planning, health and children's departments, shortcomings that might have been mitigated to some extent by the adoption of a few structural reforms.

Structural reform, however, does not guarantee improvement. As Supervisors Edmund Edelman, Zev Yaroslavsky and others have argued, the expansion of the BOS to seven or more could improve representation by reducing the number of residents in each supervisorial district and allowing underrepresented groups more access to county government. But without an independent elected county executive, the larger BOS could become chaotic and difficult for an appointed executive's administration of departments and agencies. The often-sought elected executive could balance the political power of the BOS as the governor and legislative branches of California government, with one person to represent the entire county rather than the parochial interests of the various districts. But an executive such as Supervisor Pete Schabarum, who reportedly expressed interest in running for the position, or CAO Richard Dixon, who relished amassing power, might be in frequent competition with the BOS. The elected executive would be a politician working with several other elected officials, and success would depend on the attitude and attributes of the person elected.

The appointment of the sheriff, as in the LAPD with its appointed chief of police, might result in the end of the many conflicts between the sheriff and the supervisors. However, the tradition of an elected sheriff independent of the BOS might be difficult for voters to accept, and the state constitution would have to be amended for it. The appointment of a professional assessor would be more likely, especially since the position changed after Proposition 13 passed in 1978. The office of district attorney is less likely to change for good reason; the office is responsible for deciding the pursuit of charges made against top county officials, as well as others.

If any reforms could be made, how about reducing the number of special districts in the county. While each was established for a specific purpose, such as schools and mosquito abatement in small areas and those as large as the county itself, the sheer numbers of them have produced confusion, duplication of administration, and occasional mismanagement allowed by poor oversight. The consolidation of some providing similar services might go a long way in reducing expenditures and the size of the county bureaucracy in the hundreds of its special districts.[1] More transparency in BOS decision making and access for the public would also be helpful.

Beyond this critical narrative that has focused mainly on its faults and limitations, Los Angeles County government has managed to respond positively in many dire circumstances over which its leaders had limited control. As the frequently critical *Los Angeles Times* noted in early 2018, "County officials are doing some remarkable work. The task they've taken on to combat homelessness is monumental [and very slow at this writing]. Their attempt to reinvent juvenile probation is profound. The county's role in the state's economy is enormous." And since late 2018, with the ascendency of a BOS composed primarily of women (all five by the end of 2020), there has been a definite change in direction in a new era as the BOS grapples with social, environmental, economic, and other issues beyond those mentioned in Chapter 12.[2]

Despite some bad choices made in the past, and with consideration of possible reforms, the experience of the Titans of Temple Street provides an opportunity for the leaders of other counties to ponder in evaluating their own past actions and prospects in their governance.

Acronyms and Abbreviations*

BONELLI   Frank Bonelli Collection, SEAVER

BOS   Los Angeles County Board of Supervisors

BSC   Board of Supervisors Correspondence Files and County Archives, Los Angeles County Hall of Administration

BSM   Board of Supervisors Minutes of Meetings, Los Angeles County Hall of Administration and *www.lacounty.gov/wps/portal/sop*

BURKE   Yvonne B. Burke Papers, USC

CSA   California State Archives, Sacramento, California

CSL   California State Library, Sacramento, California

CSULA   Special Collections, California State University, Los Angeles

DEBS   Ernest E. Debs Papers, CSULA

EDELMAN   Edmund D. Edelman, Papers, HUNTINGTON

GARCETTI   Gilbert Garcetti Papers, HUNTINGTON

HAHN   Kenneth Hahn Papers, HUNTINGTON

HUNTINGTON   Henry E. Huntington Library, San Marino, California

JAF   John Anson Ford Papers, HUNTINGTON

LAACOC   Los Angeles Area Chamber of Commerce Collection, USC

LACCEEC   Los Angeles County Citizens' Economy and Efficiency Commission

LACGJ   Los Angeles County Grand Jury

LACHRC   Los Angeles County Human Relations Commission

LACLL   Los Angeles County Law Library

LACRC   Los Angeles City Records Center, Los Angeles

LAT   Los Angeles Times

MOLINA   Gloria Molina Papers, HUNTINGTON

POPE   Alexander Pope Papers, HUNTINGTON

---

* In most cases the words in ALL CAPS on the left of the list indicate the collection and/or institution where an item is housed. ALL CAPS are used in the chapter notes to indicate an item's location. For instance, BURKE means an item is held in the Yvonne B. Burke Papers at USC. More information can be found in the Manuscripts & Reference Collections section or other sections of the Bibliography.

SCLSSR   Southern California Library for Social Studies and Research, Los Angeles

SEAVER   Seaver Center for Western History Research, Natural History Museum of Los Angeles County

STANFORD   Special Collections, Green Library, Stanford University

UCLA   Department of Special Collections, Young Research Library, University of California, Los Angeles

USC   Department of Special Collections, University of Southern California Library, Los Angeles

All newspapers are/were published in Los Angeles unless otherwise cited.

Chapter Notes

Chapter 1

1. The term "Five Little Kings" can be found at least as early as 1966 in an article in the *Los Angeles Herald-Dispatch,* January 15, 1966, and was referred to even earlier in a 1964 community paper. They were also referred to as "The Five Little Princes" five years earlier by the editor of the *Tujunga Record Ledger,* April 9, 1959. Clippings of stories in both papers can be found in Frank Bonelli Scrapbooks for those years, SEAVER.

2. Los Angeles County Board of Supervisors and Office of Superintendent of Schools, "Los Angeles County: A Handbook of Its Government and Services," 2; Tom Sitton, *The Courthouse Crowd: Los Angeles County and its Government, 1850–1950* (Los Angeles: Historical Society of Southern California, 2013), 36.

3. Robert O. Warren, *Government in Metropolitan Regions: A Reappraisal of Fractionated Political Organization* (Davis: University of California, Davis, Institute of Governmental Affairs,1966), 59.

4. John Anson Ford newsletter, Apr. 7, 1953, box 54, JAF; "Los Angeles An Industrial Giant," Los Angeles Board of Harbor Commissioners, "Annual Report," 1951, 40; "Los Angeles Has Greatest Industry Growth," *Southern California Business* 12 (Mar. 29, 1950): 1, 3; Rachel Surls and Judith B. Gerber, *From Cows to Concrete: The Rise and Fall of Farming in Los Angeles* (Santa Monica, Calif.: Angel City Press, 2016), 75–94, 111–177; Jennifer Wolch, "From Global to Local: The Rise of Homelessness in Los Angeles During the 1980s," in Allen J. Scott and Edward W. Soja, eds., *The City: Los Angeles and Urban Theory at the End of the Twentieth Century* (Berkeley, Los Angeles, London: University of California Press, 1996), 391.

5. "Los Angeles County: A Handbook," 2; Sitton, *The Courthouse Crowd,* 296–300.

6. "Los Angeles County: A Handbook," xiv-xv.

7. *LAT,* May 28, 1972, Aug. 27, 1973; Herbert Legg motion, May 7, 1957, box 874, Hahn motion, May 4, 1972, box 27, HAHN; John Anson Ford to Jay B. Price, Oct. 3, 1958, box 18, JAF; Public Commission on County Government, *To Serve Seven Million: Report of the Public Commission on Los Angeles County Government* (Los Angeles: The Commission, 1976), 27–28, 31–34; Robert E.G. Harris, "5 Men for Five Million," *Frontier* 7 (Mar. 1956): 13–17.

8. *LAT,* Aug. 22, 1938, Sept. 5, 1953; Sitton, *The Courthouse Crowd, 214ff;* http://bos.lacounty.gov/About-Us/Board-of-Supervisors/Board-Member-Biographies.

9. *LAT,* Dec. 5, 1934, Feb. 8, 1956, Mar. 29, 1958; *Long Beach Independent Press-Telegram,* Mar. 26, 1958; *Herald & Express,* Mar. 28, 1958.

10. http://bos.lacounty.gov/About-Us/Board-of-Supervisors/Board-Member-Biographies; *Examiner,* Jun. 5, 1958; *Herald & Express,* Aug. 19, 1960; *Wilmington Press-Journal,* Sept. 2, 1960; *Mirror-News,* Oct. 17, 1960; "The Image of Frank G. Bonelli: 'Man of Distinction,'" *Los Angeles County Employee,* Sept. 15, 1964, 6; *LAT,* Feb.16, 1972. Bonelli's career can be followed in newspaper clippings in the Bonelli Scrapbooks, SEAVER.

11. *LAT,* Dec. 21, 1969; *San Francisco Chronicle,* Oct. 23, 1936; *Torrance Daily Breeze,* Mar. 31, 1960; newspaper clippings, *Los Angeles Examiner Collection,* USC; Sitton, *The Courthouse Crowd,* 222ff; http://bos.lacounty.gov/About-Us/Board-of-Supervisors/Board-Member-Biographies.

12. *LAT,* Jun. 16, 1974, Nov. 1, 1991, Dec. 2, 1992, Oct. 13, 1997; *Southside Journal,* Apr. 21, 1960; *Herald Examiner,* May 25, 1980; Edmund G. Brown to James S. Mize, Jul. 31, 1964, and Hahn motion, Jul. 21, 1964, box 478, Hahn motion, Mar. 30, 1954, box 874, HAHN; Toby Shor, "The Wizard of Ward-Heel Politics," *San Francisco Chronicle,* Oct. 25, 1981; Toby Shor, "LA's Kenny Hahn: The State's Best Politician?" *California Journal* 12 (Oct. 1981): 341–343; Alexa Bell, "The Hahn Dynasty: Kenny and Jimmy and LA Politics," *California Journal* 19 (Mar. 1988): 120–122, 126.

13. *LAT,* Nov. 4, 1983; John Anson Ford, "John Anson Ford and Los Angeles County Government" (University of California, Los Angeles, Oral History Program, 1967, passim; Sitton, *The Courthouse Crowd,* 214ff. See also John Anson Ford, *Thirty Explosive Years in Los Angeles County* (San Marino, Calif.: Huntington Library, 1961) and *Honest Politics My Theme: The Story of a Veteran Public Official's Troubles and Triumphs: An Autobiography* (New York: Vantage Press, 1978).

14. http://bos.lacounty.gov/About-Us/Board-of-Supervisors/Board-Member-Biographies;

Ernest E. Debs., Oral History Interview, Conducted by Carlos Vasquez (University of California, Los Angeles for the State Government Oral History Program, 1987), CSA, passim; Tom Sitton, *Los Angeles Transformed: Fletcher Bowron's Urban Reform Revival, 1938–1953* (Albuquerque: University of New Mexico Press, 2005), 119–121; *LAT*, Apr. 26, 27, 1977, Mar. 19, 2002.

15. *LAT*, Dec. 11, 1949, Mar. 10, 1953; *Sacramento Bee*, Jan. 17, 1950; *Los Angeles Examiner* Collection, USC; http://bos.lacounty.gov/About-Us/Board-of-Supervisors/Board-Member-Biographies.

16. http://bos.lacounty.gov/About-Us/Board-of-Supervisors/Board-Member-Biographies; *LAT*, Aug. 23, 26, 1972.

17. *LAT*, Apr. 6, 1942, Mar. 10, 1953, Jan. 25, 1956, Jan. 22, 1971 (quote); *San Francisco Chronicle*, Apr. 10, 1942, Feb. 5, 1945; Sitton, *The Courthouse Crowd*, 214ff; Ford weekly newsletter, Dec. 5, 1944, box 53, JAF.

18. *LAT*, Aug. 25, 1974, Jan. 11, 2006; "The Image of Warren M. Dorn: "Apostle of Purity,'" *Los Angeles, County Employee*, Nov. 16, 1964, 7.

19. *LAT*, Jul. 7–20, December 9, 1952, May 28, 1972; Harris, "5 Men for 5 Million," 13–17.

20. *LAT*, Nov. 27, 1957, Dec. 2, 1958, May 18, 1960, Mar. 6, 10, 1965, Jul. 18, 1966, Dec. 14, 1973; *North Hollywood Valley Times*, Apr. 8, 1959; *Westchester Citizen*, Mar. 11, 1965; *West Los Angeles Independent*, Apr. 1, 1965; *Herald-Dispatch*, Jan. 15, 1966.

21. *LAT*, Jan. 13, 1954, Jan. 15, 1969, Dec. 7, 1970; Harris, "5 Men for 5 Million," 15–16; Ford, *Thirty Explosive Years*, 28–34; Sitton, *The Courthouse Crowd*, 234ff.

22. *LAT*, Oct. 14, 1954, Apr. 25, 1956, May 29, 1960; *Pomona Progress-Bulletin* (Nov. 29, 1967; copy of Kennedy press release, Nov. 21, 1956, box 82, Goodwin Knight Papers, CSA; Ford, *Thirty Explosive Years*, 66–72; Sitton, *The Courthouse Crowd*, 277, 280, 289, 298.

23. On Postwar America see, among many others: Steve Fraser and Gary Gerstle, eds., *The Rise and Fall of the New Deal Order, 1930–1980* (Princeton, N.J.: Princeton University Press, 1989); James T. Patterson, *Grand Expectations: The United States, 1945–1974* (New York: Oxford University Press, 1996); William Henry Chafe, *The Unfinished Journey: America Since World War II* (New York: Oxford University Press, 1991).

24. Copy of BOS resolution, Mar. 25, 1947, box 46, JAF; "True Copy of County Loyalty Oath," box 1, Orilla Winfield Papers, SCLSSR; Harold W. Horowitz, "Report on the Los Angeles City and County Loyalty Programs," *Stanford Law Review* 5 (February 1953): 233–234; *LAT*, Mar. 3, 14, 1947, Mar. 1, 1960; Harold W. Kennedy, "Special Report of the County Counsel on problem created by recent United States Supreme Court cases affecting the Communist Party and the twenty year fight of the County of Los Angeles against subversion and Communism," Aug. 19, 1964, quote on 9, LACLL;

Herald & Express, Oct. 14, 1948; Sitton, *The Courthouse Crowd*, 275–280.

25. Ford weekly newsletter, Aug. 1, 22, 1950, box 54, Ford statement for KTTV, Aug. 23, 1950, Judge Stanley Moffatt to Ford and other friends, Oct. 14, 1950, box 46, JAF; *LAT*, Aug. 23, 29, 1950; Sitton, *The Courthouse Crowd*, 149–152; Carey McWilliams, "The Registration of Heretics," *Nation* 171 (Dec. 9, 1950): 526–528.

26. Congressman Gordon McDonough to Ford, Nov. 3, 1945, copy of E.P. Conser to BOS, Oct. 9, 1945, James H. Burford to Ford, Jul. 22, 1946, " Report of Los Angeles County Board of Supervisors' Committee on Rent Control Practices and Procedures in the County of Los Angeles," Dec. 4, 1945, box 65, Ford weekly newsletters, Oct. 9, Dec. 4, 1945, box 53, and Jul. 9, 23, 1946, box 54, JAF; *LAT*, Jul. 10, 1946; Sitton, *Los Angeles Transformed*, 114–115.

27. *Daily News*, Jul. 16, 1949; Minutes of Chamber of Commerce directors meetings, Jun. 3, 1948, 63, February 24, 1949, 22, carton 029, LAACOC; Armando Torrez to BOS, Aug. 25, 1949, copy of Thomas O'Dwyer to BOS, Sept. 13, 1949, newsletter of the California Housing Association (n.d. 1949), County Counsel Harold Kennedy to BOS, Jun. 24, 1949, box 65, Ford weekly newsletter, Sept. 27, 1949, box 54, JAF; Don Parson, *Making a Better World: Public Housing, the Red Scare, and the Direction of Modern Los Angeles* (Minneapolis and London: University of Minnesota Press, 2005), 90–91, 98–102.

28. Copy of BSM transcript, Nov. 22, 1949, Arthur Miley memo to Ford, Dec. 27, 1949, box 65, Ford weekly newsletter, Dec. 27, 1949, box 54, JAF; *LAT*, Nov. 16, 18, December 28, 1949.

29. Ford weekly newsletters, Sept. 29, 1949, Sept. 12, 1950, box 54, JAF; *LAT*, Aug. 2, Sept.13, 1950.

30. *LAT*, Nov. 3, 19, 1950; Dale Gardner to Ford, Jan. 18, 1951, box 65, JAF; Parson, *Making a Better World*, 75–135; Sitton, *Los Angeles Transformed*, 157–160, 165–187.

31. *LAT*, Dec. 15, 1950, Sept. 19, 1954, Aug. 8 (second quote), 9, 16, Oct. 31, Nov. 1, 9, 13, 1961, Sept. 19, 1962; Ford newsletters, Feb. 1, Mar. 15, 1955, box 55, JAF; Hahn press release, Nov. 2, 1961 (first quote), Hahn to John F. Kennedy, Dec. 7, 1961, box 1013, Andrew J. Fink to Phil Pennington, Aug. 7, 1964, and Joseph M. Quinn to BOS, Jan. 10, 1967, box 1015, HAHN; Sitton, *The Courthouse Crowd*, 252–261, 310.

32. *LAT*, Apr. 30, Aug. 23, Dec. 27, 1950, Feb. 28, 1951; *Herald Examiner*, Jun. 26, 1964; Gordon T. Nesvig to Harold W. Kennedy, Jun. 4, 1954, Hahn motion, Sept. 29, 1964, box 876, and other material in boxes 598, 599, HAHN.

33. *LAT*, Jul. 13, 1951, Nov. 15, 1952, Dec. 14, 1957, Mar. 1, 1960, May 17, Dec. 22, 1967; Ford statement, Mar. 8, 1948, *Alert* newsletter, Feb. 21, 1949, 262, and copy of Jimmie Tarantino telegram to *Daily News*, May 26, 1952, box 46, JAF.

34. Kennedy, "Special Report of the County

Counsel," Jun. 9, 1964, LACLL; *LAT*, Mar.12, 1958, Feb. 2, 1962, Aug. 20, 1964; Hahn motions, Aug. 25, 1964, box 876, and Jan. 24, 1967, box 878, Maurice Chez presentation transcript, Mar. 9, 1971, box 148, HAHN; Minutes of Chamber of Commerce directors meetings, Feb. 20, 1969, 16, carton 035, LAACOC; Debs motion, Dec. 8, 19–64, Harold Kennedy Report on Nazis (n.d.), box 404, DEBS.

35. Paul Jacobs, "Assault on UNESCO," *The Commonweal* 62 (May 27, 1955): 210–211; Jo Hindman, "Los Angeles--City in Turmoil," *American Mercury* 84 (Apr. 1957): 146–147; Glen W. Adams, "The UNESCO Controversy in Los Angeles, 1951–1953: A Case Study of the Influence of Right-Wing Groups on Urban Affairs" (PhD diss., University of Southern California, 1970), passim.

36. Mrs. Eugene E. Finkle to Frank Bonelli, Jan. 19, 1971, box 29, DEBS; *LAT*, Jan. 28, 1971; "Film Collection Attacked in Los Angeles County," *Library Journal* 96 (Mar. 1, 1971): 771–772.

37. Sarah Schrank, *Art and the City: Civic Imagination and Cultural Authority in Los Angeles* (Philadelphia: University of Pennsylvania Press, 2009), 64–71, 79–94; Sitton, *The Courthouse Crowd* (first quote, 309; Sitton, *Los Angeles Transformed*, 153.

38. *LAT*, Jul. 6, 1952, Jun. 25, 1953, May 2, 1954, Jul. 15, 2006; Duncan Gleason to Supporting Organizations, Jul. 15, 1951, American Legion Malibu Post No. 605 resolution, Aug. 25, 1956, Ford to Donald Hughes, Jr., Oct. 2, 1956, box 46, JAF.

39. *LAT*, Aug. 19, 1950, Feb. 1954, Jul. 6, 1955; Ford newsletters, Aug. 12, 1952, Feb. 24, 1953, box 54, JAF; Robert Gottlieb and Irene Wolt, *Thinking Big: The Story of the Los Angeles Times, Its Publishers, and Their Influence on Southern California* (New York: G.P. Putnam's Sons, 1977); 525–526.

40. *LAT*, May 1, 1957, Jun. 10, 1958, Jun. 11, 1959, Apr. 20, 1964, Jun. 10, 1967; letters to/from Ford and Chamber of Commerce leaders, box 67, JAF; Minutes of Chamber of Commerce directors' meetings, 1950–1972, esp. Jul. 23, 1970, 61, carton 039, and cartons 033–039, LAACOC; material on Chamber of Commerce retreats in 1970s, box 625, HAHN, and 1980s and 1990s, box 373, EDELMAN; Ford, *Thirty Explosive Years,* 35–39. Note: "Area" was added to the Chamber of Commerce title in 1967.

41. *LAT*, May 30, 1950, Dec. 31, 1952; Ford newsletters, Feb. 20, Mar. 20, Apr. 3, 1951, Mar. 11, Dec. 30, 1952, Jan. 6, 20, Apr. 28, 1953, box 54, JAF; Ford, *Thirty Explosive Years* 43–46.

42. *LAT*, Mar. 25 (first quote), 26 (second quote), 30, 31, Apr. 5 (third quote), 6, 10, 1966; newspaper clips in box 454, *LAT* Records, HEH; Schrank, *Art in the City*, 129–130.

43. *LAT*, Apr.6, 20, 1955, Jun. 30, 1956, Apr. 11, 1957, Mar. 18, 1959, May 20, 1965, Jun. 7, 1967, Nov. 16, 2014; "Financial Goal Nearing for Music Center," *Southern California Business* 25 (Apr. 14, 1963): 3–4; "Brightness in the Air," *Time*, Dec. 18, 1964, 46, 55–58; Gottlieb and Wolt, *Thinking Big*, 526. Some of the 1958–1970 scandals appear in

newspaper clippings, especially in the *Examiner Collection* at USC and in the Frank Bonelli Scrapbooks, SEAVER.

44. *LAT*, Sept. 29, 1954, Nov. 9, 1956, Mar. 7, May 7, 1957, Sept. 30, 1959, et al; Ford newsletters, Jun. 9, 1953, box 54, Sept. 28, 1954, Sept. 17, 1957, box 55, JAF: Neil J. Sullivan, *The Dodgers Move West* (New York: Oxford University Press, 1987), passim; Jerald E. Podair, *Dodger Stadium and the Birth of Modern Los Angeles* (Princeton, N.J.: Princeton University Press, 2017), passim.

45. Robert E.G. Harris, "Showman Saint of Temple Street," *Frontier* 7 (Jan. 1956): 12–15; *LAT*, Oct. 21, 2007; Ford, *Thirty Explosive Years*, 80; Sitton, *The Courthouse Crowd,* 203, 226, 243, 254,261, 277, 305.

46. *LAT*, Mar. 24, 1953, Jan. 25, Dec. 6, 1961, Nov. 17, 1965, Dec. 30, 1966, Feb. 27, Jun. 30, 1967, Apr. 5, 1999; *Santa Monica Evening Outlook*, Apr. 21, 1967; Bob Gottlieb, "Is it Time to take the Reins Away from Pistol Pete?" *Los Angeles* 23 (Jun. 1978): 126–128, 243–247; Gottlieb and Wolt, *Thinking Big*, 528–529; Alice Catt Armstrong, *Who's Who in California, 1973* (Los Angeles: Who's Who Historical Society, 1972), 111.

47. *LAT*, Jun. 18, 1958, Dec. 9, 1959, Feb. 10, 1961, Nov. 13, 1963, Dec. 14, 1964, Nov. 30, 1966, Feb. 28, 1970, Dec. 16, 2016; *Santa Monica Evening Outlook*, Apr. 21, 1967; Hahn press releases, Apr. 21, 1967, Mar. 5, 1969, Hahn to Pitchess, Dec. 8, 1967, Pitchess press release, Apr. 20, 1967, Pitchess to BOS, Oct. 21, 1965, Apr. 16, Aug. 3, Dec. 7, 1967, copy of Los Angeles branch of NAACP to Biscailuz, May 26, 1954, John P. Kearney to Hahn, Jun. 22, 1967, Interim Report of Special? Jail Committee, in 1953 County Grand Jury, "Annual Report," box 367, Carman W. Combs to BOS, Apr. 27, 1955, box 147, Eason Monroe to Hahn, Nov. 25, 1966, box 305, HAHN; Sub-Committee on Crime and Correction, Control of Juvenile Delinquency, etc., 1953; Los Angeles County Sheriff's Department, *150 Years: A Tradition of Service?* (Paducah, Ky.: Turner Pub. Co., 2000), 47–55; Gerald Horne, *Fire This Time: The Watts Uprising and the 1960s* (Charlottesville: University Press of Virginia, 1995); 153, 304; Sitton, *The Courthouse Crowd*, 262, 304.

48. *LAT*, Feb. 1, 1961, May 19, 1965, Nov. 19, 1970; *Herald Examiner*, Jul. 12, 1965; Ford newsletter, Jan. 16, 1951, box 54, JAF; Hahn press release, Jul. 3, 1953, Bell Gardens Secret Civic Committee to Hahn, received Aug. 11, 1953, copy of Peter Pitchess to Mrs. Charles J. Jones, Mar. 2, 1966, box 367, Harold Kennedy to Hahn, Dec. 23, 19, 1966, box 1026, Joseph A. Wapner to Hahn, Nov. 20, 1970, box 1027, HAHN.

49. California Legislature, Assembly, Interim Committee on Judiciary, Subcommittee on Rackets, "Organized Crime in California: Report of the Subcommittee on Rackets of the Assembly Interim Committee on Judiciary," 1953 and 1957, CSA; *LAT*, Apr. 24, 1968, Nov. 14, 1970; Sitton, *The Courthouse Crowd*, 304–307.

50. "The Pattern of Vice Protection: A Report of

the Los Angeles County Grand Jury of 1950," 1951, box 62, California Ephemera Collection, UCLA; *LAT*, Jan. 13, Dec. 17, 1950, Jul. 7, Sept. 5, 1951; *Daily News* clipping, Aug. 1953, and Bell Gardens Secret Civic Committee to Hahn, received Aug. 11, 1953, box 367, HAHN.

51. George Putnam Broadcast notes, April 11 (initial quotes) to May 10, 1956, box 650, *LAT* Records, HEH; Putnam to Governor Goodwin J. Knight, Mar. 21, 1956, and Theodore H. Jenner to Knight, Mar. 26, 1956, box 82, Goodwin Knight Papers, CSA; *LAT*, May 5, 1956 (last two quotes).

52. *Examiner*, Dec. 5, 6, 1954; *LAT*, Apr. 29, May 2, 1951, Oct. 27, Dec. 3, 1956; Homer Bell to Goodwin J. Knight, Nov. 1956, Knight Papers, CSA; Jo Hindman, "LA City in Turmoil," *American Mercury* 84 (Apr. 1957): 142–3.; Ford, *Thirty Explosive Years*, 75–76; Sitton, *The Courthouse Crowd*, 181–182, 206–207, 261–262, 304–306.

53. *LAT*, Jun. 3, Aug. 8, 1958, Jun. 5, 1960, Feb. 25, 1964, Dec. 2, 6, 1970, Jun. 28, 1975.

54. *LAT*, May 28, 1972 (quote). On earlier juries see Sitton, *The Courthouse Crowd*, 180–182, 220–222.

55. *LAT*, Mar. 29, 1961; Hahn to Bonelli, Sept. 22, 1965, box 241, John R. Leach memo to Hahn, Oct. 10, 1067, L.S. Hollinger to Lloyd S. Nix, Sept. 7, 1967, Hahn statement, Jun. 17, 1970, box 387, Hahn statement, Sept. 11, 1973, box 245, HAHN.

56. On the 1930s and 1940s budgets see Sitton, *The Courthouse Crowd*, 200–203, 230, and 293–296.

57. *LAT*, May 3, Jun. 10, 14, 1950, Jun. 12, 1952, Apr. 28, Jun. 16, 1954, Feb. 27, Jun. 14, Nov. 27, 1957, Jun. 10, 11, 13, 1958, Jun. 11, 28, 1959; Hahn press statement, Nov. 25,1969, box 880, HAHN; Chace statement, Feb. 17, 1958, box 22, JAF.

58. *LAT*, Feb. 28, Apr. 24, 1961, Apr. 30, Jun. 27, 1962, Apr. 26, May 25, Aug. 14, 1964, May 4, Jun. 22, 1966, Aug. 27, 1967; *Covina Argus-Citizen*, Mar. 4, 1965; *Whittier Daily News*, Mar. 5, 1965; Hahn statement, Jun. 17, 1970, box 387, Hahn statement, Sept. 11, 1973, box 245, HAHN.

59. *LAT*, Aug. 8–19, Dec. 9, 1970, Jan. 27, Apr. 21, Jun. 30 (first quote), Oct. 10, 31, 1971, Jun. 24, 1972; Arthur G. Will to BOS, Jan. 5, 1971 (second quote), box 27, DEBS.

60. *LAT*, May 30, 1950, Dec. 13, 1953, Apr. 1, 20, 1955, Feb. 3, 1957, Oct. 12, 1960, Jan. 21, 1961, Oct. 11, 2016; *Southside Journal*, Oct. 27, 1960.

61. *LAT*, May 28, 1972 (quote).

62. "A Monument to Democracy" brochure, 1954, n.p. (all quotes), SEAVER; Ford to Cecil R. King, Oct. 30, 1944, Kelvin Vanderlip to Ford, Sept. 15, 1950, box 73, JAF; Russell A. Kazal, "Sculpting Interracialism in Mid-Century Los Angeles: Multicultural Boosterism and the Monument to Democracy," Paper delivered at the Annual Meeting of the Social Science History Association, Boston, Nov. 2011, 1–3.

63. Ford to Douglas MacArthur, Jun. 20, 1950, Ford to Conrad Hilton, Mar. 31, 1955, Ford

to Harry Truman, Jun. 7, 1955, Ford to Howard Hughes, May 9, 1957, and other material in box 73, JAF; *Tokyo Nippon Times*, Oct. 3, 1954; *LAT*, Oct. 5, 1958, Mar. 22, 1959, Sept. 8, 1967.

64. Sitton, *The Courthouse Crowd*, 111.

65. *LAT*, Dec. 6, 1971 (quote). See also material earlier in this chapter.

66. *LAT*, Apr. 30, 1950; *People's World*, Jun. 6, 1964, Mar. 26, Apr. 29, 1972; *Herald Examiner*, Jun. 1, 1976; William C, Taylor statement, Mar. 20, 1964, box 594, and other material in boxes 594, 595, and 599, HAHN.

67. Ford to Tom Goff, May 1958, Ford to Carl Cheek, Oct. 15, 1958, box 48, JAF; *LAT*, Nov. 4, 1958.

68. Copy of Benjamin S. Hite to Hahn, Nov. 10, 1958, box 48, JAF; *LAT, Nov.* 6, 13, 19, Dec. 7, 9, 1958, Oct. 22, 1989; Jane and Tom Apostal, "Grassroots Democratic Activism in Altadena," *Southern California Quarterly* 96 (Fall 2014): 287; Gloria Molina, Oral History Interview Conducted 1990 by Carlos Vasquez, 2 vols. (University of California, Los Angeles for the State Government Oral History Program, 1990), CSA, 2: 474.

69. *LAT*, Nov. 24, 26, 1960, Jun. 6, 8, 1968, Jul. 8, 1969; Ray Lee to Hahn, Jun. 14, 1968, box 621, James S. Mize to Registrar-Recorder, Jul. 10, 1969, box 880, HAHN.

70. *LAT*, Jun. 4, 13, 19, 24, Jul.8, 1970; *Long Beach Independent Press-Telegram*, Jun. 4, 1970 (quote); *Los Angeles Enterprise*, Jul. 6, 1970; Hahn statement, Jun. 5, 1970, Ray Lee to Hahn, Jun. 4, 1970, box 609, and copies of lawsuit and other material in box 618, HAHN.

71. John Maharg to Louise Huebner, Dec. 29, 1969 (quotes), box 5, Anne Flynn to Robert Donohue, Nov. 6, 1969, box 283, DEBS.

72. Louise Huebner to Maharg, Jan. 6, 1970 (first two quotes), box 283, DEBS; *Hollywood Citizen-News*, Jan. 18, 1970 (third, fourth and fifth quotes); *LAT*, Jan. 25, 1970 (last quote).

Chapter 2

1. Los Angeles County Grand Jury, "Final Report," 1973, 85, LACGJ website.

2. Richard G. Lillard, *Eden in Jeopardy: Man's Prodigal Meddling with His Environment, The Southern California Experience* (New York: Alfred A. Knopf, 1966), 53–54 (quote on 53); Tom Sitton, *The Courthouse Crowd: Los Angeles County and Its Government, 1850-1950* (Los Angeles: Historical Society of Southern California, 2013), passim.

3. Kimball Garrett, Interview by author, Los Angeles, Calif., August 23, 2013; *LAT*, Feb. 22, Mar. 1, 1979; Mike Davis, *Ecology of Fear: Los Angeles and the Imagination of Disaster* (New York: Vintage Books, 1999), 57–91, esp. 79; John Anson Ford, *Thirty Explosive Years in Los Angeles County* (San Marino, Calif.: Huntington Library, 1961), 51.

4. *LAT*, Nov. 8, 1963, Jun. 11, 1964, Jan. 26, 27, 1972; *Mirror* clipping (n.d.), box 14, JAF; Ernest

Debs to Evelle Younger, Jun. 7, 1967, box 404, DEBS; Bill Boyarsky and Nancy Boyarsky, *Backroom Politics: How Your Local Politicians Work, Why Your Government Doesn't, and What You Can Do About It* (New York: Hawthorn Books, 1974), 52–70, 156–160; Victor Valle, *City of Industry: Genealogies of Power in Southern California* (New Brunswick, N.J.: Rutgers University Press, 2009), 53–62, 79–80; Tom Sitton, *Los Angeles Transformed: Fletcher Bowron's Urban Reform Revival, 1938–1953* (Albuquerque: University of New Mexico Press, 2005), 119–121.

5. *LAT,* Mar. 6, 7, Apr. 11, Jul. 22, 1953.

6. *LAT,* Jan. 20, 1975; Bob Geoghegan memo to Edmund Edelman, Jul. 27, 1976 (quote), box 752, EDELMAN; Boyarsky and Boyarsky, *Backroom Politics,* 52–70.

7. *LAT,* Feb. 4, 1976, Jan. 3, 24, 25, 1980; protest letters and other material, 1976, box 740, EDELMAN; copy of Sherman W. Griselle to Peter Schabarum, Dec. 5, 1979, Owen Lewis to BOS, Jan. 24, 1980, box 352, HAHN; Valle, *City of Industry,* 190–192, 194 (quote on 191).

8. Ford, *Thirty Explosive Years,* 51–58; Milton Breivogel, "Seven Decades of Planning and Development in the Los Angeles Region." (University of California, Los Angeles, Oral History Program, 1989), 118–180; Ernst & Ernst, "Review of the Department of Regional Planning for the 1978–79 County Grand Jury Audit Committee," April 24, 1979, Von KleinSmid Library, USC.

9. *LAT,* Apr. 4, 6, 1967, Oct. 5, 1970 (quotes); Seismic Safety Element for Los Angeles County General Plan, Oct. 11, 1974, Introduction, box 350, HAHN.

10. *LAT,* Aug. 15, 16, 18, 22, Sept. 7, 20, Oct. 12, 19, 20 (quote), 1972; James Mize notice for Aug. 21, 1972, BOS hearing, box 45, DEBS; Harry Marlowe memo to Hahn, Feb. 8, 1973, John Maharg to BOS, Oct. 19, 1972 (quote), box 354, HAHN; Geoghegan memo to file, Jul. 29, 1975, box 743, EDELMAN.

11. *LAT,* Apr. 14, May 22, Jul. 28, 1973, Mar. 13, 19, 1975; Evelle Younger to Pete Schabarum, Apr. 11, 1973, box 354, "Professional Planners Challenge L.A. County's General Plan," Center for Law in the Public Interest *Public Interest Briefs,* Summer 1973, 2–3 (quote), box 570, HAHN; Geoghegan memo to file, Jan. 14, 1977, box 743, EDELMAN.

12. *LAT,* Mar. 24, Apr. 11, 1975, May 17, Jul. 27, 1979, Apr. 3, 1980, May 21, Sept. 30, 1981; William R, Robertson to BOS, Nov. 7, 1980, box 352, HAHN; Norman Murdoch to Edelman, Jan. 5, 1978, box 738, and Jan. 22, 1980, box 742, Jeff Seymour memo to Edelman, Nov. 12, 1980, box 741, EDELMAN.

13. Harold W. Kennedy, "The History, Legal and Administrative Aspects of Air Pollution Control in the County of Los Angeles, A Report submitted to the Board of Supervisors of the County of Los Angeles," May 9, 1954, 7–14; Sitton, *The Courthouse Crowd,* 267–270, 288–290.

14. Ford, *Thirty Explosive Years,* 122–125 Sitton, *The Courthouse Crowd,* 290–291.

15. *New York Times,* October 8, 1950; *LAT,* Mar. 19, 1977.

16. *Herald & Express,* Oct. 19, 21, 1954; *LAT,* Dec. 11, 1952, Jan. 11, Apr. 15, 1953; Dorn to Ford, Dec. 4, 1953, and correspondence between Ford and representatives of the groups and many citizen complaints noted in this paragraph, box 25, JAF.

17. LAT Sept. 23, Oct. 14, 16, Nov. 26, 29, 1953, May 31, 1955; copy of Gordon Larson to Norris Poulson, Sept. 24, 1953, Poulson statement, Oct. 24, 1954, box 25, Poulson radio broadcast, Jun. 12, 1955, box 30, JAF; Jeffrey Fawcett, *The Political Economy of Smog in Southern California* (New York and London: Garland Publishing, 1990), 82–83.

18. Ford correspondence with representatives of the California Incinerator Association, 1954, box 25, JAF; *LAT,* Aug. 6, 1960; A.J. Haggen-Smit, "Air Conservation: With Discovery of the Sources and Chemical Reactions of Pollutants, the Stage is Set for Conservation," *Science* 128 (Oct. 17, 1958): 869–878; Fawcett, *The Political Economy of Smog,* 83.

19. Minutes of Chamber of Commerce directors' meetings, Apr. 9, 1953, Sept 22, 1955, 46, 2–4, carton 033, LAACOC; Arthur J. Will to JAF, Oct. 11, 1954, L.B. Hitchcock to Fred D. Fagg, Jr., Apr. 8, 1954, box 26, JAF; "Los Angeles Pinpoints Auto Exhaust as Uncontrolled Air Pollution Source," *American City* 73 (May 1958): 126.

20. *LAT, Dec.* 22, 1952, Jun. 11, Dec. 17, 1953, Mar. 17, 1954; Ford newsletter, Feb. 17, 1953, box 54, JAF; Robert E.G. Harris, "5 Men for Five Million," *Frontier* 7 (Mar. 1956): 16 (quote); James E. Krier and Edmund Ursin; *Pollution and Policy: A Case Essay on California and Federal Experience with Motor Vehicle Air Pollution, 1940–1975* (Berkeley and Los Angeles: University of California Press, 1977), 66–74.

21. *Daily News,* Oct. 16, 1954; *LAT,* Nov. 30, 1954, Oct. 9, 1957, Oct. 29, 1959; Krier and Ursin; *Pollution and Policy,* 67.

22. Correspondence with automobile companies, Hahn's booklets and Hahn to Kennedy, Sept.14, 1953, box 736, Hahn Statement, Oct. 6, 1964, box 565, HAHN; Scott Dewey, "The Antitrust Case of the Century: Kenneth E. Hahn and the Fight Against Smog," *Southern California Quarterly* 81 (Fall 1999): 341–376.

23. Jim Gilbert, Jr., "SMOG from the Auto," *Car Life* 8 (Aug. 1961): 6–13; Fawcett, *The Political Economy of Smog,* 84–89.

24. Dorn motion, Jan. 26, 1965, and BOS resolution Jan. 26, 1965, box 566, HAHN.

25. *New York Tribune,* Apr. 10, 1966; *LAT,* Sept. 25, Nov. 1, 4, 1967; *Monrovia Daily News-Post,* Jun. 29, 1966; James S. Mize to Gov. Ronald Reagan, Mar. 6, 1967, box 474, Hahn motion, Apr. 2, 1968, and David D. Mix to Hahn, Nov. 20, 1968, box 566, and additional material in boxes 565, 567, and 568, HAHN.

26. *LAT,* Mar. 5, Sept. 13, 19, 1969; Hahn to John Mitchell, Mar. 7, 1969, box 880, Hahn to Mitchell, Sept. 4, 1968, Hahn to Ralph Nader, Jan.16, 1969, and James Mize to County Counsel, Sept. 19, 1969,

box 567, Robert Bush memo to Hahn, Nov. 9, 1973, box 570, HAHN; Dewey, "The Antitrust Case of the Century," 353–370.

27. Mize to the President and each member of Congress, et al, Nov. 29, 1972, box 883, HAHN; Fawcett, *The Political Economy of Smog*, 89–91.

28. Hahn motion, Sept. 24, 1974, KFWB Radio editorial, Dec. 3, 1974, box 572, Hahn to editor of the *Los Angeles Times*, Dec. 18, 1974, Hahn press statement, Dec. 23, 1974, box 571, People's Lobby press release, Jan. 14, 1975, box 574, Hahn to Gov. Edmund G. Brown, Jr., Mar. 13, 1975, box 475, HAHN; *San Gabriel Valley Tribune*, Apr. 25, 1975; Daniel Judge, "Highway Robbery: Retrofit Smog Device Fiasco," *Motor Trend*, Aug. 1975, 38–41, 110.

29. *LAT, Sept.* 3, 1972, Jan. 10, 1973; Fawcett, *The Political Economy of Smog*, 84–85; Dewey, "The Antitrust Case of the Century," 370–371.

30. *LAT*, Jan. 25, Apr. 6, 1955, Feb. 19, 1958; Arthur Will to BOS, Dec. 6, 1973, box 28, and J.H. Stuart to SCAPCD board, Jul. 25, 1975, Robert G. Lunche to BOS, Sept. 19, 1975 (quote), Harry Hufford to BOS, Jul. 2, 1976, box 573, HAHN; Baxter Ward statement, Sept. 2, 1976, box 544. EDELMAN.

31. Ford newsletter, March 1, 1949, box 54, JAF; Sitton, *The Courthouse Crowd*, 292.

32. *LAT*, Feb 11, 1954; Hahn motion Mar. 5, 1970, box 881, Hahn motion, Feb. 6, 1968, box 879, Hahn motion, Feb. 11, 1969, box 880, copy of John D. Parkhurst to Burton W. Chace, Dec. 17, 1970, box 363, HAHN; Debs to Kimmi Nakano, Jul. 21, 1972 (quote), box 347, DEBS; Arthur Pickett, "Stop Ground-Water Pollution," *American City* 69 (Aug. 1954): 95–96.

33. LAT, Feb. 26, 1968; Blake Gumprecht, *The Los Angeles River: Its Life, Death, and Possible Rebirth* (Baltimore and London: Johns Hopkins University Press, 1999), 240.

34. Sitton, *The Courthouse Crowd*, 291–292.

C.E. Arnold, "Report on Refuse and Rubbish Disposal in Los Angeles County," April 1949, box 30, JAF; "More Powers for Los Angeles County Sanitary Districts," *National Municipal Review* 39 (Jan. 1950): 44; C.E. Arnold, "Cut and Cover Refuse Disposal." *American City* 66 (May 1951): 92–93.

35. BOS meeting transcript, Sept. 10, 1952, box 30, Ford newsletter, Apr. 12, 1955, box 55, JAF.

36. Ford newsletter, Apr. 12, May 10, 1955, box 55, JAF; California Legislature, Assembly, Interim Committee on Judiciary, Subcommittee on Rackets, Report of the Subcommittee on Rackets of the Assembly Interim Committee on Judiciary, House Resolution No. 224, 1957, "Organized Crime in California" (Sacramento: Assembly of the State of California, 1959), 47–56, quotes on 47; *Huntington Park Daily Signal,* July 14, 1955; *LAT*, Sept. 23, Oct. 14, 16, 1953, May 26, 31, Jun. 1, 3,12, 29, Aug. 1, 3, 1955, May 10, 1956, Sept. 20, 1958.

37. *LAT*, Oct. 6, 12,18, 25, 27, Nov. 2,10,15, Dec. 21, 1955, Jan. 23, 26, 27, Feb. 1, 2, 3,4, 8, Mar. 5, 24,

1956; George Putnam broadcast, Apr. 13, 1956, KTTV, box 650, *LAT* Records, HEH.

38. *LAT*, Jan. 26, Feb. 8, 14, Apr. 12, 16, 21, Jul. 24, 1957.

39. *LAT*, Jan. 1–30 (quote), Feb. 2, 1, 3, 15, May 7, Jun. 14, Oct. 14, 1959, Sept. 24, 2019; *Examiner*, Feb. 1, 2, 3, 6, 1959; *Herald & Express*, Feb. 2, 1959.

40. *LAT*, Jan. 24, 1957, Mar. 2, 1958, Jan. 6, 1960; Boyarsky and Boyarsky, *Backroom Politics*, 169–170.

41. Copy of John D. Parkhurst to Thomas Bradley, Feb. 8, 1974, Mission Canyon timeline prepared by the CAO, 1978, box 366, HAHN; Boyarsky and Boyarsky, *Backroom Politics*, 168–170; "Los Angeles County Loses Landfill Fight," *American City and County* 92 (Jun. 1977): 30.

42. Baxter Ward motion, Mar. 3, 1977, box 366, Bradley to Parkhurst, Apr. 13, 1977, *Brentwood-Westwood Hills Press*, Mar. 16, 1978 (quote), Hahn Statement, Mar. 23, 1978, Hahn to John Ferraro, et al., May 25, 1978, box 363, HAHN; *LAT*, Jan. 5, 1981; *Daily News,* May 13, 1981.

43. *LAT*, Feb. 9, 12 (quotes), 22, 26, 27, Mar. 1, Oct. 11, 1972; Hahn motion, Feb. 29, 1972, Arlen V. Weber to writers of letters to Hahn, Mar. 1, 1972, box 1034, HAHN.

Chapter 3

1. Refrain from *Seventy-Six Cities,* music and lyrics by Steve, Paul, and Ralph Colwell, and Cecil Broadhurst, Copyright©1965 by Up with People, used by permission, Up with People Archive (MS 491), courtesy of University of Arizona Libraries, Special Collections; *LAT*, Sept. 26, 1965, Dec. 7, 1966. In 1941, the county CAO declined to recommend that a song written by a Los Angeles composer be approved as the county song. The CAO was "at a loss to know why the county should have an official song." *LAT*, March 31, 1941.

2. Tom Sitton, *The Courthouse Crowd: Los Angeles County and Its Government, 1850-1950* (Los Angeles: Historical Society of Southern California, 2013), 170–175, 297–298; Richard Bigger and James D. Kitchen, *How the Cities Grew*, Vol. 2 of *Metropolitan Los Angeles: A Study In Integration*, ed. by Edwin A. Cottrell, 16 vols. (Los Angeles: Haynes Foundation, 1952), 93.

3. Sitton, The Courthouse Crowd, 296–298; *LAT*, Oct. 25, 1950, Jul. 21, 1951, Sept. 8, 1953.

4. Sitton, The *Courthouse Crowd*, 298–299. Downey and Commerce were two new cities that did not take advantage of contracting for most services.

5. Martin J. Schiesl, "The Politics of Contracting: Los Angeles County and the Lakewood Plan, 1954–1962," *Huntington Library Quarterly* 45 (Summer 1982): 227–229, quotes on 227 and 229. Robert O. Warren, *Government in Metropolitan Regions: A Reappraisal of Fractionated Political Organization* (Davis: University of California, Davis, Institute of Governmental Affairs, 1966),

141–161; Gary J. Miller, *Cities by Contract: The Politics of Municipal Incorporation* (Cambridge, Mass.: MIT Press, 1981), 16–23; Victor Valle, *City of Industry: Genealogies of Power in Southern California* (New Brunswick, N.J.: Rutgers University Press, 2009), 60–63; *LAT,* Dec. 2, 3, 1953, Feb. 21, Mar.16, 1954.

6. *LAT,* Nov. 6, 1953; Miller, *Contract Cities,* 37–41, 54–57.

7. *LAT,* Nov. 29, 1953, Sept. 18, 1955, Apr. 1, Oct. 9, 1956, May 23, 1958, Jan.8, 1959, Mar. 24, 1960; Miller, *Contract Cities,* 57–59; Charles John Hoch, "City Limits: Municipal Boundary Formation and Class Segregation in Los Angeles Suburbs, 1940–1970" (PhD diss., University of California, Los Angeles, 1981), 229–238, 290–306; Winston W. Crouch and Beatrice Dinerman, *Southern California Metropolis: A Study in the Development of Government for a Metropolitan Area* (Berkeley and Los Angeles: University of California Press, 1963), 234.

8. *LAT,* Nov. 27, 1955, Jul. 22, Sept. 2, 1956; Hoch, "City Limits," 217–227, 239–250; Miller, *Contract Cities,* 41–53; Valle, *City of Industry,* 75; Crouch and Dinerman, *Southern California Metropolis,* 236.

9. *LAT,* Feb. 26, 1953, Jan. 13, Feb. 3, 1957, Jun. 21, 1962; Miller, *Contract Cities,* 87–97; Crouch and Dinerman, *Southern California Metropolis,* 236–237.

10. *LAT,* Oct. 28, 1956, Jan. 27, 1957, Feb. 7, 1957, May 17, 1959, Oct. 20, Nov. 16, 27, 1960, Aug 8, 1962, Mar. 8, 1964; Miller *Contract Cities,* 35–37.

11. *LAT,* Jul. 3, 1961; Schiesl, "The Politics of Contracting," 233, 239. Early positive assessments of the Lakewood Plan include, among others, Guy Halferty, "A Unique Experiment in City-County Relationships: How the 'Lakewood Plan' Operates," *American City* 70 (May 1955): 134–135; "California's 'Contract Cities,'" *American City* 75 (Dec. 1960); 100; Samuel K. Gove, "Los Angeles County Works for Cities," *National Civic Review* 50 (Jan. 1961): 40–42; and Richard M. Clon, "Accommodation Par Excellence: The Lakewood Plan," in Michael N. Danielson, ed., *Metropolitan Politics: A Reader,* 2nd ed. (Boston: Little, Brown and Co., 1971), 224–231.

12. Schiesl, "The Politics of Contracting," 229–230, 236–238, 239; *LAT,* May 17, 1959; Morton J. Goldman to Harry A. Marlow, Aug. 20, 1954, box 25, HAHN; Judith Norvell Jamison and Richard Bigger, "Metropolitan Coordination on Los Angeles," *Public Administration Review* 17 (Summer 1957): 165–166.

13. Richard Bigger, Evan A. Iverson and Judith N. Jamison, "Escape from the County," *National Municipal Review* 46 (Mar. 1957): 126–130 (quotes on 128, 129); Schiesl, "The Politics of Contracting," 234–236.

14. Hoch, "City Limits," passim; Miller, *Contract Cities,* esp. 8–19, 132–140,190–196; Valle, *City of Industry,* 60–129.

15. *LAT,* Nov. 27, 1962, Apr. 9, 26, May 3, Sept. 28, 1970, Feb. 17, Jul. 29, 1971; Schiesl, "The

Politics of Contracting," 236; Crouch and Dinerman, *Southern California Metropolis,* 202–205. Robert Warren, "Changing Patterns of Governmental Organization in the Los Angeles Metropolitan Area" (Ph. D.)—University of California, Los Angeles, 1964 PhD diss., University of California, Los Angeles, 1964), 203–262; Robert R. Mitchell to Ernest E. Debs, Mar. 29, 1971, box 29, Verne Orr to Debs, Nov. 23, 1962, box 147, DEBS; Los Angeles County Grand Jury, "Final Report," 1962, 61–65, and 1969, 14–15, LACGJ website.

16. *LAT,* Jan. 27, Feb. 17, Sept. 29, Oct. 25, 1963, Sept. 28, 1966, Aug. 4, 1968, Sept. 26, 1971; *Torrance Daily Breeze,* Sept. 16, 1971; Los Angeles County Local Agency Formation Commission, "Six Year Report, 1963–1969," 1969, 1–14; Schiesl, "The Politics of Contracting," 238–239; Miller, *Contract Cities,* 126–130; Christopher Hoene, Mark Baldassare and Michael Shires, "The Development of Counties as Municipal Governments: A Case Study of Los Angeles County in the Twenty-First Century," *Urban Affairs Review* 37 (Mar. 2002): 575–591; Crouch and Dinerman, *Southern California Metropolis,* 225–228.

17. *LAT, Dec.* 9, 1973, Mar. 13, 1975, Jun. 15, 1976, Feb. 13, Jun. 1, Jul. 21, Nov. 27–1977; Valle, *City of Industry,* 133–140; Los Angeles County Grand Jury, "Final Report," 1984–1985, 27–37, and many other such probes, 1975–1994, LACGJ website.

18. *LAT,* Jun. 28, 1968, Jan.7, Jun. 24, Oct. 29, 1969, Dec. 29, 31, 1970; Hollinger to BOS, Sept. 4, 1969, box 25, HAHN; Tom Bradley to Baxter Ward, Jul. 11, 1973, box 764, Bradley Papers, UCLA; Arthur G. Will to BOS, Aug. 30, 1973, box 49, DEBS; Alan Saltzstein, "Quasi-City Departments: Joint Powers Authorities and Intergovernmental Relations," in Hynda L. Rudd, et al., eds., *The Development of Los Angeles City Government: An Institutional History, 1850–2000,* 2 vols. (Los Angeles: Los Angeles City Historical Society, 2007), 2: 805–815. See Chapter 2 for more on Poulson's Administration.

19. Hufford to BOS, Dec. 27, 1974, box 30, John Larson to BOS, Mar. 21, 1980, box 390, HAHN; Larson to BOS, Nov. 17, 1981, box 1007, Bob Geoghegan memo to Edelman, Feb. 16, 1982, box 81, DeWitt Clinton to BOS, Dec. 20, 1983, box 184, Clinton to BOS, May 21, 1984, box 77, EDELMAN; *Daily Journal,* Nov. 17, 1981, Oct. 13, 1983; *LAT,* Dec. 11, 1958, Oct. 11, 1975, Apr. 3, May 1, 1977.

20. *LAT,* Jul. 9, Oct. 23, 1975, Sept. 26, 1976; Raphael J. Sonenshein, *Politics in Black and White: Race and Power in Los Angeles* (Princeton, N.J.: Princeton University Press, 1993), 167–169 (quote on 167–168); Mara A. Cohen-Marx, "Community Redevelopment" in Rudd, et al, eds., *The Development of Los Angeles City Government,* 1: 429–440.

21. *LAT,* May 4, 1989; Marvin Freedman to Gov. Edmund G. Brown, Jr., Sept. 18, 1975 (quote), box 32, HAHN; KFWB editorial, Jan. 8, 1976, and response Jan. 12, 1976, Larson to BOS, Dec. 7, 1976, and DeWitt Clinton to Edelman, March 7, 1985,

box 155, Ernani Bernardi to Edelman, Apr. 19, 1989, box 154, EDELMAN.

22. Hufford to BOS, Jun. 16, 1981, box 201, EDELMAN.

23. Sitton, *The Courthouse Crowd*, 230–234, 296–302.

24. Samuel Leask, Jr., to Los Angeles City Council, Mar. 15, 1961 (quote on 1), CSA; Sitton, *The Courthouse Crowd*, 230–234, 296–302.

25. *LAT*, Oct. 19, 1958, Jan. 22, 1961, Jan. 17, 1963; *Baldwin Park Bulletin*, Oct. 14, 1971; Edelman to David Carrino, Mar. 5, 1976, box 573, EDELMAN.

26. *LAT*, May 22, 27, Sept. 16, 17, 27, 30, Oct. 10, 28, Nov. 14, 1971, Mar. 2, Apr. 20, May 15, 22, Jun. 27, Aug. 29, 1972. See also Hoch, "City Limits," 345–349.

27. *LAT*, Sept. 29, Dec. 19, 1974; notes on the "County Formation Law," (AB 4271—Knox), box 573, EDELMAN.

28. *LAT*, Jan. 20, Jul. 23, Aug. 31, Dec. 21, 1975; Hufford to BOS, Jan. 7, Feb. 8, 1976, box 33, HAHN; County Citizens' Economy and Efficiency Commission, Report 70, October 1976, LACCEEC website.

29. *LAT*, Aug. 18, 22, Oct. 17, Nov. 4, Dec. 5 (quotes), 1976; Peter L. Shaw, "L.A. Voters to Decide on Creation of a New County," *National Civic Review* 65 (Oct. 1976): 471.

30. *LAT*, Jun. 20, 1976, Jun. 12, 1977; LACCEEC report 78, May 1978, 23–52, website; Bob Simmons, "The Move to Secede from Los Angeles County," *California Journal* 7 (Apr. 1976): 117–119.

31. *LAT*, Oct. 10, 1976, May 15, 1978; County Citizens' Economy and Efficiency Commission, Report 78, May 1978, 29–34, LACCEEC website.

32. *LAT*, Oct. 10, 1976, Mar. 13, May 15, 1977, Feb. 9, Apr. 26, 27, 1978; County Citizens' Economy and Efficiency Commission, Report 78, May 1978, 24–29, LACCEEC website.

33. *LAT*, Mar. 25, 1976, Feb. 27, Jun. 12, Aug. 25, 1977; charts on state legislation affecting Los Angeles County in 1977, box 39, HAHN; Mike Cullen to Edelman, box 565, EDELMAN.

34. *LAT*, May 15, 30, Jun. 8, 1978. For efforts to create new counties in other areas of California at the same time see Rosaline Levensen, "California Changes Law on New Counties," *National Civic Review* 67 (Jan. 1978): 44–45.

35. *LAT*, Nov. 9, 1978, Sept. 27, 1979.

36. *LAT*, Apr. 13, 1981, Aug. 8, 1990, Nov. 3, 1995, Mar. 30, Jul. 11, 1997; material in San Gabriel County 1995 file, box 784, MOLINA.

Chapter 4

1. Population figures derived from a Los Angeles County Human Relations Commission research report in HRC RESEARCH, July 1972, box 2, HAHN, and other sources also basing the

totals on the U.S. Department of the Interior, Census for 1950 and 1960.

2. Tom Sitton, *The Courthouse Crowd: Los Angeles County and Its Government, 1850–1950* (Los Angeles: Historical Society of Southern California, 2013), 254–257, 262–266, 284–285; *LAT*, Nov. 27, 1977, Nov. 11, 2007, Oct. 17, 2020; Loren Miller to Pasadena Realty Board, Sept. 28, 1948, box 8, and examples of racial covenants in box 25, Loren Miller Papers, HEH; Nita Blackwell to Raymond Darby, Jun. 21, 1951, and Dale Gardner to Human Relations Commission Executive Committee, Sept. 19, 1950, box 72, Anti-Defamation League memo, Dec. 31, 1948, box 75, John Anson Ford to Robert C. Wian, Oct. 2, 1956 (quotes), Samuel Ishikawa to Ford, Sept. 30, 1949, box 76, JAF; Scott Kurashige, *The Shifting Grounds of Race: Black and Japanese Americans in the Making of Multi-Ethnic Los Angeles* (Princeton, N.J.: Princeton University Press, 2008), esp. 234–258; Stephen Grant Meyer, *As Long as They Don't Move Next Door: Segregation and Racial Conflict in American Neighborhoods* (Lanham, Md.: Rowman & Littlefield, 2000), 64–66, 75–77, 115–116, 126–129.

3. *Sentinel*, Jun. 10, 1949; *LAT*, Mar. 9, 1987 (quote); Welfare Council of Metropolitan Los Angeles material, 1950, in box 9, Miller Papers; newspaper clippings and other material on "rat packs" or "wolf packs," 1953–1954, in box 72, JAF, and box 32, Edward Roybal Papers, UCLA.

Josh Sides, *L.A. City Limits: African American Los Angeles From the Great Depression to the Present* (Berkeley and Los Angeles: University of California Press, 2003), passim.

4. Kenneth Hahn to William H. Nicholas, Sept. 17, 1959, Hahn resolution, Jan. 6, 1960, box 421,

Commission, Sept. 5, 1963, box 875, HAHN; *LAT*, Sept. 18, Oct. 30, 1963; *Sentinel*, Jan. 4, Apr. 7, Jul. 14, 1960; Arthur Youtan to Gov. Goodwin Knight, Jul. 20, 1956, box 82, Goodwin Knight Papers, CSA.

5. Dale Gardner memos to Ford, Oct. 18, Nov. 6, 1951, Nov. 25, 1952, Mrs. Edward M. Lazard to Ford, Aug. 31, 1955, box 72, JAF; Howard Shorr, "'Race Prejudice is Not Inborn—It is Learned': The Exhibit Controversy at the Los Angeles Museum of History, Science and Art, 1950–1952," *California History* 90 (Fall 1990): 276–83, 311–12.

6. *LAT*, Jun. 6, 8, 10, 25 (second, third quotes), 27, Jul. 12, Sept. 4, 1963; Hahn motion, Jun. 4, 1963 (quote), box 875, HAHN; Minutes of Chamber of Commerce directors' meetings, June. 6, 20, 1963, 67, 73, carton 035, LAACC.

7. *LAT*, Dec. 6, 1963, Oct. 18, 1964; *Culver City Star News*, Sept. 21, 1964; Gordon Nesvig to Los Angeles County Representatives in Congress and Senator Engle, May 21, 1964, box 876, HAHN; Raymond E. Wolfinger and Fred I. Greenstein, "The Repeal of Fair Housing in California: An Analysis of Referendum Voting," *American Political Science Review* 62 (Sept. 1969): 753–769. Assemblyman

John G. Schmitz later tried to repeal the Rumford Act again but failed. *LAT,* Jan. 7, Feb. 14, 1968.

8. "California Governor's Commission on the Los Angeles Riots, Violence in the City—An End or a Beginning?" Dec. 2, 1965, 1, 10–25; Gerald Horne, *Fire This Time: The Watts Uprising and the 1960s* (Charlottesville: University Press of Virginia, 1995), 54–133; Robert Conot, *Rivers of Blood, Years of Darkness* (New York: Bantam, 1967), passim; Robert M. Fogelson, *Violence as Protest: A Study of Riots and Ghettos* (Garden City, N.Y.: Doubleday, 1971), 191–192.

9. Phil Pennington description of his and Hahn's experience on August 11 and 12, 1965 (quote), and Hahn, "Sequence of Events—Southeast Los Angeles Riot," August 12–17, 1965, box 1043, HAHN.

10. *Herald Examiner,* Sept. 13, 1965; Hahn statement, Sept. 5, 1965, box 1043, HAHN. Parker was praised by the entrepreneurial elite for his actions in responding to the violence, but he has been a major contributor to it because of his racism and LAPD policies. Minutes of Chamber of Commerce directors meeting, Aug. 19, 1965, 89, carton 036, LAACOC; Sides, *L.A. City Limits,* 169–176; Ethan Rarick, *California Rising: The Life and Times of Pat Brown* (Berkeley and Los Angeles: University of California Press), 321–340.

11. *LAT,* Aug. 24, 25, 1965; Los *Angeles Newsletter,* Nov. 27, 1965, 1–2; Fogelson, *Violence as Protest,* 191–216; Horne, *Fire This Time,* 341–348; Lawrence B. de Graaf, "The Changing Face and Place of Race," in Hynda L. Rudd, et al., eds., *The Development of Los Angeles City Government: An Institutional History, 1850–2000,* 2 vols. (Los Angeles: Los Angeles City Historical Society, 2007), 2: 268; Minutes of Chamber of Commerce directors meeting, Oct. 19, 1965, 104, carton 035, LAACC.

12. *LAT,* Aug. 24, 25, Nov. 10, Dec. 22, 1965; *Herald Examiner,* March 22, 1966; Los Angeles County Human Relations Commission, "Proposals for Improvement of Human Relations in the Los Angeles Metropolitan Area," Nov. 2, 1965, Stafford R. Grady to Gov. Edmund G. Brown, Nov. 22, 1965, box 1042, Hahn to Brown, Sept. 22, 1965, Nesvig to Brown, Nov. 12, 1965, box 474, HAHN.

13. *LAT,* Aug. 19, Nov. 23, 25, 27, 1966, Mar. 7, Jul. 2, 1967, Apr. 16, 1968, Jul. 9, 1975, Aug. 11, 1985, Aug. 5, 1990, Aug. 11, 1995, Aug. 11, 2005, Aug. 6, 2015; Lindon Hollinger to BOS, Apr. 11, 1978, box 1042, Hahn statement, Aug. 4, 1967, box 1043, Hahn statement, Nov. 22, 1966, box 877, James S. Mize to The President, et al., Mar. 6, 1968, box 879, HAHN; *Report of the National Advisory Committee on Civil Disorders* (New York: Bantam Books, 1968), passim.

14. *LAT,* Feb. 27, Dec. 20, 1963, Feb. 11, May 27, 1969, Jul. 5, Aug. 30, 1970, Mar. 4, 2018, Aug. 23, 29, 2020; De Graaf, "The Changing Face of Race and Place," 2:768–769; Horne, *Fire This Time,* 259.

15. Herbert L. Carter to Human Relations Commissioners, Sept. 3, 1970 (quotes), box 212, HAHN; *LAT,* Sept. 1, 1970; Juan Gómez-Quiñones, *Chicano Politics: Reality and Promise, 1940–1990* (Albuquerque: University of New Mexico Press, 1990), 126–128.

16. *LAT,* Sept. 18, 1970, Jan. 11, Feb. 2, ,3, Jul. 28, 31, Aug. 11,1971, Dec. 19, 1973; Gómez-Quiñones, *Chicano Politics,* 127–128; James S. Mize to Anthony Day Feb. 5, 1971, box 662, *LAT* Records, HEH; John H. Larson to BOS, Dec. 11, 1973, box 108, HAHN.

17. De Graaf, "The Changing Face of Race and Place," 2:771; James P. Allen and Eugene Turner, *Changing Faces, Changing Places: Mapping Southern Californians* (Northridge: California State University, Northridge, 2002), 11.

18. De Graaf, "The Changing Face of Race and Place," 2:771; *LAT,* Apr. 22, 24,30, May 3, 1975, Jan. 5, 1976, Aug. 22, 24, 1979; Harry Hufford to BOS, Apr. 24, 1975, box 31, Tom Bradley to Hahn, Oct. 10, 1979, box 513, copy of David G. Galloway to Edelman, Oct.7, 1983, box 90, HAHN; James Hayes motion, Mar. 15, 1977, box 365, EDELMAN.

19. De Graaf, "The Changing Face of Race and Place," 2:757, 764–65; Edelman motion, Mar. 11, 1975, box 364, Edelman statement, May 20, 1976 (quote), Bob/Gil memo to Edelman, Sept. 17, 1986, Bunny Hatcher to Roger Ragan, n.d. [October 1989], box 276, EDELMAN.

20. Allen and Turner, *Changing Faces, Changing Places:* 11; Ellis P. Murphy to BOS, Jul. 1, 1974, box 310, HAHN; De Graaf, "The Changing Face of Race and Place," 2:757–758, 763–764, 770–774.

21. *LAT,* Mar. 26, 1975, May 15, 1976, Jan. 9, 1977, Apr. 26, 1978, Mar. 28, 1980; *Herald Examiner,* Jan. 22, 23, 1986; John Larson press release, Feb. 19, 1975, box 109, Larson to BOS, Nov. 21, 1979, box 192, Larson to BOS, May 1, 1980, box 390, Hahn to George Deukmejian, Jan. 10, 1979, Beverlee A. Myers to Hahn, Jan. 12, 1979, box 498, Hahn to Gov. Edmund G. Brown, Jr., May 7, 1980, box 475, HAHN; Keith Comrie to BOS, Jun. 2, 1976, and David M. Ager (for John Larson) to Liston A. Witherill, Feb. 24, 1977, box 12, Bert Corona Papers, STANFORD; Marion J. Woods to Edelman, Feb. 5, 1976, box 332, EDELMAN. See also Thomas Muller and Thomas J. Espenshade, *The Fourth Wave: California's Newest Immigrants* (Washington, D.C.: The Urban Institute, 1985), esp. Chapters 4 and 5.

22. Sitton, *The Courthouse Crowd,* 152–153, 207, 255–256; Los Angeles Branch of the NAACP to E.W. Biscailuz, Sheriff, May 26, 1954, box 367, HAHN.

23. Ford newsletters, Feb. 26, 1956, Jun. 26, 1956 (quote), Feb. 4, 1958, Sept. 2, 1958, box 55, Harold Kennedy to BOS, Feb. 28, 1958, transcript of BOS meeting, Feb. 4, 1958, Max Mont memo to Steering Committee of the Committee for Equal Employment Opportunity, n.d., box 31, JAF; *LAT,* Jun. 27, 1956, Mar. 19, Nov. 2, 4,1958.

24. Transcript of BOS meeting, Jan. 9, 1962 (quotes), LACLL; *LAT,* Jan. 10, 1962, Dec. 20, 1963,

May 27, 1969; Debs motion, Jan. 30, 1968, Deputy Stevely memo to Debs, Jun. 28, 1968, box 4, DEBS.

25. *LAT*, Sept. 3, 8, Oct. 6, Nov. 27, 1969.

26. *LAT*, Jan. 12, Feb. 7, 1973; Clyde Johnson, et al., to Hahn, Feb. 2, 1973, Gordon Nesvig memo to department heads, Feb. 13, 1973, Arthur G. Will to BOS, Mar. 1, 1973, box 1, HAHN.

27. Edelman motion, Jun. 27, 1978, Hahn motion, Jul. 5, 1978, box 1, *Public Interest Briefs*, Summer 1973, 2, box 570, HAHN. Examples of some of the letters sent to county officials include Joe G. Avila to Baxter Ward, Sept. 30, 1976, Assemblyman Art Torres to Pete Schabarum, Jan. 5, 1978, box 82, Congressman Edward R. Roybal to Harry Hufford, Jan. 24, 1978, box 236, Clyde Johnson to Liston A. Witherill, Jun. 7, 1976, box 312, HAHN.

28. *LAT*, Dec. 20, 1967.

29. *LAT*, Feb. 6, 12, Dec.10, 19, 1958, Jun. 3, 1959, Dec. 12, Nov. 15, 1961, Sept. 30, 1966, Oct. 18, Dec. 8, 1967; Burton Chace to other supervisors, Nov. 3, 1958 (quote), box 89, Los Angeles Examiner Collection, USC; Hahn motion, Sept. 27, 1966, box 877, *Los Angeles Newsletter*, Nov. 11, 1961, 2–3, box 1014, HAHN.

30. *LAT*, Dec. 8, 13, 20, 1967; *San Gabriel Valley Tribune*, Dec. 7, 1967.

31. *LAT*, Dec. 26, 1967, Aug. 4, 14, 28,1968, Feb. 22, 23, 1969; Debs media release, Jul. 9, 1968, L.S. Hollinger to BOS, Aug. 7, 22, 1968; Chace motion, Aug. 13, 1968, Thomas Noguchi to Chace, Aug. 22, 1968, L.E. McKee to Chace, Oct. 9,1968, box 1, DEBS.

32. *LAT*, Feb. 26 (quote), Mar. 5, 11,14,19, 24,1969; letters from Asian Americans and others supporting Noguchi in box 75, HAHN, and in box 15, DEBS; Hollinger to BOS, Mar. 4, 1969, box 290, BOS to Noguchi, Mar. 14, 1969, box 15, DEBS. For more on Dr. Noguchi's predicament and personality see Anne Soon Choi, "The Japanese American Citizens League, Los Angeles Politics, and the Thomas Noguchi Case," *Southern California Quarterly* 102 (Summer 2020): 158–192.

33. *LAT*, Mar. 25, Jul. 16, 1969; *Long Beach Independent Press-Telegram*, Mar. 2, 1969; KFWB radio editorial, Mar. 25, 69, box 290, DEBS; George Schwartz to George Putnam, Mar. 6, 1969, John Maharg to Hahn, May 26, 1969, George H. Takei to Hahn, Aug. 4, 1969, and statement from JUST Noguchi Defense Committee, n.d. 1969, box 75, HAHN. Examples of newspaper entries in *Rafu Shimpo*, *Kashu Mainichi*, and *Pacific Citizen* can be found in box 15, DEBS.

34. *LAT*, Apr. 2, May 16, 20, 21, 23, 24, 27, 29, 30, Jun. 6, 10, 13, 24, 25, Aug.1 (quote), 2, 1969; Hahn motion, Apr. 1, 1969, box 880, HAHN.

35. Debs to George Takei, Aug. 1, 1969, Noguchi to Chace, Aug. 8, 1969, box 15, and Debs to Takei, Mar. 24, 1970, and Hollinger to BOS, Feb. 27, 1970, box 23, DEBS; Japanese American Citizens League resolution, Jan. 28, 1970, box 648, Peat, Marwick, Mitchell & Co. audit, "Report No.2, Chief Medical Examiner-Coroner's Department," Jun. 21, 1971,

box 148, HAHN; Kashu *Mainichi*, Jan. 29, 1970; *LAT*, Aug. 2, 6, 10,13, 1969, Aug. 10, 2015.

36. *LAT*, Apr. 15, Jul. 26, 1978, Sept. 28, 1979, Dec. 28, 1981; *Santa Monica Evening Outlook*, Jul. 24, 1980.

37. *LAT*, Oct. 14, 21, Dec. 27 (quote), 28, 29, 30, 1981, Jan. 20, 1982; Noguchi memo to staff, Dec. 28, 1981, box 47, HAHN.

38. *LAT*, Jan. 21, 26, Mar. 3, 8, 9, 10, 11,12,13,16, 17,18, 26, Apr. 7, 16, 27, 1982; "The Celebrity Corner," *Newsweek* 99 (Mar. 22, 1982): 57; Harry Hufford to BOS, Apr. 29, 1982, box 177, HAHN.

39. *LAT*, May 20, 1982 (quote), Jul. 20, 21, 22, 30, Aug. 20, 24, Sept. 8,10,15, 21, Nov. 5, 6,12, 1982; *Daily News*, Mar. 21, 1982; *Rafu Shimpo*, Apr. 6, 1982; copy of Godfrey Isaac to Civil Service Commission, Apr. 5, 1982, copy of Joe Fallin to Michael Antonovich, Mar. 29, 1982, copy of William A. Masterson to Civil Service Commission, May 17, 1982, box 79, Yaneo Yamamoto to Hahn, Jul. 2, 1982, Ruth Pratt to Hahn, Apr. 25, 1982, Jules L. Beasley to BOS, Apr. 22, 1982, box 75, HAHN; Frank Sinatra to Edelman, Mar. 10, 1982, statement to Antonovich from thirty-nine Asian Americans, Nov. 22, 1982, box 177, Edelman to Yaneo Yamamoto, Jul. 20, 1982, box 194, EDELMAN.

40. *LAT*, Feb.12,13,15, 23, Mar. 31, Oct. 16, Nov. 10, 1983, Jun. 23, 1984, Dec. 14, 1986, Mar. 2, 1987, Jul. 18, 1990; *Daily News*, Feb. 24, 1983; Hearing Officer Sara Adler report, Feb. 10, 1983, box 79, HAHN; Rob Saltzman memo to Edelman, Feb.14, 1983, Tommy Hon to Edelman, Feb. 18, 1983, box 177, EDELMAN; Thomas T. Noguchi, *Coroner* (New York: Pocket Books, 1983); Thomas T. Noguchi, *Coroner At Large* (New York: Pocket Books, 1985).

41. *LAT*, Dec. 12, 1969, Mar. 7 (quote), Apr. 8, 12 (quote), 17, 22, 28, May 6, 1970.

42. "L.A. County vs. Lone Black Architect," *Perspective* 1 (Winter 1983/84): 1,4; *LAT*, Feb.14, 16, 23, 29, Mar. 14, Sept. 8, 1984; De Witt Clinton to BOS, Mar. 14, 1984, box 52, Hahn motion, Feb. 28, 1984, Burke Roche memo to Hahn, May 17, 1984 (quote), James Silcott to Carlos Hernandez, Aug. 21, 1984, box 81, HAHN.

43. *LAT*, Oct. 31, Nov. 1, 19, 1984; *Sentinel*, Nov. 15, 1984; Edward Cano memo to Hahn, Jul. 20, 1984, Hahn statement, n.d. (Dec. 1984), box 81, HAHN; additional material on the Silcott case can be found in box 81, HAHN, and in boxes 679 and 680, EDELMAN.

44. Robert A. Arias to BOS, Aug. 13, 1987, with completed California Department of Fair Employment and Housing form, Aug. 4, 1987, box 63, Richard Dixon and De Witt Clinton to BOS, Aug. 29, and Sept.6, 1988, and Richard Llewellyn memo to Edelman, Sept. 12, 1988, box 18, EDELMAN.

Chapter 5

1. *LAT*, Dec. 1, 1975 (epigraph); and Jun. 15, 1977 (quote).

2. *LAT*, Feb. 22, Jun. 12, 1981, Mar. 13, 1990, Jun. 12, 1997; Toby Shor, "Pete Schabarum—Fifth Wheel Turned County Boss of L.A. County," *California Journal* 12 (Jun. 1981); 199–202.

3. http://bos.lacounty.gov/About-Us/Board-of-Supervisors/Board-Member-Biographies; *LAT*, Aug. 17, 2000; James Hayes to Ernest Debs, Oct. 20, 1970, box 23, DEBS; James A. Hayes, Oral History Interview Conducted 1990 by Carlos Vasquez (University of California, Los Angeles for the State Government Oral History Program, 1990), CSA, passim.

4. http://bos.lacounty.gov/About-Us/Board-of-Supervisors/Board-Member-Biographies; *LAT*, Apr. 16, 1978, Oct. 31, 1988, Jan. 16, 1981, Jan. 15, 1989, Feb. 5, 2002; Jeanie Kasindorf, "Baxter Ward: His Own Best Human Interest Story," *Los Angeles*, Oct. 1972, 44–45, 80; "The Crusader," *Newsweek*, Apr. 8, 1973, 26.

5. Los Angeles City Council biography file, Jul. 12, 1967, Los Angeles Public Library; *LAT*, Nov. 5, 1994, Sept. 13, 2016. See also material throughout EDELMAN.

6. *LAT*, Jun. 15, 16, 1979; *Sentinel*, May 11, 2009; *Herald Examiner*, Jun. 23, 1975, Oct. 27, 1977; *Civic Center NewSource*, Jul. 4, 1994.

7. *LAT*, Oct. 8, 29, Nov. 9, Dec. 6, 1972, Aug. 27, 1973, Dec. 14, 1973, Apr. 8, 1979; Bob Gottlieb, "The Supervisors: Five Angry and Threatened Men," *Los Angeles*, Jun. 1978, 129–130.

8. *LAT*, Jan. 19, May 10, Jul. 12, Sept. 12, 19, Oct. 30, 1973, Mar. 21, May 23, 1974, Apr. 27 (quote), Jun. 15, 1977, Sept. 4, 1978, May 7, 1980; *Van Nuys Valley News*, Jun. 27, 1974; *Herald Examiner,* Apr. 12, 1973; Baxter Ward to Debs, May 4, 1973, box 630, transcript of BOS meeting, Jan. 22, 1974, 8, box 64, HAHN.

9. *LAT*, Dec. 28, 1972, Jul. 24, 1973, Mar. 21, 1974.

10. *LAT*, Jun. 15, 1977, Jun. 15, 1978; *Long Beach Independent Press-Telegram*, Jun. 17, 1974; Hahn statement, May 31, 1974, box 29, Giles Mead to Ed Harrison, Apr. 10, 1978, John Larson to Harrison, May 9, 1978, Mead to Joel R. Bennett, May 18, 1978, Hayes to Harrison, Jun. 15, 1978, Hahn to Harrison, Jun. 21, 1978, Harrison to Hahn, Jul. 10, 1978, box 251, HAHN; Alma Fitch memo to Edmund Edelman, Jun. 1978, box 366, EDELMAN.

11. Hayes to Edelman, Jul. 7, 1977, box 90, EDELMAN; Edmund D. Edelman, interview by author, Los Angeles, June 17, 2011; Gottlieb, "The Supervisors: Five Angry and Threatened Men," 130.

12. *LAT*, Aug. 27, 1973, Nov. 25, 1975, Jan. 24, 1979. On the BOS "Divide by Five" see Gary W. Cox and Timothy N. Tutt, "Universalism and Allocative Decision Making in the Los Angeles County Board of Supervisors," *Journal of Politics* 46 (1984): 546–555.

13. *LAT*, Oct. 30, 1973, Oct. 1, 12, 13, 24, Nov. 23, Dec. 21, 26, 1974, Jan. 11, Apr. 19, Oct. 14, 1975, Jun. 9, 1977; Baxter Ward to Joseph Busch, Jan. 9, 1973, box 48, Busch to Ward, Mar. 8, 1973, box 51, DEBS.

14. John Maharg to Hahn, Oct. 7, 1968, box 106, Hahn to County Grand Jury, Mar. 2, 1973, box 148, HAHN; Philip Watson to Ward, Apr. 18, 1973 (quotes), box 48, DEBS; Carmine S. Bellino to Watson, Nov. 23, 1976, box 5, Jonathan Beaty (for Ward) to Pat Vecchio, et al., Jan. 27, 1977, box 6, Edelman motion, Feb. 10, 1977, Watson to Edelman, Feb. 28, 1977, box 9, POPE; *LAT*, Oct. 25, 1972, Jun. 4, 1977, Oct. 11, 1978; *Herald Examiner*, May 5, 1977, Feb. 19, 1982.

15. *LAT*, May 15, Jun. 6, 1973; *Long Beach Independent Press-Telegram*, Jun. 6, 1973; *Hollywood Independent*, Jun. 7, 1973; Peter Pitchess news release, May 30, 1973 (quote), John Larson to Pitchess, Aug. 9, 1973, box 58, DEBS.

16. *LAT,* May 10, Sept. 28, Oct. 2, 3,7, 9, 25, 29, Nov. 26, Dec.18, 1974; Ward news release, Sept. 30, 1974, box 368, Ward to Jessie L. Robinson, Nov. 12, 1974, Pitchess news releases, Oct. 21, Nov. 17, 1974, box 63, HAHN.

17. *LAT*, Dec. 24, 1974, Feb. 8, 13, 17, 22, Mar. 8, Apr. 19, 1975; Jessie L. Robinson to BOS, Dec. 23, 1974, Mar. 6, 1975, Ward to Pitchess, Feb. 19, 1975, box 63, Harry Hufford to BOS, Feb. 5, 1975, box 369, HAHN.

18. *LAT*, Jun. 2, 1979; City News Service Wire, Oct. 27, 1976 (quote), Pitchess news release, Mar. 10, 1978, Hayes statement, Mar. 11, 1978, box 369, HAHN.

19. *LAT, Aug.* 26, 31, Sept. 2, 29, Oct. 3, 1971, Dec.27, 1972, Sept. 4, 6, Oct. 10, 20, 1978, May

20, Dec. 21, 1981, Jun. 25, 1983; Hahn to Governor Edmund G. Brown, Aug. 20, 1959, box 474, anonymous letters to BOS, Feb. 7, 1981, Jan.? 1982, Hufford to Hahn, Mar. 13, 1981, Robert Philibosian to BOS, Jun. 24, 1983, box 402, HAHN; Baldo Kristovich to Debs, Nov. 19, 1970, box 23, DEBS.

20. *LAT*, Aug. 26, 27, 1971, May 14, 16, 1974, Jul. 13, 1975, Apr. 6, 1977, Apr. 30, 1988, Apr. 3, 1992, Feb. 11, 2016; Leo D. Epstein and Christian W. Planje to BOS, Aug. 24, 1971, box 148, Arthur Will to BOS, Dec. 8, 1971, box 29, Judge Charles J. Loring to BOS Aug. 17, 1972, box 388, Ward to Judge Robert A. Wenke, Jul. 18, 1975, box 63, Larson to Hahn, Aug. 7, 1975, box 109, HAHN; draft of ACLU report requesting a grand jury investigation of the Sirhan case, c.1992, box 149, DEBS.

21. *LAT*, Jan. 6, 1973, Jun. 7, 8, Aug. 13, Nov. 20, 1974, Mar. 4, May 15, Nov. 12, 16, 1975, Apr. 6, 1976, Dec. 23, 1978, Oct. 14, 1981; Ernest Sanchez to Emmet Sullivan, Apr. 28, 1975, box 71, file on Kirkpatrick suit against County Civil Service Commission in 1975, box 72, Kirkpatrick to BOS, Aug. 12, 1974, box 80, Larson to BOS, Sept. 1, 1974, box 108, Hahn to Kirkpatrick, Jun. 13, 1972, box 291, memos from Robert Bush to Kirkpatrick, May 3, 1973, May 10, 1974, box 292, James S. Mize to Kirkpatrick, Nov. 19, 1974, Hahn statement, Dec. 11, 1975, box 293, Hahn statement, Feb. 24, 1978, Larson to BOS, Sept. 4, 1980, box 294, Larson to BOS, Sept. 30, 1981, box 295, HAHN.

22. *LAT*, Oct. 5, 6, 12, 1973, Jan. 24, Feb. 6, Aug. 13, Oct. 30, Nov. 30, 1974, Jan. 28, May 20, 1975,

Jun. 12,1977; Hahn to Timothy Sperl, Oct. 18, 1973, box108, Donald N. Eastman to Busch, Nov. 15, 1973, box 630, Busch to Hahn, Jun. 27, 1974, box 123, Hufford to Busch, Sept. 26, 1974, Ward to BOS, Nov. 25, 1974, Ward memo to BOS, Dec. 9, 1974, box 63, HAHN.

23. *LAT*, Jan. 4, 9, 16, 18, 23, 24, 25, 1980.

24. *LAT*, Mar. 29, 19, Aug. 4, 7, 11, 1976; Grillo to BOS, Mar. 30, 1976, Larson to Ward, Aug. 10, 1976, box 246, Larson to Grillo, Aug. 5, 1976, Hufford to BOS, Aug. 6, 1976, James B. Czarnecki to Hufford, Aug. 9, 1976, Mark Bloodgood to Ward, Aug. 9, 1976, box 34, HAHN.

25. *LAT,* Aug.-Oct. 1976, Apr. 30, May 22, Aug. 17, Nov. 8, 23, 1977; Grillo to Hahn, Jan. 19, 1977, box 246, HAHN; Edelman to Grillo, Jan. 28, 1977, box 203, EDELMAN.

26. *LAT*, Jan. 11, 12, Jul. 4, 1975, May 29, 1980; *Santa Monica Evening Outlook*, Jan. 11, 1979; *Daily Journal*, Jan. 17, 1979; Larson to BOS, Jan. 11, 1979, Robert Bush memo to Hahn, Jan. 8, 1979, Donald K. Byrne (for Larson) to BOS, Jan. 11, 1979, Hahn motion, Jan. 16, 1979, box 247, correspondence on the case in box 40, HAHN.

27. *LAT*, Jan. 18, 22, 23, 25, Sept. 17, 1974, Feb. 5, 2002; transcript of BOS meeting, Jan. 22, 1974, Ward to BOS, Jan. 16, 1974, and receipts signed by Hugh Dynes, box 64, KH.

28. *LAT*, Jan. 5, 1973, Jan. 30, Mar. 20, 23, 27, May 3, Jul. 11,17, Aug. 20, 30, Sept. 2, 9,11, Oct. 3, Nov. 8, 1974, Jun. 20, 1975; Jessie L. Robinson to BOS, Oct. 2, 1974, box 148, HAHN; "Illegal Attorney Referral Activity in Los Angeles County," report, Aug. 1974, Von KleinSmid Library, USC; material related to other Ward investigations can be found scattered in HAHN.

29. *LAT*, May 28, 1972, Jul. 9, 1978; Debs motion, Jan. 30, 1973, box 51, DEBS; Ralph L. Inglis, et al, to Members of State Senate Judiciary Committee, Nov. 27, 1972, in Los Angeles County Grand Jury, "Final Report," 1977–1978, 15–17, box 150, HAHN and LACGJ website.

30. *LAT*, Mar. 27, 29, Apr. 2, 3, 8, 9, 10, May 7 (quote), Jun. 19, 1980; *Santa Monica Evening Outlook*, Jul. 2, 1980.

31. *LAT*, May 29, Jun. 1, 4, 8, Aug. 23, 25, Oct. 1, 29, Nov. 9, 1972; Hahn campaign material in boxes 598, 599, HAHN.

32. *LAT*, Oct. 24, Nov. 2, 1971, Feb. 8, May 11, 28, Jun. 1, 8, Sept. 7, Oct. 4, 23, Nov. 9 (quote),

11, 1972; Robert Gottlieb and Irene Wolt, *Thinking Big: The Story of the Los Angeles Times, Its Publishers, and Their Influence on Southern California* (New York: G.P. Putnam's Sons, 1977), 526.

33. *LAT*, Nov. 1, 3, 1973, Jan. 4, 7, 26, Apr. 4, 17, May 15, 28, Jun. 2, 5, 1973, Jun. 6, Jul. 20, Oct. 17, 23, 25, 29, 30, Nov. 6,7,1974; *Long Beach Independent Press-Telegram*, Aug. 2, 1974; Edelman news releases, Aug. 2, Sept. 12, 1974, and other campaign material in box 850, EDELMAN.

34. *LAT,* Feb. 1, May 30, Jun. 9, 1976; *Herald Examiner,* Jun. 1, 1976; Hahn campaign material in boxes 599 and 600, HAHN.

35. *LAT*, Mar. 11, Jun. 7, 1978; Coalition for Economic Survival Newsletter, Feb.-Mar. 1978, 1, "Los Angeles County Times" flier, Spring 1978, box 37, Bert Corona Papers, STANFORD.

36. *LAT*, Jun. 5, 15, 1979, Sept. 13, Oct. 5, 22, 25, 26, 31, Nov. 1, 29, Dec. 29, 1979, Jan. 24, Feb. 5, 25, Apr. 26, May 13, 30, Jun. 29, Jul. 27, Sept. 7, Oct. 26, Nov. 2, 5, 19, 25, 1980, Jan. 11, 1990; Burke motions, May 5, 1980, box 60, and May 13, 1980, box 341, BURKE.

37. *LAT*, Mar. 4, 1977, Oct. 19, 31, 1979; LASD, "The Contract Law Enforcement Program: A Discussion and Review Issues and Values," Jun. 1978, box 531, EDELMAN; Hahn news release, Nov. 16, 1979, box 369, HAHN; Los Angeles County Sheriff's Department, *150 Years: A Tradition of Service* (Paducah, Ky.: Turner Pub. Co., 2000) 58–59. Among many Pitchess requests for more funding see, Pitchess to Hahn, Jun. 29,1973, box 368, Pitchess to BOS, Jun. 23, 1975, box 369, HAHN; Pitchess to BOS, Aug. 23,1977, Pitchess to Edelman, Jun. 20, 1979, Edelman to Pitchess, Jun. 28, 1979, box 531, EDELMAN.

38. *LAT*, Nov. 19, 20, 1970, Jul. 2, 1975, May 19, Jul. 24, 1977, Apr. 20, 1978, Sept. 3, 1980; Neil Abramson to Hahn, Aug. 15, 1966, Harry Marlow memo to file, Aug. 23, 1966, box 305, Judge Joseph A. Wapner to Hahn, Nov. 20, 1970, James S. Mize to Governor Ronald Reagan, Apr. 13, 1973, box 1027, HAHN. See also Chapter 1.

39. Pitchess to Hahn, May 13, 1974 (first quote), Pitchess to Hahn, Nov. 4, 1975, Pitchess to BOS, Oct. 6, 1975 (second quote), Pitchess to BOS, Dec. 1, 1975, Ed Davis to BOS, Nov. 17, 1975, Hahn to Pitchess, Nov. 29, 1977 (last quote), Hahn press release, Oct. 29, 1975, box 369, LASD, "The Status of Organized Crime in LA County," April 1983, box 370, HAHN; *Valley News*, Mar. 19, 1980; John Van de Kamp to BOS, Mar. 31, 1980, and other material in box 109928657, BSC.

40. *LAT*, Jul. 27 (quote), Aug. 21, 1978; *Daily Journal*, Aug. 28, 1980; Pitchess to Hahn, May 29, 1974, box 368, Hufford to BOS, Feb. 21, 1978, box 369, HAHN; William Bradford Reynolds to Edelman, n.d., received Oct. 21, 1985, Sherman Block to BOS, May 19, 1989, with "Projected Fiscal Impact of the Custody Crisis" report, box 533, EDELMAN; LASD, *150 Years*, 60–61, 69–70.

41. *LAT*, Apr. 10, 1973, Jul. 24, 1974, Nov.12, 1975, Apr. 21, Jun.30, Nov. 17, 1976, Jun. 28, 1977; Yvonne Johnson to Hahn, Sept. 9, 1976, Pitchess to BOS, Oct. 7, 1976, box 369, Hufford to BOS, Oct. 7, 1975, box 32, Ed Davis to Hahn, Jun. 10, 1975, Lynn Beyer to BOS, Jul. 11, 1975, Los Angeles Coalition for Youth and Justice statement, Jul. 11, 1975, box 293, HAHN; inmate complaints about Sybil Brand Institute, 1975–1976, and minutes of Los Angeles County Commission on the Status of Women, late 1976, box 536, EDELMAN.

42. *LAT*, Feb. 7, 1971, Feb. 9, 1973, May 17, Jul. 9,11, 24, 1974, Dec. 1975, Feb. 2, Sept. 21, Oct. 21, 29, 1980; Congressman Augustus Hawkins, et al, to Hahn, Nov. 30, 1972, Hahn statements, Jan. 24,

1973, Dec. 3, 1973, Hank Allison, "Juvenile Delin-quency: A Progress Report," KFWB radio broad-cast, Oct. 8, 1973, box1001, Ed Davis to Art Snyder, Dec. 8, 1972, Hahn statement, Jan. 31, 1974, J.C. Chambers to Schabarum, Mar. 28, 1973, Alonzo A. Crim to Hahn, Apr. 13, 1973, box 1002, and juvenile murderer reports in boxes 1001 to 1005, HAHN; probation and juvenile delinquency material in boxes 667, 897 to 898, and 943 to 947, EDELMAN.

43. *Sentinel*, Nov. 22, 1973; Edelman to Capt. Craig Carpenter, Jan 23, 1978, Edelman to Acting Capt. George A. Corbett, Mar. 7, 1978, Edelman to Pitchess, May 21, 1981, box 531, EDELMAN; Mr. and Mrs. Clarence E. Lee to Hahn, May 24, 1973, Rev Donald Grant to Hahn, Feb. 4, 1974, Pitchess to Hahn, Jul. 27, 1973, Hahn to Pitchess, Aug. 6, 1973, box 368, and many other constituent letters, 1970s, box 367 to 370, HAHN.

44. *LAT*, Nov. 7, Dec. 12, 15, 19, 1979, Jan. 12, Aug. 14, 1980; several complaints of deputy mis-treatment at the at Firestone jail in 1973, box 368, anonymous Deputy Sheriff to Hahn, Nov. 9, 1979, Pitchess to Hahn, Dec. 5, 1979, copy of Humberto Camacho to Sheriff's Department, Jun. 20, 1979, box 369, HAHN; copy of Mrs. Felix Tevis to Pitchess, Apr. 8, 1981, box 531, EDELMAN.

45. *LAT*, Nov. 19, Dec. 8,10,1977; Gerald F. Uel-man, "Varieties of Police Policy: A Study of Police Policy Regarding the Use of Deadly Force in Los Angeles County," Loyola *of Los Angeles Law Review* 6 (1973): 1-65, Pitchess to Edelman, Dec. 2, 1977, box 536, Dave Glascock to Edelman, Aug. 16, 1977, box 18, "Reporter's Transcript of Proceed-ings" of Dec. 9, 1977, hearing, box 537, EDELMAN.

46. *Herald Examiner,* Jul. 3, 1979; *LAT*, Oct. 21, 1977, Jun. 25, 26, 27, 28, 30, Jul. 24, Oct. 24, 1979, Mar. 13,14, 1980; Richard Lawrence memo to Edel-man, May 21, 1979, box 531, Lawrence memo to Edelman, Jun. 26, 1979, District Attorney's final report on the death of Steven Conger, March 13, 1980, box 536, EDELMAN.

47. *LAT*, Dec. 12, 15, 19 (quotes), 1979; Barry S. King to Michael Zinzun of the Coalition Against Police Abuse, Jul. 9, 1979, box 536, EDELMAN.

48. Tom Sitton, *The Courthouse Crowd: Los Angeles County and Its Government, 1850-1950* (Los Angeles: Historical Society of Southern Cal-ifornia, 2013), 190-200, 223-229, 293-295; Los Angeles Department of Public Social Services, "A History of Public Welfare in Los Angeles County," 1975, Part 3, 3.

49. *LAT*, Feb. 1, 2, 1950, Jan. 25, 1952, Feb. 7, 1960, Sept. 17, Oct. 1, 2, 1964, Jan. 3, 1965, Mar. 9,15, Apr. 12, 28, 1967, Jan. 22, Apr. 24, 1968; Hahn motion, Aug. 25, 1959, box 874, Hahn motion, Feb. 2, 1965, box 305, Hahn motion, Feb. 3, 1966, Hahn statement, Sept. 20, 1967, box 306, HAHN; James Mize to California Congressional Delegation, Feb. 21, 1968, box 14, DEBS.

50. *La Mirada Herald American*, Jan. 8, 1966; *LAT*, Feb. 16, 1966, Mar. 2, Aug. 1967, Mar. 13, 1968, Feb. 2, Apr. 22, Jun. 13, Jul. 1, Dec. 16, 19,

1969; L.S. Hollinger to BOS, Mar. 2, 1967, Ellis P. Murphey to Hahn, Mar. 13, 1967, and Apr. 12, 1967, box 307, HAHN.

51. *LAT,* Mar. 17, May 24, 1970, Jan. 20, 27, Mar. 14, May 4, Jul. 9, 1971; Hahn statement, Nov. 17, 1970 (quote), Hahn statement, Jan. 12, 1971, box 307, BOS resolution, Mar. 10, 1971, box 478, HAHN.

52. *LAT,* Sept. 29, Dec. 10, 1972, Apr. 24, Sept. 15, 1973, Dec. 24, 1974; Hahn statement, Mar. 28, 1973, Arthur G. Will to BOS, Dec. 27, 1973, box 308, Keith Comrie to Edelman, Jan. 10, 1977, box 312, Comrie to BOS, Aug. 7, 1977, box 313, HAHN; CAO news release, Dec. 19, 1973, box 56, DEBS.

53. Murphy to BOS, Feb. 26, 1973, box 308, Murphy to BOS, Aug. 22, 1975, Murphy to BOS, Jan. 15, 1976, BOS meeting memo, Nov. 4, 1975, box 311, Comrie to BOS, Jun. 3, 1977, box 312, and Sept. 20, 1977, and Oct. 18, 1977, box 313, and Comrie to BOS, Mar. 22, 1978, box 314, HAHN; Los Angeles County Grand Jury, "Final Report," 1973, 63, LACGJ website.

54. *LAT,* Jan. 25,1975, Nov. 11, 1977, Jun. 14, 1978, Dec. 24, 1980; BOS meeting memo, Oct. 10, 1972, box 883, Comrie to BOS, Sept. 27, 1979, box 315, Murphy to BOS, Jan. 27, 1975, box 310, Mur-phy to BOS, Apr. 21, 1975, Richard W. Canton to Murphy, Oct. 27, 1975, Comrie to BOS, Mar. 31, 1976, box 311, Eddy Tanaka to BOS, Dec. 18, 1980, box 316, HAHN.

55. *Alhambra Post Advocate*, Jul. 30, 1971; *LAT,* Jul. 28, 31, Aug. 4, 11, 1971, Jan. 16, 1978; Murphy to BOS, Jan. 11, 1974, box 309, HAHN.

56. *LAT,* Sept. 22, 1964, Mar. 14, Apr. 20, Jul. 12, 14,15, Aug. 6, 27, Sept. 2, 1965, Jan. 20, Feb. 15, Apr. 24, 1966, May 28, 1969, May 9, Jul. 1, 1972; Samuel Yorty to BOS, Sept. 8, 1964, Congressman Augustus F. Hawkins news release, Jan. 3, 1966, Hahn to Sargent Shriver telegram, Jan. 6, 1966, box 304, BOS resolutions, Jan. 26, 1966, and Nov. 9, 1966, Hahn statement, April 26, 1966, box 877, William A. Leone to BOS, Feb. 5, 1971, Donald D. Newman to Alex Aloia, Nov. 15, 1971, box 431, Assemblyman Bill Greene to Hahn, Mar. 21, 1972, box 481, HAHN; material in folder 169, Office of Economic Activities Records, CSA; Dale Rog-ers Marshall, *The Politics of Participation in Pov-erty: A Case Study of the Board of the Economic and Youth Opportunities Agency of Greater Los Ange-les* (Berkeley, Los Angeles: University of California Press, 1971), passim; Robert Bauman, *Race and the War in Poverty: From Watts to East L.A.* Norman: University of Oklahoma Press, 2008), 17-66.

57. *LAT,* Jun. 10, 1973, Mar. 29, 1974, Mar. 23, 26, Dec. 24, 1975, Jan. 13, 1976, May 4, Dec. 15, 1977, Jun. 28, Oct. 17, 26, Dec. 13, 1978; Arnold Martinez memo to Debs, Feb. 26, 1974, Ralph D. Fertig to Debs, Mar. 11, 1974, Debs news release, April 4, 1974, Arthur G. Will to BOS, Apr. 19, 1974, box 388, DEBS; Jessie L. Robinson to BOS, Mar. 18, 1975, box 148, Hufford to Hahn, Dec. 3, and 19, 1975, box 32, Hufford to BOS, Jan.12, 1976 (quote), box 33, David G. Galloway to BOS, Jul. 12, 1982,

box 87, HAHN; Bauman, Race *and the War on Poverty*, 66–68.

58. *LAT*, Jan. 23, 1976, Jul. 23, 1977, Feb. 3, 16, Nov. 15,17, 29, 1978, Jan. 24, 28, Feb. 8,16, Jun. 13 ,20, 27, 1979, Feb. 21, Apr. 8, 9, 10, May 7, Jun. 19, 29, Oct. 1, 1980; Dan Farcas to Edelman, Mar. 13, 1978, box 255, EDELMAN; Hufford to Schabarum, Dec. 21, 1977, box 37, Hayes to Hahn, Jul. 21, 1977, Bob Bush memo to Hahn, Nov. 17, 1978, and Galloway to BOS, Dec. 18, 1978, box 83, Galloway to BOS, Sept. 21, 1979, Oct. 18, 1979, and Dec. 10, 1979, box 84, Galloway to BOS, Feb. 14, and 16, 1980, box 85, Galloway to BOS, Feb. 23 and Jul. 30, 1981, box 86, Galloway to BOS, Apr. 6, and Nov. 16, 1982, box 87, and many others on the same subject in these boxes, HAHN.

59. *LAT*, Jan. 15, 1973, Apr. 1, 1980, Mar. 28, 29, 30, May 18, 26, Sept. 18, Nov. 12, 16, Dec. 2, 21, 1982, Apr. 17, Jun. 15, 1983, Sept. 25, 1994; Galloway to BOS, Mar. 24, 1980, box 86, Sept. 2, 1981, box 87, and Jan. 18, 1983, box 89, HAHN; John R. Chávez, *Eastside Landmark: A History of the East Los Angeles Community Union, 1963-1993* (Stanford: Stanford University Press, 1998), passim.

60. From "The State of the County," Los Angeles County Grand Jury, "Final Report," 1978–1979, 8, LACGJ website.

Chapter 6

1. Epigraph quote from a presentation by Supervisor Mark Ridley-Thomas, in Los Angeles County Civil Grand Jury, "Final Report," 2015–2016, 254, LACGJ website.

2. Tom Sitton, *The Courthouse Crowd: Los Angeles County and its Government, 1850-1950* (Los Angeles: Historical Society of Southern California, 2013), 230–234.

3. Nathaniel Fitts to BOS, Dec. 18, 1951, box 5, JAF; 1958 Grand Jury resolution for BOS (quote), box 147, HAHN; *Daily Journal*, Dec. 4, 1972 (quote); *Examiner*, Feb. 26, 1956; many Citizens' Economy and Efficiency Commission reports on the LACCEEC website (the commission was initially a committee until 1973); *LAT*, Jun. 15, 1959, Dec. 1, 1975.

4. *LAT*, Jan. 16, 1952, May 22, 1958, Mar. 28, 1969.

5. *Herald & Express*, Oct. 19, 1961; "Metro" pamphlet, 1959, and other material in box 13, Marie Koenig Collection, HEH; Bruce Thomas, "1313's Hidden History," (Chicago) *Hyde Park Herald*, May 23, 2004.

6. Hamilton Beamish to John Anson Ford, Aug. 8, 1958, box 5, JAF; *LAT*, Feb.7, April 28, Aug. 18, Dec. 10, 1958; Jo Hindman, *Terrible 1313 Revisited: A Compilation of Speeches and New Metro Articles with the Metrochart* (Caldwell, Ida.: Caxton Printers, 1963), esp. 32–33 (second quote on 33); Michelle M. Nickerson, *Mothers of Conservatism: Women and the Postwar Right* (Princeton, N.J.: Princeton University Press, 2012), 69–70 (first quote on 69), 99–101.

7. *LAT*, May 22, 1958, Jun. 21, 1959, Jan. 4, 1961, Mar. 21, 1962, Jun. 15, 1969; Edwin A. Cottrell and Helen L. Jones, eds., *Metropolitan Los Angeles: A Study in Integration*, 16 vols. (Los Angeles: Haynes Foundation, 1952-1955); Los Angeles Chamber of Commerce, "Proceedings: Metropolitan Government Symposium, April 8, 1958," UCLA Library; Winston W. Crouch and Beatrice Dinerman, *Southern California Metropolis: A Study in the Development of Government for a Metropolitan Area* (Berkeley and Los Angeles: University of California Press, 1963), 137–138, 189–210, 364–371, 379–80; California Governor, "Metropolitan California: Papers Prepared for the Governor's Commission on Metropolitan Area Problems," edited by Ernest A. Engelbert (Sacramento: 1961), passim; David Y. Miller and Raymond W. Cox, III, *Governing the Metropolitan Region: America's New Frontier* (Armhonk, New York: M.E. Sharpe, 2014), 153–207.

8. *LAT*, Sept. 2, Oct. 3, Dec. 12, 1965; "Plan New California Agency for Regional Problems," *National Civic Review* 52 (Jul. 1963): 384–385. On SCAG prior to 1975 see Joke Hilde Wiersema Johnson, "The Southern California Association of Governments: A Study of Its Record and Possible Future" (PhD diss., Claremont Graduate School, 1976).

9. *LAT*, Jan. 5, 12 (quote), Mar. 30, Oct. 30, 1966, Jul. 10, 1967; *Huntington Park Signal*, Jan. 5, 1966; *Claremont Courier*, Jan. 12, 1966; *Herald Examiner*, Feb. 27, 1966; *Torrance Daily Breeze*, Mar. 30, 1966; Gordon Nesvig to each city in Los Angeles County, Apr. 1, 1966, box 585, Milton Breivogel to BOS, Sept. 18, 1967, box 348, HAHN; Davis Mars, "Regional Activity in Los Angeles," *National Civic Review* 58 (Apr. 1969): 169–170.

10. *LAT*, Feb. 1, Nov. 15, 1970, Mar. 10, 15, Jun. 23, 1971; *Arcadia Tribune*, Sept. 29, 1971; Hahn motion, May 25, 1971, box 882, HAHN; John Maharg to Warren Dorn, Mar. 9, 1971, Katherine Dunlap to Ernest Debs, Jun. 7,1971, John Conlan to Debs, Jun. 7, 1971, Richard Donohue memo to Debs, Dec. 10, 1971, box 324, DEBS.

11. *LAT*, Feb. 16, May 9, Aug. 24, 1973; Thomas Bradley, "Regional Governance and Racial and Ethnic Minorities," in Kent Mathewson, ed., *The Regionalist Papers* (Southfield, Mich.: Metropolitan Fund, 1978), 122–129; Hahn motion, Mar. 19, 1974, box 885, George Wakefield to BOS, Feb. 4, 1974, box 482, HAHN; "Los Angeles County Sues on Federal Transit Rule," *National Civic Review* 66 (Jan. 1977): 34.

12. *LAT*, Jul. 1, 1975 (quotes), Sept. 25, 1980; Harry Hufford to BOS, Jul. 21, and Dec. 19, 1975, Larry Gotlieb memo to Edelman, April 4, 1977, box 551, EDELMAN; Hufford to BOS, Jun. 28, 1978, box 38, Hufford to BOS, Jan. 8, 1979, box 40, HAHN.

13. *LAT* Feb. 13, 16, Jun. 1, 1977; Arthur G. Will to BOS, Dec. 6, 1973, box 28, HAHN.

14. Hahn motion, Apr. 22, 1980, Jack W. Salyers to BOS, May 12, 1980, box 151, HAHN:

David Roberti to James Mize, Aug. 26, 1981, box 109927605, BSC; Tom Sitton, *The Courthouse Crowd: Los Angeles County and Its Government, 1850-1950* (Los Angeles: Historical Society of Southern California, 2013), 172.

15. Sitton, *The Courthouse Crowd*, 172.

16. William J. Fox bulletin, Jan. 17, 1955, box 82, Goodwin Knight Papers, CSA; *LAT*, Jul. 7, 1976, Jan. 10, 1989, Jul. 26, 1993, May 6, 1994; Robert A. Wenke to James Hayes, Mar. 18, 1976, box 388, HAHN; Hufford to BOS, Sept. 9, 1983, box 201, Kerry Gottlieb memo to Edelman, Jul. 16, 1993, box 63, EDELMAN; Herald *Examiner*, Sept. 12, 1984.

17. See Los Angeles County Grand Jury, "Final Reports" for 1967, 1968, 1969, 1972, 1978-79, 1979-80, 1980-1981, and 1983-84, LACGJ website; Sally Reed to BOS, Oct. 22, 1993, Sherman Block to BOS, Dec. 21, 1993, and De Witt Clinton to BOS, Dec. 27, 1993, and many letters from Municipal Court judges in box 119, MOLINA; and many *Times*, editorials from the 1960s to 1990s.

18. Mize to CAO, Jun. 22, 1973, box 309, Maurice Rene Chez to Hahn, Mar. 19, 1973, box 432, "Task Force on Chief Administrative Office" report, June 1983, box 51, HAHN; *Herald Examiner*, Sept. 7, 1983; Molina motion, Jul. 20, 1993, box 290, MOLINA.

19. John Anson Ford, *Thirty Explosive Years in Los Angeles County* (San Marino, Calif.: Huntington Library, 1961), 18-19; Sitton, *The Courthouse Crowd*, 245.

20. *LAT*, Mar. 11, 1959, Sept. 21, 1961; L.S. Hollister to BOS, Sept. 22, 1964, box 25, HAHN.

21. *LAT*, Dec. 24, 1962, Nov. 8, Dec. 30, 1963, Jan. 8, 9, Feb. 5, 19, 20, 27, Apr. 16, 1964.

22. Michael Mont Harmon, "The Consolidation of the Los Angeles City and County Health Departments: A Case Study" (PhD diss., University of Southern California, 1968), passim. *LAT, Jun.* 15,18, 1964, Jan. 10,13, 1967, Sept. 23, 1973, Aug. 21, 1974, Apr. 30, 1975, Jan. 27, 1980; Tom Bradley to Hahn, Jul. 3, 1974, box 625, Milton G. Gordon to Maurice Weiner, Nov. 1, 1973, box 634, Will to BOS, Jul. 8, 1974, box 30, and Ann Boren to BOS, Feb. 18, 1981, box 448, HAHN; Hufford to BOS, Jun. 16, 1981, box 201, EDELMAN.

23. *LAT*, Jul. 8, Aug. 5, 1956, Feb. 7, 1958, Jun. 15, 1969 (quote), Sept. 15, 1985; *Star*, Apr. 6, 27, 1861; Hufford to BOS, Jun. 16, 1981, box 201, EDELMAN; Samuel Leask, Jr., to Los Angeles City Council, Mar. 15, 1961, CSL; letters of complaint on Ford's borough plan, 1943-1944, in box 2, Los Angeles County and City Consolidation Collection, UCLA. For more on city-county consolidations in the U.S. see Suzanne M. Lemand, and Kurt Thurmaier, eds., *Case Studies in City-County Consolidation: Reshaping the Local Government Landscape* (Armonk, N.Y.: M.E. Sharpe, 2004).

24. Sitton, *The Courthouse Crowd*, 135-139.

25. *LAT*, Nov. 24, 1926.

26. *Examiner*, Feb. 26, 1956; *LAT*, Dec. 1, 1975; Ford newsletter, Jul. 24, 1956, box 55, JAF.

27. Ford newsletters, Apr. 16, Jul. 30, 1957 (quotes), box 55, Ford to Charles F, Davis, Jun. 23, 1958, box 5, JAF.

28. *LAT*, Oct. 30, 1957, Aug. 20, 1958.

29. *LAT*, May 30, 1958, Aug. 1, 6, 13, Sept. 3, 1958; *Examiner*, Nov. 3, 1958; Resolution of the Los Angeles County Grand Jury, May 27, 1958, box 147, HAHN; Ford newsletters, Jun 4, Jul. 22, Sept. 2, 1958, box 55, and Warren Dorn to Ford, Aug. 14, 1958, box 5, JAF.

30. *Downey Champion*, Mar. 24, 1959; *LAT,* Apr. 10, May 15, 1959; *San Fernando Sun*, May 17, 1959; *Whittier News*, Nov. 20, 1959.

31. *LAT*, Feb. 2, May 9, 22, Jun. 7, Jul. 18, Nov. 11, 1962; Los Angeles County Charter Study Committee, "Recommendations of the Charter Study Committee Presented to the Board of Supervisors," June 6, 1962, quote on 1; Minutes of Chamber of Commerce directors meeting, Jul. 12, 1962, 68, carton 035, LACCOC; and various materials in box 633, HAHN.

32. *LAT*, Oct. 22, 1964, Jun. 5, 1966, Nov. 29, 1967.

33. *LAT*, Mar. 26, 28 (quote), 1969; Hahn motion, Mar. 25, 1969, box 106, HAHN.

34. Los Angeles County Grand Jury, "Final Reports," 1970, 74, 1972, 33-34, 1973-74, 1975-76, LACGJ website; County Citizens' Economy and Efficiency Commission, Reports18, 26, 33,35, 43, 68, 69 (1970-1976), LACCEEC website; *LAT*, Apr. 23, 29, 1970.

35. Hahn statement, Sept. 11, 1970, box 431, Hahn to editor of *Times*, Jul. 27, 1973, box 632, HAHN; *LAT*, Jul. 20, 29, Aug. 3, 1970; County Citizens' Economy and Efficiency Committee, Report 18, Jul. 1970, LACCEE website.

36. *Whittier Daily News*, Jul. 28, 1971; *LAT*, Dec. 9, 1971; John H. Larson to Hahn, Apr. 7, 1975, box 109, HAHN.

37. Hahn motion, Apr. 18, 1972, box 883, HAHN; Los Angeles County Grand Jury, "Final Report," 1972, 33-34, LACGJ website; *LAT*, Jul. 12, 1972.

38. Hahn motions, Jul. 24, 1973, box 885, May 1, 1973, box 884, Hahn to editor of *Times*, Jul. 27, 1973, box 625, HAHN; *LAT,* Jul. 26, 1973; County Citizens' Economy and Efficiency Committee, Report 35, Mar. 1973, LACCEEC website.

39. *LAT*, Jan. 24, 30, Jun. 18, Jul. 24, Aug. 4, 7, 1974; County Citizens' Economy and Efficiency Commission, Report 43, Jul. 1974, LACCEEC website.

40. Hahn motion, Jan. 21, 1975, box 625, HAHN; *LAT*, Jan. 22, 1975 (quote in editorial).

41. Warren Christopher to Francis Lindley, Nov. 12, 1974 (quote), plus the amended grant proposal in Grant File 2118, box 13, Haynes Foundation Records, Los Angeles; Robert Gottlieb and Irene Wolt, *Thinking Big: The Story of the Los Angeles Times, Its Publishers, and Their Influence on Southern California* (New York: G.P. Putnam's Sons, 1977), 528-29.

42. Christopher to Lindley, Jan. 23, 1975, box 13, Haynes Foundation Records.

43. Seth Hufstedler to Lindley, Mar. 24, 1975, box 13, Haynes Foundation Records; *LAT*, Aug. 8, 1973, Jan. 22, Feb. 19, Mar. 14, May 1,1975; Daily *Journal*, Mar. 5, 13, 14, 1975.

44. Christopher to Lindley, May 30, 1975, box 13, Haynes Foundation Records; LAT, Aug. 27, Oct. 31, Nov. 25, Dec. 9, 1975; Steven P. Erie, interview by author, San Marino, Calif., December 15, 2016.

45. Public Commission on County Government, *To Serve Seven Million: Report of the Public Commission on Los Angeles County Government* (Los Angeles: The Commission, 1976), passim; Rosaline Levenson, "Major Changes Sought in L.A.: County Study Commission Wants Structural Reform," *National Civic Review* 65 (Jul. 1976): 353–4. During the commission's research work the 1975 County Grand Jury again recommended the elected county executive. *LAT,* Jun. 27, 1975.

46. *LAT*, Feb. 12, 13, 20, 1976; constituent request form, Feb. 20, 1976, box 200, EDELMAN.

47. Larry Gotlieb memo to Edelman, Feb. 18, 1976, box 374, EDELMAN; Hahn motion, Mar. 3, 18, 1976, box 889, HAHN; *LAT,* Feb. 13, Mar. 13, 19, 21, 29, May 5, 20, Jun. 23, 1976.

48. *LAT*, Jun. 28, Sept. 17, Oct. 3, 10, 17, 21, 1976; *Herald Examiner*, Jun. 28, 1976; Gottlieb and Wolt, *Thinking Big*, 529; County Citizens' Economy and Efficiency Commission, Reports 68 and 69, Sept. and Oct. 1976, LACCEEC website.

49. *LAT*, Nov. 3, 4, 7, Dec. 21, 26, 1976; Lindley to Francis Wheat, Dec. 3, 1976 (quote), box 13, Haynes Foundation Records.

50. Los Angeles County Grand Jury, "Final Report," 1977–78, 13–14 (quotes), LACGJ website; Hahn statement, Jun. 21, 1978, box 150, Hufford to BOS, Jul. 14, 1978, box 632, HAHN; *LAT, Mar.* 28, Jun. 22, Jul. 20, Aug 6, 13, Sept. 4, 1978.

51. Walter Zelman to Hahn, Aug.11, 1978, box 633, HAHN; Larry Fisher to Proposition C Planning Group, Sept. 26, 1978, box 8, Braun & Company Records, CSA; *LAT*, Sept. 30, Oct. 8, 29, Nov. 3, 5, 1978; *Herald Examiner,* Oct. 3, 1978; *Santa Monica Evening Outlook*, Nov. 3, 1978; KNX 1090 radio editorial, Oct. 18, 1978, box 509, EDELMAN.

52. *LAT,* Sept. 4, 9, 1978; various materials on the 1978 election in box 199, EDELMAN.

53. County Citizens' Economy and Efficiency Commission, "Challenge for the 1980s: Can We Govern Ourselves?" Report 83, Jan. 1979, LACCEEC website; Rosaline Levenson, "Changes Urged for L.A. Area," *National Civic Review* 68 (Jul. 1979): 375–376.

Chapter 7

1. The sources for the epigraphs are *LAT,* Apr. 30, 1978, and Norman Macrae in the *San Francisco Chronicle*, Jan. 13, 1979, as quoted in Howard Jarvis, *I'm Mad as Hell: The Exclusive Story of the Tax Revolt and Its Leader* (New York: Times Books, 1979), 181.

2. Tom Sitton, *The Courthouse Crowd: Los Angeles County and Its Government, 1850–1950* (Los Angeles: Historical Society of Southern California, 2013), 200–203, 230, 293–296.

3. *LAT*, May 3, Jun. 10, 13,14, 16, 28, 1950, Apr. 4, 19, 28, Jun. 16, 1954, Jun. 11,14,19, Dec. 7, 11, 14,18, 1957, Mar. 13, Jun. 11,13, 1958, Sept. 30, Oct. 2,1959; Bates S. Himes to Burton Chace, Nov. 7, 1955, and other tax complaints in box 82, Goodwin Knight Papers, CSA.

4. *LAT*, Jan. 6, Jun. 11, 15, Jul. 3, Aug. 21, Sept. 18, Dec. 15, 1960, Mar. 19, 20, 21, 22, 1961.

5. *LAT*, Feb. 27, 28, Jun. 4, 1961, Jul. 30, 1962, Oct. 30, 1963, Jan. 4,1966; Hahn to Assemblyman John T. Knox, Jan. 26, 1966, Hahn to Governor Edmund G. Brown, Feb. 1, 1966, box 481, HAHN.

6. *LAT*, Apr. 30, Jun. 27, 1962, Jul. 2, 1963, Jul. 15, Nov. 11, 13, 18, 22, 24, 1964, Nov. 13, 16, 1966, Sept. 27, 1979.

7. *Herald Examiner*, Jul. 14, 1967; *LAT*, Jan. 5, Feb. 17, 1965; Los Angeles County Grand Jury, "Final Report," 1964, 29–30, LACGJ website; Hahn to Ronald Reagan, Nov. 29, 1967, box 494, James S. Mize to Los Angeles County delegation to the State Legislature, Nov. 1, 1967, box 878, HAHN.

8. *LAT*, Nov. 8, 1962, Mar. 10, Aug. 7, 8, 1963, Jul. 15, 1964, Jun. 9, Nov. 22, Dec. 16, 1966, Feb. 7, 21, Apr. 24, May 4, Jun. 13, Jul. 7, 22, Oct. 17, 1967; Steven P. Erie, interview by author, San Marino, Calif., Dec. 15, 2016.

9. *LAT*, Aug. 9, 14, Sept. 9, Oct. 9, 17, 28, Nov. 1, 3, 5, 6, 1968; James Beebe report on Watson Initiative, in Minutes of Chamber of Commerce directors meeting, Aug. 22, 1968, 63, carton 035, LAACOC; De Witt Clinton (for John Maharg) to Hahn, Oct. 7, 1968, box 106, HAHN.

10. *LAT,* Dec. 5, 1962, Jun. 13, 1967, Feb. 25, Apr. 17, 1968, Dec. 17, 1971; Richard White memo to Ernest Debs, Mar. 26, 1968, box 9, DEBS; Jarvis, *Mad as Hell*, 31–39.

11. *LAT*, Dec. 17, 1971, Nov. 1, 2 (quote), 1972; *Sacramento Bee*, Aug. 22, 1972; Governor Ronald Reagan to Dr. Norman Topping, Sept. 26, 1972, and other material in Proposition 14 files, box 1, Braun & Co. Records, CSA; Jarvis, *Mad as Hell*, 31–39.

12. Jarvis, *Mad as Hell*, 40–54; *LAT, Aug.* 1, 1976, Dec. 30, 1977.

13. *LAT,* Oct. 12, 13, 24, 1973; copy of Debs to Ronald Reagan, Sept. 2, 1970, BOS resolution, Jan. 18, 1972, box 474, HAHN; Arthur Will to BOS, Mar. 10, 1972, box 347, Will to BOS, Oct. 19, 1973, box 49, DEBS; Jarvis, *Mad as Hell*, 39.

14. *Daily Journal*, Jul. 13, 1971; *LAT*, Jun. 27, 1974, Jun. 21, Dec. 6, Oct. 10, 1975; Hahn statement, May 4, 1972, box 27, Hahn motion, Sept. 14, 1973, box 885, Hahn statement, May 30, 1974, box 29, Hahn motion, Dec. 9, 1975, box 479, HAHN; Will to BOS, Feb. 7, 1973, Will to BOS, May 1, 1973, box 49, DEBS.

15. *LAT*, May 4, 5, 1976; Robert J. Downey to BOS, Jan. 14, 1976 (first quote), box 432, HAHN; County Citizens' Economy and Efficiency Commission, "The New York City Crisis and Los

Angeles County Government: Organization, Employment and Compensation," Report 63, May 1976 (quotes on ii and 1), LACCEEC website; Eugene Garaventa, "Los Angeles County Seeks to Avoid Disaster," *National Civic Review* 66 (Feb. 1977): 103–104.

16. *LAT,* Jan. 8, 23, Jun. 29, Jul. 1, 1976, Aug. 11,19, 31, Sept. 9, 17, 21, 22, 30, Oct. 25, Nov. 7, Dec. 16, 1976; Jarvis, *Mad as Hell,* 40–41.

17. *LAT, Jun.* 30, Jul. 1, Dec. 9, 1977; Bob Geoghegan memo to Edelman, Dec. 13, 1976, Hufford to BOS, Dec. 13, 1976, box 78, EDELMAN; Hufford to BOS, Dec. 9, 28, 1977, box 37, HAHN.

18. *LAT,* Nov. 25, Dec. 3, 1977; Gary J. Miller, *Cities by Contract: The Politics of Municipal Incorporation* (Cambridge, Mass.: MIT Press, 1981), 190–196.

19. *LAT,* Mar. 31,1977, Jan. 12, Apr. 12, 1978; Bob Geoghegan memo to Edelman, Mar. 17, 1978, box 77, EDELMAN; John M. Allswang, *California Initiatives and Referendums, 1912–1990* (Los Angeles: Edmund G. "Pat" Brown Institute of Public Affairs, 1991), 135–136; League of Women Voters of Los Angeles County memo to BOS, Apr. 20, 1978, box 643, HAHN; David O. Sears, *Tax Revolt: Something for Nothing in California* (Cambridge, Mass: Harvard University Press, 1982), 26–27, 194 (quote).

20. *LAT,* Jan. 25, Feb. 10 (first quote), Mar. 15, 22, 30 (second quote), May 3, 1978; *Torrance Daily Breeze,* Mar. 28, 1978; Hufford to BOS, Feb. 2, 1978, Edelman press release, Mar. 24, 1978, box 643, HAHN.

21. *LAT,* Apr. 12,16, 21, 25, 26, 30,1978; County Citizens' Economy and Efficiency Commission, "Statement on Proposition 13, The Jarvis Gann Initiative," Report 77, Apr. 5,1978, LACCEEC website; Harry Hufford to BOS, Apr. 14, 1978, box 643, HAHN; Dan Farcas memo to Edelman, April 25, 1978, box 181, EDELMAN.

22. *LAT, May* 2, 1978; *Long Beach Independent Press-Telegram,* Jun. 10, 1979 (*Independent* was dropped in 1981); *Daily News,* May 29, 1988; Sears, *Tax Revolt,* 192–194.

23. *LAT,* May 25, 1978; *Herald Examiner,* May 23, 1978; Hahn motions, May 2 and 9, 1978, Hufford to BOS, May 8,10, 1978, box 643, HAHN; Bob Geoghegan memo to Edelman, May 5, 1978, box 250, Geoghegan memo to Edelman, May 8,1978, box 512, EDELMAN; Edelman quote in transcript of "Proposition 13: The Causes and Consequences" Conference, September 27, 2003, Huntington Library, HEH, 25; Joel Fox, *The Legend of Proposition 13: The Great California Tax Revolt* (Philadelphia: Xlibris, 2003), 71; Sears, Tax Revolt, 30, 191–192.

24. *LAT,* Jun. 7, 8, Aug. 18, 1978, Jun. 6, 1983; *New York Times,* Jun. 8, 1978 (quote); Jarvis, *Mad as Hell,* 177–184.

25. *LAT,* Jun. 8, 28, 30, Jul. 30, Aug. 16, 1978; Mark Bloodgood to BOS, Jun.15,1978, box 16, Hahn motion, Jun. 13, 1978, box 643, Hahn news release, Jun. 28, 1978, box 497, Harry Marlow,

"Life With Proposition 13" report, Feb. 22, 1979, Hufford to Lloyd G. Hild, May 4, 1979, box 644, HAHN.

26. *LAT,* Jun. 24, Aug. 12, 15, 22, 24, 1978; Edelman essay in *Philadelphia Inquirer,* October 2, 1978 (quote); Hufford to BOS, Nov. 14, 1978, box 513, Edelman to Congressman Jim Lloyd, Jul. 27, 1978, box 236, EDELMAN; Hufford to BOS, Dec. 18, 1978, box 40, Hufford to Lloyd G. Hild, May 4, 1979, box 644, HAHN; Roseline Levenson, "California Plans Urban Strategy," *National Civic Review* 67 (Sept. 1978): 368–369.

27. *LAT,* Sept. 1, 6, 20, Oct. 19, Nov. 1, 1978, Jul. 29, Aug. 5, 1979; *Daily Journal,* Dec. 6, 1978, Apr. 24, 1979; *Herald Examiner,* Feb. 21, 1979; *Long Beach Independent Press-Telegram,* Jun. 10, 1979; Peter Pitchess to Edelman, Jun. 2, 1979, and Edelman to Pitchess, Jun. 28, 1979 (quote), box 531, EDELMAN; Howard Jarvis telegram to Hahn, Jun. 20, 1979, box 645, HAHN.

28. *LAT,* Nov. 18, 1978, Feb. 17, May 7, 1980, Apr. 5, 1983, Sept. 5,13,16,1984; Proposition 9 1980 (Jarvis II) file, box 511, EDELMAN; Hufford to BOS, Nov. 27, 1979, box 43, HAHN; Allswang, *California Initiatives and Referendums,* 138–139, 142–143, 149–150.

29. *LAT,* May 30, Jun. 21, 1980, Apr. 5. Jun. 6, 1983, Apr. 24, 25, 30, Jun. 29, Jul. 1, 17, 1984, Jun. 30, 1985; Hahn to Alan Robbins, Jul. 24, 1980, box 480, draft of article for "County Digest," Sept. 30, 1983, box 52, HAHN; Bob Geoghegan memo to Edelman, May 20, 1982, box 188, Hufford to Edelman, Oct. 26, 1982, box 180, Geoghegan memo to Edelman, Apr. 19, 1983, box 146, Hufford to BOS, Jun. 2, 1983, box 190, EDELMAN.

30. *LAT,* Oct. 10, 1976.

31. *LAT,* Apr. 21, 1978, Jun. 5, 1983, Dec. 9, 1984, Apr. 3, 1988, Mar. 3, 1991, Nov, 29, 2010, Jan. 30, Jun. 8, 30, Dec. 29, 2014, Jun. 10, Nov. 2, 2015, Jan. 14, Jun. 4, Aug. 19, Oct. 11, 16, 17, 2018, Mar. 31, 2019; *Daily Journal,* Jun. 6, 1988; *Daily News,* Jun. 4, 1991; Terry Schwadron, ed., *California and the American Tax Revolt: Proposition 13 Five Years Later* (Berkeley and Los Angeles: University of California Press, 1984), 1–97, 180–194; Sears, *Tax Revolt,* passim; Jack Citrin and Isaac W. Martin, eds., *After the Tax Revolt: California's Proposition 13 Turns 30* (Berkeley, Calif.; Berkeley Public Policy Press, Institute of Governmental Studies, University of California, 2009), esp. 101–134; Fox, *The Legend of Proposition 13, 2003,* esp. 57–124.

32. Dan Walters. "Despite Proposition 13, California Property Tax Revenue Has Soared," *CALmatters,* Jul. 18, 2017; Citron and Martin, *After the Tax Revolt,* esp. 1–49, 135–156; Sears, *Tax Revolt,* esp. 33–49, 207–244; Fox, *The Legend of Proposition 13,* 94–175, 207–233; California Legislative Analyst Office, "Common Claims About Proposition 13," 2016, passim; Transcript of "Proposition 13: The Causes and Consequences," 8, 13–15, 38–39.

33. *LAT,* Apr. 8, 1979, Jun. 30, 1985, Jan. 10, 2011, Aug. 18, 26, 2019; Schwadron, ed. *California and the American Tax Revolt,* 98–179.

Chapter 8

1. On another "Solid Three" supervisor majority active in the earlier 1900s see Tom Sitton, *The Courthouse Crowd: Los Angeles County and Its Government, 1850–1950* (Los Angeles: Historical Society of Southern California, 2013), 112–113, 122–127.

2. *LAT*, Dec. 2, 1996, Apr. 22, 2005; http://were.lacounty.gov/About-Us/Board-of-Supervisors/Board-Member-Biographies.

3. *LAT*, Feb. 11, 1978, Apr. 8, 1979, Jan. 18, 1983, Dec. 5, 1985; http://bos.lacounty.gov/About-Us/Board-of-Supervisors/Board-Member-Biographies; *Herald Examiner*, Jun. 12, 1985; Michele Willens, "A Second Political Hat for LA Chairman Mike Antonovich," *California Journal* 14 (May 1983): 183–185.

4. *LAT*, Jan. 29, Jun. 5, Nov. 1, 29, Dec. 29, 1979, Jan. 24, Feb.5, 25, Apr. 26, May13, 30, Jun. 29, Jul. 27, Sept. 7, 13, Oct. 5, 22, 25, 26, 31, Nov. 2, 5,19, 28, 1980, Jan. 11, 1990; J. Morgan Kousser, *Colorblind Injustice: Minority Voting Rights and the Undoing of the Second Reconstruction* (Chapel Hill: University of North Carolina Press, 1999), 92–95.

5. *LAT*, Feb. 2, 9 (quote), 19, 23, 25, Mar. 5, 26, 28, May 20, 31, Jun. 1, 5, 10, 1982.

6. *LAT*, Apr. 18, Jul. 11, Aug. 22, Sept. 23, 1983, Jan. 14, Mar. 3, 8, 18, Apr. 25, May 11, 18, 20, 24, 31, Jun. 1, 6, 10, 1984; *Herald Examiner*, May 3, Jun. 3, 1984; California Commission on Campaign Financing, *Money, and Politics in Local Elections: The Los Angeles Area* (Los Angeles: Center for Responsive Government, 1989), 170–172; 1984 campaign material in boxes 142,143, Alexander Pope Papers, HEH.

7. *LAT*, Oct. 30, 1985, Feb. 25, Mar. 30, May 22, 23, Jun. 1, 5, Oct. 16, Nov. 2, 1986; Bob Geoghegan memo to Edmund Edelman, Jun. 2, 1986, box 419, EDELMAN.

8. *LAT*, Jan. 12, Apr. 12, Sept. 19, Oct. 9, 1987, Jan. 28, 29, Feb. 4, May 31, 1988; *Daily News*, Feb. 9, 1988; *Torrance Daily Breeze*, Jun. 1, 1988; Herald *Examiner*, Feb. 3, May 19, Jun. 6, 1988; *Sentinel*, Feb. 18, 1988; Julian Dixon draft announcements, Feb. 3, 1988, box 125, Julian Dixon Papers, CSULA; Tom Johnson, "Kenny's Last Stand," *Los Angeles*, 33 (May 1988): 133; election material in boxes 605 and 606, HAHN.

9. *LAT*, Apr. 27, Jul 2, 1987, Jan. 14, 28, Mar. 28, May 12, 22, 27, Jun. 6, 12, Sept. 17, Oct. 22, 26, 27, Nov. 1, 5,10, 1988; *Daily News*, Aug. 2, 1988; Wallace for Supervisor biographical statement, 1994, box 184, MOLINA; Michael Antonovich to Dixon, Aug. 23, 1988, box 124, and Michael Antonovich, Sr., to Dixon, Aug. 6, 1988 (quote), box 123, Dixon Papers.

10. *LAT*, Mar. 3, May 25, 29, Jun. 9, 1988.

11. *LAT*, Feb 7, Mar. 9, Apr. 27, May 22, 26, 31, Jun. 2, 7, Oct. 14, Nov. 2, 7, 1990.

12. *LAT*, Jun. 12, 1981, Jul. 15, Dec. 2, 21, 1988; *Herald Examiner*, Oct. 9, 1986.

13. *LAT*, Dec. 1, 1980 (quote), Jan. 9, Apr. 10,

May 3, 1981, Dec. 21, 1983; James S. Mize to Senator S.I. Hayakawa, Jul. 2, 1981, box 236, EDELMAN; *San Pedro News Pilot*, Nov. 17, 1988. In 1986 the BOS voted 4–0 against an English-only initiative in California because it was too divisive. *LAT*, Apr. 23, 1986.

14. John Stodder memo to Edelman, Feb. 10,1986, box 59, EDELMAN; Dan Wolf memo to Hahn, Nov. 26, 1986, box 56, HAHN; *LAT*, Feb. 11,18,19, 1986.

15. *LAT*, Jul. 30,1958, Sept. 26, 1973, Jan. 22, 1978, Sept. 7, 1984, Feb. 23, 26, Mar. 8, May 30, 1986; *Daily News*, Jan. 19, 1986; Dana motions, Jan. 9, 1986, and Feb. 25, 1986, Geoghegan memo to Edelman, Dec. 30, 1985, Sam Duca to BOS, Mar. 4, 1986, box 75, EDELMAN; James Hankla to BOS, Jan. 30, 1986, box 57, KFWB editorial, Feb. 13, 1986, box 13, Hahn to Los Angeles County Court Commissioners, Apr. 10, 1986, box 392, HAHN.

16. *LAT*, Jun. 9, 1986, Mar. 17, Nov. 5,19, 1987, Nov. 8, 1990; *Daily News*, Aug. 19, Dec. 10, 1986, May 26, 1987, Apr. 16, 1990; Mark H. Bloodgood to BOS, May 19,1987, box 74, Rosa Mora to John Lynch, Nov. 10, 1989, Kerry Gottlieb memo to Edelman, Jan. 8, 1990, box 73, Hahn to Lynch, Jun. 27, 1989, Tom Bradley press release, Nov.1, 1990, box 75, EDELMAN.

17. *Herald Examiner*, Nov. 4, Dec. 29, 1981, Dec. 21, 1983, Mar. 19 (quote), Jun. 29, Oct. 17, 1984, Jun. 14, 1988, Sept. 29, Dec. 22, 1989, Jul. 26, 1990; Hahn to Cruz Reynoso, Feb. 10, 1982, transcript of BOS meeting, Jan. 19, 1982 (quote), box 499, HAHN; *Daily News*, Feb. 7, 1988.

18. Schabarum to Edelman, Aug. 25, 1981, box 745, Geoghegan memo to Edelman, Apr. 12, 1988, box 200, EDELMAN; *Herald Examiner*, Oct. 22, 1981, Jun. 13,1989; *Daily News*, Apr. 20, Jun. 26, 1988, Jan. 27, 1991; *Sentinel*, Dec. 17, 1981; LAT, Oct. 22, Dec. 9, 1981, Apr. 20, 1982, Jun. 28, Aug. 8, 1988, Jan. 10, 1989, Mar. 14, 1990; Hahn motion, Jan. 5, 1982, box 633, HAHN.

19. *LAT*, Mar. 19, 1984; *Herald Examiner*, Sept. 1, 1988.

20. *LAT*, Mar. 9, 1982, Dec. 6, 1984; Dana news release, Apr. 4, 1982, box 234, Minutes of BOS meeting, Jan. 31, 1984, CAO Harry Hufford to BOS, Aug. 24, 1984, box 236, Schabarum motion, Apr. 1, 1986, box 237, Alice Carreon memo to Geoghegan, Aug. 17, 1982, box 560, EDELMAN; County of Los Angeles *Digest*, March 1982, 1–3; S. Kenneth Howard, "Renewing the Federalism Debate," *National Civic Review* 17: (Apr. 1983) 188–189, 244.

21. *LAT*, Oct. 18,1986; Edelman motion, Nov. 6, 1981, Minutes of BOS meeting, May 3, 1988, box 237, EDELMAN; Hahn statement, Jun. 1, 1982, box 87, HAHN.

22. *LAT*, Apr. 27, Nov. 10, Dec. 29, 1982, Apr. 29, May 25, 26, 1983, May 31, Jun. 5, 1985; Joan Zyda, "Los Angeles Gets a New DA," *California Journal* 14 (Feb. 1983): 86.

23. *Daily Journal*, Jul. 31, 1985; *LAT*, Jul. 1, 2, 1988; *Herald Examiner*, Jul. 18, 1988; copy of CSAC Executive Director Larry E. Naake to Governor

Deukmejian, Sept. 19, 1985, box 251, EDELMAN; Hahn statement, Jul. 8, 1987, Hahn statement, Jul. 13, 1988, box 501, HAHN. Deukmejian also declined to appoint his friend Schabarum as state treasurer after the death of incumbent Jess Unruh in 1988. *LAT*, Jul. 15, 1988; Willens, "A Second Political Hat for Mike Antonovich," 183.

24. *LAT*, May 23, Jun. 17, 23, Jul. 1, 8, 1981; *Daily News*, Jul. 14, 1981 (quote); copy of Richard Robinson to Herb Jackson, Jun. 6, 1981, box 483, HAHN; Clyde Johnson to Robert C. Gates, Sept. 16, 1987, box 562, Geoghegan memo to Edelman, Sept. 25, 1987, Diane E. Watson to Robert Quiroz, Aug. 20,1987, Richard G. Polanco to Gates, Sept. 24, 1987, box 563, EDELMAN.

25. *LAT*, Apr. 8, 1991, Nov. 10,1992; Schabarum motion, Jun. 18, 1985, box 567, Hankla to BOS, Feb. 22, 1985, Richard Dixon to BOS, May 1,1989, box 551, Geoghegan memo to Edelman, Feb. 26, 1985, box 521, EDELMAN; Alan L. Saltzstein, "Los Angeles: Politics Without Governance," in H.V. Savitch and Ronald K. Vogel, eds., *Regional Politics: America in a Post-City Age* (Thousand Oaks, CA: Sage Publications, 1996), 58–70.

26. *LAT*, Nov. 16,1988, Sept. 23,1989; *Daily News*, Dec. 10, 1989; Los Angeles 2000 Committee, *LA2000: A City of the Future* (Los Angeles: Los Angeles 2000 Committee, 1988), passim; The 2000 Partnership, "Managing Growth in Southern California: A Proposal," 1990, box 553, EDELMAN; William B. Fulton, *The Reluctant Metropolis: The Politics of Urban Growth in Los Angeles* (Point Arena, Calif.: Solano Press Books, 1997), 163–164.

27. *LAT*, Sept. 23, 1989 (quote), Jan. 19, Mar. 25, Apr. 8, 1991; Richard Dixon to BOS, Aug. 8, 1990, and CSAC resolution, box 251, Dixon to BOS, Apr. 22, 1991, box 57, EDELMAN; Doris M. Ward, "Regional Governance Issues in California: Citizen and Policy Implications," *National Civic Review* 79 (Mar.-Apr. 1990): 132–137; Craig Hamley and A.G. Block, "Regional Government: Everyone Wants to Land on Boardwalk," *California Journal* 21 (Nov. 1990): 530–534; Fulton, *Reluctant Metropolis*, 163–166.

28. *LAT*, Mar. 15, 1984, Jan. 27, 1985 (first quotes); Maria Elena Harris, "Is Ideology a Determinant of Local Government Fiscal Policy? A Case Study of the Los Angeles County Board of Supervisors" (PhD diss., University of Southern California, 1995), 142 (last quote), 155.

29. *LAT*, Apr. 8, 1979, Jun. 27, 1983, Mar. 15, Aug. 29, 30, 1984, Dec. 26, 1999; Hufford biography, August 1984, box 59, EDELMAN.

30. *LAT*, Aug. 30, 1984, Jan. 27, Feb. 15, 1985, Nov. 19, 1986, Aug. 21, 1998; *Daily News*, Feb. 3, 1986; Hankla to Edelman, Dec. 20, 1985, and Nov. 19, 1986, County of Los Angeles *Digest*, 20 (March 1, 1985): 1–2, box 59, EDELMAN.

31. *LAT*, May 23, 1984, Jan. 27, 1985, Dec. 10, 1986, Jan. 10, 1989, Aug. 28, 1991, Feb. 1, 1992, Sept. 29, 1993; *Torrance Daily Breeze*, Dec. 3,1986; Ron Curran, "Richard Dixon: Powerful Politician You Never Elected," *L.A. Weekly*, Feb. 21–27, 1992, 18–25.

32. *LAT*, Jul. 28, 1983, Jan. 27, 1985, Jan. 10, 1989, Aug. 23, 1991, Feb. 25, 1992; Harris, "Is Ideology a Determinant," 121, 125–126, 136, 140–155.

33. *LAT*, Jun. 6, Aug. 7, 1983, Apr. 30, Jul. 17, 1984, Jun. 7, 30, 1985, May 24, 1986, Jul. 1,1988, Jul. 21,1989; Hufford to BOS, Feb. 3, 1983, box 49, KNBC4 editorial, Jun. 22, 1983, box 50, HAHN; Dixon to BOS, May 23, 1989, box 184, EDELMAN. For more on county budgeting in these years see material in boxes 58–61, 180, and 184, EDELMAN, and boxes 46–59, HAHN. On Los Angeles CAOs after this period see Mark Pisano and Richard F. Callahan, "Case Study 1: Fiscal Sustainability in Los Angeles County," *National Civic Review* 101 (Spring 2012): 11–17.

34. John Anson Ford, *Thirty Explosive Years in Los Angeles County* (San Marino, Calif.: Huntington Library, 1961), 32–33; *LAT*, Apr. 8, 1979 (quote); Winston W. Crouch, *Organized Civil Servants: Public Employer-Employee Relations in California* (Berkeley and Los Angeles: University of California Press, 1978), 14–19, 258–261; Thomas Wilson Vinson, "The 1966 Changeover from a Civil Service to a Personnel Department" (M.A. thesis, USC, 1968), passim; "Los Angeles Task Force Studies Civil Service," *National Civic Review* 63 (Jun. 1974): 328–329; "Report of the Los Angeles County Employee Relations Commission, 1968–1977," August 1978,1–8, box 128, HAHN; and many other sources in LAT, the HAHN and EDELMAN Collections, reports of county agencies, and other county records. On the 1966 social workers strike see Fred B. Glass, *From Mission to Microchip: A History of the California Labor Movement* (Oakland: University of California Press, 2016), 353–355.

35. *LAT*, Dec. 3, 6 (quote) 10, 17, 31, 1980, Jan. 28, 1981, Dec. 11, 1982, and many more throughout the decade; Minutes of BOS meeting, Jan. 12, 1988, BOS section of County website.

36. James Hankla to BOS, Aug. 14, 1985, box 54, Hahn press statement, Nov. 5, 1985, Mark H. Bloodgood to BOS, Oct. 30, 1985, box 54, HAHN; Schabarum motion, Apr. 28, 1981, box 698, Rob Saltzman memo to Edelman, Sept. 23, 1983, box 1007, Rob Saltzman memo to Edelman, Mar. 28, 1984, box 59, Jim Petzke memo to Edelman, May 12, 19, 1988, box 201, EDELMAN; Rosaline Levenson, " California Supreme Court Decision Gives Public Employees Right to Strike," *National Civic Review* 74 (Jul.-Aug. 1985): 320. Edmund D. Edelman, "Contracting Out: The County of Los Angeles Experience," 1987 (Revised November 1988), box 187, EDELMAN. On U.S experiences in the 1980s and after see, among many others, C.J. Hein, "Contracting Municipal Services: Does it Really Cost Less?" *National Civic Review* 72 (Jun. 1983): 321–326; Eugene Garaventa, "Private Delivery of Public Services May Have a Few Hidden Barriers," *National Civic Review* 75 (May-Jun. 1986): 153–157; Paul Seidenstat, ed., *Contracting Out*

Government Services (Westport, Conn.: Praeger, 1999, passim).

37. *LAT,* Jan. 30, Oct. 21, 26, Nov. 7, 1974, Nov. 9, Dec. 6, 1978, Apr. 28,1980; John H. Larson to BOS, Jul. 10, 1974, box 108, HAHN; Charles Weissburd to Jim Petzke, Aug. 9, 1986, with ballot arguments for and against Proposition A,1978, box 186, EDELMAN; County Grand Jury, "Final Report," 1982–1983, 10–15, esp. 13, LACGJ website.

38. *LAT,* Apr. 26, May 2, 4, 11, 20, Aug. 4, Nov. 19, 22, 1983; *L.A. Weekly,* Nov. 22–28, 1985, 30; Hahn to Edelman, Apr. 5, 1984, box 52, HAHN; County Grand Jury, "Final Report," 1984–1985, 88–98, LACGJ website; transcript of Assembly hearing, Aug. 3, 1983, box 10, Series 001, Richard Alatorre Papers, CSULA; John Stodder memo to Edelman, Oct. 18, 1983, box 186, EDELMAN.

39. *LAT,* Nov. 4, Dec. 27, 1988; Minutes of BOS meeting, Feb. 17, 1987, BSM; Jim Petzke memo to Edelman, Dec. 4, 1986, Bob Ballinger memo to Edelman, Sept 17, 1987, box 186, Edelman presentation, Nov. 1988, 5, box 187, EDELMAN; County Citizens' Economy and Efficiency Commission, Report 106 on contracting out, Aug. 1987, LACCEEC website.

40. Dixon to department and special district heads, March 16, 1987, Bob Ballinger memo to Edelman, Sept. 21, 1987, Marshall Langberg memo to Edelman, Sept. 24, 1987, Dixon to BOS, Dec. 5, 1988, box 186, Dixon to BOS, Apr. 15, 1988, box 185, EDELMAN; Dan Wolf to Hahn, Jul. 8, 1988, box 58, HAHN.

41. *LAT,* Jul. 20 (quote), Oct. 5, 10, 1988, Jan. 5, Feb. 17, Sept. 22, Nov. 10, Dec.22, 1989; County Grand Jury, "Final Report," 1986–1987, 88–89, LACGJ website; Ballinger memo to Edelman, Jun. 19, 1987, Dixon to BOS, Jun. 19, 1987, box 186, James Gilson memo to Edelman, May 28, 1986, DeWitt W. Clinton to BOS, Oct. 3, 1988, box 191, EDELMAN; Hahn motion, Oct. 11, 1988, box 191, HAHN.

42. *LAT,* Sept. 21, 1989 (quote), Apr. 10, 1992, Feb. 8, Jun. 20, 2000; Kerry Gottlieb memos to Edelman, Aug. 31, Dec. 12, 1989, box 185, EDELMAN; Rodney E. Cooper to Gloria Molina, Oct. 19, 1999, box 459, MOLINA.

43. *LAT,* Jun. 6, Dec. 25, 30, 1981, Jan. 6, Feb. 25, 1982, May 17, 1987; *Daily Journal,* Jan. 5, 1982; *East Los Angeles Tribune,* Jan. 13, 1988.

44. *LAT,* Mar. 18, Jun. 8, 1981, Feb. 26, Oct. 28,1983, Jul. 31, 1985, Mar. 26, Apr. 27, 1986; *Wall Street Journal,* Dec.29, 1988; Los Angeles County Sheriff's Department, "The Status of Organized Crime in Los Angeles County," April 1983, and "Update" on the report, May 1984, box 370, Hahn statement, Apr. 2, 1988, and Apr. 5, 1988, box 477, Douglas R. Woodworth to Robert Quiroz, Mar. 27, 1986, box 392, Hahn press release, Feb. 5, 1986, box 371, Hahn press release, Aug. 1, 1988, Hahn to Sherman Block, Jan. 22, 1988 (quote), box 372, HAHN; Dixon to BOS, Jun. 23, 1989, box 530, EDELMAN.

45. *Daily News,* Nov. 15, 1982; *Herald Examiner,*

Nov.17,1982; *LAT,* Feb. 27, Mar. 23, Jun. 5, 1985; Edelman press release, Mar. 20, 1975, box 769, Sheila Kuehl to BOS, n.d. (postmarked May 9, 1985), box 96, EDELMAN: De Witt Clinton and James Hankla to BOS, Mar. 22, 1985, box 1036, Clinton to BOS, Mar. 22, 1985, Minutes of Obscenity and Pornography Commission meeting, Apr. 5, 1985, Fred Okrand to Hahn, Jun. 8, 1985, Betty W. Brooks to Hahn, May 30, 1985, box 1035, HAHN.

46. *Herald Examiner,* Sept. 11, 1985; *LAT,* Feb. 12, Jul. 27, 1986, Dec. 2, 4, 1987; *Daily Journal,* Sept. 30, 1985; Hankla to BOS, Jun. 18, 1985, box 732, James Gilson memo to Edelman, Feb. 9, 1987, box 1008, EDELMAN. The County Obscenity and Pornography Commission had less to do and fewer funds over the next decade and was disbanded by the BOS in 2001. *Bakersfield Californian,* Nov. 14, 2001; Minutes of BOS meeting, Feb. 20, 2001, box 641, MOLINA.

47. *LAT,* Jan. 1, Apr. 6 (quote), 1986, Mar. 28, 1987, Mar. 8, Aug. 30, 1989; William Bradford Reynolds to Edelman, c.Mar. 1985, box 238, Reynolds to Edelman, May 5, 1986, box 533, Chinese American Citizen Alliance to Edelman, Jul. 25, 1988, Councilman Richard Alatorre to Antonovich, Mar. 9,1989, box 535, EDELMAN; Reynolds to Edelman, c. October 1985, Hahn motion, Nov. 19, 1985, and Hahn press release, Nov. 19, 1986, box 371, HAHN; Los Angeles County Sheriff's Department, *150 Years: A Tradition of Service* (Paducah, Ky.: Turner Pub. Co., 2000), 69–70; Sitton, *The Courthouse Crowd,* 104, 150.

48. *LAT,* Feb. 2, Sept. 21, Oct. 5, Dec. 28, 1989, May 27, Dec. 5, 1990, Aug. 18, 1991; *Long Beach Press Telegram,* Dec. 2, 4, 5, 1990; Hahn to Block, Dec. 13, 1984, box 370, copy of Enrique H. Lopez to Los Angeles County Grand Jury, Aug. 9, 1984, Melanie Lomax to Hahn, Jan. 8, 1985, box 371, HAHN.

49. *LAT,* Jun. 30, Jul. 11, Aug. 30, 1981, May 17, 1983, Dec. 20, 1988; Eddy S. Tanaka to BOS, Mar. 29, 1983, box 317, KNX Radio editorial, May 23, 1983, box 318, HAHN; Jennifer Wolch, "From Global to Local: The Rise of Homelessness in Los Angeles During the 1980s," in Allen J. Scott and Edward W. Soja, eds., *The City: Los Angeles and Urban Theory at the End of the Twentieth Century* (Berkeley, Los Angeles, London: University of California Press, 1996), 394–400; Kousser, *Colorblind Injustice,* 134–137.

50. *LAT,* Oct. 1, 1983, Feb. 18, 1984, Aug. 13, 1989; Eddy S. Tanaka to BOS, Oct. 5, 1984, Tanaka to Hahn, Aug. 2, 1983, Jo Anne B. Ross to Tanaka, Jun. 4, 1985, box 318, Hahn motion, Aug. 22, 1989, box 319, HAHN.

51. *LAT,* Apr. 12, Jul. 13,17,1985, May 24,1986, Feb. 27, 1987, Jul. 21, Sept. 6,1989; Tanaka to BOS, Oct. 12, 1983, box 317, Hahn statement, Sept. 15, 1986, box 319, Hankla to BOS, Feb. 25, 1985, box 52, HAHN; Los Angeles County Grand Jury, "Final Report," 1986–1987, 28–35, LACGJ website.

52. *LAT,* Jan. 20, 1983, Aug. 3, 15, 20, 1984; Hufford to BOS, Feb. 23, 1983, box 49, Hahn resolution,

May 8, 1984, Stephanie Klopfleisch to BOS, Aug. 3, 1984, box 1022, HAHN; Wolch, "From Global to Local," 394–421.

53. *LAT,* Jan. 16, 17, 21, Feb. 22, Oct. 3, 1985; Hankla to BOS, Mar. 29, 1985, box 52, Hahn to Bradley, May 13, 1985, box 1022, "Homeless in Los Angeles County" report of task force, Aug. 16, 1985, box 1023, HAHN; Los Angeles Grand Jury, "Final Report," 1984–1985, 73–74, LACGJ website.

54. *LAT,* Mar. 25, Jul. 23 (quote), 1987, Jun. 28, 1988, Jun. 3, Sept. 24, 1989; Dixon to BOS, Mar. 20, 1987, James Moreno memo to Edelman, Apr. 18, 1988, box 701, Minutes of BOS meeting, Jul. 23, 1987, Clinton to BOS, Jun. 15, 1989, Dixon to BOS, Oct. 12, 1989, box 147, Moreno memo to Edelman, Jun. 1, 1989, box 172, EDELMAN.

55. *LAT,* Dec. 10, 1980, Mar. 18, 26, 31, May 30, Jun. 3, 24, Jul. 3, 5, 9, Aug. 12, 1981, Jan. 12, 1982; Wolch, "From Global to Local," 396- 398.

56. *LAT,* Feb. 12, Jun. 21, 1982, Dec. 18, 1983; Hufford to BOS, Mar. 4, 1982, box 47, HAHN.

57. *Herald Examiner,* Aug. 15, 1985; Rob Saltzman to Don Kilhefner, May 15, 1984, box 249, Los Angeles City/County AIDS Task Force, "Summary of AIDS Hearings Held, May 8, 1985," Neil R. Scram, "Testimony Before the California AIDS Advisory Committee, Sept. 20, 1985," box 248, EDELMAN; Lillian Faderman and Stuart Timmons, *Gay L.A.: A History of Sexual Outlaws, Power Politics, and Lipstick Lesbians* (New York: Basic Books, 2006), 301–322.

58. *Herald Examiner,* Aug. 23, Nov. 4, 1985; *LAT,* Aug. 23, Sept. 9, 16 (quote), Oct. 20, Nov. 11, 1985; John Stodder memo to Edelman, Aug. 15, 1985, Scram, "Testimony Before the California AIDS Advisory Committee, Sept. 20,1985," box 248, Schabarum motion, Oct. 29, 1985, box 247, EDELMAN. CAO Hankla reported the county had budgeted almost $11 million for AIDS care and education for 1985–1986. Hankla to BOS, Sept. 10, 1985, box 248, EDELMAN.

59. *LAT,* Apr. 30, May 3, 27, 1987, Jan. 28, May 3, 10 (quote), 23, Jun. 1, 27, 1989, Mar. 15, 27, 1991; *Daily News,* Jun. 13, 1990; Jim Petzke memo to Edelman, Oct. 28, 1986, box 247, EDELMAN; Jim Cleaver memo to Mas Fukai, Jul. 26, 1987, and Minutes of meeting of Obscenity and Pornography Commission, May 28, 1987, box 440, HAHN; Veronica Gutierrez memo to Gloria Molina, Mar. 21, 1991, box 278, MOLINA; Faderman and Timmons, *Gay L.A.,* 307–322.

60. *LAT,* Jul. 8, 1982, Aug. 21, 24, 31, 1983; Edelman news release, Apr. 1, 1983, box 130, Jami Warner memo to Edelman, Aug. 17, 1983, Stodder memo to Edelman, Oct. 21, 1983, box 136, EDELMAN; Los Angeles County Grand Jury, "Final Report," 1982–1983, 16–20, LACGJ website.

61. *Daily Journal,* Nov. 12, 1985, Feb. 6, 1986; *LAT,* Jan. 27, Feb. 2, May 30, Dec. 6, 1986, Jan. 19, 1990; *Herald Examiner,* Dec. 13, 18,1984, Feb. 2, 1986 (quote); *Torrance Daily Breeze,* Jan. 24, 28, 1990; Frankye Schneider memo to Edelman, Nov.

26, 1985, box 130, Dixon to BOS, Feb. 13, 1990, box 137, EDELMAN.

62. *LAT,* Mar. 9, 1984; Herald *Examiner,* Apr. 12, Aug. 6, 1984; Edelman news release, Apr. 10, 1984, Rich Callahan memo to Edelman, Jul. 19, 1984, box 136, Callahan memo to Edelman, Jun. 18, 1984, John Stodder memo to Edelman, Jul. 19, 1984, box 130, Hufford to BOS, Nov. 20, 1984, box 129, EDELMAN.

63. *Daily News,* Mar. 6, Apr. 5, 1985; *LAT,* Apr. 2, 13, Nov. 27, 1985; *Torrance Daily Breeze,* Jul. 23, 1985; *Herald Examiner,* Nov. 8, 19, 1985; Stodder memos to Edelman, Mar. 8, 12,1985, BOS press release, Apr. 11, 1985 (quote), box 130, transcript of television news story, Mar. 11, 1985, Moreno memo to Edelman, Mar. 14, 1985, Frankye Schneider memos to Edelman, Jul. 19, Aug. 5,1985, box 1008, EDELMAN.

64. *Herald Examiner,* Jul. 31 to Aug. 6, 11, 18, 24, 1989; *Daily News,* Jun. 7, 1990; *LAT,* Jul. 17, 1990; Helen A, Kleinberg to Edelman, Jun. 18, 1990, box 128, Jennifer Roth memo to Edelman, Jul. 6, 1990, Antonovich news release, Jul. 19, 1990, Dixon to Clifford L. Allenby, Aug. 2, 1990, box 131, EDELMAN.

Chapter 9

1. Ron Curran and Lewis MacAdams, "The Selling of L.A. County," *L.A. Weekly,* Nov. 22–28, 1985 (quote on 31).

2. Curran and MacAdams, "The Selling of L.A. County," 24–49; California Commission on Campaign Financing, *Money, and Politics in Local Elections* (Los Angeles: the author, 1989), 176–179; *LAT,* Oct. 23, 1983, Apr. 27, 1987.

3. Curran and MacAdams, "The Selling of L.A. County," 27, 32; *LAT,* May 28, 1980, Jan. 30, 1983. See also Chapters 2 and 5.

4. Curran and MacAdams, "The Selling of L.A. County," 31, 37; *LAT,* Aug. 13, 1983, Jun. 1,1989; Betty Fisher memo to Edelman, in March 1988, Bob Geoghegan memos to Edelman, Jul. 1, Aug. 11, 1988, Mark Slavkin memo to Edelman, Jul. 12, 1988, box 737, EDELMAN.

5. *LAT,* Jun. 7, 1987; *Daily News,* Mar. 1, 12, 1988; Gary J. Miller, *Cities by Contract: The Politics of Municipal Incorporation* (Cambridge, Mass.: MIT Press, 1981, 126–130; Slavkin memos to Edelman, Nov. 30, 1987, Mar. 8, 1988, box 707, EDELMAN.

6. *Daily Journal,* Apr. 23, 1987; *LAT,* 29, 1987, Dec. 29, 1998; Edelman to editor, *Herald Examiner,* Dec. 2, 1987, box 576, EDELMAN; "Zoning Laws Can Be Cause for Suit," *National Civic Review* 76 (Nov.-Dec. 1987): 515.

7. *LAT,* Mar. 29, 1981, May 17, 1981, May 13, Nov. 4, 1982.

8. *LAT,* Jan. 20, 1983, Feb. 27, 1986, Jun. 7, 10, 11, Jul. 10, 1987, Sept. 7, Oct. 24, 31, Nov. 1, 1987; *Newhall Signal,* Jun. 12, Nov. 1, 1987; *Daily News,* Jun. 6, Nov. 20,1987; Slavkin memos to Edelman,

Apr. 21, 1987, May 14, 1987, Jul. 31, 1987, box
709, Ed Davis to Edelman, Nov. 2, 1987, box 708,
EDELMAN.

9. *LAT*, May 10, 1985, Jun. 7, 1987, Aug. 4, 1988,
Sept. 11, 13, Oct. 20, 1990; *Daily News*, Nov. 20, 21,
1987, Apr. 27, Aug. 11, 1988; Ed Davis to Edelman,
Nov. 2, 1987, Slavkin memos to Edelman, Nov. 13,
1987, Feb. 24, 1988, box 708, EDELMAN.

10. *LAT*, Dec. 10, 1965; Bill Boyarsky and Nancy
Boyarsky, *Backroom Politics: How Your Local Poli-
ticians Work, Why Your Government Doesn't, and
What You Can Do About It* (New York: Hawthorn
Books, 1974), 157–166.

11. *LAT*, Dec. 29, 1982, Jan. 2, Mar. 23, 1983,
Aug. 22, 1985, Feb. 18,1987, Jun. 1, Sept. 1, 29, Oct.
20, Dec. 15, 1988; *L.A. Weekly*, Nov. 22–28, 1985;
Johanna Bernstein to Tom Hayden, Aug. 6, 1986,
Carl Randall to Cliff Gladstein, Sept. 19, 1986,
LP322:399, state Senator Gary K Hart to Dana,
Sept. 24, 1986, LP322:400, Hayden to BOS, Jan.
12, 1989, LP322:401, Tom Hayden Papers, CSA;
CAO Richard Dixon to BOS, Jul. 20, 1988, Geoghe-
gan memo to Edelman, Aug. 4, 1988, Jon Freed-
man memo to Edelman, Oct. 18, 1988, box 759,
EDELMAN.

12. *LAT*, Jun. 29, 1988, Sept. 10, 1989, Mar. 4, 7,
29, Dec. 30, 1990, Mar. 8, Apr. 21, 1991, Nov. 13,
2000, Jan. 13, 2015; *Malibu Times*, Sept. 21, 1989;
Malibu Surfside News, Oct. 26, 1989; Kerry Gottlieb memo to Edelman, Mar. 21, 1991, box 709,
Gottlieb memos to Edelman, Aug. 21, 1991, May
26,1992, Jun. 28, 1993, box 760, T.A. Tidemanson
to BOS, Jun. 3, 1993, box 758, EDELMAN. See also
material in LP322–399 and 400, Hayden Papers,
CSA.

13. *LAT*, Dec. 10, 1978, Oct. 7, 1982, Mar. 10,
1989; Boyarsky and Boyarsky, *Backroom Politics*,
60–70.

14. *Pico Post*, Jul. 31, 1980; *LAT*, May 31, Oct. 14,
25, 31, Nov. 7, 30, 1984, Jun. 28,1985; Lillian Faderman and Stuart Timmons, *Gay L.A.: A History of
Sexual Outlaws, Power Politics, and Lipstick Lesbians* (New York: Basic Books, 2006), 231–234,
276–279.

15. *LAT*, Oct. 12,1973, Jan. 27, 1983, Mar. 22,
27, 1986, Jun. 1, 5, 2003, Elizabeth Wagner memo
to Edelman, Jul. 22, 1983, box 708, EDELMAN;
LAFCO Executive Officer report, Jan. 25, 2012, box
159, MOLINA.

16. Department of the Interior, National Park
Service, "Proposed Public Ownership" Plan, Santa
Monica Mountains National Recreation Area, May
1979, Jeff Seymour memo to Edelman, Jun. 12,
1979, box 762, EDELMAN.

17. *LAT*, Jul. 26, 1979, Dec. 31, 1981; *Herald
Examiner*, Dec. 13, 1981; Anthony Beilenson to
Edelman, May 30, 1979, Edelman to Beilenson,
Aug. 21, 1979, box 236, EDELMAN.

18. *LAT, Jul.* 4, Dec. 5, 29, 1982, Jan. 6, 1983;
Anthony Beilenson to Edelman, Dec. 1, 1982,
Edelman to Beilenson, Dec. 8, 1982, box 235,
EDELMAN.

19. *Daily Journal*, Feb. 23,1983; Russell E.

Dickenson to James S. Mize, Feb. 14, 1983, box 763,
EDELMAN; *Daily News*, Dec. 10, 1993; *Metropolitan News-Enterprise*, Dec. 8, 1993.

20. *LAT*, Feb. 22, 1979, Jul. 29, 1982, Nov. 14,
20, 1986, Jan. 20, 1991, Mar. 21, 1994; Betty Fisher
to Edelman, Feb. 11, 1987, box 739, Don Wallace
memo to Edelman, Feb. 14, 1991, box 525, and Rosi
Dagit, "Where Have all the Oak Trees Gone?: A
Status Report on the Effectiveness of the Los Angeles County Oak Tree Ordinance," Dec. 3, 1991, box
754, EDELMAN; Allan A. Schoenherr, *A Natural
History of California* (Berkeley and Los Angeles:
University of California Press, 1992), 387–390.

21. *LAT*, Dec. 13, 1982, Nov. 4, 1990 (quote), Joel
Bellman memo to Edelman, Oct. 26, 1990, Jennifer
Roth memos to Edelman, Oct. 29, 1990, Aug. 15,
1991, box 745, EDELMAN.

22. *LAT*, Nov. 4, 7,1990; James E. Hartl to BOS,
Dec. 6, 1990, Kerry Gottlieb memo to Edelman,
Nov. 9, 1990, box 745, EDELMAN.

23. *LAT*, Jan. 20, Mar. 20, 28, Apr. 3, Jun. 12, 28,
1991, Jun. 2, 1992, Feb. 20, Mar. 21, 1994; Jennifer
Roth memos to Edelman, Oct. 29, 1990, Aug. 15,
1991, Gottlieb memo to Edelman, Nov. 9, 1990, box
745, EDELMAN.

24. *LAT*, Feb. 25, 26, 1976; Carla Lazzareschi,
"The Pressure Tactics of Smog Boss Tom Quinn,"
California Journal 8 (Jul. 1977): 224–226, quote
on 224; Richard B. Harvey, *The Dynamics of Cal-
ifornia Government and Politics*, 2nd ed. (Monte-
rey, CA: Brooks/Cole, 1985), 193–197; Wyn Grant,
*Autos, Smog and Pollution Control: The Politics of
Air Quality Management in California* (Aldershot,
UK: Edward Elgar, 1995), 52–55.

25. See Tom Sitton, *The Courthouse Crowd: Los
Angeles County and Its Government, 1850–1950*
(Los Angeles: Historical Society of Southern California, 2013), 288–291 and Chapter 2 in this book
for more on smog prior to 1976.

26. *LAT*, Jun. 9, Jul. 7, Sept. 25, 1978, May 12,
1979; Geoghegan memo to Edelman, May 10, 1977,
box 544, H.L. Richardson to BOS, Nov. 15, 1978
(first quote), box 543, EDELMAN; Ralph A. Die-
drich to HAHN, April 6, 1979 (remaining quotes),
Schabarum motion, April 3, 1979, box 41, HAHN.

27. *Herald Examiner*, Jul. 29, 1979, Jun. 30,
1981; *LAT*, Jul. 2, Aug. 2, 25, Sept. 15, 1979, Dec.
12, 1980; Geoghegan memo to Edelman, Aug. 13,
1979, Maybelline Griffith memo to Edelman, Apr.
26, 1984, box 547, Berkhemer & Kline, Inc. news
release, Sept. 4, 1979, KNXT editorial, Feb. 2, 1981,
Geoghegan memos to Edelman, Jan. 7, 1981, Jan.
26, 1983, Thomas F. Heinsheimer to Anne Gor-
such, Jan. 14, 1983, box 548, EDELMAN; Hahn
news release, Mar. 9, 1984 (quote), box 573, HAHN;
Grant, *Autos, Smog and Pollution Control*, 107–
121.

28. *LAT*, Oct. 9, 1980, Apr. 4, Sept. 11, 1981,
Mar. 26, 29, Dec. 10, 1982; *Daily News*, Apr. 1, Sept.
1, 1982; Geoghegan memo to Edelman, Jul. 30,
1982, box 543, Melanie Piech memo to Geoghegan,
Aug. 14, 1984, box 544, EDELMAN; James S. Mize
to Edward J. Rollins, Jan. 12, 1983 (quote), Edward

Camerena to Harry Hufford, Apr. 17, 1984, box 109927605, BOS Subject files; Builder and Graubard, "A Conceptual Approach to Strategies for the Control of Air Pollution in the South Coast Air Basin," v–ix.

29. *LAT,* Jul. 14, 1984; *L.A. Weekly,* May 22–28, 1987; Hahn news release, Sept. 24, 1982, box 577, HAHN.

30. *LAT,* Feb. 6, 14 (quote), 18, 1987; *L.A. Weekly,* May 22–28, 1987; Hahn to County Grand Jury foreman Edward Roseman, May 18, 1987, box 577, HAHN.

31. *LAT,* Sept. 5, 1987, Jan. 6, 1988 (quote); James M. Letts to SCAQMD Board, Sept. 22, 1987, Geoghegan memo to Edelman, Oct. 5, 1987, box 542, EDELMAN.

32. Sitton, *The Courthouse Crowd,* esp. 105–106, 139–142, 165–168, 240–241; Blake Gumprecht, *The Los Angeles River: Its Life, Death, and Possible Rebirth* (Baltimore and London: Johns Hopkins University Press, 1999), passim; Jared Orsi, *Hazardous Metropolis: Flooding and Urban Ecology in Los Angeles* (Berkeley, Los Angeles, London: University of California Press, 2004), passim.

33. Los Angeles Department of Water and Power plan for a Snake River pipeline, 1963, and Ralph M. Parsons Company plan for a Columbia and Snake River pipeline to U.S., Canada, and Mexico sites, 1960s, Hahn statement, Aug. 27, 1981, box 1010, Hahn statement, Jun. 4, 1982, box 493, Hahn to Los Angeles Area Chamber of Commerce, Sept. 9, 1981, box 82, HAHN; James Mize to James G. Watt, Aug. 31, 1981, box 232, EDELMAN. On California water history see Norris Hundley, *The Great Thirst: Californians and Water, 1770s-1990s* (Berkeley and Los Angeles: University of California Press, 1992).

34. *LAT,* Jun. 6, 1990; Esteban Torres to Richard Callahan, May 19, 1989, box 235, EDELMAN; Los Angeles County Grand Jury, "Final Report," 1988–1989, 120–128, LACGJ website; Edmund Edelman, "Los Angeles County Water Advisory Council," Southern California Water Committee *Newsletter* 6 (Dec. 1990); 2,7.

35. *LAT,* May 4, 6, 10, 19, 1990; *Torrance Daily Breeze,* May 9, 1990 (last quote); *Portland Oregonian,* May 9, 1990; Jack Metcalf to Hahn, Jul. 8, 1990 (first 2 quotes), box 1012, Hahn to Governor-elect Pete Wilson, Nov. 9, 1990, box 477, HAHN; Los Angeles County Grand Jury, "Final Report," 1990s, LACGJ website. A plan like Hahn's was resurrected in 2015. See *LAT,* Apr. 21, 27, 2015.

36. *LAT,* Mar. 1, 20, 28, Apr. 12, 24, May 22, 1985; *Santa Monica Evening Outlook,* Feb. 28, Apr. 18, May 22, 1985; *Sacramento Bee,* Apr. 16, 1985; transcript of KCBS television news investigation, Feb. 26, 1985, Tom Hayden to Edelman, Apr. 16, 1986, Edelman to Hayden, May 1, 1985, box 565, EDELMAN; Kenneth W. Kizer to Tom Hayden, Apr. 11, 1985, LP322:428, Hayden Papers, CSA. On the clash of scientists involved in analyzing the degree of toxicity and danger in the mid-1980s see Bill Sharpsteen, *Dirty Water: One Man's Fight*

to Clean Up One of the World's Most Polluted Bays (Berkeley, Los Angeles, London: University of California Press, 2010), passim.

37. *LAT,* Jun. 29, 1990, Jul. 10, 1991, May 1, 1996, Mar. 14, April 27, 2021; Robert C. Gates to BOS, Jun. 24, 1994, box 81, EDELMAN.

38. *LAT,* May 13, Jul. 14, 21, 25, Aug. 22, Sept. 5, 6, Oct. 29, Dec. 18, 1985, Aug. 21, 1987; Hayden timeline flier, c. Sept. 1986, LP322:428, Hayden Papers, CSA; Anna Sklar, *Brown Acres: An Intimate History of the Los Angeles Sewers* (Los Angeles: Angel City Press, 2008), 179–197.

39. *LAT,* Jun. 12, 1986, Sept. 11, 1988; Tom Hayden to Ira Reiner, Jun. 12, 1987, LP:322:429, Hayden Papers; Minutes of BOS meeting, Oct. 27, 1987, T.A. Tidemanson to BOS, May 15, 1989, box 520, EDELMAN.

40. *LAT,* Jan. 5, 22, May 5, 1981, Jan. 8, 14, 1982, Jun. 2, 1985; *Daily News,* May 13, Nov. 18, 1981, Jul. 26, 1982; Stephen J. Koonce to BOS, Jul. 28, 1980, box 366, HAHN; Geoghegan memo to Edelman, May 6, 1981, James S. Mize to BOS, City Council, and Chairperson of City County Consolidation Commission, Jan. 18, 1982, box 520, Walter E. Garrison to BOS, Jul. 14, 1982, box 524, EDELMAN. On Mission Canyon before 1980 see Boyarsky and Boyarsky, *Backroom Politics,* 161–171. On waste disposal in the nation overall at this time see Martin V. Melosi, *Garbage and the Cities: Refuse, Reform, and the Environment* (Chicago: Dorsey Press, 1987), 190–226.

41. *LAT,* Jun. 2, 1985, Jun. 25, Jul. 16, Sept. 8, 1987; Deane Dana news release, Oct. 2, 1985, Geoghegan memo to Edelman, Oct. 11, 1985, box 160, Schabarum motion, Sept. 8, 1987, box 520, Dixon to BOS, Dec. 7, 1987, box 523, Jon Freedman memo to Edelman, Dec. 17, 1987, box 147, De Witt Clinton to BOS, Jan. 11, 1988, box 525, EDELMAN.

42. *LAT,* Apr. 6, May 29, 1988, Jun. 29, 1989, Feb. 22, Mar. 28, 1990; Hahn motion, Jul. 20, 1989, box 365, HAHN; Robert H. Collins to Edelman, Aug. 29, 1990, box 520, Jennifer Roth memo to Edelman, Oct. 6, 1990, box 708, Roth memo to Edelman, Jan. 28, 1991, T.A. Tidemanson to Councilman Hal Bernson, Jan. 15, 1991, box 525, Tidemanson to Edelman, Jan. 1, 1993, box 523, EDELMAN; Assemblywoman Paula Boland to Gloria Molina, Oct. 1, 1993, box 856, MOLINA.

43. *LAT,* Jul. 23, Aug. 10, Sept. 7, Oct. 27, 30, 1980, Jun. 26, 1986; Los Angeles County Grand Jury, "Final Report," 1980–1981, 199–213, LACGJ website.

44. *LAT,* Aug. 12, 21, Sept. 12,1980, Dec. 27, 1981, Aug. 21, 1982, Apr. 3, 1985; *Herald Examiner,* Dec.19, 1980; Baxter Ward to Robert White, Aug. 8, 1980, White to Edelman, Aug. 15, 1980, White to BOS, Aug. 18, 1980, White to Maureen Kindel, Dec. 15,1980, R.L. Dennerline to Marie Stephens, Mar. 9, 1981, box 522, EDELMAN.

45. *LAT,* Oct. 30, 1983, Nov. 18, 1984 (quote), Dec. 8, 1985, Dec. 14, 1986, Nov. 1, 1987, Dec. 8, 1988, Jan. 5, 1989; Charles W. Coffee to Jim Moreno, Nov. 16,1982, box 524, EDELMAN.

46. *LAT,* Jul. 12, 13, 25, Aug. 2, Sept. 27, 30; Schabarum motion, Sept. 22, 1981, box 521, EDELMAN.

47. *LAT,* Oct. 30, 1980, May 8, 1983, Mar. 3, 1985, Jan. 26, 1989; *Daily News,* Oct. 24, Dec. 7,1984; Hahn motion, Mar. 22, 1983, Robert Philibosian to BOS, Apr. 11, 1983, box 364, BKK Corporation to Interested Persons, Aug. 10,1984, box 365, HAHN; California Department of Health Services, "BKK Update," Jun. 1990, box 522, Geoghegan memo to Edelman, Feb. 26, 1985, box 521, EDELMAN.

48. *LAT,* Dec.10, 1989.

Chapter 10

1. The source of the epigraph is Morgan Kousser, *Colorblind Injustice: Minority Voting Rights and the Undoing of the Second Reconstruction* (Chapel Hill: University of North Carolina Press, 1999), 75. The source of "Fiefdoms Under Fire" is *LAT,* Jun. 12, 1988.

2. On the Voting Rights Act see, among others, Kousser, *Colorblind Injustice*; J. Douglas Smith, *On Democracy's Doorstep; The Inside Story of How the Supreme Court Brought "One Person, One Vote" to the United States* (New York: Hill and Wang, 2014); Charles S. Bulloch, Ronald Keith Gaddie, and Justin J. Wert, The *Rise and Fall of the Voting Rights Act* (Norman: University of Oklahoma Press, 2016).

3. Royce D. Delmatier, et al., The *Rumble of California Politics, 1848-1970* (New York: John Wiley & Sons, 1970), 355–357.

4. *LAT,* Jun. 28, Nov. 21, 27, 1985.

5. *LAT,* Oct. 27, Nov. 28, Dec. 13, 18, 1985, Jan. 7, Mar. 8, 1986; *Herald Examiner,* Dec.25, 1985.

6. *LAT,* Jan. 13, 1986.

7. *LAT,* Mar. 1, Jul. 1,3, 9, 16, 20, 23, 31, Aug. 20, Sept. 12, 13, 23, 28, 1986; "District Court Oks Los Angeles Districts," *National Civic Review* 75 (Nov.-Dec. 1986): 374; James A. Regalado, *Political Battles Over L.A. County Board Seats: A Minority Perspective* (Los Angeles: California State University, Edmund G. "Pat" Brown Institute of Public Affairs, 1989), 6, 12–13; Raphael J. Sonenshein, *Politics in Black and White: Race and Power in Los Angeles* (Princeton, N.J.: Princeton University Press, 1993), 196–197.

8. Charter of the County of Los Angeles, Article 2, Section 7; California Election Code, Section 21500, et seq.; John Anson Ford Newsletter, Sept. 8, 1953, box 54, JAF; *LAT,* Apr. 30, 1953, Apr. 15, 1959, May 15 (quote), 16, 22, 1963, Dec. 1, 1965; *Tujunga Record-Ledger,* Apr. 5, 1959; Kousser, *Colorblind Injustice,* 73–83. See the latter for a more detailed account of these redistricting events.

9. *LAT,* Jul. 16, 28, 1971; memo from BOS executive officer to county counsel, et, al., Jan. 20, 1976, box 889, HAHN; Kousser, *Colorblind Injustice,* 83–85.

10. *LAT,* Jul. 10, 1981; Californios for Fair Representation flier, Sept. 1981, box 170, POPE; Kousser, *Colorblind Injustice,* 97–100,109–115.

11. Leticia Quezada to Los Angeles County Supervisors District Boundary Committee, Jul. 29, 1981, box 197, Philip Montez to Los Angeles Area Reapportionment Project Participants, Jun. 7, 1983, box 238, EDELMAN; *Daily News,* Jul. 30, 1981; *LAT,* Aug. 4, 1981.

12. *Daily News,* Aug. 6, Sept. 23, 1981; *LAT,* Aug.4, 26, Sept. 19, 23, 25, 1981; Californios for Fair Representation flier, Sept. 1981, box 170, POPE; Kousser, *Colorblind Injustice* 111–128.

13. *LAT,* Sept. 25, 1981, Jun. 9, 1982; Kousser, *Colorblind Injustice,* 122–125.

14. *LAT,* May 26, 27, Jun. 7, 1988; De Witt W. Clinton to Tom Hibbard, Dec. 21, 1989, Clinton to William Bradford Reynolds, Jul. 8, 1988, box 196, EDELMAN.

15. *Daily News,* Jul. 28, 1988 (quotes); *LAT,* Jun. 7, Jul. 29, 1988; *Herald Examiner,* Jul. 21, 29, 1988; Bob Geoghegan memo to Edelman, Jul. 22, 1988, box 197, EDELMAN; Regalado, *Political Battles Over L.A. County Board Seats,* 15–16, 27–28.

16. *Herald Examiner,* May 23, Jun. 13, Jul. 21, 27, 1988; *Daily News,* Jul. 28, Aug. 12, 1988, Feb. 5, 1989; *LAT,* Jun. 12, Jul. 29, 1988, May 18, Dec. 6, 1989, Jan. 3, Jun. 11, Nov. 15, 1990; *Long Beach Press-Telegram,* Jan. 11, 1989.

17. *LAT,* Jul. 20, 25, 27, Sept. 9, 1988; *Herald Examiner,* Jul. 21, 1988; Geoghegan memo to Edelman, Jul. 6, 1988, and Los Angeles County Chicano Employees Association press release, Aug. 24, 1988, box 196, and U.S.A. v. County of Los Angeles Civil Action 88–05435, U.S. District Court for Central District of California, box 197, EDELMAN; Regalado, *Political Battles Over L.A. County Board Seats,* 28–29.

18. *Herald Examiner,* Sept. 29, 1988; *Whittier Daily News,* Sept. 17, 1988, Feb. 10, 1989; *LAT,* Sept. 28, Oct. 3, 1988; Clinton to BOS, Dec. 28, 1988, box 196, EDELMAN.

19. "Eric Bucy, Lawsuits Threaten LA Supervisors Fiefdoms," *California Journal* 20 (Jan. 1989): 41–43. *Daily News,* Oct. 1, 1989; James W. Sweeney, "One Little, Two Little … Nine Little Kings?" *Golden State Report* 5 (Nov. 1989); 13–17; *LAT,* Jan. 25, 1989, Feb. 23, 1990; *Santa Monica Evening Outlook,* Jul. 17, 1989; Clinton to Hibbard, Dec. 21, 1989, box 196, EDELMAN. Copies of some of the 1989 depositions are in boxes 196 and 197, EDELMAN.

20. *LAT,* Oct. 21, Nov. 29, Dec. 6, 13, 14, 15, 18, 19, 20, 22, 23, 24, 28 (last quotes), 1989; *Daily News,* Dec. 7, 13 first (quote), 19, 1989.

21. *LAT,* Jan. 4, 9,12, 15, Feb. 23 (quote), Mar. 7, 11, 14, Apr. 5, 1990; *Daily News,* Jan 9, Apr. 7, 1990; *Daily Journal,* Apr. 6, 1990; *Torrance Daily Breeze,* Mar. 4, 1990; *San Gabriel Valley Tribune,* Jan. 24, 1990; Joel Bellman memo to Edelman, Apr. 6, 1990, box 196, EDEMAN.

22. *LAT,* Apr. 4, 5, 8, 11, Jun. 5 (quotes), Jun. 6, 1990; *Garza* v. *Los Angeles County,* especially 43–44, quote on 43.

23. *Daily News*, Jun. 11, Jul. 3 (first quote), 1990; *LAT,* Jun. 5, 8, 11, 22, 27, 29 (quotes), 1990; *San Gabriel Valley Tribune*, Jun. 28, 1990; Kousser, *Colorblind Injustice*, 130–132.

24. *LAT,* Jun. 30, Jul. 1, 6, 26, Aug. 2 (quote), 4, 1990; *Long Beach Press-Telegram*, Jul. 5, 1990.

25. *LAT,* Aug. 10, 17, Nov. 2, 1990, Jan. 8, 1991(quote); *Daily News*, Nov. 7, 1990; Kousser, *Colorblind Injustice*, 132–134.

26. *LAT*, Mar. 19, May 3, 1991; De Witt Clinton to BOS, Apr. 19, 1991, box 911, MOLINA.

27. *LAT,* Dec. 21, 1988 (quote), Dec. 24, 1989; *Daily News,* Jul. 31, 1989.

28. *LAT,* Mar. 10, 13, 15, 16,18, 1990; *Sentinel,* May 31,1990; *Daily News*, Jul. 30, 1990; Tom Waldman, "Schabarum Bails Out: Surprise Exit Stiffs Wannabes." *California Journal* 21 (May 1990): 227–230. Schabarum's retirement announcement spurred several newspaper articles that thanked him in a highly sarcastic manner. See, for example, *LAT*, Mar. 14, 25, 1990, Feb. 15, 1991.

29. *San Gabriel Valley Tribune*, May 19, 27, 1990; *LAT,* May 25, 26, 1990.

30. *LAT,* May 20, Jun. 5, 6, 7, 8, 19, Jul. 1, 1990.

31. *LAT,* Jun. 19, Jul. 28, Aug. 4, 1990.

32. *LAT,* Oct. 6, 31, 1990.

33. *LAT,* Aug. 12, Nov. 10, 13, 14, 15, 22, Dec. 1, 6, 7, 9, 17, 19, 1990, Jan. 2, 13, 17, 20, 21, 1991.

34. *LAT*, Jan. 20, 23, 27, Feb. 1, 5, 6, 14, 17, 20, 1990.

Chapter 11

1. "Los Angeles An Industrial Giant," Los Angeles Board of Harbor Commissioners, "Annual Report," 1951, 40; "Los Angeles Has Greatest Industry Growth," *Southern California Business* 12 (Mar. 29, 1950):1, 3.

2. *LAT*, Dec. 5, 1982, Aug. 11, 1991, Dec. 5, 6, 7, 1993, Oct. 25, 2015; Jennifer Wolch, "From Global to Local: The Rise of Homelessness in Los Angeles During the 1980s," in Allen J. Scott and Edward W. Soja, eds., *The City: Los Angeles and Urban Theory at the End of the Twentieth Century* (Berkeley and Los Angeles: University of California Press, 1996), 391–393; Los Angeles County Grand Jury, "Final Report," 1991–1992, 65–89, LACGJ website; Michael Storper, Thomas Kemeny, Naji Makarem, and Taner Osman, *The Rise and Fall of Urban Economies: Lessons From San Francisco and Los Angeles* (Stanford, CA: Stanford University Press, 2015), passim.

3. Gloria Molina, Oral History Interview Conducted 1990 by Carlos Vasquez, 2 vols. (University of California, Los Angeles for the State Government Oral History Program, 1990), CSA.; *LAT,* Feb. 5, 1987; *Herald Examiner*, Oct. 27, 1977; Robert Greene, "Spotlight on Gloria Molina," *Civic Center NewSource*, Nov. 27, Dec. 4, 1995; http://bos.lacounty.gov/About-Us/Board-of-Supervisors/Board-Member-Biographies.

4. *LAT,* Oct. 17, 1992, Mar. 1, 2006; *Sentinel,*

May 11, 2009; http://bos.lacounty.gov/About-Us/Board-of-Supervisors/Board-Member-Biographies.

5. *LAT,* Dec. 5, 1994, Apr. 10, 2002, Apr. 6, 2008; Robert Greene, "Spotlight on Zev Yaroslavsky," *Civic Center NewSource*, Jun. 12, 19, 1995; Raphael J. Sonenshein, *Politics in Black and White: Race and Power in Los Angeles* (Princeton, N.J.: Princeton University Press, 1993), esp.179,192–200, 259–260; http://bos.lacounty.gov/About-Us/Board-of-Supervisors/Board-Member-Biographies.

6. *LAT,* Nov. 19, 1987, Nov. 10, 1988; "Don Knabe: New Fourth District Supervisor," Los Angeles "County Digest," January 1997, 1, 4; http://bos.lacounty.gov/About-Us/Board-of-Supervisors/Board-Member-Biographies.

7. *LAT,* Apr. 29, Sept. 6, Nov. 1, 9, 19, 1991, Jan. 21, Feb. 22, Apr. 25, May 26, 28, Oct. 17, 22, 25 (quote), 31, Nov. 5, 17, Dec. 25, 1992; "County Politics," *LATAX Report* 15 (Feb. 3, 1993): 3, box 78, EDELMAN; Yvonne Burke to Ira Reiner, Nov. 10, 1992, and other material on the 1992 election in box S500, BURKE; Diane Watson, Oral History Interview Conducted 1999 by Susan Douglass Yates, 2 vols. (UCLA Oral History Program, for the California State Archives Government Oral History Program, 1999), 265–267.

8. *LAT,* May 18, 23, 28, Jun. 4, 12, 10, Oct. 23, 25, 1992, Feb. 9, 1993.

9. *LAT,* Dec. 16, 1982, Nov. 22 (quote), 27, 1991, Mar. 27, Apr. 1, 16, May 31(second quote), Jun. 4, Aug. 2, Sept. 18, 19, Oct. 26, Nov. 5, 1992; *Daily Journal*, Jun. 1, 1992; *Torrance Daily Breeze*, Jun. 4, 1992. See also 1992 election material in box 52, GARCETTI.

10. *LAT,* Jul. 28, 29, Dec. 2, 1993, Feb. 24, Mar. 18, Apr. 30, May 16, 24, 26, 28, 29, Jun. 9,1994. See also 1994 election material in box 184, MOLINA.

11. *LAT,* Nov. 15, 1994, Jul. 23, 1995, Feb. 12, 20, 23, Mar. 1, 12, 18, 19, 20, 24, 28, Sept. 21, 23, Oct. 13, 21, 25, Nov. 7, 1996; *Wilshire Independent*, Mar. 6, 28, 1996; "Notice of Intention to Recall Yvonne Braithwaite Burke," n.d, and Connie B. McCormack to Howard A. Sands, Jan. 26, 1996, box S484, BURKE.

12. *LAT,* Feb. 13, 25, Mar. 17, 28, Aug. 1, Oct. 9, 17, 18, 20, 22, Nov. 22; Daily *News*, Mar. 20, 1996; *Civic Center NewSource*, Mar. 4, 1996; *Daily Journal,* Nov. 7, 1996; Sherman Block to *Times* editor, Mar. 21, 1996, box 6, Fairbank, Maslin, Maullin & Associates to Gilbert Garcetti Reelection Campaign, Mar. 7, 1996, box 59, GARCETTI; Martin Berg, "Are We Lucky or What? Gil Garcetti wants another Term as D.A.; Does He Deserve it?" *Los Angeles* 41 (Mar. 1996): 18–20.

13. *LAT,* Jan. 23, Feb. 17, Mar. 3, 13, 19, Apr. 10, 17, 30, May 2, 19, 21, 24, Jun. 2, 5, 30, Aug. 13, 29, 9–23, Oct. 25, 30, Nov. 1, 1996; Gregory Gutierrez, "Running for Your Life," *Los Angeles*, 43 (May 1998): 50–53.

14. *LAT,* Dec. 9, 15, 1999, Feb. 20, 23, 25, 28, Mar. 1, 9, 19, 23, 24, Apr. 11, May 9, 17, Jul. 28, Sept.

21, Oct. 20, 26, 27, 29, Nov. 5, 2000; *Daily News*, Jan. 10, 2000; Report by Garcetti political consultants, box 64, and other 2000 election material in boxes 59 and 64, GARCETTI; election returns at Los Angeles County Registrar-Recorder/County Clerk website.

15. *Torrance Daily Breeze*, Feb. 17, 1991; *LAT*, Feb. 20 (quote), 1991; *L.A. Weekly*, Mar. 7, 1991.

16. *LAT*, Mar. 27, Jun. 16, Jul. 23, Oct. 11, 1991, Mar. 6, 1992, May 26, 1994; Hector Tobar, "The Politics of Anger," *Los Angeles Times Magazine*, Jan. 23, 1993, 10–12, 32–33; *Pomona Daily Bulletin*, Nov. 14, 1992; Robert Greene, "Spotlight on Gloria Molina," *Civic Center NewSource*, Nov. 27, 1995; Jim Moreno memo to Edelman, Jun. 4, 1992, box 178, copy of a "Co-worker" to Gloria Molina, Nov. 24, 1992 (quote), box 190, Moreno memo to Edelman, May 5, 1993, Box 357, Larry J. Monteilh to BOS, Oct. 14, 1993, Richard Llewellyn memo to Edelman, Sept. 17, 1993, and Burke motion, Oct. 19, 1993, box 93, EDELMAN; Edmund Edelman, interview by author, Los Angeles, Jun. 17, 2011; Zev Yaroslavsky, interview by author, Los Angeles, Mar. 6, 2017.

17. *LAT*, Jan. 10, 1989; Ron Curran, "Richard Dixon: The Most Powerful Politician You Never Elected," *L.A. Weekly*, Feb 21–27, 1992; Maria Elena Harris, "Is Ideology a Determinant of Local Government Fiscal Policy? A Case Study of the Los Angeles County Board of Supervisors" (PhD diss., University of Southern California, 1995), 126, 139–140, 147–149.

18. *Daily News*, Mar. 4, 1991; *LAT* May 29, Jul. 23, Aug. 23, 28, 30, 1991, Dixon to BOS, May 16, 1991, box 659, Dixon to BOS, Aug. 14, 1991, box 74, and other material in boxes 633 and 659, MOLINA.

19. *LAT*, Sept. 26, Oct. 10,1991, Feb. 1, Sept. 19, 1992; Los Angeles County Grand Jury, "Final Report," 1991–1992, 5–48, LACGJ website; Molina newsletter, Jan. 14, 1992, box 143, MOLINA; Joanne Sturges to BOS, Sept. 26, 1994, box 89, EDELMAN.

20. *LAT*, Jan. 15, Feb. 1, 2, 5, Mar. 26, Apr. 7, 25, 1992; *Daily News*, Aug. 20, 1992; Molina newsletter, Jan. 14, 1992, box 143, MOLINA; Los Angeles County Grand Jury, "Final Report," 1991–1992, 161–172, LACGJ website.

21. *LAT*, Jan. 15, Feb. 2, Jun. 10, Jul. 17, 18, 22 (second quote), 1992, Sept. 29, 1993; Molina to Dixon, Jan. 14, 1992 (first quote), Dixon to BOS, Feb. 1, 1993, box 143, MOLINA.

22. Molina motion, Feb. 25, 1992, box 757, Jackie Goldberg memo to Molina, Feb. 12, 1992, box 192, MOLINA; *LAT*, Mar. 6, 1992.

23. *LAT*, Apr. 22, 1992; *Daily News*, Jun. 12, Jul. 1, 1992; Llewellyn memo to Edelman, Jan. 27, 1992, Molina motion, Jul. 21, 1992, box 919, EDELMAN; Jackie Goldberg memo to Molina, May 8, 1992, box 487, Goldberg memo to Marjorie Kaufman, Apr. 28, 1992, Larry Monteilh to BOS, Aug. 21, 1992, box 192, MOLINA.

24. *LAT*, Dec. 16, 1992, Mar. 12, 24, May 9, 1993; *San Gabriel Valley Tribune*, Dec. 18, 1992, Burke motion, May 5, 1980, box 60, BURKE; David E. Janssen and De Witt Clinton to BOS, Sept. 5, 1997, box 191, MOLINA.

25. *LAT*, Sept. 25, Oct. 2, 1991; Kerry Gottlieb memo to Edelman, Jul. 15, 1991, box 772, EDELMAN; Minutes of BOS meeting, Sept. 24, 1991, box 239, Affirmative Action files in box 8, MOLINA.

26. *LAT*, Feb. 21, Apr. 21, May 1, 1991; *Daily News*, Apr. 24, 25, May 25, 1991; Llewellyn memo to Edelman, Jan. 17, 1991, box 189, Llewellyn memos to Edelman, Apr. 10, and Jun. 17, 1991, De Witt Clinton to BOS, Apr. 19, 1991, box 195, County Bar Association Reorganization Survey on expansion and elected executive, Jul. 1991, box 201, EDELMAN; Richard P. Fajardo to Molina, Apr. 23, 1991, box 35, MOLINA.

27. *Daily News*, Feb. 15, 26, 1992; *LAT*, Apr. 14, 15, 1992; Llewellyn memo to Edelman, Jan. 29, 1992, box 189, Edelman news release, Feb. 14, 1992, box 199, Llewellyn memos to Edelman, Feb. 18, 24, 1992, box 195, EDELMAN: "Probable Impact of Elected Executive on voting rights...," for Los Angeles County Boundary Review Committee, Feb 1992, box 757, MOLINA.

28. *LAT*, Jul. 22, 23, Aug, 2, Sept. 4, Oct. 12, Nov. 4, 8, 21, Dec, 1,1992; *Pasadena Star-News*, Jul. 1, 1992; *Torrance Daily Breeze*, Oct. 18, 1992; *San Gabriel Valley Tribune*, Oct. 30, 1992; *Long Beach Press-Telegram*, Oct. 28, 1992; ballot arguments, Aug, 5, 1992, Llewellyn memos to Edelman, Aug. 21, Sept. 8, 1992, Larry Fisher to Edelman, Sept. 4, 1992, box 201, and newspaper clippings in boxes 199 and 200, EDELMAN; Rodd Zolckos, "L.A. County Contemplates New Form of Government," *City and State* 9 (Aug. 10–23, 1992): 3, 23.

29. *LAT, Nov.* 14, 1998, Feb. 27, Aug. 25, 30 (quote) 1999; Los Angeles County Grand Jury, "Final Report," 1996–1997, 49–50, LACGJ website; Richard Polanco to Bion Gregory, Jan. 25, 1991, LP441: 787, Richard Polanco Papers, CSA; Sally R. Reed to BOS, May 16, 1996, box 488, Lloyd W. Pellman to BOS, Dec. 21, 1998, box 34, Pellman to Yaroslavsky, Aug. 18, 1999, box 35, Yaroslavsky motion, Aug. 24, 1999, box 36, MOLINA.

30. *LAT*, Sept. 6, 1999; *Daily News*, Sept. 22, 1999; Molina to Seth Hufstedler, Sept. 2, 1999, box 36, Molina motion, Sept. 7, 1999, box 428, Julie Matsumoto to Yaroslavsky, Sept. 12,1999, Minutes of BOS meeting, Sept. 21, 1999, box 37, MOLINA.

31. *LAT*, May 19, Jun. 20, 21, 28, Jul. 6, Oct. 19, Nov. 2, 4, 5, 15, 2000; *Whittier Daily News*, Apr. 24, 2000; Zev Yaroslavsky interview, Mar. 6, 2017; *Metropolitan News-Enterprise*, Jun. 21, 28, 2000; League of Women Voters of Los Angeles County circular for Nov. 7, 2000, election, box 35, MOLINA.

32. *LAT*, Feb. 17, 2007, May 15, Jun. 14, 21, 2015, May 4, Jul. 18, 2017, Feb. 23, 2018; Dan Walters, "For the Powerful Five 'Kings' of Los Angeles County, Change is in the Air," *CALmatters*, Jun. 25, 2017; Los Angeles County Grand Jury, report on county structure, "Final Report," 2015–2016, 247–263, LACGJ website.

33. *Cal-Tax News*, Dec. 1, 1989; *LAT*, Feb. 28, May 31, Jul. 25, Sept. 30, Nov. 8, 1990; Dixon to BOS, Feb. 18, 1991, box 868, MOLINA; John M. Allswang, *California Initiatives and Referendums, 1912-1990* (Los Angeles: Edmund G. "Pat" Brown Institute of Public Affairs, 1991), 180–181.

34. *LAT*, Dec. 1, 1999, Jul. 6, 2000, Aug. 6, 2001; *Daily News*, Apr. 23, 2000, Aug. 8, 2001; Pellman to BOS, Dec. 15, 1999, box 868, MOLINA; Schabarum to BOS, Jul. 24, 2000, Connie McCormack to David J. Butler, Aug. 25, 2000, box S431, BURKE.

35. *LAT*, Oct. 2, 2001, Feb. 19, Mar. 7, 2002, Mar. 15, 2006, Jan. 6, 2008, Jul. 24, 25, 29, 31, Aug. 1, 2012; *Daily Journal*, Oct. 24, 2001; *Pasadena Star-News*, Mar. 1, 2002; Steven Holguin to Joseph D. Rich, Oct. 1, 2001, box S431, BURKE; Pellman to BOS, Jan. 27, 2003, box 868, MOLINA.

36. *LAT*, Dec. 28, 1989, Feb. 13, 24, Mar. 16, Apr. 19, May 27, Jun. 24, Dec. 12, 1990, Mar. 14, May 15, 1991, Dec. 2, 3, 1993, Aug. 30, 1994; Los Angeles County Sheriff's Department, *150 Years: A Tradition of Service* (Paducah, Ky.: Turner Pub. Co., 2000), 72.

37. *LAT*, Aug. 4, 6, 24, 29, Sept. 4, 11, 12, 13, 14, 19, 21, Oct. 5, 30, Dec. 11,18, 22, 1991; *Daily News*, Sept. 13, 1991; Richard Polanco to Edelman, Aug. 19, 1991, Lucille Roybal-Allard to Edelman, Aug. 22, 1991, Margarite Archie-Hudson to Edelman, Sept. 5,1991; Diane Watson to Edelman, Sept. 21, 1991, box 528, Llewellyn memo to Edelman, Sept. 11, 1991, box 529, EDELMAN.

38. *LAT*, Feb. 28, May 26, 1992; "The County Sheriff's Department: A Report by Special Counsel James G. Kolts and Staff," July 1992.

39. *LAT*, Dec. 4, 1990, Nov. 21, 1991; George V. Denny to Block, Sept. 24, 1990, box 529, EDELMAN; Kevin Brazile to Los Angeles County Claims Board, Jan. 8, 1996, box 810, Robert Garcia to BOS, Dec. 15, 1992, box 825, MOLINA; Kolts, "The County Sheriff's Department," 323–332, quotes on 332. On later reports of LASD "gangs" see *LAT*, Sept. 4, 5, 1998, Mar. 24, May 4,1999, Jul. 10, 11, 2018, and in 2019 and 2020.

40. *LAT*, Jul. 21, 23, 30, Oct. 15, Dec. 12, 1992; LASD, "A Response to the Kolts Report," October 1992, box 931, EDELMAN.

41. "LASD: A Status Report by Special Counsel James G. Kolts and Staff," December 1992, box 931, EDELMAN; *LAT*, Dec. 12, 31, 1992, Jan. 5, 6, 1993.

42. *LAT*, Oct. 10, 11, 1993, Sept. 3, 1995, Sept.18, 1996, Apr. 5, 1999, Sept. 23, 2011, Mar. 20, Aug. 8, 2014; *Witness L.A.*, Aug. 8, 2014; ACLU news release, Sept. 10, 1997, box S436, Merrick J. Bobb to Burke; May 2, 1997, box S447, BURKE, Lisa Proft memo to Molina, Oct. 8, 1997, box 4, MOLINA. Many of the early semi-annual reports can be found in boxes S436 and S447, BURKE, and boxes 825, 827 and 828, MOLINA.

43. *LAT*, Apr. 25, 1990, Jan. 9, 1994, Jul. 18, 1995, Jan. 20, Oct. 24, Dec. 31, 1996, Mar. 23, 1997, Aug. 15, 2001; LASD, *150 Years*, 69–70, 75 (quote on 69); Pellman to BOS, Sept. 24, 1998, box 426,

Molina; Kolts Report, 237–248; and material in box 528, EDELMAN.

44. *LAT,* Aug. 21, Nov. 3, 6, 22, 1996, Feb. 28, Mar. 4, Apr. 2, Jun. 10, Jul. 9, 1997, Dec. 7 (quote), 1998, Feb. 10, 1999, Dec. 28, 2000, Sept. 30, 2001; Randi Tahara memo to Burke, Jun. 24, 1997, box S449, BURKE.

45. *LAT*, May 28, 1999, Feb. 20, 2000, May 7, 2001; *Daily News*, Sept. 19, 1992; *Daily Journal*, Feb. 23, 1998, Apr. 14, 1998; District Attorney budget history, 1981–1993, and budgets, 1993–1995, box 4, material on child support in box 3, GARCETTI; Jennifer Roth memo to Frankye Schneider, Aug. 11, 1994, box 171, EDELMAN; material on domestic abuse in box 143, MOLINA; Michael Parrish, *For the People: Inside the Los Angeles County District Attorney's Office,1850-2000* (Santa Monica, Calif.: Angel City Press, 2001), 70–71, 77, 118–123, 135, 160–161. See also 1990s investigations and audits in the final reports of the Los Angeles County Grand Jury, LACGJ website.

46. *Daily News*, Jul. 4, 1993; *LAT*, Mar. 4, Jun. 10, Sept. 3, 1992, Jun. 24, 1993, Jul. 11, 1995; *L.A. Weekly*, Jul. 23, 1995; Diane Watson to Hahn, Jul. 22, 1992, Watson to Edelman, Jun. 14, 1993, box 563, Hufford to BOS, Oct. 14, 1993, box 559, County Supervisors Association of California, "Budget Flash" newsletter, May 3, 1993, box 251, EDELMAN; Kathy Zimmerman McKenna, "No Cash on the Horizon for Parched Counties," *California Journal* 20 (Aug. 1989); 333–336; Mark Baldassare, *When Government Fails: The Orange County Bankruptcy* (Berkeley and Los Angeles: University of California Press, 1998), 75–85.

47. *LAT*, Jul. 31, Aug. 1, 1990; Molina to Dixon, Jun. 19, 1991, box 179, Dixon to All Department Heads, Jan. 29, 1992, box 41, MOLINA.

48. *LAT*, May 16, Jul. 6, 30, Sept. 4, 5, 15, 30, Oct. 1, 8, 1992; *Daily News*, Sept. 16, Oct. 7, 14, 1992; *Metropolitan News Enterprise*, Sept. 30, 1992; Jim Moreno memos to Edelman, Jun. 4, Sept. 17, 1992, box 178, EDELMAN; John Redmond memo to Molina, Sept. 16, 1992, box 41, MOLINA.

49. *LAT*, Jan. 6, 1993, Jan. 27, Mar. 27, Apr. 7, May 28, Jun. 7, 23, 24, 25, Jul. 7, 13, 16, 21, 22, 26, 27, 29, 30, 31, Sept. 14, 15, 19, 21, 1993, Aug. 4, Oct. 18, 1993; *Pasadena Star-News*, Jul. 20, Sept. 11, 1993; *LATax Report*, Feb. 3, 1993; Hufford to BOS, Jun. 15, 1993, box 43, MOLINA; Molina motion, Mar. 2, 1993, box 178, EDELMAN.

50. *LAT*, Jan. 25, Mar. 8, 13, 20, 22, 24, Apr. 6, May 17, 18, Jul. 15, Aug. 10, Oct. 5, 1994.

51. *LAT*, Dec. 7, 8, 11, 1994, Mar. 13, 1995; Larry J. Monteilh to BOS, Dec. 1, 1994 (quote), box S436, BURKE; Baldassare, *When Government Fails*, passim.

52. *LAT*, Jan. 14, 20, Feb. 8, 17, 24, Mar. 13, Apr. 21, May 11, Jun. 15, 16, 18, 20, 21, 28, Jul. 13, 1995; Alan T. Sasaki to BOS, Jan. 12, 1995, Barbara Maynard memo to Molina, et. al, May 3, 1995, California Legislative Office, "An Overview and Assessment of Los Angeles County's 1995-96 Budget Problem," July 11, 1995, box 44, Molina motion,

Mar. 6, 1995, and Antonovich motion, Dec. 12, 1995, box 35, Emergency Coalition to Save LA, "Alternative Plan to keep LA Working," June 1995, box 45, MOLINA: Los Angeles County Grand Jury, "Final Report," 1994–95, 47- 53, LACGJ website.

53. *LAT*, Jul. 1, 3, 4, 6, 7, 12, 14, 19, 20, Aug. 2, 3, 4, 10, 11, 15, 29, 1995; Sally Reed to BOS, Aug. 9, 1995, box 44, MOLINA.

54. *LAT*, Sept. 15, 21, 22, 23, 1995.

55. *LAT*, Jan. 11, 23, Apr. 12, 13, 21, May 7, 22, Jun.7, 25, 28, Aug. 2, Sept. 11, 1996; minutes of Sally Reed Budget Meeting, n.d., box 47, Molina motion, Sept. 12, 1996, box 46, California State Auditor, "LA County: … Financial Uncertainties Linger," Mar. 1997, box 48, MOLINA.

56. *LAT*, Feb. 21, Mar. 20, Nov. 15, 2000, Dec. 28, 2002, Apr. 20, May 21, 2004; Los Angeles County news release, Apr. 15, 2002, box 54, MOLINA.

57. *LAT*, Nov. 15, 28, Dec. 5, 1990, Mar. 1, Dec. 31, 1992, May 12, Jul. 10, 29, Sept. 7, 1993, Jun. 15, Jul. 15, Aug. 13, 1994; *Daily News*, Apr. 20, 1992; Molina motion, Apr. 14, 1992, box 258, Yolanda Vera to BOS, Apr. 30, 1993, Burke motion, Jul. 5, 1994, Dana motion, Jun. 28, 1994, box 257, EDEL-MAN; Virginia A. Collins to Gary W. Wells, Dec.14, 1992, De Witt Clinton to BOS, May 17, 1993, box 291, MOLINA; Robert Tranquada, "The Healthcare Conundrum," in Michael J. Dear, H. Eric Schockman and Greg Hise, eds., *Rethinking Los Angeles* (Thousand Oaks, CA: Sage Publications, 1996), 213–229.

58. *LAT*, Mar. 22, Jun. 18, 21, 27, Jul. 12, 14, 16, 20, 23, 26, 29, Aug. 11,15, 16,18, Sept. 15, 19, 22, 23, 24, 26, Oct. 14, 15, 29, 1995; Burt Margolin to BOS, Jul. 24, 1995, box 34, Mark Finucane to BOS, Apr. 9, 1997, box 93, staff memo to Molina, Jun. 3, 1997, box 294, MOLINA.

59. DHS timeline for LAC+USC Medical Center Restructure, 1984–1997, box 446, MOLINA; Jim Moreno memo to Edelman, Apr. 11, 1994, box 305, EDELMAN.

60. *LAT*, Mar. 8, Jun. 29, Nov. 9, 12, 13, 1997; *Los Angeles Business Journal*, Jun. 9, 1997; Molina Report on LAC+USC project, with summary of reports by auditor Harvey M. Rose (1995) and Drs. Robert Tranquada and Henry Zaretsky (1996), box 445, Antonovich to Sylvester Graff, Mar. 25, 1997, Antonovich news release, Jun. 11, 1997, box 957, Minutes of BOS meeting, Nov.12, 1997, box 439, Molina.

61. *LAT*, Aug. 16, 18, 19, 22, Sept. 14, 20, 1998, Apr. 14, 15, Jun. 21, Jul. 5, Sept. 6, 15, Oct. 10, 23, 28, 1999; *San Gabriel Valley Tribune*, Jul. 26, 29, 1999; Molina to "LAC+USC Community," Aug. 12, 1998, box 436, Timeline for LAC+USC and Harbor-UCLA Hospital plans, 1997–1999, box 439, Mark Finucane to Xavier Becerra, Jun. 8, 1999, box 445, MOLINA.

62. *Torrance Daily Breeze*, 1-3-2000; *LAT*, Jan. 17, Feb. 3, 2000; LAC+USC Medical Center Replacement Project Strategy Paper, n.d, box 439, MOLINA.

63. *LAT*, Jul. 9, 1975, Aug. 11, 1985, Aug. 5,

1990, Aug. 11, 1995, Aug. 11, 2005, Aug. 6, 2015; Melvin O. Oliver, James H. Johnson, Jr., and Walter C. Farrell, Jr., "Anatomy of a Rebellion: A Political-Economic Analysis," Chapter 9 of Robert Gooding-Williams, ed., *Reading Rodney King, Reading Urban Uprising* (New York: Routledge, 1993), 117–141; Roger Keil, *Los Angeles: Globalization, Urbanization and Social Struggles* (Chichester, Eng., New York; John Wiley & Sons, 1998), 205–226.

64. Los Angeles County Human Relations Commission and Los Angeles City Human Relations Commission, "McCone Revisited," Jan. 1985, 16.

65. *LAT*, Feb. 17, 18, 19, May 11, 1992; Eugene S. Mornell to Robert Habersham, Oct. 27, 1986, box 703, EDELMAN; Regina Freer, "Black-Korean Conflict," Chapter 8 in Mark Baldassare, ed., *The Los Angeles Riots: Lessons for the Urban Future* (Boulder, Colo.; Westview Press, 1994), 175–204; Sumi K. Cho, "Korean Americans vs. African Americans: Conflict and Construction," Chapter 13 of Gooding-Williams, ed., *Reading Rodney King*, 96–211.

66. *LAT*, Sept. 30, 1991, Jan. 9, 11, May 11, 1992, Mar. 19, 2016; Brenda Stevenson, *The Contested Murder of Latasha Harlins: Justice, Gender, and the Origins of the LA Riots* (New York: Oxford University Press, 2013), passim.

67. *LAT*, Apr. 30, May 1to 6, 14, 15, 1992; Jim Miyano memo to Edelman, May 4, 1992, box 151, EDELMAN; Dixon to BOS, May 4, 1992, box 775, MOLINA; Lou Cannon, *Official Negligence: How Rodney King and the Riots Changed Los Angeles and the LAPD* (New York: Times Books, 1997), 175–346.

68. *LAT*, Jun. 18 (quote), 1992; "Los Angeles Civil Unrest Fact Sheet, May 28, 1992," box S287, BURKE; Employment Development Department Report, "Analysis of the 1992 Los Angeles Civil Unrest," Feb. 1993, box 150, EDELMAN; Joan Petersilia and Allan Abrahamse, "A Profile of Those Arrested," Chapter 6 of Baldassare, ed., *The Los Angeles Riots*, 135–148.

69. *LAT*, May 29, 1992, Apr. 9, 18, 1993; Victor memo to Molina and staff, Oct. 2, 1992, box 775, MOLINA; Edelman to Rodney E. Cooper, Feb. 14, 1993, Edelman to Mark Hoffman, Feb. 23, 1993, Hufford to Edelman, Mar. 12, 1993, box 937, outline of plan for BOS and Sheriff news conference on preparation for verdicts, Apr. 8, 1993, Hufford to BOS, Apr. 12, 1993, box 150, EDELMAN.

70. *LAT*, Jun. 12, 13, Nov. 4, 1992, Apr. 28, 29, 30, May 22, Jun. 9, Jul. 13, 29, 1993, Apr. 14, 1994, Sept. 7, Oct. 10, 1996, Mar. 2, 1997. Several of the post-riot essays include Jane Pisano, "After the Riots," *National Civic Review* 81 (Summer/Fall 1992): 313–318; J. Eugene Grigsby, "Rebuilding Los Angeles: One Year Later," *National Civic Review* 82 (Fall 1993): 348–353; and Harlan Hahn, "Los Angeles and the Future: Uprisings, Identity, and New Institutions," in Dear, Schockman, and Hise, eds., *Rethinking Los Angeles*, 77–95.

71. Some of the many examples of the sources noted in this section are: *LAT*, Jul. 13, 31, 1996, Nov. 30, 1998, Sept. 10, 2002, Dec.10, 2006, Jun. 24, Nov. 25, 2007, Jul. 25, 2008, Apr. 1, 2016, Apr. 26, 28, 29, Aug. 20, 2017, Aug. 9, 2021; Philip J. Ethington, "Segregated Diversity: Race, Ethnicity, Space, and Political Fragmentation in Los Angeles County, 1940–1994," Final Report to the Haynes Foundation, Presentation to the USC Population Studies Lab, Sept. 13, 2000," http://www.usc.edu/college/historylab/Haynes_FR/index.

72. *LAT*, Feb. 10, May 11, 2000; Evelyn Gutierrez to Alma Martinez, et al., Jan. 28, 2000, Gutierrez to Barbara Nack, Mar. 9, 2000, box 110, MOLINA.

Chapter 12

1. *LAT*, May 23, 1999, Aug. 21, Oct. 25, 2007, Jan. 6, May 11, 2008, Sept. 30, 2019, Feb. 16, Nov. 4, 5, 2020; Jon Regardie, "Political Evolution," *Los Angeles Downtown News*, Jan. 5, 1998; http://bos.lacounty.gov/About-Us/Board-of-Supervisors/Board-Member-Biographies.

2. http://hildalsolis.org/biography; Jon Matthews, "Spotlight on Hilda Solis," *Civic Center NewSource*, Apr. 3, 1995; *LAT*, Sept. 12, 1995, Apr. 10, Dec. 1, Nov. 5, 13, 2014; http://supervisorkuehl.com; file LP402, Sheila Kuehl Papers, CSA.

3. http://hahn.lacounty.gov/about-Janice/; *LAT*, May 17, Jun. 9, 12, Nov. 6, 9, 2016; http://kathrynbarger.lacounty.gov/supervisor-kathryn-barger/.

4. *LAT*, Jan. 17, 1997, Sept. 20, 1998, Apr. 15, 1999, Dec. 31, 2001, May 10, 2006, Nov. 28, Dec. 1, 2014, Feb. 24, 2015, Mar. 30, Dec. 6, 2016; Zev Yaroslavsky, interview by author, Los Angeles, March 6, 2017; review of BOS meetings since 2014 by the author, BSM.

5. *LAT*, Nov. 10, Dec. 6, 2016; author observation of BOS meetings since 2014, BSM.

6. *LAT*, Oct. 19, 2000, Feb. 11, 2007, May 9, 2011, Aug. 17, 2014, Feb. 21, Jul. 7, 2015; Dan Walters, "For the Powerful Five 'Kings' of Los Angeles County, Change is in the Air," *CALmatters*, Jun. 25, 2017; Los Angeles County Grand Jury, report on county structure in "Final Report," 2015–2016, 247–263, LACGJ website.

7. *LAT*, Jun. 27, 2001, Aug. 6, 10, 17, 20, Sept. 7, 28, 2011; *Metropolitan News-Enterprise*, Jan.4, 2002; *L.A. Weekly*, Sept. 28, 2011; Yvonne Burke to Elaine Jones, Jan. 18, 2001, box S506, BURKE; Alan Clayton to Joseph Rich, Jan. 4, 2002, Los Angeles County Chicano Employees Association news release, Jun. 28, 2005, Raymond G. Fortner to BOS, Jul. 25, 2005, box 103, redistricting maps in box 764, Sean Andrade, et. al, to BOS, Jul. 13, 2011, box 767, MOLINA.

8. *LAT*, Jun. 13, Dec. 3, 2013, Jul. 13, 22, Oct. 20, 2014, May 7, 2015, Apr. 6, Sept. 26, Oct. 1, 2016; *LAT* Essential California Newsletter, Mar. 3, 2019.

9. *LAT*, Feb. 19, 21, Apr. 11, May 17, 23, Jul. 3,

Oct. 18, 20, Dec. 19, 2012, Jul. 22, 2016, May 23, Jul. 20, 2020; *Park La Brea News*, May 31, 2018.

10. *LAT,* Jan. 28, 1972, Mar. 3, 1998, May 23, Oct. 2, 2012, Nov. 12, 24, 2014, Mar. 16, 2017, Oct. 11, Nov. 5, 2018, Jan. 31, 2019.

11. For some examples see *LAT,* May 21, 2002, Apr. 15, 2003, May 21, 2004, Feb. 4, 2009, Feb. 5, 2011; David Janssen statement, Apr. 19, 2004, Molina talking points on Gov. Schwarzenegger's "obscene and offensive" budget plan, c2004, box 58, Antonovich motion for budget augmentation targeting terrorism, Jun. 23, 2003, box 57, and Janssen to BOS, Sept. 12, 2001, box 868, MOLINA.

12. *LAT,* Aug. 15, 2001, May 12, 2005, Feb. 6, Aug. 25, 2006, Feb. 20, 2009, Dec. 25, 2011, Feb. 17, 2012, Feb. 7, 2013, Jun. 29, Jul. 2, 2013; Michael Gennaco, Office of Independent Review, "First Year Report," Oct. 2001, i–v, box 596, Brian Center memo to Gloria Molina, Apr. 26, 2004, box 597, MOLINA.

13. *LAT,* Sept. 30, 2001, Mar. 1, Apr. 7, May 30, Jun. 21, Oct. 14, 16, Dec. 18, 2002, Mar. 20, 28, Jun. 28, Jul. 21, Oct. 6, Nov. 10, 2004, Sept. 16, 2006, Jun. 9, 2007, Oct. 25, Dec. 10, 2010, Jan. 14, 15 (quote), May 29, 2011, Mar. 7, Jul. 11, 2012, Feb. 1, Dec. 19, 2013, Feb. 1, 2014; KABC stories Jan. 30, 31, 2014, https//abc7.com.

14. *LAT,* Dec. 30, 2006, Jul. 12, 2007, Sept. 23, Oct. 16, 23, 2011, Apr. 14, Dec. 10, 2013, Jan. 26, Feb. 8, Jul. 2, Sept. 17, 2014; 2006–2007 County Grand Jury, "Final Report," 271–278, LACGJ website.

15. *LAT,* Jan. 11, 2015 (quote), Feb. 16, Mar. 25, Apr. 2, 11, Nov. 2, Dec. 23, 2016, Mar. 16, 2017, Jul. 10, Aug. 12, Oct. 7, 9, 26, 27, Nov. 27, 29, Dec. 2, 5, 2018, Jan. 19, 28, 31, Jul. 14, Sept. 20, 2019; Mar. 4, 6, 27, Apr. 1,4, 13, Jun. 3, 9, 6, 20, 25, Jul. 25, 27, 31, Aug. 5, 14, 23, 27, Nov. 11, Dec. 4, 2020, Jan. 23, Mar. 24, Jul. 1, 2021, Jul. 8, 2022; BOS meeting minutes, April 4, 2020, 13, BSM; ABC Channel 7 reports, Jul. 31, Nov. 11, 2020.

16. *LAT,* May 21, 2004, Jun. 8, 16, 24, 2010, Jan.10, Aug. 30, 2011, Feb. 21, Apr. 4, Sept. 5, 2012, Apr. 14, Oct. 13, 2013, Apr. 10, 16, Dec. 16, 2015, Oct. 13, 2016, Feb. 13, Apr. 4, May 2, 2018, Dec. 7, 8, 2020; *Daily News*, Aug. 12, 2017; LASD contract material in boxes 808 and 810, and material on Probation Department in boxes 1068 and 1069, MOLINA; 2012–2013 County Grand Jury, "Final Report,"19–22, and 2013–2014 "Final Report," 81–95, LACGJ website.

17. *LAT,* Mar. 15, 2001, Oct. 13, 2004, Dec. 5 to 10, 2005, Aug. 11, Sept. 9, 2007, Apr. 24, 2008, Jul. 9, 2009, Jul. 7, 8, 2015, Sept. 25, 2017; Molina and Ridley-Thomas motion, Jul. 6, 2010, box 436, MOLINA; Janice Hahn to Thomas Garthwaite, Oct. 29, 2004, Genevieve Clavreul to BOS, Sept. 20, 2004, Garthwaite to BOS, Dec. 23, 2003, Fred Leaf to Raymond Fortner, Apr. 11, 2005, box S301, and other material in boxes S301 and S313, BURKE.

18. *LAT,* Feb. 4, 2000, Oct. 2, 18, 28, Nov. 6, 2002, Mar. 31, May 18, 2014, Sept. 29, 30, 2015, Aug. 12, 16, Sept. 6, Nov. 9, 10, 15, Dec. 2, 9, 2020,

Feb. 2, 2022; Yaroslavsky motion, Jul. 30, 2002, box 882, Mark P. Robinson Jr., to BOS, Nov. 17, 1998, box 874, Mark Finucane to BOS, Feb. 28, 2000, box 875, MOLINA; 2004–2005 County Grand Jury, "Final Report," Rose Audit, 1–165, LACGJ website; Minutes of BOS meetings, Dec. 12, 2017, Oct. 9, 2018, BSM.

19. *LAT,* Jan. 12, Dec. 20, 1988, Aug. 22, 1996, Aug. 23, 1997, Jan. 8, May 22, Aug. 20, 22, 1998, Apr. 1, Jul. 6, Aug. 29, 1999, Aug. 2, 2000; *L.A. Weekly,* Jun. 8, 1995; Jennifer Wolch and Heidi Sommer, "Los Angeles in an Era of Welfare Reform: Implications for Poor People and Community Well-being," Human Services Network, 1997, passim; Ellen Reese, *They Say Cut Back, We Say Fight Back!* (New York: Russell Sage Foundation, 2011), 105–126.

20. *LAT,* Feb. 8, 1998, Feb. 8, Jul. 12, Oct, 20, 2000, Jul. 1, Oct. 19, 2006, Nov. 7, 2007, Jun. 20, Oct. 8, 2008, Jun. 12, 2009, Jun. 11, 2012, Jul. 8, 2015; *Daily Journal,* Apr. 14, 2000; DPSS press releases, Mar. 31, 1999, and Jun. 30, 1999, Economic Roundtable, "On the Edge: A Progress Report on Welfare to Work in Los Angeles," April 1999, esp. 38–42, and Los Angeles County Chief Administrative Office, Urban Research Division, "Monitoring the Implementation of CalWORKS: "Welfare Reform and Welfare Service Provision in Los Angeles County, 1998," August 1999, box 703, MOLINA; Reese, *They Say Cut Back,* 4–15, 74–83, 108–125.

21. *LAT,* Apr. 1, 1998, Jul. 23, 2005, Mar. 5, 2006, and Steve Lopez series on homeless, Oct.16 to 19, 23, 2005; *Santa Monica Evening Outlook,* Dec. 14, 1993; Jim Moreno memos to Edmund Edelman, Dec. 3, 23, 1991, box 701, EDELMAN; Robert G. Medina to BOS, May 27, 1993, box S163, BURKE; Stephanie Klopfleisch to BOS, May 5, 1997, box 376, MOLINA; Los Angeles County Grand Jury, "Final Report," 2006–2007, 216–225 (quote on 218), LACGJ website; Jennifer Wolch, "From Global to Local: The Rise of Homelessness in Los Angeles During the 1980s," in Allen J. Scott and Edward W. Soja, eds., *The City: Los Angeles and Urban Theory at the End of the Twentieth Century* (Berkeley and Los Angeles: University of California Press, 1996), 406–419, esp. 406.

22. *LAT,* Jul. 5, 2014, Jan. 25, Dec. 10, 2015, Feb. 10, May 5, Nov. 15, 18, 2016, Jun. 1, 14, 20, 2017, Feb. 1, 19, 25 to 28, Mar. 1, 2, Jun. 1, Oct. 24, 28, Dec. 19, 2018, Jan. 22, Jun. 5, 2019; 2015–2016 County Grand Jury, "Final Report," 75–91, LACGJ website.

23. *Long Beach Press-Telegram,* Jul. 14, 1990; *LAT,* Jul. 17, 1990, Mar. 28, 1993, May 14, Jul. 5, Dec. 11, 1999; *Daily News,* Jun. 7, 1990, Jan. 30, 1992, Mar. 23, 1993; Gerald Davis to BOS, Feb. 8, 1990, box 135, Jennifer Roth memo to Edelman, Aug. 10, 1990, box 131, Roth memos to Edelman, Nov. 20, 1990, Sept. 24, 1992, box 133, Peter Digre to BOS, Mar. 30, 1993, box 127, EDELMAN; Rob Gurwitt, "The Man with Too Many Children, *Governing* 11(Sept. 1998): 32–37.

24. *LAT,* Jan. 12, 19, 2000, Feb. 11, Mar. 12, Jul. 18, 2002, Feb. 10, 2003, Apr. 22 (quote), Aug. 5, Sept. 16, Oct. 11, Nov. 22, 2009, Feb. 5, Mar. 20, 24, Aug. 18, Oct. 22, Nov. 21, Dec. 14, 19, 2010, Apr. 4, May 2, Aug. 7, 11, Oct. 11, 2011.

25. *LAT,* Mar. 30, 2012, Feb. 14, May 31, 2013, Jun. 2, 26, Jul. 31, Oct. 7, Dec. 18, 19, 2013, Jun. 11, 21, 28, 2014, Apr. 5, Jun. 8, 2015, Apr. 8, 2016, Mar. 21, 2017, Jun. 22, 23, 26, 28, Sept. 14, 2018, Jan. 8, 2020; Minutes of BOS meeting, Aug. 14, 2018, 34–36, BSM.

26. *LAT,* Jan. 10, 1994, May 22, Jun. 27, 2002, Apr. 19, 2004, Jan. 28, 2012, Feb. 13, 2018; 1993–1994 County Grand Jury, "Final Report," 99–117, 2003–2004 "Final Report," 529–554, 2014–2015 "Final Report," 1–24 , LACGJ website; Ralph Shafer, interview by author, Jan 4, 2017, Covina, Calif.; material on county contracts in boxes 808 and 810, MOLINA; Mara A. Cohen Marks, "Community Redevelopment," in Hynda L. Rudd, et al., eds., *The Development of Los Angeles City Government: An Institutional History, 1850–2000,* 2 vols. (Los Angeles: Los Angeles City Historical Society, 2007) 1: 415–445; Roger Keil, *Los Angeles: Globalization, Urbanization and Social Struggles* (Chichester, Eng., New York; John Wiley & Sons, 1998), 153–171.

27. *LAT,* Feb. 2, Jun. 27, Jul. 8, 2001, Jan. 30, Mar. 11, 2003, Mar. 21, 2006, Jan. 29, Sept. 22, 2010, Apr. 8, 2013, Apr. 28, 2015, May 13, Aug. 10, Oct. 18, Dec. 20, 2016, Mar. 29, 30, 2017, Feb. 11, 2018, Jan. 5, 2019.

28. *LAT,* Jun. 24, 2010, Jul. 3, 15, 26, 30, Sept. 1, 16, 22, 2010, Aug. 3, 2012, Nov. 6, 13, 2013, Apr. 9, 10, 14, 16, 17, Aug. 2, 2014, and many more; Thom Reilly, *The Failure of Governance in Bell, California: Big Time Corruption in a Small Town* (Lanham, Md.: Lexington Books, 2016), passim.

29. *LAT,* May 17, 1964, Jan. 27, Aug. 15, 1973, Nov. 9, 1974, Jan 8, Aug. 15, 1975, May 28, 1976, Apr. 2, 1978, Oct. 27, 1980; *Long Beach Independent Press-Telegram,* Oct. 30, 1980; 1980 General Election sample ballot, box 965, and other material on Proposition A in box 961, 962, and 963, HAHN; Ethan N. Elkind, *Railtown: The Fight for the Los Angeles Metro Rail and the Future of the City* (Berkeley and Los Angeles: University of California Press, 2014), 5–37.

30. *Daily News,* May 30, 1985; *LAT,* Jul. 1, Nov. 1, 1984, Feb. 9, Dec. 17, 1986, Jan. 24, Feb. 12, 18, Mar. 2, Apr. 4, Oct. 17, 1987, Dec. 2, 9, 1988, Nov. 10, 1989, Jan. 3, 1990; Kenneth Hahn to John Dyer, Feb. 6, 1985, Hahn statement, Mar. 25, 1988, Hahn motion, Dec. 6, 1988, box 965, Hahn to David Roberti, May 20, 1987, Hahn to Richard Katz, Sept. 9, 1987, Hahn to Tom Bradley and the Los Angeles City Council, May 25, 1988, box 501, Hahn statement, Jul. 1, 1985, box 964, Hahn to Alan Pegg, Oct. 26, 1988, box 963, James Hankla to BOS, Jan. 27, 1987, box 57, Hahn to Ted Reed, Nov. 9, 1989 (quote), box 858, HAHN; 1986–1987 County Grand Jury, "Final Report," 175–180, LACGJ website.

31. *LAT*, Feb. 15, Mar. 28, Jul. 15, 16, Dec. 26, 1990, Sept. 19, 1992, Apr. 29, 1993, May 23, Sept. 4, Oct. 6, 1994, Mar. 31, Aug. 8, 1995, Dec. 6, 1996, May 30, Aug. 20, 1997, Apr. 3, 10, 24, Jun. 1, 22, Aug. 3, Oct. 20, 1998; *Daily News*, Jul. 7, 1993, Mar. 12, 1998; Edelman to Burke, Dec. 7, 1992, box 428, Mike Bohlke memo to Burke, Mar. 10, 1998, box S484, BURKE; Tim W, Ferguson, "Who Said Anything About Transportation?," *Forbes* 156 (Dec. 4, 1995): 130–134; Martin Wachs, "If I were in Charge," *Los Angeles,* 41 (Jan. 1996): 18; Elkind, *Railtown*, 116–180.

32. *LAT,* Sept. 28, Oct. 18, 2000, Jun. 1, Nov. 2, 2003, Jul. 26, Aug. 13, 2008, Nov. 3, 2009, Feb. 18, Mar. 31, 2013, Jan. 27, 2014, Mar. 14, 2016, Oct. 13, Nov. 20, 2018; James K. Hahn to Yvonne Burke, Jan. 8, 2002, box S248a, BURKE; Yaroslavsky interview, Mar. 6, 2017; Elkin, *Railtown*, 181–216.

33. *LAT,* Apr. 27, 2012, Dec. 25, 2013, Jan. 19, Mar. 29, Nov. 8, 2014, May 10, 2015, Mar. 22, Jun. 21, Sept. 29, Oct. 7, 25, Nov. 6, 7, 2016, Jan. 5, 2017, Jul. 3, 2019; May 25, 2021; Elkind, *Railtown*, 210–216.

34. *LAT,* Jun. 28, Sept. 13, 2017; Minutes of BOS meetings, Dec. 20, 2016, Feb. 7, Mar. 14, Sept. 5, Dec. 19, 2017, Mar. 20, May 1, Jun. 19, Sept. 4, Oct. 2, 2018, BSM.

35. *LAT,* Nov. 20, Dec. 20, 2016, Mar. 17, 22, Apr. 1, May 9, Jun. 23, Jul. 14, Aug. 11, 13, 2017, Jun. 21, Oct. 1, 2018; minutes of BOS meetings, Oct. 17, 2017, BSM. See also "I.C.E. in L.A." report in 2015–2016 County Grand Jury, "Final Report," 149–157, LACGJ website.

Epilogue

1. On the vast number of special districts in Los Angeles County, California and the nation see, among many others: Los Angeles County Citizens' Economy and Efficiency Commission, "Review of the Relationship between Los Angeles County and State Government," Report 167, Feb. 1997, esp. 34–36, LACCEEC website; John C. Bollens, *Special District Governments in the United States* (Berkeley and Los Angeles: University of California Press, 1957), passim; California Little Hoover Commission, "Special Districts: Relics of the Past or Resources of the Future?" May 3, 2000, http://www.lhc.ca.gov/studies/155/report155.html; and Joe Mathews, *California Crackup: How Reform Broke the Golden State and How We Can Fix It* (Berkeley: University of California Press, 2010), 160–163.

2. *LAT*, Jan. 12, 2018 (quote), Feb. 2, Jun. 5, 2019, Dec. 7, 2020.

Bibliography

Manuscripts and Reference Collections

Bancroft Library, University of California, Berkeley.
  Edmund G. Brown Papers
  Robert W. Kenny Correspondence and Papers
California State Archives, Sacramento.
  Braun & Company Records
  Goodwin Knight Papers
  Tom Hayden Papers
  Sheila Kuehl Papers
  Richard Polanco Papers
  Earl Warren Papers
  California State Library, Sacramento.
  Miscellaneous Reports, etc.
Henry E. Huntington Library, San Marino, Calif.
  Theodore J. Curphey Papers
  Edmund D. Edelman Papers
  John Anson Ford Papers
  Gilbert Garcetti Papers
  Kenneth Hahn Papers
  Los Angeles Times Records
  Loren Miller Papers
  Gloria Molina Papers
  Alexander Pope Papers
Seaver Center for Western History Research, Natural History Museum of Los Angeles County.
  Frank G. Bonelli Collection
  Map Collection
  Political Ephemera Collection
Southern California Library for Social Studies and Research, Los Angeles.
  Robert W. Kenny Collection
  Organizations Collection—Civil Rights Congress
  Henry Steinberg Collection
  Orilla Winfield Papers
Special Collections, California State University, Los Angeles.
  Richard Alatorre Papers
  Julian Dixon Papers
  Ernest E. Debs Papers
  TELACU Collection
Special Collections, Stanford University Library, Stanford, Calif.
  Bert Corona Papers
Special Collections, University of California, Los Angeles.
  American Civil Liberties Union of Southern California Records
  Eugene Warren Biscailuz Papers
  Mayor Tom Bradley Administration Papers
  California Ephemera Collection (#200)

Los Angeles City and County Consolidation Collection
Los Angeles Urban League Records
John Randolph Haynes Papers
Edward R. Roybal Papers
Special Collections, University of Southern California, Los Angeles.
Los Angeles Area Chamber of Commerce Collection
Los Angeles Examiner Collection
Yvonne Braithwaite Burke Papers

Interviews by the Author

Robert J. Banning, January 27, 2011, February 6, 2015; Pasadena, Calif.
Ernest E. Debs, July 21, 1981; Los Angeles, Calif.
Edmund D. Edelman, June 17, 2011; Los Angeles, Calif.
Steven P. Erie, December 15, 2016; San Marino, Calif.
Kimball Garrett, August 23, 2016; Los Angeles, Calif.
James Gilson, May 9. 2016; Los Angeles, Calif.
Zev Yaroslavsky, March 6, 2017; Los Angeles, Calif.

Oral History Transcripts

Breivogel, Milton. "Seven Decades of Planning and Development in the Los Angeles Region: Milton Breivo-
gel." University of California, Los Angeles, Oral History Program, 1989.
Call, Asa. "Notes With Asa Call." University of California, Berkeley, Oral History Program, 1975.
Debs, Ernest E. Oral History Interview. Conducted 1987 by Carlos Vasquez. University of California, Los
Angeles for the State Government Oral History Program, CSA.
Fox, William J. "Seven Decades of Planning and Development in the Los Angeles Region: General William
J. Fox." University of California, Los Angeles, Oral History Program, 1989.
Hayes, James A. Oral History Interview. Conducted 1990 by Carlos Vasquez. University of California, Los
Angeles for the State Government Oral History Program, CSA.
Molina, Gloria. Oral History Interview. Conducted 1990 by Carlos Vasquez. 2 vols. University of Califor-
nia, Los Angeles for the State Government Oral History Program, CSA.
Torres, Art. Oral History Interview. Conducted 2003 by Steve Edington. Center for Oral and Public His-
tory, California State University, Fullerton for the State Government Oral History Program, CSA.
Van de Kamp, John K. Oral History Interview. Conducted 2003 by Susan Douglass Yates. UCLA Oral History Program, for the California State Archives Government Oral History Program.
Watson, Diane. Oral History Interview. Conducted 1999 by Susan Douglass Yates. 2 vols. UCLA Oral History Program, for the California State Archives Government Oral History Program.

Government Documents

California. California Commission on Campaign Financing. *Money and Politics in Local Elections: The Los
Angeles Area.* Los Angeles: Center for Responsive Government, 1989.
———. *California Statutes and Amendments to Codes.* Sacramento: State Printing Office, 1950–.
———. Governor. "Metropolitan California: Papers Prepared for the Governor's Commission on Metro-
politan Area Problems." Edited by Ernest A. Engelbert. Sacramento, 1961.
———. Governor's Commission on the Los Angeles Riots. *Violence in the City—An End or a Beginning? A
Report.* Los Angeles, 1965.
———. Legislature. Assembly. Interim Committee on Judiciary. "Report of the Subcommittee on Rackets
of the Assembly Interim Committee on Judiciary, House Resolution No. 224, 1957." Sacramento: Assem-
bly of the State of California, 1959.
———. Legislature. Assembly. Interim Committee on Municipal and County Government. "Financing Los
Angeles Government in Los Angeles County." Preliminary Research Report, January 17, 1953.
———. Legislature. Assembly. Interim Committee on Municipal and County Government. "Preliminary
Report Covering Fringe Area Problems in the County of Los Angeles." Sacramento: Assembly of the State
of California, 1953.
———. Legislature. Assembly. Interim Committee on Social Welfare. Subcommittee on Crime and Correc-
tion. "Control of Juvenile Delinquency in Los Angeles County." 1953.
———. Legislature. Assembly. Interim Committee on State and Local Taxation. *The Borough System of Gov-
ernment for Metropolitan Areas.* 1951.
———. Legislature. Joint Fact-Finding Committee on Un-American Activities in California. *Report.* Sacramento: State Printing Office, 1943 and 1945.

_____. Legislature. Senate. Fact-Finding Committee on Un-American Activities. *Fifth Report*. Sacramento: State Printing Office, 1949.

_____. Little Hoover Commission. "Special Districts: Relics of the Past or Resources of the Future?" May 3, 2000. http://www.lhc.ca.gov/studies/155/report155.html, accessed Jul. 15, 2012.

_____. Special Crime Study Commission on Organized Crime. *Final Report*. Sacramento, May 11, 1953.

_____. State Auditor. "Los Angeles County: Although it Continues to Balance Current Budgets, Financial Uncertainties Linger." March 1997. CSL.

_____. State Auditor. "Los Angeles County Department of Health Services: Current proposals will not resolve its budget crisis, and without significant additional revenue it may be forced to limit services." May 2002. CSL.

Los Angeles. Bureau of Budget and Efficiency. "A Study of a Proposed City and County Government of Los Angeles within the Present City Limits." 1932.

_____. City Administrative Officer. Report to the Los Angeles City Council on a separate city and county government of Los Angeles. March 15, 1961. CSL.

_____. City Council. Minutes and Council Files. LACRC.

Los Angeles County. Air Pollution Control District. "Smog: What has been done, what must be done." 1955.

_____. Board of Supervisors. "Los Angeles County Budget." 1950–1980. SEAVER.

_____. Board of Supervisors. *Los Angeles County: A Handbook of Its Government and Services*. Los Angeles: Los Angeles County Board of Supervisors and Office of the Superintendent of Schools, 1950.

_____. Board of Supervisors. Minutes of Meetings, 1985–2020, and Statements of Proceedings and Video Recordings of Meetings, 2013–2020. www.lacounty.gov/wps/portal/sop.

_____. Board of Supervisors & Office of Superintendent of Schools. "Los Angeles County: A Handbook of Its Government and Services." 1950.

_____. *Charter of the County of Los Angeles*. Annotated, 2002. http://file.lacounty.gov/lac/charter.pdf.

_____. Charter Study Committee. "Recommendations of the Charter Study Committee Presented to the Board of Supervisors." July 22, 1958.

_____. Charter Study Committee. "Recommendations of the Charter Study Committee Presented to the Board of Supervisors." June 6, 1962.

_____. Citizens' Economy and Efficiency Commission. Reports and Correspondence. 1965–2020. http://eec.lacounty.gov/Reports.

_____. Committee on Governmental Simplification. "Activity Study of the County of Los Angeles and Incorporated Cities in the County of Los Angeles." 2 vols., 1934.

_____. Committee on Governmental Simplification. "Report." Los Angeles: Committee on Governmental Simplification, 1935.

_____. Commission to Review Public Social Services Los Angeles County, "Final Report." December 31, 1976. (In box 312, HAHN.)

_____. County Counsel. "The History, Legal and Administrative Aspects of Air Pollution Control in the County of Los Angeles." A report submitted to the Board of Supervisors of the County of Los Angeles by Harold W. Kennedy. May 9, 1954. LACLL.

_____. County Counsel. "Special Report of the County Counsel on problem created by recent United States Supreme Court cases affecting the Communist Party and the twenty-year fight of the County of Los Angeles against subversion and Communism." By Harold W. Kennedy. August 19, 1964. LACLL.

_____. Department of Health Services. "Illegal attorney referral activity in Los Angeles County: A Report on the Problem, Including an Analysis of the Handling of the Friends of the Friendless Ring by the County Department of Health Services." 1974.

_____. Department of Public Social Services. "A History of Public Welfare in Los Angeles County." 1975.

_____. Grand Jury. "Final Report." 1960–2018. http://grandjury.co.la.ca.us/gjreports.html.

_____. Grand Jury. "The Pattern of Vice Protection: A Report of the Los Angeles County Grand Jury of 1950." January 17, 1951. UCLA.

_____. Human Relations Commission. "Hate Crimes" reports. In boxes 702, 703, EDELMAN; boxes 214, 826, HAHN; boxes 389, 388, 389, MOLINA; and http://lahumanrelations.org/hatecrime/hatecrimearchivereports.htm, 1999–2020.

_____. Human Relations Commission. "The Urban Reality: A Comparative Study of the Socio-Economic Situation of Mexican Americans, Negroes, and Anglo-Caucasians in Los Angeles County." June 1965.

_____. Kolts Commission. "The Los Angeles County Sheriff's Department: A Report." By Special Counsel James G. Kolts and Staff. June 1992. And updates in boxes S436, S447, BURKE; and boxes 825, 827, 828, MOLINA.

_____. Kolts Commission. "A Status Report by Special Counsel James G. Kolts and Staff." December 1992.

_____. Local Agency Formation Commission, "Six Year Report, 1963–1969." 1969.

_____. "Los Angeles County, California. " Code of Ordinances." https://www.municode.com/library/ca/los_angeles_county/codes/code_of_ordinances.

_____. Sheriff's Department. "A Response to the Kolts Report." Sherman Block, Sheriff. October 1992.

Other Unpublished Sources

Ernst and Ernst. "Review of the Department of Regional Planning for the 1978–79 Grand Jury Audit Committee." Apr. 24, 1979.

Ford, John Anson. "Democracy Uniting the World." Los Angeles County, booklet, c. 1950. SEAVER.

Institute for Local Self Government. "Special Districts or Special Dynasties? Democracy Denied." Institute for Local Self Government, University of California, Berkeley, May 1970.

Lakewood. "The Lakewood Plan." City of Lakewood booklet, Revised, Nov. 1957.

Sonenshein, Raphael J. "The Prospects for County Charter Reform in California." Mar. 2001. Accessed at www.csus.edu/calst/Government_Affairs/faculty_fellowsprogram.html, Jun. 5, 2011.

Wolch, Jennifer, and Heidi Sommer. "Los Angeles County in an Era of Welfare Reform: Implications for Poor People and Community Well-Being." Human Services Network, 1997.

Newspapers

Long Beach Press-Telegram
Los Angeles Daily News
Los Angeles Examiner
Los Angeles Herald & Express
Los Angeles Herald Examiner
Los Angeles Sentinel
Los Angeles Times
Santa Monica Evening Outlook
Torrance Daily Breeze

Dissertations and Theses

Brienes, Marvin. "The Fight Against Smog in Los Angeles, 1943–1957." PhD diss., University of California, Davis, 1975.

Harmon, Michael Mont. "The Consolidation of the Los Angeles City and County Health Departments: A Case Study." PhD diss., University of Southern California, 1968.

Harris, Maria Elena. "Is Ideology a Determinant of Local Government Fiscal Policy? A Case Study of the Los Angeles County Board of Supervisors." PhD diss., University of Southern California, 1995.

Hoch, Charles John. "City Limits: Municipal Boundary Formation and Class Segregation in Los Angeles Suburbs, 1940–1970." PhD diss., University of California, Los Angeles, 1981.

Johnson, Joke Hilde Wiersema. "The Southern California Association of Governments: A Study of Its Record and Possible Future." PhD diss., Claremont Graduate School, 1976.

Mayer, Ernest, Jr. "Urban Growth and Annexation Policy: Problem of Unincorporated Islands." Master's thesis, University of Southern California, January 1970.

Sitton, Thomas J. "Urban Politics and Reform in New Deal Los Angeles: The Recall of Mayor Frank L. Shaw." PhD diss., University of California, Riverside, 1983.

Warren, Robert. "Changing Patterns of Governmental Organization in the Los Angeles Metropolitan Area." PhD diss., University of California, Los Angeles, 1964.

Willard, Michael Nevin. "Urbanization as Culture: Youth and Race in Postwar Los Angeles." PhD diss., University of Minnesota, 2001.

Vinson, Thomas Wilson. "The 1966 Changeover from a Civil Service to a Personnel Department in the County of Los Angeles: A Case Study." Master's thesis, University of Southern California, 1968.

Books and Articles

Abbott, Carl. *The Metropolitan Frontier: Cities in the Modern American West.* Tucson: University of Arizona Press, 1993.

Able, Emily K. *Tuberculosis and the Politics of Exclusion: A History of Public Health and Migration to Los Angeles.* New Brunswick, N.J.: Rutgers University Press, 2007.

Abrams, Richard M. *America Transformed: Sixty Years of Revolutionary Change, 1941–2000.* Cambridge, England: Cambridge University Press, 2006.

Acuña, Rodolfo. *Anything But Mexican: Chicanos in Contemporary Los Angeles.* London and New York: Verso, 1996.

Allen, Nancy E. "Have Grand Juries Outlived Their Usefulness?" *California Journal* 17 (Aug. 1986): 399–400.

Allswang, John M. *California Initiatives and Referendums, 1912–1990.* Los Angeles: Edmund G. "Pat" Brown Institute of Public Affairs, 1991.

_____. "Tom Bradley of Los Angeles." *Southern California Quarterly* 74 (Spring 1992): 55-106.

Apostol, Jane, and Tom Apostol. "Grassroots Democratic Activism in Altadena, California, in the Mid-Twentieth Century." *Southern California Quarterly* 96 (Fall 2014): 271–312.

Arnold, C. E. "Cut and Cover Refuse Disposal." *American City* 66 (May 1951): 92–93.

Baldassare, Mark. *California in the New Millennium: The Changing Social and Political Landscape.* Berkeley, Los Angles, London: University of California Press, 2000.

_____. "Citizen Support for Regional Government in the New Suburbia." *Urban Affairs Quarterly* 24 (Mar. 1989): 460–469.

_____, ed. *The Los Angeles Riots: Lessons for the Urban Future.* Boulder, San Francisco, Oxford: Westview Press, 1994.

_____. *When Government Fails: The Orange County Bankruptcy.* Berkeley, Los Angeles, London: University of California Press, 1998.

Baldassare, Mark, et al. *Risky Business: Providing Local Public Services in Los Angeles County.* San Francisco: Public Policy Institute of California, 2000.

Bauman, Robert. *Race and the War in Poverty: From Watts to East L.A.* Norman: University of Oklahoma Press, 2008.

Bell, Alexa. "The Hahn Dynasty." *California Journal* 19 (Mar. 1988): 120–123, 126.

Bemis, George W., and Nancy Basché. *Los Angeles County as an Agency of Municipal Government.* Los Angeles: Haynes Foundation, 1947.

Benton, J. Edwin. *Counties as Service Delivery Agents: Changing Expectations and Roles.* Westport, Conn.: Praeger, 2002.

Berg, Martin. "Are We Lucky or What? Gil Garcetti Wants Another Term as D.A. Does He Deserve It?" *Los Angeles* 41 (Mar. 1996): 18–20.

Berman, David R., ed. *County Governments in an Era of Change.* Westport, Conn.: Greenwood Press, 1993.

Bernstein, Shana. *Bridges of Reform: Interracial Civil Rights Activism in Twentieth Century Los Angeles.* New York: Oxford University Press, 2011.

Bigger, Richard, Evan A. Iverson, and Judith N. Jamison. "Escape From the County." *National Municipal Review* 46 (Mar. 1957): 124–130.

Bigger, Richard, and James D. Kitchen. *How the Cities Grew.* Vol. 2 of *Metropolitan Los Angeles: A Study In Integration,* ed. Edwin A. Cottrell. 16 vols. Los Angeles: Haynes Foundation, 1952.

Blanche, Tony, and Brad Schreiber. *Death in Paradise: An Illustrated History of the Los Angeles County Department of Coroner.* Los Angeles: General Publishing Group, 1998.

Bollens, John C. *American County Government, With an Annotated Bibliography.* Beverly Hills, Calif.: Sage Publications, 1969.

_____. *Appointed Executive Local Government: The California Experience.* Los Angeles: Haynes Foundation, 1952.

_____. *Special District Governments in the United States.* Berkeley and Los Angeles: University of California Press, 1957.

Bollens, John C., and Henry J. Schmandt. *The Metropolis: Its People, Politics, and Economic Life.* New York: Harper & Row, 1965.

Bollens, John C., and Stanley Scott. *Local Government in California.* Berkeley and Los Angeles: University of California Press, 1951.

Bollens, Scott A. "Fragments of Regionalism: The Limits of Southern California Governance." *Journal of Urban Affairs* 19 (May 1997); 105–122.

Bottles, Scott L. *Los Angeles and the Automobile: The Making of a Modern City.* Berkeley, Los Angeles, London: University of California Press, 1987.

Boyarsky, Bill, and Nancy Boyarsky. *Backroom Politics: How Your Local Politicians Work, Why Your Government Doesn't, and What You Can Do About It.* New York: Hawthorn Books, 1974.

Brienes, Martin. "Smog Comes to Los Angeles." *Southern California Quarterly* 58 (Winter 1976): 515–532.

Bromage, Arthur W., and Kirk H. Porter. "County Home Rule: Pro and Con." *National Municipal Review* 23 (Oct. 1934): 514–519, 535.

Bucy, Eric. "Lawsuits Threaten LA Supervisors' Fiefdoms." *California Journal* 20 (Jan. 1989): 41–43.

Bullock, Charles S., Ronald Keith Gaddie, and Justin J. Wert. *The Rise and Fall of the Voting Rights Act.* Norman: University of Oklahoma Press 2016.

Burt, Kenneth C. *The Search for a Civic Voice: California Latino Politics.* Claremont, Calif.: Regina Books, 2007.

"California's 'Contract Cities.'" *American City* 75 (Dec. 1960); 100.

Cannon, Lou. *Official Negligence: How Rodney King and the Riots Changed Los Angeles and the LAPD.* New York: Times Books, 1997.

Carr, Jered B., and Richard C. Feiock, eds. *City-County Consolidation and Its Alternatives: Reshaping the Local Government Landscape.* Armonk, N.Y.: M.E. Sharpe, 2004.

Chafe, William Henry. *The Unfinished Journey: America Since World War II.* New York: Oxford University Press, 1991.

Chávez, John R. *Eastside Landmark: A History of the East Los Angeles Community Union, 1963–1993.* Stanford: Stanford University Press, 1998.

Choi, Anne Soon. "The Japanese American Citizens League, Los Angeles Politics, and the Thomas Noguchi Case." *Southern California Quarterly* 102 (Summer 2020): 158–192.

Clary, William W. *History of the Law Firm of O'Melveny & Myers, 1885-1965.* 2 vols. Los Angeles: privately printed, 1966.

Clon, Richard M. "Accommodation Par Excellence: The Lakewood Plan," 224–231. In Michael N. Danielson, ed., *Metropolitan Politics: A Reader,* 2nd ed. Boston: Little, Brown and Co., 1971.

Cottrell, Edwin A. *Characteristics of the Metropolis.* Vol. 1 of *Metropolitan Los Angeles: A Study in Integration,* ed. by Edwin A. Cottrell. 16 vols. Los Angeles: Haynes Foundation, 1952.

Cottrell, Edwin A., and Helen L. Jones. *The Metropolis: Is Integration Possible?* Vol. 16 of *Metropolitan Los Angeles: A Study in Integration,* ed. by Edwin A. Cottrell. 16 vols. Los Angeles: Haynes Foundation, 1955.

Cox, Gary W., and Timothy N. Tutt. "Universalism and Allocative Decision Making in the Los Angeles County Board of Supervisors." *Journal of Politics* 46 (May 1984): 546–555.

Crouch, Winston W. *Intergovernmental Relations.* Vol. 15 of *Metropolitan Los Angeles: A Study in Integration,* ed. by Edwin A. Cottrell. 16 vols. Los Angeles: Haynes Foundation, 1954.

———. *Organized Civil Servants: Public Employer-Employee Relations in California.* Berkeley, Los Angeles, London: University of California Press, 1978.

Crouch, Winston W., and Beatrice Dinerman. *Southern California Metropolis: A Study in the Development of Government for a Metropolitan Area.* Berkeley and Los Angeles: University of California Press, 1963.

Crouch, Winston W., John C. Bollens, and Stanley Scott. *California Government and Politics.* 5th ed. Englewood Cliffs, N.J.: Prentice-Hall, 1972.

Crouch, Winston W., John E. Swanson, and Richard Bigger. *Finance and Taxation.* Vol. 14 of *Metropolitan Los Angeles, A Study in Integration,* ed. by Edwin A. Cottrell. 16 vols. Los Angeles: Haynes Foundation, 1954.

Crouch, Winston W., Wendell Maccoby, Margaret G. Morden, and Richard Bigger. *Sanitation and Health.* Vol. 5 of *Metropolitan Los Angeles, A Study in Integration,* ed. by Edwin A. Cottrell. 16 vols. Los Angeles: Haynes Foundation, 1952.

Dasmann, Raymond F. *The Destruction of California.* New York: Macmillan Co., 1965.

Davis, Mike. *City of Quartz: Excavating the Future in Los Angeles.* London: Verso, 1990.

———. *Ecology of Fear: Los Angeles and the Imagination of Disaster.* New York: Vintage Books, 1999.

De Graaf, Lawrence B. "The City of Black Angels: Emergence of the Los Angeles Ghetto, 1890-1930." *Pacific Historical Review* 39 (Aug. 1970): 323-352.

De Graaf, Lawrence B., Kevin Mulroy, and Quintard Taylor, eds. *Seeking El Dorado: African Americans in California.* Los Angeles: Autry Museum of Western Heritage and University of Washington Press, 2001.

Dear, Michael J., H. Eric Schockman, and Greg Hise, eds. *Rethinking Los Angeles.* Thousand Oaks, Calif.: Sage Publications, 1996.

Delmatier, Royce D., et al. *The Rumble of California Politics, 1848-1970.* New York: John Wiley & Sons, 1970.

Deverell, William, ed. *A Companion to the American West.* Malden, Mass.: Blackwell Pub., 2004.

Deverell, William, and David Igler, eds. *A Companion to California History.* Malden, Mass.: Wiley-Blackwell, 2008.

Deverell, William, and Greg Hise, eds. *A Companion to Los Angeles.* Malden, Mass.: Wiley-Blackwell, 2010.

Deverell, William, and Greg Hise, eds. *Land of Sunshine: An Environmental History of Metropolitan Los Angeles.* Pittsburgh: University of Pittsburgh Press, 2005.

Dewey, Scott. "The Antitrust Case of the Century: Kenneth E. Hahn and the Fight Against Smog." *Southern California Quarterly* 81 (Fall 1999): 341–376.

Dewey, Scott Hamilton. *Don't Breathe the Air: Air Pollution and U.S. Environmental Politics, 1945–1970.* College Station: Texas A&M University Press, 2000.

Diamond, Adam. "What a Waste: Municipal Refuse Reform and a Century of Solid-Waste Management in Los Angeles." *Southern California Quarterly* 88 (Fall 2006): 339–365.

Dreier, Peter, John Mollenkopf, and Todd Swanstrom. *Place Matters: Metropolitics for the Twenty-First Century.* Lawrence: University Press of Kansas, 2001.

Duncombe, Herbert Sydney. *County Government in America.* Washington, D.C.: National Association of Counties, 1966.

Elkin, Stephen L. *City and Regime in the American Republic.* Chicago: University of Chicago Press, 1987.

Elkind, Ethan N. *Railtown: The Fight for the Los Angeles Metro Rail and the Future of the City.* Berkeley and Los Angeles: University of California Press, 2014.

Erie, Steven P. *Beyond Chinatown: The Metropolitan Water District, Growth, and the Environment in Southern California.* Stanford, Calif.: Stanford University Press, 2006.

———. *Globalizing L.A.: Trade, Infrastructure, and Regional Development.* Stanford, Calif.: Stanford University Press, 2004.

Ethington, Philip J., and David P. Levitus. "Placing American Political Development: Cities, Regions, and

Regimes, 1789–2008." In *The City in American Political Development*, edited by Richardson Dilworth, 154–176. New York and London: Routledge, 2009.

Faderman, Lillian, and Stuart Timmons. *Gay L.A.: A History of Sexual Outlaws, Power Politics, and Lipstick Lesbians*. New York: Basic Books, 2006.

Fawcett, Jeffrey. *The Political Economy of Smog in Southern California*. New York and London: Garland Publishing, 1990.

Feldman, Frances Lomas. "Human Services in the City of Angels, Part II: 1920–1960s." *Southern California Quarterly* 85 (Fall 2003): 301–360.

———. "Human Services in the City of Angels, Part III: 1970–2000." *Southern California Quarterly* 85 (Winter 2003): 439–478.

"Film Collection Attacked in Los Angeles County." *Library Journal* 96 (Mar. 1, 1971): 771–72.

Fisher, George H. "Twenty Years of Smog in Los Angeles." *Frontier* 16 (Jun. 1965): 11–14.

FitzSimmons, Margaret, and Robert Gottlieb. "Bounding and Binding Metropolitan Space: The Ambiguous Politics of Nature in Los Angeles." In *The City: Los Angeles and Urban Theory at the End of the Twentieth Century*, ed. by Allen J. Scott and Edward W. Soja, 186–224. Berkeley, Los Angeles, London: University of California Press, 1996.

Fliedner, Colleen Adair. *Centennial Rancho Los Amigos Medical Center, 1888–1988*. Downey, Calif.: Rancho Los Amigos Medical Center, 1990.

Fogelson, Robert M. *Violence as Protest: A Study of Riots and Ghettos*. Garden City, N.Y.: Doubleday, 1971.

Ford, John Anson. *Honest Politics My Theme: The Story of a Veteran Public Official's Troubles and Triumphs: An Autobiography*. New York: Vantage Press, 1978.

———. *Thirty Explosive Years in Los Angeles County*. San Marino, Calif.: Huntington Library, 1961.

Fulton, William B. *The Reluctant Metropolis: The Politics of Urban Growth in Los Angeles*. Point Arena, Calif.: Solano Press Books, 1997.

Garaventa, Eugene. "Los Angeles Co. Seeks to Avoid Disaster." *National Civic Review* 66 (Feb. 1977): 103–104.

———. "Private Delivery of Public Services May Have a Few Hidden Barriers." *National Civic Review* 75 (May-Jun/ 1986): 153–157.

Gladfelder, Jane. *California's Emergent Counties*. Sacramento: County Supervisors Association of California, 1968.

Gómez-Quiñones, Juan. *Chicano Politics: Reality and Promise, 1940–1990*. Albuquerque: University of New Mexico Press, 1990.

Gonzalez, Elwing Su'o'ng. "Creating and Contesting Refugee Spaces: Federal Policy and Early Vietnamese Resettlement in Los Angeles." *Southern California Quarterly* 103 (Spring 2021): 99–137.

Gooding-Williams, Robert, ed. *Reading Rodney King, Reading Urban Uprising*. New York and London: Routledge, 1993.

Gottlieb, Bob. "Is it Time to Take the Reins Away from Pistol Pete?" *Los Angeles* 23 (Jun. 1978): 126–128, 243–247.

———. "Memories of Asa Call, L.A.'s Back-Room Mr. Big." *Los Angeles* 23 (Aug. 1978): 100–103.

———. "The Supervisors: Five Angry and Threatened Men." *Los Angeles* 23 (Jun. 1978): 129–133, 248, 250–259.

Gottlieb, Robert, and Irene Wolt. *Thinking Big: The Story of the Los Angeles Times, Its Publishers, and Their Influence on Southern California*. New York: G.P. Putnam's Sons, 1977.

Gottlieb, Robert, and Margaret FitzSimmons. *Thirst for Growth: Water Agencies as Hidden Government in California*. Tucson: University of Arizona Press, 1991.

Gottlieb, Robert, et al., eds. *The Next Los Angeles: The Struggle for a Livable City*. Berkeley, Los Angeles, London: University of California Press, 2005.

Gove, Samuel K. "Los Angeles County Works for Its Cities." *National Municipal Review* 50 (Jan. 1961): 40–42.

Grant, Wyn. *Autos, Smog and Pollution Control: The Politics of Air Quality Management in California*. Aldershot, UK and Brookfield, Vt.: Edward Elgar, 1995.

Grigsby, J. Eugene. "Rebuilding Los Angeles: One Year Later." *National Civic Review* 81 (Fall 1993): 348–353.

Gumprecht, Blake. *The Los Angeles River: Its Life, Death, and Possible Rebirth*. Baltimore and London: Johns Hopkins University Press, 1999.

Gurwitt, Rob. "The Man with Too Many Children." *Governing* 11 (Sept. 1998): 32–37.

Gutiérrez, David. *Walls and Mirrors: Mexican Americans, Mexican Immigrants, and the Politics of Ethnicity*. Berkeley and Los Angeles: University of California Press, 1995.

Gutiérrez, Henry. "Racial Politics in Los Angeles: Black and Mexican American Challenges to Unequal Education in the 1960s." *Southern California Quarterly* 78 (Spring 1996): 51–86.

Haagen-Smit, A. J. "Air Conservation." *Science* 128 (Oct. 17, 1958): 869–878.

Halferty, Guy. "A Unique Experiment in City-County Relationships: How the 'Lakewood Plan' Operates." *American City* 70 (May 1955): 134–135.

Hamley, Craig, and A.G. Block. "Regional Government: Everyone Wants to Land on Boardwalk." *California Journal* 21 (Nov. 1990): 530–534.

Haney-López, Ian F. *Racism on Trial: The Chicano Fight for Justice*. Cambridge, Mass., and London: Belknap Press, 2003.

Harris, Robert E. G. "5 Men for Five Million." *Frontier* 7 (Mar. 1956): 13–17.

_____. "Showman Saint of Temple Street." *Frontier* 7 (Jan. 1956): 12–15.

Harvey, Richard B. *The Dynamics of California Government and Politics*. 2nd ed. Monterey, Calif.: Brooks/Cole Pubs., 1985.

Hein, C.J. "Contracting Municipal Services: Does it Really Cost Less?" *National Civic Review* 72 (Jun. 1983): 321–326.

Hindman, Jo. "Angel City in Turmoil." *American Mercury* 84 (Apr. 1957): 141–147.

_____. *Terrible 1313 Revisited*. Caldwell, Idaho: Caxton Printers, 1963.

Hise, Greg. *Magnetic Los Angeles: Planning the Twentieth-Century Metropolis*. Baltimore and London: Johns Hopkins University Press, 1997.

Hoene, Christopher, Mark Baldassare, and Michael Shires. "The Development of Counties as Municipal Governments: A Case Study of Los Angeles County in the Twenty-First Century." *Urban Affairs Review* 37 (Mar. 2002): 575–591.

Holbrook, James G. *A Survey of Metropolitan Trial Courts, Los Angeles Area*. Los Angeles: USC Press, 1956.

Horne, Gerald. *Fire This Time: The Watts Uprising and the 1960s*. Charlottesville: University Press of Virginia, 1995.

Horowitz, Harold W. "Report on the Los Angeles City and County Loyalty Programs." *Stanford Law Review* 5 (Feb. 1953): 233–246.

Howard, S. Kenneth. "Renewing the Federalism Debate." *National Civic Review* 72 (Apr. 1983): 188–189, 244.

Hundley, Norris. *The Great Thirst: Californians and Water, 1770s-1990s*. Berkeley and Los Angeles: University of California Press, 1992.

Jackson, Kenneth T. *Crabgrass Frontier: The Suburbanization of the United States*. New York: Oxford University Press, 1985.

Jacobs, Chip, and William J. Kelly. *Smogtown: The Lung-Burning History of Pollution in Los Angeles*. Woodstock, N.Y.: Overlook Press, 2008.

Jamison, Judith N. *Regional Planning*. Vol. 3 of *Metropolitan Los Angeles: A Study in Integration*, ed. Edwin A. Cottrell. 16 vols. Los Angeles: Haynes Foundation, 1952.

Jamison, Judith Norvell, and Richard Bigger. "Metropolitan Coordination on Los Angeles." *Public Administration Review* 17 (Summer 1957): 164–169.

Jarvis, Howard. *I'm Mad as Hell: The Exclusive Story of the Tax Revolt and Its Leader*. New York: Times Books, 1979.

Jelinek, Lawrence J. *Harvest Empire: A History of California Agriculture*. San Francisco: Boyd and Fraser, 1979.

Johnson, Tom. "No More Mr. Nice Guy." *Los Angeles* 33 (May 1988): 128–136.

Judge, David, Gerry Stoker, and Harold Wolman, eds. *Theories of Urban Politics*. London and Thousand Oaks, Calif.: Sage Publications, 1995.

Kasindorf, Jeanie. "Baxter Ward: His Own Best Human Interest Story." *Los Angeles* 17 (Oct. 1972): 44–45, 80.

Keil, Roger. *Los Angeles: Globalization, Urbanization and Social Struggles*. Chichester, Eng., New York; John Wiley & Sons, 1998.

Klein, Norman M., and Martin J. Schiesl, eds. *20th Century Los Angeles: Power, Promotion, and Social Conflict*. Claremont, Calif.: Regina Books, 1990.

Koehler, Cortus. *Managing California's Counties: Serving People, Solving Problems*. Sacramento: County Supervisors Association of California, 1983.

Kousser, J. Morgan. *Colorblind Injustice: Minority Voting Rights and the Undoing of the Second Reconstruction*. Chapel Hill: University of North Carolina Press, 1999.

_____. "How to Determine Intent: Lessons for L. A." *Journal of Law and Politics* 7 (Summer 1991): 591–732.

Krier, James E., and Edmund Ursin. *Pollution and Policy: A Case Essay on California and Federal Experience with Motor Vehicle Air Pollution, 1940-1975*. Berkeley and Los Angeles: University of California Press, 1977.

Kun, Josh, and Laura Pulido, eds. *Black and Brown in Los Angeles: Beyond Conflict and Coalition*. Berkeley and Los Angeles: University of California Press, 2014.

Kurashige, Scott. *The Shifting Grounds of Race: Black and Japanese Americans in the Making of Multiethnic Los Angeles*. Princeton, N.J.: Princeton University Press, 2008.

Lamb, Barbara. "Los Angeles County Master Plan Addresses Area Problems of Suburban Sprawl and Middle-Class Out-Migration." *Architectural Record* 163 (Apr. 1978): 34.

Laslett, John H.M. *Sunshine was Never Enough: Los Angeles Workers, 1880-2010*. Berkeley and Los Angeles: University of California Press, 2012.

Lazzareschi, Carla. "The Pressure Tactics of Smog Boss Tom Quinn." *California Journal* 8 (Jul. 1977): 224–226.

League of Women Voters of Los Angeles County. *Los Angeles County Government*. Rev. ed. Los Angeles: League of Women Voters of Los Angeles County, 1968.

Lee, Eugene C. *California Votes 1928–1960*. Berkeley: University of California, Berkeley, Institute of Governmental Studies, 1963.

Lemand, Suzanne M., and Kurt Thurmaier, eds. *Case Studies in City-County Consolidation: Reshaping the Local Government Landscape*. Armonk, N.Y.: M. E. Sharpe, 2004.

Levenson, Rosaline. "California Changes Law on New Counties." *National Civic Review* 67 (Jan. 1978): 44–45.

_____. "California Legislature Ends First Year of 1977–1978 Session." *National Civic Review* 67 (Feb. 1978): 87–89.

_____. "California Plans Urban Strategy." *National Civic Review* 67 (Sept. 1978): 368–369.

_____. "California Supreme Court Decision Gives Public Employees Right to Strike." *National Civic Review* 74 (Jul.-Aug. 1985): 320.

_____. "Changes Urged for L.A. Area." *National Civic Review* 63 (Jul. 1979): 375–376.

_____. "Major Changes Sought in L.A.: County Study Commission Wants Structural Reform." *National Civic Review* 65 (Jul. 1976): 353–354.

Lillard, Richard G. *Eden in Jeopardy: Man's Prodigal Meddling with His Environment, The Southern California Experience*. New York: Alfred A. Knopf, 1966.

Logan, John R., and Harvey L. Molotch. *Urban Fortunes: The Political Economy of Place*. Berkeley and Los Angeles: University of California Press, 1987.

Looking Back—A Century of Nursing: The History of the Los Angeles County Medical Center School of Nursing, 1895–1995. Los Angeles: Los Angeles County Medical Center School of Nursing, 2000.

Los Angeles County Agricultural Commissioner Department. *Centennial, 1881–1981: A Headstart on the Future*. Los Angeles: the author, 1981.

Los Angeles County Sheriff's Department. *150 Years: A Tradition of Service*. Paducah, Ky.: Turner Pub. Co., 2000.

"Los Angeles County Sues on Federal Transit Rule." *National Civic Review* 66 (Jan. 1977): 34.

"Los Angeles Pinpoints Auto Exhaust as Uncontrolled Air Pollution Source." *American City* 73 (May 1958): 126.

Lotchin, Roger W. *Fortress California, 1910–1961: From Warfare to Welfare*. New York: Oxford University Press, 1992.

Marshall, Dale Rogers. *The Politics of Participation in Poverty: A Case Study of the Board of the Economic and Youth Opportunities Agency of Greater Los Angeles*. Berkeley, Los Angeles, London: University of California Press, 1971.

Marshall, Eliot. "Clean Air? Don't Hold Your Breath." *Science* 244 (May 5, 1989): 517–120.

Martin, Helen Eastman. *The History of the Los Angeles County Hospital, 1878–1968, and the Los Angeles County-University of Southern California Medical Center, 1968–1978*. Los Angeles: University of Southern California Press, 1979.

McCune, Ellis. *Recreation and Parks*. Vol. 9 of *Metropolitan Los Angeles, A Study in Integration*, ed. by Edwin A. Cottrell. 16 vols. Los Angeles: Haynes Foundation, 1954.

McKenna, Kathy Zimmerman. "No Cash on the Horizon for Parched Counties." *California Journal* 20 (Aug. 1989): 333–336.

McWilliams, Carey. "The Registration of Heretics." *Nation* 171 (Dec. 9, 1950): 526–528.

_____. *Witch Hunt: The Revival of Heresy*. Boston: Little, Brown, 1950.

Menzel, Donald C., ed. *The American County: Frontiers of Knowledge*. Tuscaloosa and London: University of Alabama Press, 1996.

Merritt, Bruce G. "Faith and Fair Housing: An Episcopal Parish Church in the 1964 Debate over Proposition 14." *Southern California Quarterly* 95 (Fall 2013): 284–317.

Meyer, Stephen Grant. *As Long as They Don't Move Next Door: Segregation and Racial Conflict in American Neighborhoods*. Lanham, Md.: Rowman & Littlefield, 2000.

Miller, David Y., and Raymond W. Cox, III. *Governing the Metropolitan Area: America's New Frontier*. Armonk, N.Y.: M.E. Sharpe, 2014.

Miller, Gary J. *Cities by Contract: The Politics of Municipal Incorporation*. Cambridge, Mass.: MIT Press, 1981.

Muchnik, Suzanne. *LACMA So Far: Portrait of a Museum in the Making*. San Marino, Calif.: Huntington Library, Art Collections, Botanical Gardens, 2015.

Muller, Thomas, and Thomas J. Espenshade. *The Fourth Wave: California's Newest Immigrants*. Washington, D.C.: Urban Institute Press, 1985.

Nelson, Howard J. *The Los Angeles Metropolis*. Dubuque, Iowa: Kendall-Hunt, 1983.

Nevins, Jane. "No Wonder Everyone Wants to Be a Supervisor." *Los Angeles* 17 (May 1972): 40–41, 64–66.

Nicolaides, Becky M. *My Blue Heaven: Life and Politics in the Working-Class Suburbs of Los Angeles, 1920–1965*. Chicago: University of Chicago Press, 2002.

Noguchi, Thomas T., M.D. *Coroner*. New York: Pocket Books, 1983.

_____. *Coroner at Large.* New York: Pocket Books, 1986.

O'Connor, Janine. "Is Los Angeles County Unmanageable?" *California Journal* 6 (Jun. 1975): 28.

Olson, Bruce T. *Grand Juries in California: A Study in Citizenship.* Modesto, Calif.: American Grand Jury Foundation, 2000.

Orsi, Jared. *Hazardous Metropolis: Flooding and Urban Ecology in Los Angeles.* Berkeley, Los Angeles, London: University of California Press, 2004.

_____. "Restoring the Common to the Goose: Citizen Activism and the Protection of the California Coastline, 1969–1982." *Southern California Quarterly* 78 (Fall 1996): 257–284.

Packard, Francis H. "The Politics of Smog." *Frontier* 7 (Apr. 1956): 11–12.

Parrish, Michael. *For the People: Inside the Los Angeles County District Attorney's Office, 1850–2000.* Santa Monica, Calif.: Angel City Press, 2001.

Parson, Don. *Making a Better World: Public Housing, the Red Scare, and the Direction of Modern Los Angeles.* Minneapolis and London: University of Minnesota Press, 2005.

Pastor, Manuel, Jr., et al. *Regions That Work: How Cities and Suburbs Can Grow Together.* Minneapolis: University of Minnesota Press, 2000.

Patterson, James T. *Grand Expectations: The United States, 1945–1974.* New York: Oxford University Press, 1996.

Pickett, Arthur. "Stop Ground Water Pollution." *American City* 69 (Aug. 1954): 95–96.

Pisano, Jane G. "After the Riots: Multiculturalism in Los Angeles." *National Civic Review* 81 (Summer/Fall 1992): 313–318.

Pisano, Mark, and Richard F. Callahan. "Case Study 1: Fiscal Sustainability in Los Angeles County. *National Civic Review* 101 (Spring 2012): 11–17.

"Plan New California Agency for Regional Problems." *National Civic Review* 52 (Jul. 1963): 384–85.

Public Commission on County Government. *To Serve Seven Million: Report of the Public Commission on Los Angeles County Government.* Los Angeles: The Commission, 1976.

Queenan, Charles. *Long Beach and Los Angeles: A Tale of Two Ports.* Los Angeles: Harbor Department, 1983.

Rawls, James J., and Walton Bean. *California: An Interpretive History.* Seventh ed. New York: McGraw-Hill, 1998.

Reese, Ellen. *They Say Cut Back, We Say Fight Back!* New York: Russell Sage Foundation, 2011.

Regalado, James A. *Political Battles Over L.A. County Board Seats: A Minority Perspective.* Los Angeles: California State University, Edmund G. "Pat" Brown Institute of Public Affairs, 1989.

Roderick, Kevin. "Hidden Powers: The County's Supervisors Enjoy Job Security and Enormous Influence—But Not a Lot of Attention." *Los Angeles* 51 (Aug. 2006): 88, 90, 92, 94, 96.

Rodriguez, Gregory. "Politics: Running for Your Life." *Los Angeles* 43 (May 1998): 50–53.

Rogin, Michael P., and John L. Shover. *Political Change in California: Critical Elections and Social Movements, 1890-1966.* Westport, Conn.: Greenwood Publishing Corp., 1970.

Rothman, Hal. *The Greening of a Nation? Environmentalism in the United States Since 1945.* Fort Worth: Harcourt Brace, 1998.

Sackman, Douglas Cazaux, ed. *A Companion to American Environmental History.* Malden, Mass.: Wiley-Blackwell, 2010.

Salant, Tanis J. "County Governments: An Overview." *Intergovernmental Perspectives* 17 (Winter 1991): 5–9.

Savitch, H.V., and Ronald K. Vogel, eds. *Regional Politics: America in a Post-City Age. Urban Affairs Annual Reviews 45.* Thousand Oaks, Calif.; Sage Publications, 1996.

Schiesl, Martin J. "Airplanes to Aerospace: Defense Spending and Economic Growth in the Los Angeles Region, 1945–1960." In Roger W. Lotchin, ed. *The Martial Metropolis: U.S. Cities in War and Peace,* 135–149. New York: Praeger, 1984.

_____. "The Politics of Contracting: Los Angeles County and the Lakewood Plan, 1954–1962." *Huntington Library Quarterly* 45 (Summer 1982): 227–243.

Schiesl, Martin J., and Mark M. Dodge, eds. *City of Promise: Race and Historical Change in Los Angeles.* Claremont, Calif.: Regina Books, 2006.

Schoenherr, Allan A. *A Natural History of California.* Berkeley, Los Angeles, London: University of California Press, 1992.

Schrank, Sarah. *Art and the City: Civic Imagination and Cultural Authority in Los Angeles.* Philadelphia: University of Pennsylvania Press, 2009.

Schwadron, Terry, ed. *California and the American Tax Revolt: Proposition 13 Five Years Later.* Berkeley and Los Angeles: University of California Press, 1984.

Scott, Allen J., and Edward W. Soja, eds. *The City: Los Angeles and Urban Theory at the End of the Twentieth Century.* Berkeley, Los Angeles, London: University of California Press, 1996.

Sears, David O. *Tax Revolt: Something for Nothing in California.* Cambridge, Mass: Harvard University Press, 1982.

Seidenstat, Paul, ed. *Contracting Out Government Services.* Westport, Conn.: Praeger, 1999.

Sharpsteen, Bill. *Dirty Water: One Man's Fight to Clean Up One of the World's Most Polluted Bays.* Berkeley, Los Angeles, London: University of California Press, 2010.

Shor, Toby. "LA's Kenny Hahn—The State's Best Politician?" *California Journal* 12 (Oct. 1981): 341–343.
_____. "Pete Schabarum—Fifth Wheel Turned Boss of L.A. County." *California Journal* 12 (Jun. 1981): 199–202.
Shorr, Howard. "'Race Prejudice is Not Inborn—It is Learned': The Exhibit Controversy at the Los Angeles Museum of History, Science and Art, 1950-1952." *California History* 90 (Fall 1990): 276–83, 311–12.
Sides, Josh. *L.A. City Limits: African American Los Angeles from the Great Depression to the Present.* Berkeley and Los Angeles: University of California Press, 2003.
Simmons, Bob. "The Move to Secede from Los Angeles County." *California Journal* 7 (Apr. 1976): 117–119.
Sitton, Tom. *The Courthouse Crowd: Los Angeles County and Its Government, 1850-1950.* Los Angeles: Historical Society of Southern California, 2013.
_____. *The Haynes Foundation and Urban Reform Philanthropy in Los Angeles: A History of the John Randolph Haynes and Dora Haynes Foundation.* Los Angeles: Historical Society of Southern California, 1999.
_____. *Los Angeles Transformed: Fletcher Bowron's Urban Reform Revival, 1938-1953.* Albuquerque: University of New Mexico Press, 2005.
Skerry, Peter. *Mexican Americans: The Ambivalent Minority.* Cambridge, Mass.: Harvard University Press, 1993.
Sloane, David C., ed. *Planning Los Angeles.* Chicago: American Planning Association, 2012.
Sokolow, Alvin D. "The Limited and Contrary Uses of County Charter Reform: Two California Cases." *State and Local Government Review* 36 (Fall 2004): 7–19.
Sonenshein, Raphael J. *Politics in Black and White: Race and Power in Los Angeles.* Princeton, N.J.: Princeton University Press, 1993.
Starr, Kevin. *Coast of Dreams: California on the Edge, 1990-2003.* New York: Knopf, 2004.
_____. *Golden Dreams: California in an Age of Abundance, 1950-1963.* New York: Oxford University Press, 2009.
Stevens, Errol Wayne. *Radical L.A.: From Coxey's Army to the Watts Riots, 1894-1965.* Norman: University of Oklahoma Press, 2009.
Stone, Clarence N. "Urban Regimes and the Capacity to Govern: A Political Economy Approach." *Journal of Urban Affairs* 15 (Mar. 1993): 1–28.
Storper, Michael, et al. *The Rise and Fall of Urban Economies: Lessons from San Francisco and Los Angeles.* Stanford: Stanford University Press, 2015.
Stradling, David. *Smokestacks and Progressives: Environmentalists, Engineers, and Air Quality in America, 1881-1951.* Baltimore: Johns Hopkins University Press, 1999.
Sullivan, Neil J. *The Dodgers Move West.* New York: Oxford University Press, 1987.
Surls, Rachel, and Judith B. Gerber. *From Cows to Concrete: The Rise and Fall of Farming in Los Angeles.* Santa Monica, Calif.: Angel City Press, 2016.
Sweeney, James W. "One Little, Two Little … Nine Little Kings?" *Golden State Report* 5 (Nov. 1989); 13–17.
Torrence, Susan Walker. *Grass Roots Government: The County in American Politics.* Washington, D.C., and New York: Robert B. Luce, Inc., 1974.
Town Hall of California. *The Pension Balloon.* Los Angeles: Town Hall of California, 1979.
Turhollow, Anthony F. *A History of the Los Angeles District, U.S. Army Corps of Engineers, 1898-1965.* Los Angeles: U.S. Army Engineer District, 1975.
Valle, Victor. *City of Industry: Genealogies of Power in Southern California.* New Brunswick, N.J.: Rutgers University Press, 2009.
Van Wormer, Stephen R. "A History of Flood Control in the Los Angeles County Drainage Area." *Southern California Quarterly* 73 (Spring 1991): 55–94.
Waldinger, Roger, and Mehdi Bozorgmehr, eds. *Ethnic Los Angeles.* New York: Russell Sage Foundation, 1996.
Waldman, Tom. "Bringing Supergovernment to Southern California." *California Journal* 21 (Jun. 1990): 287–290.
_____. "Schabarum Bails Out: Surprise Exit Stiffs Wannabes." *California Journal* 21 (May 1990): 227–230.
Waldron, Granville Arthur. "Courthouses of Los Angeles County." *Historical Society of Southern California Quarterly* 41 (Dec.1959): 345–374.
Ward, Doris M. "Regional Governance Issues in California: Citizen and Policy Implications." *National Civic Review* 79 (Mar./Apr. 1990): 132–137.
Warren, Robert O. *Government in Metropolitan Regions: A Reappraisal of Fractionated Political Organization.* Davis: University of California, Davis, Institute of Governmental Affairs, 1966.
Westwick, Peter J., ed. *Blue Sky Metropolis: The Aerospace Century in Southern California.* Berkeley and San Marino: University of California Press and Huntington Library Press, 2012.
Wilcox, Robert F. *Law Enforcement.* Vol. 4 of *Metropolitan Los Angeles, A Study in Integration,* ed. by Edwin A. Cottrell. 16 vols. Los Angeles: Haynes Foundation, 1952.
Willens, Michele. "A Second Political Hat for LA Chairman Mike Antonovich." *California Journal* 14 (May 1983): 183–185.
Winter, Richard. "Problems of Satellite Cites." *Tax Digest* 36 (Apr. 1958): 76–77, 91–95.

Wolch, Jennifer, Manuel Pastor, Jr., and Peter Dreier, eds. *Up Against the Sprawl: Public Policy and the Making of Southern California*. Minneapolis and London: University of Minnesota Press, 2004.

Wolfinger, Raymond E., and Fred I. Greenstein. "The Repeal of Fair Housing in California: An Analysis of Referendum Voting." *American Political Science Review* 62 (Sept. 1968): 753–769.

Woods, Gerald. *The Police in Los Angeles: Reform and Professionalization*. New York: Garland Publishing, 1993.

Youngs, Bill. "Pepperdine's 'HAHNorable' Supervisor." *Pepperdine College Alumni Voice* 31 (Summer 1968): 14–17.

Zyda, Joan. "Los Angeles gets a new DA." *California Journal* 14 (Feb. 1983): 86.

Index